TOM REYNOLDS

JUST SAY KNOW

THE INCONVENIENT TRUTH ABOUT DRUGS
PART 1

First published in Australia by Aurora House
www.aurorahouse.com.au

This edition published 2021
Copyright © Tom Reynolds 2021

Typesetting and e-book design: Amit Dey
Cover Designer: Simon Critchell

ISBN number: 978-1-922403-19-3 (paperback)

A catalogue record for this book is available from the National Library of Australia

NATIONAL LIBRARY OF AUSTRALIA

Distributed by: Ingram Content: www.ingramcontent.com
Australia: phone +613 9765 4800 |
email lsiaustralia@ingramcontent.com
Milton Keynes UK: phone +44 (0)845 121 4567 |
email enquiries@ingramcontent.com
La Vergne, TN USA: phone +1 800 509 4156 |
email inquiry@lightningsource.com

DEDICATION

For the three most important people in my life:
My mother, who has been my inspiration
My father, who has been my rock
My girl, who has been my light

ACKNOWLEDGMENTS

This project would simply not have been possible without the help of many people. First and foremost, my family—my parents and wife, who have supported me through everything, and who endure my endless rants about all that is wrong with drug policy.

To the team at Aurora House, who have worked tirelessly to ensure that this journey has been as smooth as possible and so that no stone is left unturned in the quality of this work. And to all of the past and present individuals who have dedicated their lives to bettering drug policy throughout the world in the face of such staunch opposition. If it weren't for you, the world would be in a much worse place than what it is now. Current and future generations are eternally indebted to you.

CONTENTS

1

WHY I HAD TO WRITE THIS BOOK

We cannot live in a society that is both free, and drug free.

— Lester Grinspoon

On a typical Thursday afternoon in 2007, being the academic and conscientious Year Eleven student that I was, homework was the last thing on my mind (if it was ever on my mind). It was only about an hour since school had finished for the day, but I had already managed to park myself in front of the television in my room to immerse myself into the world of *Need for Speed*. Lying in bed, glued to the screen, taking the occasional small break to consume whatever junk food I had scored on the way home was where you would find me... Well, until I was inevitably dragged out for dinner.

In fact, dinner was a somewhat inconvenient ritual, as it involved pausing the game, getting out of bed, walking approximately ten metres to the dinner table, and replacing my preferred junk food with something unquestionably healthier. Vegetables and meat versus chips and soft drink to a sixteen year old boy is a no-brainer.

Sitting around the dinner table with my mother and father, chatting about each other's day and whatever news was floating around at the time, my mind was somewhere else—time missing out on *Need for Speed*. I had kind of made a deal with myself though. If I ate all of my vegetables really quickly, that would somehow impress my mum, and then I'd be back in front of the screen faster!

Little did I know, my worst nightmare was around the corner. Both Mum and Dad had work to do, leaving me with no option; the dishes were not going to wash themselves. I endured twenty minutes of pure torture. I was washing and drying so quickly that half of the plates and cutlery went back into the drawers and cupboards with suds or food still attached but I didn't care. *Need for Speed* was calling. Occasionally I would run back inside, however, dishwashing police can be ruthless when on duty, and I was repeatedly apprehended for my sub-par wash-ing/drying skills.

Just as I was about to put the tea towel down, I paused mid-air after hearing a click in the laundry, and I knew that meant one thing. There was washing to hang out. As far as I was concerned, this was the worst night of my life. The strugs were real, and I couldn't even deal. I couldn't believe that I had missed out on so much time! My soft drink had probably gone flat, my chips had most likely gone mushy, and my enthusiasm was killed. All because I was subjected to the torture of eating healthy food, making conversation, washing a handful of dishes and hanging up a few shirts. Keeping in mind that I was an only child (probably with only-child syndrome), which meant there were about three plates and six pieces of cutlery to wash, and all of the washing to hang up was likely to be mine. That was a rough night – I think I diagnosed myself with clinical depression after this traumatic evening.

Not to worry though, I eventually made it back to my room, back to my utopia. The cloud of anxiety increasingly lifted as I reclaimed my happy place. The next time I would leave this room would be in the morning when I had to go to school (which for me was really just another obstacle in the way of achieving *Need for Speed* world dominance). But maybe if I could stay up for long enough, then I would be really tired, miss my alarm clock, get up too late 'accidently' and have no choice but to get driven to school! You could say I was good at working the system.

This time when I went back to my room, I decided to check my phone next to the dresser before I lay down. Getting out of bed again, walking halfway across the room was energy that could be potentially channelled into dominating on the PlayStation. The phone that I had at the time was one of those old Nokia bricks—the one where, apart from texts and calls, the only thing you could do was play *Snake*. There was a message on it from one of my friends, who I will call Lilly.

Lilly was one of my closest friends who went to a girls' school nearby and lived in the same area. Almost every day we would get the bus or walk home together. She was a beautiful looking girl—blonde, slim, with big eyes, perfectly straight teeth and a gorgeous soft smile.

Although Lilly on the outside was stunning, on the inside, she was screaming. She had lost her mother at an early age, lived in a house with her stepdad who she didn't get on with, was disconnected with the rest of her family, longed to be with her mother and did not have a wide group of friends. She found it difficult to fit in at school. She was not all that interested in sport or extracurricular activities and was not terribly academic. You could say that Lilly was a lost sock in the laundry of life.

Lilly battled eating disorders and depression and used a variety of drugs to self-medicate throughout the time I knew her. She often sent me worrying text messages that warranted concern, but since she had sent so many over the years, I had become somewhat desensitised to what was obviously a call for help. The message that she sent me read 'How much vodka would I have to drink for it to kill me?'

To be honest, I don't remember what I did for Christmas, Easter or my birthday that year. I don't remember what sports I played that year at school or how I did in my exams. But writing this story over a decade later, I vividly remember that message, even though at the time I took it with a grain of salt. Firstly, I had no idea that alcohol could actually kill someone or how much it would take to kill them. Alcohol was a drink, not a drug—if it was harmful, then it would be illegal, right? Just 'enjoy responsibly'. I mean, everyone in my life drank or, at least, had tried alcohol, and it wasn't a 'bad' drug like cocaine, heroin or ecstasy. The primary message that I got from this text was that she needed attention, so I did not respond. I have no idea if she actually ended up drinking that night, but she was okay when I saw her after school the next day.

Throughout our school years, I received countless messages from Lilly like that, and the more she sent them, the more deaf I became to her cries for help. I just assumed that I would see her at the bus stop the next day, and she would laugh it off.

When we graduated from school, the contact between us became less frequent. I was reassured, however, by her social media images with lots of smiles, holidays, friends and happy times. She had a boyfriend who loved her, and her life appeared to have turned around. Facebook and Instagram (or for us oldies back in the day, Myspace) had the ability to portray a life that differed from reality or, at the very least, differed from what was going on inside of that individual. On the inside, Lilly was still screaming. She lost her battle in late February 2013. She was twenty-one years old.

About a month before she passed, Lilly reached out to me and we messaged each other a few times. We planned to catch up the following week. I told her I would let her know over that weekend which day would suit best. I messaged her over the weekend, but by Tuesday I knew something was wrong because she still had not seen the message. A day later, I found out she was gone. The last time I had seen Lilly was at her school formal, where I was her partner. I saved that unseen message and still have it.

In the months following her death, I blamed myself relentlessly—thinking what a pathetic friend I had been for ignoring the warning signs and, more importantly, not beginning to know how to help or be there for her.

Her story raised so many questions and issues, but the saddest realisation was that nobody knew how to help her, and she had no supportive networks in her life that could have protected and saved her. Despite the fact that her friends went to the same school, had the same teachers, did the same assignments, caught the same buses and trains to school and home, lived in the same suburb, attended the same parties, played the same sports and used the same drugs, their lives did not unravel like Lilly's.

For a long time, like many people, I held the view if someone ended up like Lilly, it was because of poor decisions they had made in their life. I thought that people who didn't use drugs, or at the very least didn't get into any trouble with drugs, stood on a higher moral ground than others. I understand now that we blame weakness or poor moral fibre when there are more complex reasons that we don't understand.

We now know that the most important elements in an individual's life to protect them from harm are the supportive networks that surround them. When Barack Obama, Steve Jobs, Justin Bieber, David Cameron, Lady Gaga, Arnold Schwarzenegger, Boris Johnson, Andre Agassi, Bill Gates, Al Gore, Rihanna, George Bush and millions of other highly successful individuals used illicit drugs in their younger days but did not end up dependent, it was because of the supportive networks around them. Blaming or punishing the friends or acquaintances of these celebrities who, in the same environment, took the same drugs but did become problematic users due to circumstances outside of their control is entirely unfair.

It also highlights that if you take drugs, you can often get away with it if you are a person of enough importance. It is disturbing that many policymakers as well as those who work in the media continue to perpetuate myths and misunderstandings underpinning drug policies, particularly considering that many of them have used drugs but did not get into trouble of any sort for reasons outside their control, such as genetics, environment or even good luck.

Losing Lilly was one of the reasons I decided to work with young people, and reflecting back on that experience has also changed my entire perspective on *how* I work with young people. When I first started working with school students, I very much fitted the mould of an anti-drugs campaigner. I was against drugs, and this often led me to be against the *people* who used drugs. As my upbringing was conservative, if you chose to use drugs, then that was your irresponsible choice. If you were harmed by those drugs, then it was a fitting outcome, and the punishment or consequences you faced would deter you from future drug use. (Of course, this approach would have been entirely useless when it came to helping Lilly.)

Lilly's death (among other events) not only inspired me to do what I do, but it also shined a light on so many areas where we fail as a society in our approach to drugs: in policy, in legislation, in the media, on the streets, in the classroom and in the home. Why did none of Lilly's friends (including myself) know what to do for her or how to look after her if she was under the influence of drugs? Why did she not get help, or if she did get help, why did it fail? Why did she end up going down an entirely different road to all of her friends, despite the fact that they shared the same school, neighbourhood, opportunities and experiences? Why is the drug that was the biggest contributing factor to her death freely available and actively promoted, while many drugs that could have been the answer to her illness were denied to her due to their illegality? Trying to answer these questions requires going deep down the rabbit hole, and often what we find at the bottom is not what we want to hear. The ways in which we as a society have chosen to respond to people like Lilly and the issues they face are highly complex.

The evidence is, however, clear. We do not learn from our mistakes.

2

WHAT ARE DRUGS, AND
WHY ARE THEY IMPORTANT?

If you ask ten different people what the definition of a drug is, you are likely to get ten very different answers. If you ask a young person, the typical answer is either 'something that can harm you', 'something that can be addictive' or 'something that can make you high'.

In pure pharmacological terms, a drug is classified as any chemical that produces a physiological change in the body when ingested through whatever means of administration (intravenous, oral, inhaled etc.). In general, society divides drugs into two categories: safe and good (legal) or unsafe and bad (illegal). The reason society views drugs through a safe/unsafe lens is because of their respective legal status—it has very little to do with the actual harm of the drug.

Drugs and poisons are regulated in Australia through the Therapeutic Goods Administration (TGA), the *Therapeutic Goods Act 1989* and are published in the Standard for the Uniform Scheduling of Medicines and Poisons (SUSMP), otherwise known as the Poisons Standard. Drug offences are regulated in Australia according to the *Narcotic Drugs Act 1967* (Cth) as well as various pieces of state-specific legislation such as the *Drug Misuse and Trafficking Act 1985* (NSW), the *Drug Misuse Act 1986* (QLD) and the *Drugs, Poisons and Controlled Substances Act 1981* (VIC).

The SUSMP contains ten ordering Schedules (Schedule 1, however, is not currently in use), which are theoretically used to categorise chemicals according to their harm potential. Although the Australian Department of Health acknowledges that the intrinsic toxicity of chemicals covered in the SUSMP is only one of many factors involved in scheduling, drugs seem to be categorised in a somewhat haphazard fashion.

Schedule number	Schedule classification	Examples
Schedule 1	Currently void Schedule	-
Schedule 2	Pharmacy medicine: Available only in a pharmacy	Hydrocortisone, clotrimasol, benzoyl peroxide
Schedule 3	Pharmacist medicine: Available only from a pharmacist	Salbutamol, pseudo-ephedrine, flavoxate
Schedule 4	Prescription medicine: Available only through prescription	Codeine, cortisone, venlafaxine
Schedule 5	Caution: Low harm potential	Mandipropamid, turpentine oil, oxadixyl
Schedule 6	Poison: Moderate harm potential	Hydrazine, nickel sulphate, diphacinone
Schedule 7	Dangerous poison: High harm potential—only available to authorised personnel	Methazole, aldicarb, phosphine
Schedule 8	Controlled drug: Restrictions on use, manufacture, possessions and sale	Cocaine, Amphetamine, secobarbital
Schedule 9	Prohibited substance: Prohibited for all purposes, other than research	Desomorphine, lysergic acid, diamorphine
Schedule 10	Entirely prohibited substance: Entirely prohibited	1,4 Butanediol, dimethylamylamine, triparanol

The UK categorises drugs in a similar fashion. Drugs are either class A, B or C, with Class A supposedly containing the most harmful drugs, and their misuse, therefore, attracting the most severe penalties. Drugs in the UK are controlled under the *Misuse of Drugs Act 1971* as well as the *Medicines Act 1968*. In the United States, drugs are categorised across five Schedules according to the *Controlled Substances Act 1971*, with Schedule 1 containing drugs classified as illegal with supposedly a high potential for abuse. These drugs also attract the highest penalty and cannot be used in medicine.

In Australia, the SUSMP has very significant implications for the community, not only for the availability and accessibility to these chemicals, but also how they are viewed in terms of their toxicity and potential for harm.

I remember being in a classroom of Year Eleven students recently and asking the students which drugs they thought were the most harmful. One student said morphine or heroin (Schedules 8 and 9 respectively), the next one said acid (assuming they are referring to LSD, Schedule 9), the third one said he had heard of a really potent drug called fentanyl (Schedule 8) and, of course, one student said methamphetamine (Schedule 8) because, despite reports of global warming, Australia is apparently in the middle of an ice age.

In reality, it is likely that every student in that classroom will be administered with heroin, morphine or fentanyl at some point in their life, probably for post-operative pain management, and there may be some students in that year who are currently using a type of amphetamine to treat their ADHD or narcolepsy. It is unlikely that any of them will become dependent, end up problematic users or be harmed by any of those drugs at any point in their life.

It is also interesting that none of the students mentioned alcohol or tobacco (both of which are exempt from scheduling), which kill about 27,000 Australians together annually, and it is almost certain that some of the students in that classroom will die as a result of their tobacco or alcohol use or both.

Although two of the drugs mentioned, LSD and heroin, share the same Schedule (9), people have survived 100 times the average dose of LSD on a blotter (square tab placed on tongue), whereas the difference between an effective dose of heroin and a lethal dose is very small. Heroin is also highly addictive, whereas LSD is not considered an addictive drug. Morphine and fentanyl were two other drugs mentioned by the students. However, none of them mentioned carfentanil, an analogue of fentanyl, that is at least 100 times as potent as fentanyl, as well as at least 3,000 times as potent as morphine. (They all share the same Schedule, however).

These are simplistic examples; however, it is apparent that there are disparities between actual drug harm, how the drug is represented in scheduling, and a young person's perception of drug harm. The same inconsistencies exist in other parts of the world, such as in the US, where cannabis, lysergic acid diethylamide (LSD), 3,4-methylenedioxy-methamphetamine (MDMA) and peyote are Schedule 1 drugs, while fentanyl, cocaine, and oxycodone are Schedule 2. Not only can scheduling affect how the community perceives the harmfulness of a drug, but the scheduling itself results in very real and severe direct consequences.

In the United Kingdom, a man was imprisoned for twenty-five years for manufacturing LSD tablets. Similarly, in the USA, a man was imprisoned for twenty-four years for possessing and distributing LSD. The movie *Snitch*, starring Dwayne Johnson, is based on the true story of eighteen year old Joey Settembrino who was sentenced to ten years in prison for intent to sell LSD tablets. Richard Paey from Florida was sentenced to twenty-five years and fined $500,000 for being in possession of a large quantity of legally prescribed opioids. Similar cases have occurred in Australia, and the drug laws have expanded in a random fashion over the years.

The relationship between objective drug harm and perceived drug harm is very complex, and many factors need to be taken into consideration when we examine these issues. We cannot ignore the fact that the media plays possibly the most important role in regulating the community's perspectives on drug harms. This is why it is so important not to make drugs a 'conversation' per se with your child, but rather have an ongoing dialogue, as not a day goes by when drugs don't end up in the news. Chances are a young person's perception has already been strongly affected by the media, and their views on what the most harmful drugs are is likely very different from the reality.

This is not, however, the only reason why it is important to start the conversation at a young age. In fact, almost every seminar that I run with young people, particularly if it is the first time that I have seen the students, will begin with why we even broach the subject. If the topic is not important, or even more so, if it does not relate to their life, a young person will always be your harshest critic. Their attention span is already short, so if it doesn't matter to them, they can fall asleep pretty quickly!

Drug use matters specifically to young people because it is generally one of the first things they do in their life that has very real and tangible risks for themselves and also for others. The other experience early in their life with a high degree of risk is driving a motor vehicle. These two activities go hand in hand. All significant aspects of human life involve drugs, whether it is medication during pregnancy and/or childbirth; caffeine, consumed daily by almost all Australians; alcohol, used in celebrations well as commiserations; pain relief and other drugs used in palliative care; or taking LSD, which many people report being as one of the most important experiences of their life.

Young people need to be aware that many of the leading causes of death are exacerbated by drug use, for example, use of contaminated needles spreading HIV/AIDS, the contribution of alcohol to cancer and drink driving to road traffic statistics, Chronic Obstructive Pulmonary Disease (COPD) driven by tobacco and heart disease driven by alcohol/tobacco consumption. On the flip side, many diseases, such as smallpox, have been eradicated by drugs (vaccines).

The regulated drug industry (caffeine, alcohol, tobacco and pharmaceuticals) is the largest industry in the world, and with a global ageing population, the pharmaceutical industry is not going to slow down any time soon. The drug trade is second only to arms in terms of scale, yet is greater on profitability measures. Hundreds of millions of people throughout the world use drugs every single year, and the illicit drug trade is a mammoth industry in its own right—larger than many small national economies.

And when it comes to drugs, the more you know, the more you realise how much you do not know! I was not eased gently into this work—I was pushed from personal, peer, academic and societal angles. When I left school, I didn't know what to do, but I liked the idea of PE teaching, so I studied that for a bit before moving into a similar health-related degree. While learning about drugs at University, I worked at a school as a sports coach, and because I was not a qualified teacher, the students didn't have their guard up when talking about risky behaviour that they or their friends engaged in.

The biggest lesson I learnt from those students is that they were never taught what they needed and wanted to hear about drugs, nor how to look after their friends. They were taught what their teachers thought they needed to hear, which was 'don't take drugs, they are bad', as one student told me. During this time, Lilly passed away, and I couldn't turn on the news without hearing a drug-related story. I interpreted it as someone sending me a message. I started writing facts, figures, quotes, information and ideas. Pretty soon, I had an absurd amount of random information written down, which I decided to put into a presentation. All of the information I had written down, however, was one-sided, anti-drugs. But could you blame me?

I had seen my friend die because of drugs; I saw people on the news die because of drugs. I had been told growing up that drugs were bad; drug-related deaths exceeded all other preventable causes of death such as suicide or traffic accidents. I learnt through my studies that drugs were a massive problem at a societal level, and the kids I was teaching were not getting the message because they still took drugs!

I thought that we just weren't shouting the message loudly enough, which is sort of like driving in the wrong direction and thinking that continuing the same way but just driving faster will get you where you need to go. I was doubling and tripling down on what already existed, and then it hit me... All of my efforts had been put into finding evidence to support my predetermined position that drugs were intrinsically bad, when I should have been forming a position based on the evidence.

My views in the beginning were unbalanced, unscientific, close minded, clouded with judgements, morals and opinions, and I was doing a disservice to young people. Getting into the drugs space was the easy part, and my reasons for doing so were straightforward—protecting young lives meant protecting their future. But even though my reasons for working in the drug space never changed—keeping young people safe and giving them the best possible start in life—as I read, watched, listened and soaked in all that I could, my position stood on increasingly shakier grounds. The aim of both Part One and Part Two of this book is to give you bulletproof clarity and understanding on drug-related issues, so that you don't buy into the myths that I did for most of my life.

Most of the drugs that young people are interested in are drugs which affect the brain, such as alcohol, cannabis and ecstasy. The first experience a young person has with a psychoactive (psycho/psyche = brain, active = activity, therefore changing brain activity) drug is generally the most powerful because they have no previous experience or tolerance.

If the initial experience is a positive one, it can lay down overwhelmingly positive memories, which can lead to future drug use and possible dependence later in life. This is particularly true if they are predisposed by factors outside their control, such as genetics or trauma. Negative experiences can actually be beneficial. For example, if the first time someone smokes tobacco, they cough, splutter, feel nauseous and dizzy, they are less likely to try it again. Most young people are not mature, experienced drugs users, meaning they do not employ harm-reduction strategies—they scull their drinks, blaze their joints and down their pills, instead of sipping their drinks, smoking slowly and 'starting low, going slow'.

One of the main reasons drugs which affect the brain are so important is because of the complexity of the human brain. No computer can compete when it comes to the computing power of the human brain. Paradoxically, drugs can damage the brain, and yet when a brain malfunctions, it may be treated with drugs. In Australia, the leading brain disease is dementia. Dementia-related deaths have doubled over the past decade, and it is predicted that within a decade it will be the leading cause of death in the country. The effects of alcohol on the brain will be detailed in later chapters. However, in regards to a young person's brain and alcohol, the evidence is clear: delay any form of alcohol consumption for as long as possible.

At a parent session one night, a mother recounted her later school years to me. She would occasionally get drunk and insisted everyone did it. It was a rite of passage. This has been proven time and again to be incorrect, as the vast majority of secondary school students do not drink or get drunk regularly. What was interesting was that she justified her actions by saying that her drinking didn't harm her at all.

Individual or subjective cases are weak foundations for forming arguments and taking stances on public health issues. They ignore dozens of variables. What if that logic of accepting that 'everyone does it' was applied to those children who were predisposed to dependence because they had parents who were alcoholics? When a child has parents who are or were alcoholics, the child can be born with gamma aminobutyric acid (GABA) receptor alterations in their brain, meaning that when they start drinking at a younger age, they have a higher tolerance to alcohol because they are less sensitive to its effects. They can drink more when they are younger and are more likely to become dependent later in life. What if such a child was in the same situations as Lilly, with no support networks around them to protect them from developing drug problems? Public or social health concerns are exactly that—the public and all of society, not exceptions to the rule.

The statement 'it didn't harm me' is also naïve because it is difficult for an individual to be objective. How would she know if it did harm her? How intelligent or successful could she have become if she hadn't gone out every weekend when her brain was developing and flood it with a toxic chemical? We often hear about brain damage. However, for a young person's brain, what we are really concerned about is the loss of potential.

Parents make so many sacrifices and go to so much effort for their children to give them the best opportunities to reach their potential. Why would a parent give with one hand but then take with the other? Those who justify the allowance of their child's alcohol consumption on the basis of 'I drank, and there's nothing wrong with me' often don't want to look at their own drinking. Is there anything wrong with them? Many people are dependent on alcohol without realising it. Many consume alcohol outside recommended limits and believe the myth that there is a safe level of alcohol consumption.

A child's brain is about the size of their two fists put together. It grows in a way comparable to how a broccoli grows, with one of the last parts of the brain to develop being the prefrontal cortex. The prefrontal cortex governs decision making, and so we have to keep in mind when a young person makes the decision to use a drug at a young age, be it alcohol, cannabis, ecstasy or something else, to an extent, they are missing the part of their brain that, in five, ten or fifteen years' time, would make a different decision. They simply have not lived enough life to experience events that showcase the harm that drugs can cause, and their perception of risk is small compared to the level of reward. Attempting to scare a young person into not using drugs by using extreme examples is futile, because it is either not part of their reality, or whenever serious adverse consequences of someone using a drug do occur, the rarity of them fosters a belief that 'it is never going to happen to me'.

Many of the harms caused by drugs also occur due to chronic and/or long-term use, so scaring a sixteen year old by saying they will end up with oral, breast or liver cancer by middle age because of consistent alcohol consumption will not make a big dent in their judgement. As far as a young person's experience goes, once they sober up and the hangover is behind them, the risks evaporate. They cannot see the long-term harms on their horizon, and since those harms appear to be a lifetime away, they assume their habits can be reversed and they can recover long before then. Plus, one of my favourite reasons as to why a young person is apathetic towards health issues later in life is that they assume by the time they actually end up at that age with a health problem, the medical system will have invented a cure for the illness. Over a decade ago, when I was towards the end of high school, this was the primary justification used by one of my close friends in regard to his smoking. He still smokes today, and is still hoping that a cure for head, neck and lung cancer is discovered.

If you give a young person black and white messages, such as if they use ecstasy, they will die, or if they smoke cannabis, it will make them psychotic, or if they take LSD, they will be stuck in a trip for the rest of their life, what are you going to tell them when a handful of their friends are regular ecstasy users and have suffered no serious adverse reactions? Or when a third of their friends have used cannabis and none are psychotic? Or when someone uses LSD and they describe the trip as life changing and have no long-term side effects? Credibility is very fragile, and sensationalist claims, which attempt to 'scare' the public or young people, provide no benefit in terms of safety.

Professor Charles Yesalis, a world expert on performance-enhancing drugs in sports from Penn State University states in the film *Bigger Stronger Faster*:

> *Education is important, but what you have to watch out for, is embellishing. If you look at 'Reefer Madness', it [cannabis] causes you to be a stark raving murdering lunatic—very funny to watch because it goes so over the edge. Physicians and sport scientists have done*

that with the best of intentions in this area—Oh steroids are going to cause you to drop over dead in your tracks, and so on. Athletes are looking around saying—gee, I haven't seen that many guys die.

So it is important that the conversations around drugs come from a place of objectivity, not of extremes, and instead of messages such as 'if you take x drug, this will happen to you', you can say 'if you use x drug, these are the risks you potentially run'.

If you are unsure of the effects, particularly with illicit drugs due to their purity/adulterant inconsistency as well as emerging psychoactive substances (EPS), explain that they are effectively being a guinea pig for the future, due to the effects being unknown. This is often a more powerful message than using simplistic scare tactics. When you don't know what you are taking, you cannot rule out *any* side effect.

When young people learn about drugs, the overwhelming focus is on how the drugs can affect their health (physical and psychological), both in the short term and in the long term. In my opinion, young people need to be at least aware of the consequences of getting caught with a drug or passing a drug on to one of their friends. More often than not, the criminal sanction that a young person receives in regard to their drug offence will do significantly more harm to them than the drug will to their body.

Not only do we need to be very careful about using the law to harm people, particularly young people, but we also need to ensure that they are fully aware of both the effects of the drug on their health and the criminal sanctions that apply if they are caught in possession, dealing, manufacturing or driving under the influence. Additionally, drug legislation is not uniform throughout the world.

Getting caught with cannabis may land you a fine or caution in Australia, but getting caught with cannabis in parts of South East Asia may land you decades in prison or capital punishment. This should be made very clear to young people, particularly considering the number of high-school leavers who now travel to countries such as Indonesia or Thailand for schoolies or other holidays after school.

South East Asian destinations are popular with Australian school leavers because they are low cost. It is often cheaper to holiday there than domestically or in other international destinations. Many of these countries not only have different punishments, but also completely different criminal justice systems. Young people must be aware that a criminal record at a young age will significantly affect their future, most notably employment. A very large number of employers will do criminal record checks, and even if having a criminal record does not bar the young person from gaining employment, for many employers, the existence of a criminal record will alter the perception of a potential employee. It will also alter friend's and acquaintance's perceptions of the convicted person.

It is important to note that the additional problems created by handing someone a criminal record, particularly a young person, are problems that are not limited to the convicted. Increases in criminal records inevitably generate greater stresses on social security, particularly unemployment benefits, housing and public health care—all of which are footed by the taxpayer. And this is one of the most important points when it comes to why drugs are important. Young people must understand that if they choose to use a drug, it is not just them who could be affected.

For a very short period of time, I worked at a drug rehabilitation facility in Sydney. When I tell people that I work in drug education, they always ask if I talk about alcohol as well. And of course, that begs the question: does the community think alcohol is a drug? We will come to that later.

One seventeen year old boy from the north coast of New South Wales (NSW) I worked closely with was undergoing treatment, primarily for crack cocaine use. Although he had attempted to complete the program multiple times, he never managed to get over the finish line. Towards the end of a particular week, I took him to a nearby bank to withdraw his most recent Centrelink payment of approximately $600, which had been deposited the previous day. We had a chat about a lot of things while we were walking to the bank, including what he was planning to do when he finished treatment. I got the feeling that this boy was going to self-discharge as soon as he got his payment, and because he was not bailed to treatment, there would be no warrant out for his arrest if he was to leave, so there was little incentive to stay. He made a comment that has stuck with me. I asked him what he was planning to do with his money, and he immediately replied, 'I can't wait—I'm going to go get some crack'.

He said this as we were walking through a busy shopping and business area. I had to restrain myself from grabbing this kid by the collar, belting him and screaming at him, 'You see all these people here—all of these people who are busting their ass, working ten to twelve hour days in jobs they hate to pay their mortgage and put food on the table for their family? Much of their income is forcibly taken away from them through taxation, and some will even lose half of their income through taxation. That money goes to the government to pay for services, such as education, defence and healthcare. However, the largest cost is social security and welfare, which is exactly what you are receiving to help your disadvantaged situation.'

I felt like telling him that he was not entitled to use their money for illicit drugs, and if that was how you chose to use it, your financial assistance should be denied, as it is both not your money, and those who fund your life should be able to put conditions on how it is spent.

This boy would be oblivious to the concept that hard-working Australians are providing him with financial assistance to improve his life, and for him to take that opportunity for a ride seemed like an abuse of that privilege. Individuals do have the right to choose what they put into their body, but only as long as they are not asking others to pay for the consequences of that choice. This is precisely the reason why we place heavy taxes on tobacco, as well as alcohol, and why there is a strong push to implement a sugar tax. All these products place significant strain on the public health system, and the taxation acts, not only as a deterrent to curb the usage of these products but also to offset the cost to public health.

One of the most fundamental concepts that a young person learns growing up is that every action and choice they make has a knock-on effect to others in some way, and drugs are no exception. Young people are inherently self-focused, often lacking insight into how their actions affect others, and part of the developmental process is learning to function within society, not that society functions around them, or as psychology professor Jean Twenge puts it better in her outstanding 2006 book, *Generation Me*:

> *Children are naturally self-centred; growing up is the process of learning how to empathise with other people. Instead of children doing 'all about me' projects, or writing 'commercials' advertising themselves, perhaps they could learn about another child in the class... Children would learn a lot more from this type of project and might also develop empathy.*

Much of this has to do with basic brain development; however, evidence suggests that young people are a lot more self-focused than previous generations. It is argued that this is a result of Western culture moving towards individualism, away from collectivism. There are dozens of examples that reflect this, such as the sharp decrease within books and music of the words 'we', 'us', 'our' and 'them', while an equal increase in the words 'I', 'me', 'my' and 'you' as well as the phrases 'I love me', 'just be yourself' and 'love yourself'. The delay and decline of people getting married are said to be a result of people wanting to pursue careers, travel, education and finding themselves before starting a family—all of these reasons are focused on the self. Over the past fifty years, secondary school students have progressively assigned less value to helping others, making friends or enjoying and finding interest in work, while progressively assigning more value to vacation time, money and respect from work colleagues—again, a movement towards the self.

A 2012 study of Finnish adolescents in the *Journal of Adolescence* showed that from 1983 to 2007, collective fears such as war, terrorism, crime, economic instability and the harsh judgement of society decreased, while individualistic fears such as relationships, loneliness, education, personal health and death increased dramatically.

Across the Western world, children are decreasingly being given common names at birth, which is a testament to the individualistic ethos of uniqueness and standing out, rather than belonging and fitting in. In Australia, the average house size has doubled in the past fifty years, despite family sizes shrinking, meaning the average floor area per person has tripled—each person has more of their own individual space. My mother was one in a family of seven living in a three-bedroom, one-bathroom house, yet I was one in a family of three living in a four-bedroom, two-bathroom house.

The fact that everything is personalised—media service providers such as Netflix, Stan and Foxtel allow individuals to personalise entertainment by electing exactly what they want. It's not a coincidence that iTunes, iPod and iPhone all start with the letting 'I' or that YouTube's slogan is 'broadcast yourself'. Or that you can personalise your own vehicle license plate or that you can get a bottle of Coke with your name on it or that everyone has their own personal ringtones or that you can go to Nike and get your own custom-designed shoes. If you went back twenty to thirty years, and saw someone taking a picture of themselves, let alone with a selfie stick, that would be considered extremely strange behaviour, but now it's common. Everyone is considered special, even though the intrinsic meaning of the word does not allow for this—nobody is special if everyone is.

The individualism movement has however led to some wonderful changes in society such as equal rights, regardless of race, gender or sexual orientation. Some argue that the use of any drug for psychoactive pleasurable effects is selfish in its nature, as it ignores the potential harm which others face, either in the short term, such as violence or traffic accidents, or in the long term, such as losses in economic productivity or increased strain on health care system. Many young people are not particularly concerned or aware of how drugs affect others, while other young people who have suffered difficult lives, such as through trauma, are self-focused because it has developed as a natural mechanism to protect themselves.

While someone may justify using a drug by saying it is their choice and they aren't harming anyone else, the reality is that often others *are* paying for it. Only if nobody loved you and you lived on an isolated island would no one else be affected. The primary reason legislation exists in regard to drugs is not to protect the person using the drug, but to protect society, which is ultimately damaged, whether it be through measurable costs, such as loss of productivity, health care or policing time, or through immeasurable costs, such as familial emotional suffering or an individual's loss of potential.

A student disagreed with me once on this concept by using the analogy of a seatbelt, arguing that if someone chooses to not wear a seatbelt, then they also choose the consequences, and since the driver will be the only one harmed, why do we need seatbelt regulations? I explained that if the person has an accident and becomes a permanent quadriplegic due to not wearing a seatbelt, then the public health system would have to take charge of their life, which is not only emotionally distressful for the family and friends but also horrendously expensive for taxpayers. The societal costs of drugs exceed $55,000,000,000 in Australia, and young people need to be aware of this, as they will be the ones paying for it in the future. Even if someone chooses to be a non-smoker, non-drinker, and never touches an illicit drug, they as a taxpayer bear the cost.

3

WHY DO WE HAVE DRUGS,
WHERE DO THEY COME FROM,
AND HOW ARE THEY USED?

Drug-related issues are almost unrivalled in terms of the controversy and intensity of debate they generate. Whether it be decriminalisation, pill testing, opioid-substitution therapy or incarceration, drug-related topics are guaranteed to produce limitless, fiery debates. Although society typically views a schism in the drug space between drugs that have medical uses and drugs that do not, drugs at an organic level have existed for thousands of years.

There are suggestions that fermented beverages have been around for 10,000 years; however, the oldest drugs are alkaloids contained in the coca leaf—approximately 8,000 years, alkaloids contained in the peyote cactus—approximately 5,500 years, alkaloids contained in the opium poppy—approximately 5,000 years, and cannabis, containing tetrahydrocannabinol (THC—the 'stoning' psychoactive compound), and cannabidiol (CBD—non-psychoactive compound)—approximately 4,500 years, but evidence from Egyptian tombs suggests cannabis being used possibly as long as 6,000 years ago.

During the 1960s, archaeologists suggested that the first known use of a psychoactive compound occurred around 9000 BC in Asia and comprised chewing areca nuts and the betel leaf to release arecoline, a stimulant comparable to nicotine. It is fairly clear that the instinctive human desire to explore the depths of our own mind and to experience a somewhat different form of reality existed well before the law stepped in to control these behaviours. In fact, laws controlling the use and distribution of such drugs are not much more than 100 years old.

These earliest discovered drugs were all derivatives of plant material, and it is hypothesised that the word 'drug' originated from the Dutch word *droge-vate* or *droog*, both essentially meaning 'dried plant'. But why would plants produce chemicals that produce psychoactive properties? This is probably best rationalised by the model of natural selection, which biologist Charles Darwin conceptualised in the mid-1800s. Natural selection was a keystone feature of Darwin's theory of evolution, where organisms such as humans, plants and animals survived by passing on the characteristics that fostered survival to their offspring.

It was also during the 1800s that large pharmaceutical companies began to emerge, largely due to the discovery that compounds could be isolated and extracted from plants, providing the commercial opportunity for patenting. Plants develop multiple defences to ensure their survival such as thorns to shield themselves from insect predators, and some of these defences are of chemical nature. When insects land on a plant, and attempt to consume its nutrients, the plant releases natural insecticides that, at certain levels, poison the insect by overloading its nervous system, thereby ensuring the plant's survival.

Nicotine is a natural insecticide produced in the *Nicotiana tabacum* tobacco plant, as is cocaine produced in the *Erythroxylon coca* plant and caffeine in the guarana and *Camellia sinensis* plant. The psychedelic drug LSD is derived from lysergic acid produced by the ergot fungus, while psychedelic psilocybin is derived from hundreds of different varieties of mushrooms, and another psychedelic N,N-dimethyltryptamine (DMT) is produced from the plant *Psychotria viridis*. The stimulant MDMA is synthesised from safrole, which can be extracted from the root bark of the sassafras tree, aspirin is derived from the bark in willow trees, while some depressants such as morphine, heroin and oxycodone all part of the opioid family, derived from the opioid poppy. Some plants also contain chemicals that hold high ultraviolet absorption properties, which protect the plant from sun exposure damage, such as tetrahydrocannabinol (THC) in the cannabis plant.

From a historical perspective, the initial discovery that plants produced chemicals that had physiological effects on humans came about inadvertently. More recently, scientific and technological advancements have allowed researchers to artificially produce chemicals in a more systematic and sophisticated process. Paclitaxel, which is a chemotherapy drug, part of the taxane family, is yielded from the pacific yew tree. However, now due to plant cell fermentation, it can be produced by isolating molecules from the twigs of the tree, and growing the cells artificially. Natural cannabis has been used for thousands of years. However, the primary active chemical in cannabis THC can now be synthesised artificially using column chromatography. THC is the active chemical in dronabinol—one of the very few cannabis-based medicines. Other synthetic cannabis compounds, known as synthetic cannabinoids (SC), have also been created. However, this has been to the detriment of public health because, although these drugs were originally invented as an improvement on cannabis as a medicine and bind to the same receptors, they are much more powerful and can be highly toxic.

⁓

Drugs were initially discovered by accident, but now exist as a key component in the practice of medicine, and as the practice of medicine has developed over thousands of years, so have drugs and how they are used as treatments. Drugs are nothing more than chemicals producing physiological changes in the body and were naturally formed through evolution, and it is critical that young people appreciate drugs from this context and do not buy into the media rhetoric, which portrays drugs as evil or a product of the devil.

When drugs possessing medical value are consumed for other reasons or in other ways, they often end up on media or political platforms, and here enters the concept of recreational drugs, or more correctly 'drugs used for recreational purposes', as there is no such thing as an intrinsic recreational drug. When drugs were initially discovered, humans viewed them as tools to derive spiritual or medicinal value from; they were not consumed for hedonism. Sadly, researchers and practitioners have been forced in recent history to keep some drug discoveries quiet in the fear that particular drugs will make their way into the recreational market, become a political football and subsequently be banned.

An example of this is MDMA (drug in ecstasy), which was originally synthesised in 1912 by the oldest pharmaceutical company in the world, Merck. MDMA was referred to in medical literature as methylsafryla-min, and was essentially untested on humans until 1960. Originally, the substance was just a precursor in a new chemical pathway that was patented as a means of avoiding an existing patent used in the synthesis of hydrastinine, which is a clotting agent.

There was limited and erratic use of MDMA by therapists until the 1970s, until the 'godfather of psychedelics', Alexander Shulgin, resynthesised the drug, and suggested to his colleagues that they use it in conjunction with psychotherapy. In 1977, Shulgin introduced MDMA to one of his colleagues Leo Zeff—another pioneer in the use of psychoactive drugs in psychotherapy—who then subsequently spread the popularity of MDMA through training thousands of therapists. It is estimated that by the time of Zeff's passing in 1988, approximately 4,000 therapists were using MDMA in clinical settings. Zeff was so impressed by the therapeutic value of MDMA, claiming that one MDMA-assisted therapy session was equal to at least six months of traditional therapy.

In the early days of its use in psychotherapy, MDMA was not well known, and therapists attempted to keep it that way to avoid it being taken up by the recreational drug scene, which would likely lead to its prohibition. It was not long after the drug had spread through clinical networks that it leaked into the recreational scene, and a small market was born. With its growing popularity in nightclubs throughout the 1980s, politicians pressured the Drug Enforcement Administration (DEA—established 1973) to illegalise MDMA, and despite enormous protest from the entire medical community due to its efficacy in treatment, the drug was placed in Schedule 1. The scheduling of MDMA in the USA sparked a movement to illegalise the drug internationally.

No research has been undertaken that evaluates whether illegalising a drug actually deters usage, although it certainly prohibits or, at the very least, makes it difficult for clinicians to use or study. Although the populist belief is that MDMA, the active ingredient in ecstasy, is a party or recreational drug, the drug has its roots in a clinical setting. The law is an extremely powerful force when it comes to changing the public's perception of drugs, what their harms are and why they are used. If you ask someone what ecstasy is and why people use it, the response is typically that it is a dangerous drug used for fun, but if those same people knew of the MDMA's efficacy in treating illnesses that are extremely difficult to treat, such as post-traumatic stress disorder (PTSD), would they see the same drug in the same light? Would the public view LSD in the same light if they knew that it was the most effective treatment for alcoholism? Would the public see ketamine in the same light if they knew of its use in the treatment of depression? Of course, the tension point with every drug is whether the benefits outweigh the harms. Basically, every drug that is prohibited in Australia was previously used for its medical value. However, when a drug is banned, its medical utility is dismissed, and it can no longer be viewed as a chemical that humans can extract any value from, other than recreational value with the potential for serious harm, and that is often how illegal drugs are viewed.

I run sessions with primary school students and one of the first things I cover is what a drug is and some examples of drugs. It always amazes me that while very few students mention alcohol, tobacco or pharmaceuticals, they usually know all the illegal drugs. Straight away you know that their main source for information about drugs is the media, and this is typically focused on the most obvious aspects of drug harm. Drugs tend to end up on the news when someone dies, is hospitalised or is arrested overseas.

When a young person thinks of drugs, a dark cloud forms in their mind and they conjure up negative connotations. It does not register that they were brought into the world with drugs, treated or cured by drugs at various points in their life, and that they are spared from dying before reaching their teen years from infectious diseases due to vaccinations.

One of the questions I ask students is why people use drugs. The most common response is that they are addicted, or they started using drugs for fun and then they ended up addicted. Both of these answers are true; however, they only paint a very small part of the picture. People use drugs for a wide variety of reasons, and the majority of people are not causing substantial harm to themselves or others. This is one of the arguments that the alcohol industry uses, not only to justify their product as a legal drug, but also an argument to block any legislative reform that aims to curb use and harm of alcohol. What is interesting is that all young people are able to give examples of how drugs cause harm, either to the user or to others, but I have only met a handful of students who can give examples of the factors that influence drug harm other than the drug itself.

It is important to know that the drug choice and the amount used are only two aspects that dictate harm potential. The product may contain other drugs or adulterants that are more toxic than the intended drug. The product may be used in an unsafe environment such as in a back alley with no supervision, or in an isolated area without access to medical assistance, or it may be taken in haste if the user notices police near them and attempts to avoid prosecution. The cost of the drug may change the harmfulness. Products that are less expensive may contain harmful additives whereas an expensive drug may be highly potent, increasing financial pressure on user if dependent as well as possibly a greater chance of overdosing. The psychological state of the user at the time of ingestion is another factor; it is advised that if someone is going to use a psychedelic drug, that they do it when they are in a positive state of mind, where they feel safe and not scared, as opposed to being alone and anxious. It is not only the type of drug, or amount of drug, but also the time between each dose; an adult drinking an entire bottle of bourbon evenly over two weeks is unlikely to be significantly intoxicated at any time, however consuming the same amount over a couple of hours is likely to be fatal.

The projected effects of a drug, based on its chemical make-up in a test tube or the effect the drug produces in animals do not predict what effects it will have on humans, and this is why rigorous clinical trials exist. Despite the fact that loperamide (anti-diarrhoea medication) and diamorphine (heroin used for pain relief) are both opioids and chemically almost identical outside of the body, loperamide does not cross the blood-brain barrier and produces no psychoactive effects, whereas diamorphine crosses the blood-brain barrier rapidly and has very powerful psychoactive effects.

Clinical trials are experiments containing several progressive (group size etc.) phases designed to answer questions regarding the safety and efficacy of drug and non-drug interventions in a methodological manner. The gold standard for clinical trials is randomised (subjects are assigned drug or placebo on a random basis), double-blind (neither subjects or experimenters know the placebo or drug assigning), or triple-blind (subjects, administrators and evaluators don't know assignment of drug or placebo) and placebo controlled (fake treatment). This type of study reduces or eliminates any bias or confounding factors and is important for public health because it can illustrate the efficacy of medical intervention in a more reliable and accurate fashion. An example of this is hormone replacement therapy, which population observations suggested to be beneficial for postmenopausal women. However, when controlled trials were conducted, they consistently showed significant cardiovascular and thromboembolic (clotting) risks.

A significant number of clinical trials exclude specific groups for safety reasons such as women for fertility risks, and only a very small number of drugs trialled progress to approval. Two of the most spectacular drug failures in recent history were theralizumab (TGN1412), which underwent clinical trials in London as an immunotherapeutic drug, and BIA 10-2474, which underwent clinical trials in France for the treatment of a wide range of illnesses. Three pre-clinical trials suggested safety in human administration. However, in the first human clinical trial of TGN1412, despite the fact all volunteers were healthy and were administered with doses approximately 500 times lower than had been tested safely in animals, all suffered disastrous reactions. Most suffered multiple organ failures, with one volunteer losing fingers and toes. All volunteers needed extensive hospitalisation, and all have likely suffered permanent damage to their immune system.

During the trial of BIA 10-2474, all volunteers were healthy and none had reported any side effects. However, on the fifth dose level, a volunteer reported experiencing neurological problems and was subsequently hospitalised. He lapsed into a coma the following day and was pronounced dead one week later. Other volunteers survived; however, they required hospitalisation and were left with irreversible neurological disabilities. Both of these drugs were trialled in animals with no reported negative outcomes. Administering these drugs to healthy human volunteers, well below clinical doses, while following correct protocols resulted in outcomes that were catastrophic in both studies.

Even if a drug gains approval after clinical trials, there is no guarantee that it will not cause significant harm following long-term use. All drugs are harmful because even the safest drugs have lethal doses, as well as the potential for issues, such as side effects, allergic reactions and withdrawals. There have been drugs that were deemed safe in clinical trials, such as thalidomide and fenfluramine, which have now been withdrawn due to safety issues. Although used initially for its antiemetic (anti-nausea) properties, primarily morning sickness, thalidomide was later withdrawn due to the drug causing birth defects, liver damage, blood clots and cardiovascular and neurological problems. Fenflura-mine was initially used to suppress appetite, typically in significantly overweight patients, but was later withdrawn due to the drug causing damage to heart valves as well as increases in insomnia, anxiety, cognitive impairments and the risk of serotonin syndrome.

~⁓~

The method in which the drug gets into the body (route of administration—ROA) is one of the most important aspects contributing to overall drug harm, possibly the most important, and there are over 100 pathways for a drug to enter the body. Drugs that are injected, particularly intravenously (into the vein), or smoked reach the brain fastest and in the greatest concentration. However, they both carry higher risks when compared to other routes, such as topical or oral use. Inhaling any burnt substance will damage the mouth, throat and lungs. This is one of the reasons why using a vaporiser (vaping) is significantly less harmful than smoking, as it heats the substance to the point where it can be inhaled but not to the point where it is burnt.

Injecting any drug carries the risk of transmitting infections, damaging the skin or veins, a higher risk of overdose as well as a higher risk of dependence due to the drug entering and exiting brain more rapidly. When injected, drugs are also not metabolised by the liver or digested by the stomach. Users who inject often want to either conserve their drugs by making each hit go further or achieve the biggest high possible, regardless of the risks. If someone is not injecting, they should not start, but if they are injecting, they should switch to a safer method, such as snorting, or at least avoid injecting into the veins.

Injecting into a vein (intravenous) rather than the muscle (intramuscular) is the riskiest method, and the most hazardous sites include the neck and groin. Injecting into the neck is exceptionally risky because of the risk of abscesses, nerve damage and, if the carotid artery is hit, severe bleeding. The neck area can also swell, which can obstruct the airway, and vein clots can stop blood flow because of close proximity to the heart. Injecting into the groin is also very risky because veins, arteries and nerves cross over each other, and like injecting into the buttocks, it can be hard for users to see. The feet and armpits are also highly risky sites.

It cannot be overstated how much greater the risk is to inject any drug. Oral anabolic steroid users, for example, may face minor side effects, such as acne, male pattern baldness and gynecomastia. However, if they switch to injecting, they can collapse veins and potentially contract terminal diseases—which are far more harmful than the risks associated with oral use. This is particularly so if the user is inexperienced, untrained or lacks basic understanding of injection safety, such as the bevel of the syringe facing upwards, not frontloading or backloading, not injecting into a pulse or simpler strategies, such as washing hands prior to touching any equipment. Using sterile equipment does not eliminate all risks, but it certainly reduces them.

Safer methods, such as oral use, are not without their dangers, however. As the drug is absorbed at a slower rate, the person may mistake the delayed effects as a low dose and subsequently take more. An example of this is the common belief that instead of smoking cannabis, eating cannabis brownies or cookies is safer. While this avoids smoking harms and the drug is absorbed at a slower rate, the user may consume more, unaware that they have taken a large dose. When drugs are absorbed at a slower rate, regulating intake becomes increasingly difficult.

Oral administration is thought to be the safest way of using a drug, particularly with certain illicit drugs, such as cocaine, where chewing a coca leaf to administer the drug at a slower rate to the brain is safer compared to the hazards associated with smoking or injecting the same drug. Users may not only increase the dosage, but also change routes of administration as their habit develops, such as a user moving from snorting, to smoking, to injecting in order to achieve the same or greater high as their tolerance builds. Only a very small number of drug users inject, but it can be a very slippery slope.

Drugs are often not used in singular fashion, and polydrug use (using two or more drugs at or near the same time) changes both the effects of each of the drugs as well as the potential harms. Polydrug use essentially has three primary considerations: synergistic interactions, antagonistic interactions and new chemicals created. Mixing two or more drugs that have parallel effects, such as alcohol and methadone, results in a potentiating effect. In this case, much greater respiratory depression than if either drug was used in isolation. Mixing two or more drugs that have contrasting effects, such as alcohol and caffeine or MDMA, will result in the intoxicating effects being diminished. The alcohol and hospitality industry have attempted to utilise this concept by going into partnership with energy drink companies such as Red Bull and V. Combining alcoholic beverages with energy drinks to create products such as Vodka Red Bulls and Jägerbombs encourages the consumer to drink more alcohol due to the caffeine acting as a masking agent to hide the intoxicating effects of the alcohol. This, of course, is very effective in making people consume more alcohol, therefore, generating more profits for the vendor.

In this case, the user may not be consciously attempting to mask alcohol intoxication, but in other cases of polydrug use, users often combine drugs in an attempt to enhance the high as well as minimise or offset the negative side effects or comedown of individual drugs. A number of celebrities have died over the years engaging in a particularly risky example of this, known as 'speedballing' or 'powerballing', where users typically consume cocaine and heroin or morphine simultaneously. The cocaine, being a stimulant, reduces the drowsy effect of the heroin, and the heroin, as a depressant, reduces the anxiety experienced in cocaine use. However, it is extremely difficult to create equilibrium in the concentration and effects of these drugs. Coupled with suppressing the side effects, so the user cannot gauge their own level of intoxication, this activity is exceptionally risky. The user is also at risk of administering a lethal dose if the drugs do not wear off in unison, and the user experiences the effects of one of these drugs in isolation. In this case, the user is given a false sense of tolerance until it is too late, due to the effects of each drug temporarily cancelling out the negative side effects of the other.

The final consideration in polydrug use occurs when two drugs are taken in conjunction and create a new chemical, which often is more toxic than the two chemicals individually. Cocaethylene is a cardiotoxic compound created when alcohol and cocaine are used concurrently. It is thought that due to the majority of cocaine users also simultaneously consuming alcohol, the subsequently generated metabolite, cocaethylene, is why cocaine is frequently reported in emergency department presentations.

Mixing drugs can also have a number of other complications. Two of the drugs most commonly used together are alcohol and cannabis. One of the most common outcomes for a person drinking to excess is vomiting, which is due to the body rejecting the substance. On the other hand, cannabis contains THC, which is an antiemetic drug, that is, a drug used to treat nausea and vomiting, typically associated with motion sickness, anaesthetics and, in THC's case, chemotherapy.

If a person consumes alcohol to the point where they need to vomit, but have also used cannabis, they run the risk of the cannabis negating the body's ability to rid itself of the alcohol. Therefore, they may be at greater risk of either choking on their vomit or not clearing the contents and thus increasing their risk of alcohol poisoning.

Although many people never intend to use illicit drugs, this can often change if they are under the influence of alcohol, as alcohol is one of the very few drugs that actually alters judgement. Not only may a person use another drug on top of the alcohol, but they may take more or too much of another drug if they are disinhibited. Although this will be covered later, polydrug use is not specific to non-medical drugs, and examples of this are taking antidepressants with stimulants, which increases the risk of serotonin syndrome, and taking alcohol with antibiotics or the contraceptive pill. In the case of antibiotics, this can make it harder for the person to recover, and in the case of the contraceptive pill, the pill will be rendered ineffective if the individual vomits it up after drinking.

It should also be noted that not only are there drug-drug interactions, but also food-drug interactions, and this is particularly important for those who take specific medication on a regular basis. Foods high in vitamin K, such as kale and spinach, interact with blood-thinning medication, such as warfarin, rivaroxaban and heparin, and some citrus fruit juices, such as grapefruit, interact with more than eighty medications, including benzodiazepines and amphetamines.

The drugs that are the primary focus of this book are those used to improve hedonic tone (to feel better), through either the increasing of pleasure, or the reduction of suffering. Although many of these drugs were initially synthesised for medical or spiritual purposes, they are often used today for recreational purposes, that is, for reasons other than their medicinal value.

Almost every person in the world has used a drug at some point, however, only a small percentage of those users become dependent at any stage in their life. Most people who have experimented with illicit drugs left it at that—an experiment—that is, they have come out of the other end of the experience and not continued to use. The vast majority of people who have used drugs in the past function well in society. They pay their taxes, maintain good relationships, succeed in their careers and, in some cases, end up being elected President or Prime Minister.

4

Why do People Use Drugs, How do People End up Addicted or Dependent, and Can They be Cured?

No one who ends up addicted or dependent had the intention of ending up that way, and behind every person who is, there is a story. There are many people, however, who believe that addiction does not exist, and that the reason people continue to use drugs is because they are morally weak, lack willpower and choose that lifestyle.

This logic is flawed, ignorant and exists for a variety of reasons. Addiction is a brain disorder where a person compulsively engages with rewarding and reinforcing stimuli, despite negative consequences to their life. The same can be true of other things, such as food, sex or gambling, that is, compulsive palatable food consumption despite obesity, compulsive sexual activity despite relationship failure or contracting sexually transmitted diseases, and compulsive gambling despite financial losses.

The addiction can be in the form of a substance, or it can be behavioural. Dependence differs from addiction as dependence refers to a physiological adaptive state of tolerance, where someone continues to use a drug to keep themselves out of withdrawal. The person who is dependent receives a diminishing effect every time they use the drug, and they require more of the drug to achieve the desired effect. Of course, in the space between an external stimulus and an individual's response is the power of choice. While the initial drug consumption may have been a choice, once physiological changes take place, that drive is so strong, it is hard to consider subsequent consumption truly the result of choice.

If an outsider sees a person who is affected by a drug in some way, it is easy to jump to a simplistic conclusion—as Dr Phil says 'You choose the behaviour, you choose the consequences'. However, not everyone is born with the same brain physiology or is born into the same place in society, and therefore, even if two people engage with identical stimuli, the subsequent outcomes may be very different. If John and Harry both choose to use an identical amphetamine but Harry has a significantly lower level of dopamine receptors in his brain, he will experience extreme pleasure when using the drug compared to John because a low level of dopamine receptors sensitises individuals to stimulants. This low level also tends to also predispose individuals to addiction to other drugs, such as alcohol, and animal studies have demonstrated that increasing the level of dopamine receptors results in reduced alcohol consumption.

Harry's brain now associates the drug with intense pleasure, therefore making it more likely that he repeats use. Repeated usage desensitises the receptors, which means he needs more of the drug to achieve the same high as his tolerance increases. Repeated administration of the drug creates physical changes in his brain, chaining him to the drug, because if he reduces or stops using the drug, withdrawals will kick in and drive future use. You can add background details to the hypothesis, such as Harry being abused as a child, disconnected from his family and without other supportive networks to pull him out of dependence. So, despite John and Harry engaging with the same stimuli (using an amphetamine):

- Harry was already predisposed to addiction due to his brain chemistry before he used the drug

- Harry continued to use the drug due to his brain's response
- Harry was unable to lower his drug use due to withdrawals
- Harry had no family or supportive networks to protect him from, or pull him out of, addiction
- Harry may only feel a reduction in his trauma-related suffering when using the drug.

Of course, John and Harry both had the same intention (to increase hedonic tone) and engaged with the same stimuli (using an amphetamine). However, Harry became addicted due to reasons outside of his control, not because he was morally weaker than John. People often report using drugs for pleasure, but often the pleasure that they receive is due to the drug keeping them out of withdrawal. Although smokers and drinkers may report that they use these drugs to relax, if they were to abstain for a period of time, they may experience anxiousness, irritability and sweating among other withdrawal symptoms, and the relaxation they feel is actually due to keeping the withdrawal at bay.

A collective complaint from addicts is that they do not want to continue using because the drug no longer provides them any enjoyment or pleasure. However, repeated use causes a shift in brain responses from the reward centre (nucleus accumbens) to other areas of the brain, such as the basal ganglia, that govern habits. The resulting and often permanent change in brain function means the user loses control of what was once a voluntary habit. The changes that occur in the brain can be so significant and powerful that the user can die simply from withdrawals caused by abrupt cessation. Almost 600 Australians annually undergo limb amputations for smoking-related peripheral artery disease, and these patients would have avoided amputations if they had quit, despite the fact that four out of five smokers want to quit, have tried to quit and have failed to quit.

Of course, people initiate drug use for a wide variety of reasons, and many continue to use drugs for reasons other than dependence. Initial drug uptake often occurs due to curiosity, peer pressure (desire to feel accepted by peers), or as a means of escape, due to prior events, such as childhood trauma or sexual abuse. The social and emotional environment is one of the most important factors that leads an individual to using drugs for the first time as well as whether they continue or not. The effects that someone experiences when they are using a drug for the first time are very important in regard to future usage, and often the initial effects are good predictors of future use. Many people are also dependent on drugs such as caffeine, alcohol or benzodiazepines without even being aware of it, and their withdrawals are often mild. Some people cannot get through the morning without a double espresso, some people cannot relax in the evening without a glass of wine, and some people find it difficult to fall asleep without sleeping tablets.

When someone abstains from using a drug for a period of time, withdrawals can begin within hours and can last for several months, with the first few weeks often being the most difficult. During the time a person is abstaining, their tolerance is resetting. However, this does not mean that the person is 'cured' from their addiction at any point in time during their abstinence. The reality is that addiction cannot be cured like curing influenza or a broken finger. The person will always be prone to 'falling off the wagon', as not only do they have an underlying predisposition, but their brain has changed due to repeated drug administration. Unfortunately, little research has been done into treatments that can keep people abstinent. This is also true for other mental health illnesses such as depression and related mood disorders where patients are deficient or have a dysregulation in 5-HT1A receptors. Even when treatment works, they still have a relative deficiency, meaning they are always vulnerable to relapse. In terms of treatment, individuals do not 'get rid' of depressive thoughts, but they learn not to access them.

Actor Philip Seymour Hoffman abused alcohol and a myriad of illicit drugs in his early twenties, attended rehabilitation, and then began a period of abstinence that lasted twenty-three years. He relapsed at the age of forty-six and died of a multiple drug overdose (amphetamines, benzodiazepines, heroin and cocaine). It is unclear whether every single one of these drugs contributed to his death, however, it is highly likely that the 'speedball' combination of heroin and cocaine was the primary cause. The point is that after twenty-three years of abstinence, Hoffman was still vulnerable, and he was by no means cured. Recent evidence suggests that the endorphin system may underpin many drug addictions, and some drugs used to treat addiction, such as naltrexone and nalmafene, work by blocking endorphin receptors.

The ultimate goal of abstinence-based treatment is cessation, remaining drug free, and there is little flexibility by way of harm-reduction approaches that accept that individuals may not be able to remain entirely drug free. The primary criticism of harm-reduction approaches is that the approach enables and accepts some level of drug use, while one of the primary criticisms of abstinence-based treatment is that it is unrealistic to expect individuals to remain completely drug free. Although some individuals are able to stop using and never look back, insisting that abstinence is the only option and then considering the individual 'cured' after a drug-free period is extremely risky. If the individual loses tolerance, is not monitored and relapses, they have a significantly higher mortality risk, which is what happened to Amy Winehouse.

This is particularly true for drug users who are discharged from hospital or treatment services or are released from custody. During imprisonment, if they don't use drugs, their tolerance drops, but when released, they can relapse and die, even if they use a related compound or a weaker dose because of a loss in their buffer of tolerance. In the first week of being released from prison, opioid addicts are forty times more likely to die than the general population. There is a projection of cessation in harm reduction approaches, but for the many who relapse and return to a level of drug use comparable to previous use, their risk of overdose is much greater because not only is the intrinsic pharmacological risk of overdose high with drugs like opioids, but after a period of abstinence, they are without any barrier of tolerance. And abrupt cessation of some drugs such as alcohol or benzodiazepines, without appropriate medical care, can result in fatal withdrawals.

❧

Matthew Perry, who played Chandler Bing in the hit comedy show, *Friends,* is a confessed alcoholic, and in a panel discussion on BBC *Newsnight* he recounted the nature of his addiction, despite at the time being 'recovered':

> *I am in control of the first drink, so I do all of these things to protect my body from having the first drink, but after having that first drink, the allergy [reaction] of the body kicks in, and I cannot stop after that.*

Curing should be rephrased or categorised as 'remaining in recovery', as the person is in a state of maintenance and will never be fully disconnected from their previous addicted state. Despite the fact that addiction manifests in physiological changes, addiction is a mental health disorder, and it shares many similarities with other mental health disorders. Chronic drug use, chronic depression, chronic obsessive-compulsive disorder and chronic pain are all brain disorders where a person can get locked into a rigid brain pattern. With chronic drug use, the person may repeatedly anticipate and desire the drug, with chronic depression a person may get locked into repetitive negative thinking and with chronic pain, the only thing that the person can focus on is the consistent intensity of the pain.

Unfortunately for many mental disorders, medications do not work, work partially, can make the illness worse before there is any improvement and can lose effectiveness over time. One of my closest family members is a textbook case, reflecting the ongoing battle that the medical community has with mental health. Shelly (not her real name) has been diagnosed with a form of major depressive disorder and over a number of years has been prescribed different antidepressants, antipsychotics and benzodiazepines in various combinations and concentrations. She has also undergone electro-convulsive therapy (ECT).

As I write this, she will be going back into a psychiatric hospital in two days' time, her fifth admission in just over a year. Her brain is locked in a pattern of negative and anxious thoughts, and for every good day or half day she is free of that state of mind, a bad day is just around the corner. Despite meditation, ECT, approximately a dozen different medications, lifestyle changes and psychological therapy, in the past two years she has spent more time in hospital than out. She has had all of the light drawn out of her life and she does not know if it will ever be back. Like all people with mental health disorders, she is trapped in the hardest prison on earth to break out of—her own mind.

Irish playwright George Bernard Shaw said, 'Progress is impossible without change, and those who cannot change their mind, cannot change anything'. Much of what we learn growing up is also about locked, rigid patterns of thinking and conforming to the structures of society. This is very effective if someone wants to learn a language, principles of economics or mathematical formulas but, it can constrain how the brain functions in terms of creativity, looking at life and situations from different perspectives or being freed from continual negative self-narrations. Our brains are most flexible when we are young, but as we age and our neural pathways become formed and hardwired, it becomes much harder to alter how one's brain functions, hence the phrase 'old habits die hard'. It is extremely difficult to disrupt this repetitive pattern of thought processing in the brain, which is one of the reasons why we cannot free a person from the cage of their addiction. What we can do, however, is keep them in recovery and ensure they don't tap into those negative thoughts.

The consequential question of this predicament is, of course, if some mental health disorders share the same characteristics of locked repetitive brain patterns, is there something that can unlock these brain configurations? The answer is that it is highly likely. This is where the potential utility of psychedelic drugs comes in. Psychedelic drugs such as LSD work in treating mental illnesses by switching off control centres in the brain that regulate brain patterns. Areas of the brain that are typically overactive in illnesses such as depression begin to switch off under psychedelic drugs. With the dampening down of activity in these areas of the brain, the brain increases its interconnectivity with other areas and functions in a much less rigid and disciplined way. Not only do these drugs suppress the areas of the brain that are overactive in mental illness, they also connect other areas, allowing the patient to gain some introspection and understanding into their illness.

Another example of psychedelics disrupting brain patterns is the use of these drugs to help patients cope with the anxiety and stress that inevitably follows a terminal diagnosis. Studies have demonstrated the incredible effectiveness of psychedelics in interrupting consistent negative thought patterns, significantly reducing levels of anxiety and allowing patients to spend the last period of their life in peace.

With over 350,000,000 people suffering from depression and over 40,000,000 people with generalised anxiety disorder throughout the world, psychedelic drugs could potentially be a revolutionary breakthrough in treating mental illnesses, particularly considering the difficulty that many patients experience in the short and long term with conventional medicine. So, what are the real harms?

⁓⁓

Risk is essentially a situation or activity where a person is exposed to danger. However, people do not expose themselves to the possibility of harm unless they feel that the potential harm is outweighed by the potential benefits, or they can extract at least some value from the activity.

Although perceived risk varies from person to person, there are activities that pose greater objective risk than others, and each drug is intrinsically unique in terms of the risk that it poses, both to the user and to wider society. There are a number of variables that determine drug risk, such as propensity for addiction, disparity between an effective dose and a lethal dose and typical routes of administration.

Taking any drug poses *some* risk as there is no such thing as a perfectly safe drug. Even drugs considered to be rather benign in terms of their toxicity, such as paracetamol (acetaminophen), aspirin and caffeine, all have lethal doses. As the use of all drugs includes some degree of risk, we can measure and scale the risk of a particular drug compared to other drugs, and we can also compare the risk involved in the taking of a particular drug to other activities that also involve risk such as specific sports.

5

Hooch – Alcohol

Alcohol is the second most widely consumed drug in the world behind caffeine. Beverages that contain alcohol, such as beer, wine and spirits, make up the bulk of products sold containing alcohol. However, alcohol is also present in many other products, such as mouthwash and hand sanitiser, because it is an effective chemical in killing bacteria.

There are three main types of alcohol: ethanol, methanol and iso-propanol. Isopropanol is primarily used for its antibacterial and disinfectant properties as well as in the automotive industry as a fuel additive. Methanol is primarily used for the production of plastics, explosives and paints. Ethanol is used in industries for fuel, solvents and antiseptics; however, it is also the alcohol used in alcoholic beverages, which is of primary contextual importance.

There is evidence of fermented beverages being consumed 7,000–6,500 BC in both China and the Middle East. However, some historians suggest that alcohol has been consumed since 10,000 BC. Barley was used extensively throughout the Middle East in the making of bread and cake, but if the barley was left to germinate, dry and then mixed with water, hops and yeast, beer could be produced.

During these early times, water sanitation was almost non-existent, but as the quality of water throughout the world has gradually improved, the number of cases of water-borne diseases has reduced. Before water processing and purification systems were used to provide populations with clean water, it was known that boiling water or adding alcohol were the two main ways in which water could be cleansed—and this practice was encouraged by physicians.

It is believed that the prevalence of tea consumption in Asia and beer consumption in Europe and the USA is attributable to the time when water was tainted, and it was safer to consume water that contained alcohol or had been boiled, as these methods killed any germs. Because beer was made from yeast and was considered a healthy drink, it earned the name 'liquid bread'. In the US, alcohol was consumed with every meal—even breakfast—and in many communities the town bell would ring once or twice or day to notify people to stop working, so they could drink together.

⁕

Although legally available in most parts of the world, alcohol regulations vary in every country. In Australia, restrictions are enforced, including age of purchase, hours of sale, sale to patrons based on intoxication as well as motor vehicle testing, and the public is discouraged from violating regulations by the imposition of appropriate penalties. The average Australian household spends just over thirty dollars per week on alcoholic products, and the average Australian (aged fifteen and older) consumes approximately nine to ten litres of pure alcohol annually. This equates to the average Australian consuming approximately one to two standard drinks (SD) per day (one Australian SD = ten grams of pure alcohol), about one or two bottles of wine per week or two six-packs of beer per week. Per capita alcohol consumption in Australia has been arguably decreasing slowly for some time, however, the landscape of how people drink has changed and not necessarily for the better.

Among young people, there are increasing rates of abstinence. However, those who choose to drink are drinking at more harmful levels. In 1999, approximately ten per cent of secondary school students reported never drinking alcohol but, by 2014, this had risen to about thirty per cent. This is a remarkably positive change but it should be borne in mind that these figures relate to schooled children, and once a young person become disengaged with school or leaves school, the risk of using alcohol or illicit drugs rises dramatically.

With the increased popularity of cider products, beer consumption has dropped, wine and spirit consumption has remained fairly stable, while evidence around consumption of pre-mixed products remains inconclusive. Approximately five to ten per cent more females abstain from alcohol than males up until about fourteen years of age. From fourteen to eighteen, males are more likely to be abstainers. This switch around the age of fourteen is likely to result from females beginning to socialise with males who are a few years older than they are, and this increases the chance they will come into contact with alcohol.

Around the same age is also where we begin to see parental monitoring slip, which contributes to the significant rise in risky alcohol consumption in both males and females from Year Nine to Year Ten. The change in drinking behaviour is most pronounced in the transition period and, for the first time, the number of 'risky' drinkers outweighs the number of 'moderate' drinkers. Around this time, the number of 'risky' drinkers also begins to outweigh the abstainers.

Alcohol has unfortunately become embedded within Australian culture, and the nation's relationship with alcohol is likely rooted in our historical connection to the UK, which is one of the heaviest drinking areas of the world. The Australian Capital Territory (ACT) banned alcohol in 1910 for almost two decades, and up until approximately 1960, Indigenous Australians were prohibited from consuming alcohol. Gradually each state reversed this legislation until the mid-1970s, when indigenous and non-indigenous Australians had parity in terms of alcohol consumption rights. The US banned alcohol in 1920 for almost

fifteen years, and still today alcohol is completely banned in many countries with large Muslim populations, such as Bangladesh, Iran, Yemen,
Saudi Arabia and parts of India.

❧

Despite the Rudd government introducing an alcopop (pre-mixed alcoholic drink) tax in 2008 as a proposed means of curbing young people's
consumption of alcohol, studies evaluating its efficacy are conflicting.
Some reports found reductions in youth alcohol-related hospital admissions, while other reports found areas where alcohol-related admissions
increased or plateaued. Increasing the cost of alcohol is an effective
means of reducing consumption and subsequent harm, however, the
increased levy must be applied per standard drink (per unit), and across
all alcoholic products. Increasing the cost of one type of alcoholic product simply pushes those with low disposable income, such as young people and addicts, into consuming other cost-effective products.

If three people split a box of wine (cask wine or 'goon bag' as they
are often called) evenly between each of them, they would be able to
consume ten SD's each at a cost of four dollars each (forty cents per SD).
If the same people wanted to consume the same amount of SDs but in
alcopops, UDLs and Smirnoff Cruisers currently sell in Australia from
approximately thirty dollars for packets of ten (three dollars per SD),
which equates to almost eight times the cost. Those wanting to avoid
paying extra are also able to buy a bottle of cheap spirit, such as bourbon
or vodka, and then purchase an additional mixer, such as Coca-Cola or
orange juice.

Increasing the cost of alcohol must be applied per unit of alcohol,
rather than making specific categories of beverages more expensive
than others, because the quantity of pure alcohol consumed is what
needs to decrease, not the quantity of specific products. An individual
who consumes two glasses of wine every night (three to four SDs) may
be doing more harm to themselves than an individual who consumes

a shot of whisky (one to one and a half SDs) every night. Although the notion exists that wine is a 'healthy' form of alcohol due to its antioxidant properties, and the whisky is high in alcohol content, the wine drinker is consuming at least double the amount of pure alcohol. The variable that causes harm is the amount of pure alcohol consumed, and whatever product the alcohol exists in, be it a beer, wine or spirit, is a negligible factor.

Although an argument could be made that alcoholic products with no antioxidant value or products that contain high levels of sugar or caffeine pose greater health risks, these factors are largely trivial in contributing to total alcohol harm.

Increasing alcohol excise is an effective means of reducing the number of highly dependent or addicted individuals; however, many argue against raising the cost of alcohol on the basis that it unfairly targets the poor, as well as those people who drink alcohol responsibly. On the 1 May 2018, Scotland's minimum unit pricing came into effect, which resulted in a reduction of seventy per cent in specific products, such as Frosty Jacks strong cider, an extremely popular drink among low-income earners. Scotland was able to introduce minimum pricing in the face of massive opposition from several powerful entities, such as the Scotch Whisky Association and spirits EUROPE, because Scotland has one of the worst rates of liver disease in the world. Four out of ten intensive care unit (ICU) hospital beds are occupied by individuals with alcohol-related disorders.

A representative for the company that manufactures Frosty Jacks, Aston Manor Cider, claimed that low-income earners were being unfairly penalised by being priced out of the market. This argument is flawed because one of the primary ways to prevent or reverse poverty is to not allow individuals to get trapped in dependence. Additionally, the concept that increasing alcohol excise is 'punishing the responsible drinker' is a lie because, in reality, the responsible drinker would actually save money. And the 'nanny state' argument is simply a notional concept from businesses that government is overregulating our choices and lives, despite many of these policies providing enormous benefits with minimum interference. Despite the average Australian consuming approximately ten litres of pure alcohol each year, twenty per cent of the nation's heaviest drinkers consume the vast majority of all alcohol produced, and the heaviest five per cent consume about thirty per cent of all alcohol produced. This is due to a concept known as the Pareto principle, named after Italian economist Vilfredo Pareto in 1896 (now coined Pareto's law, Pareto principle or the eighty/twenty law), where approximately eighty per cent of the effects result from about twenty per cent of causes. This can be applied in many instances such as global gross domestic product (GDP), the richest twenty per cent earn about eighty per cent of total income, or in sales where eighty per cent of sales are generated by twenty per cent of clients.

The majority of individuals who consume alcohol do so responsibly, and consume alcoholic products priced at above one dollar per SD. These individuals are not affected by excise increases as they are already consuming alcoholic products priced above the supposed floor price. They also tend to consume alcohol arguably in moderation, as drinking is an indulgence for them, meaning that they consume higher quality products, and often in licensed premises, where the cost is higher. However, the vast majority of alcohol is sold to, and consumed by, the heaviest drinking cohort, who both generate the bulk of harm and typically consume products priced below one dollar per SD. These individuals, who are drinking themselves into an early grave, are consuming the cheapest booze they can lay their hands on.

The average Australian taxpayer pays at least $1000 per year to finance alcohol-related harms. While heavy drinkers may deem this an acceptable figure, the responsible drinkers and particularly the non-drinkers are penalised unfairly because they are receiving no benefit. To be frank, governments need to grow some balls, take on the alcohol industry and price young bingers, as well as older dependent individuals, out of the market so the responsible drinkers and non-drinkers are not unfairly punished.

The Northern Territory (NT) is the first and only state in Australia to implement minimum unit floor price of one dollar and thirty cents per SD in October 2018. The primary reason for this implementation is that indigenous individuals living in the NT consume seventy per cent more alcohol than the national average, and non-indigenous individuals consume about fifty per cent more than the national average. This means that the cheapest bottle of wine would come out to be approximately nine dollars, before the wine manufacturer makes any money. One of the major problems in the NT is that those who are problem drinkers don't think they are. NT Drivers are twenty times more likely to get caught for drink diving, the road death toll is quadruple that of the nation's average, and the alcohol-related death rate is more than triple that of the nation's average. Half of the fatal road crashes in the NT are alcohol related, more than half of the suicides in the NT are alcohol related, and the alcohol-related hospitalisation rate is more than double the nation's average. Early evidence suggests that this initiative, along with the banned drink registrar (BDR—where individuals must show photo ID before purchasing alcohol and will be denied take-away alcohol if they have been flagged for offences such as drink-driving or assault) has resulted in a fall in alcohol-related violence.

I hope to be proven wrong, but it seems unlikely that minimum pricing will be rolled out across the nation, given the enormous power of the alcohol industry. While the industry may be willing to forego the NT because of the relatively small market (approximately 250,000 people), an enormous amount of pushback would be expected if the same initiative was proposed to either New South Wales (NSW) or Queensland (QLD)—two states that are thirty and twenty times the population size of NT respectively.

Based on evidence from countries that have implemented effective alcohol policies, from a political standpoint, there is absolutely no excuse for not learning from these models because the public health payback occurs within one political term. Policymakers should be aware that actually doing something constructive about alcohol harm would not result in political suicide.

Nine out of ten provinces in Canada have some form of minimum pricing (state-set floor price), and each of the provinces has seen significant improvements in public health. British Columbia introduced a ten per cent increase in alcohol excise, which resulted in an over thirty per cent reduction in wholly attributable alcohol deaths, a ten per cent reduction in alcohol-related hospital submissions and a substantial delay in morbidity and mortality from alcohol-related disease within two years. Another province, Saskatchewan, which brought in similar style increases from 2008 to 2012, saw total alcohol consumption fall by over eight per cent.

France introduced minimum alcohol unit excise almost thirty years ago as part of a three-pillar strategy (alongside decreasing drink-driving limit and the banning of alcohol advertising) and has since managed to bring liver cirrhosis and chronic liver disease rates down to less than a third of what they were during the 1970s. Contrast this with the UK, which, in the same period of time, liberalised alcohol regulations, leading to decreases in the price of alcohol, increases in consumption, and a subsequent increase in deaths from liver cirrhosis and chronic liver disease of over 500 per cent. Although it is claimed that alcohol kills about 8,000 people in the UK every year, this only covers cases where alcohol is listed on the death certificate as the direct cause. If you take into account death certificates where alcohol is listed as a contributory cause, this approximately doubles to 15,000, and this number doubles to over 30,000 once you include deaths from diseases attributable to alcohol.

Most alcohol is not consumed in licensed venues and, therefore, with the absence of regulations, drinking outside of licenced venues is where the majority of alcohol-related harm comes from. Although in Scotland, time will tell with regards to the effectiveness of their minimum pricing strategy, it is predicted to save about thirty lives and 1,500 hospital admissions within the first year, and 4,000 annual hospital admissions in years to come.

The last leader of the Soviet Union (USSR) Mikhail Gorbachev introduced a number of hard-hitting measures during the 1980s to combat widespread alcoholism in the USSR. This included raising the price of alcohol, as well as restricting sales, and although some alcohol production moved to the black market, by the time Boris Yeltsin (first President of Russia) reversed these measures five years later, over 1,200,000 lives had been saved. The policy reversal did not come as a huge surprise, however, as Yeltsin was a well-known alcoholic and this was likely to be the primary contributing factor to his death in 2007.

༎

The Australian alcohol industry is probably aware of examples of where the implementation of minimum pricing has proven enormously beneficial for both the industry as well as public health but because it is so easy to profit from heavy drinkers, their marketing plan remains unchanged.

Approximately one in every five or six Australians who have ever consumed alcohol will, at some point, become dependent (a capture rate of fifteen to twenty per cent). Dependence is extremely important as it can predict the chronicity of use, as well as the length of time it takes the individual to stop or reduce use.

Australian drinking guidelines recommend that both men and women should not consume more than two SDs on any given day, no more than four SDs on any single occasion and no more than seven SDs over a week. Adhering to these guidelines attempts to keep the consumer in the category of low risk, however, not no risk. The more a person drinks, the more harm they face, as the relationship between the level of alcohol consumption and harm is non-linear. This means that the harms of alcohol consumption increase exponentially, for example, for women consuming approximately fifteen SDs per week (one and a half glasses of wine per day), the risk of rectal cancer is approximately double that of an abstainer. However, if they consume twice this amount (thirty to thirty-five SDs per week), their risk is five times greater than an abstainer.

Generally speaking, females get hit with the subjective effects of alcohol about twice as hard per SD as males do. Although there are many physiological reasons for this, there are three key physiological differences based on average comparisons:

- lower bodyweight than males, meaning that for females, the same level of alcohol consumed takes up a greater proportion of body mass

- a smaller level of gastric alcohol dehydrogenase, the enzyme that catalyses alcohol

- a higher level of body fat, as well as a lower level of body water and muscle. Fat has very low water content, whereas muscle has a relatively high level of water content. This means that those who have higher levels of body fat have higher amounts of alcohol in their blood, because fatty tissue cannot absorb alcohol, whereas muscle can.

The alcohol industry spends over $120,000,000 annually in Australia on advertising through various mediums, and there are few to no public awareness campaigns in Australia on alcohol-related harms. There are about 160,000 hospitalisations and over 5,800 deaths each year in Australia attributable to alcohol. Some of these are wholly attributable to alcohol, such as alcohol poisoning, while others are partially attributable, for example, a person dying from pancreatic cancer, brought on by pancreatitis, brought on by high alcohol consumption. That is a death every ninety minutes, and a hospitalisation every three and a half minutes from a product we promote.

In comparison, about 1,000 Australians die annually from illicit drugs (just over 2,000 if you include pharmaceuticals), and about 20,000 are hospitalised. For illicit drug-related events as well as alcohol-related events, the average societal cost of a stay in public hospital is approximately $5,000, and recent estimates put the total cost of illicit drug-related hospitalisations at $110,000,000. In 2004/2005, the total cost of alcohol-related hospitalisations (excluding medical, ambulance etc.) was $662,200,000. Given that the Australian population has grown by twenty-five per cent in the past thirteen years, and that alcohol-related hospitalisations have risen slightly (from fifty per 10,000 women to sixty per 10,000 women, and ninety per 10,000 men to ninety-five per 10,000), we could conservatively estimate the current costs of alcohol-related hospitalisations to be at least $830,000,000. Deaths from alcohol are second to that of tobacco, however, deaths from alcohol occur across all age groups, whereas deaths from tobacco are mainly concentrated from the middle aged onwards. A significant number of highly successful individuals across many fields, such as Christopher Hitchens, Amy Winehouse, Bon Scott, F. Scott Fitzgerald and Tim Bergling (Avicii), have either had their life taken or destroyed by alcohol.

Alcohol is also a key factor in a significant amount of domestic violence cases, assaults (including sexual assaults), homicides, suicides, child abuse cases, other violent crimes and most police call-outs (particularly late night call-outs). Some cynical public health experts, however, regard tobacco-related deaths as 'good deaths' for the public system when contrasted to alcohol deaths as many tobacco-related deaths occur in middle to older age groups, and therefore those individuals who smoke pay a lot of tax in their lifetime but die before they can draw aged or disability pensions. Deaths from alcohol are net economic losses because many die young, whereas some argue that deaths from tobacco are net economic gains, as smokers pay seventeen times the cost they impose on non-smokers in terms of tangible public health costs. Aside from social harms, such as road traffic accidents, domestic/non-domestic violence and child/sexual abuse, there are a myriad of diseases that alcohol causes or contributes to. This includes mouth, throat, stomach, bowel, breast and liver cancers, pancreatitis, alcoholic-Korsakoff syndrome/ Wernicke-Korsakoff syndrome/Wernicke encephalopathy, cirrhosis, cardiovascular disease, as well as the inflammatory process that leads to early-onset dementia.

Other than methamphetamine, alcohol is the most well-documented damaging drug to the brain. Chronic, heavy consumption of alcohol can result in irreversible grey matter atrophy in the brain, particularly in the thalamus, dorsal hippocampus (up to a ten per cent reduction), precentral gyrus, middle frontal gyrus, insula and cerebellum. White matter reductions are also seen in the pons and cerebellum. Low to moderate intake also results in brain atrophy, as does nutritional deprivation as seen in many alcoholics, particularly deficiencies in thiamine or vitamin B1. These deficiencies are caused by malnutrition because alcoholics often don't consume much other than alcohol, and heavy consumption also disrupts the ability of the body to absorb thiamine. Although alcoholics can have thiamine deficiencies, which then result in brain cellular death, this is not caused directly by alcohol itself. Thiamine deficiencies can exist without alcohol, as seen in patients with genetic susceptibilities, those who consume diets high in refined carbohydrates, individuals with severe anorexia and those with renal disease.

Although alcohol does not kill brain cells, it damages dendrites on neurons, which are branched neuronal extensions that facilitate cellular communication. Dendrite damage can result in behavioural and cognitive problems, and as the brain tends to shrink with age, heavy alcohol consumption exaggerates this decrease. Pregnant women who consume alcohol run the risk of their child suffering from foetal alcohol spectrum disorder (FASD), which is characterised by a range of severe neurodevelopmental impairments; however, alcohol as an independent risk factor for SIDS remains unclear.

For the majority of diseases related to alcohol, the dose-dependent risk is exponential. There is much crossover in terms of alcohol and tobacco as both contribute risk factors to many of the same diseases. However, if an individual drinks and smokes, the synergistic effects of the two drugs mean that the risks are significantly higher than the sum of both drugs individually. Although the vast majority of drinkers in Australia do not smoke, almost every smoker drinks as well.

On the flip side, all stakeholders within the alcohol industry contribute a significant amount to the community and the economy through employment, taxation, and various other benefits. It is unarguable, however, that the benefits generated by the alcohol industry are very much outweighed by alcohol-related harm. The direct costs of alcohol in Australia range between \$14,000,000,000 and \$36,000,000,000 annually (excluding unquantifiable costs such as emotional suffering), while total revenue generated by alcohol tips just over \$7,000,000,000 annually. That is, the costs still equate to at least double the benefits at an economic level.

The widespread use of alcohol is the most prominent factor in its total harm, but for the individual, there is an intrinsic toxicity due to how alcohol is processed in the body. Alcohol goes through a number of steps from the time of ingestion to excretion. This process is called the pharmacokinetics (pharma derived from the Greek word *pharmakon* meaning medicine, and *kinesis/kenetikos* meaning mechanisms/motions) and is applicable to all drugs, as every drug is ingested, absorbed, distributed and excreted in different ways.

When a person consumes an alcoholic beverage, a small portion of the alcohol is absorbed through the stomach wall but approximately eighty per cent is absorbed through the small intestine. Beverages containing twenty to thirty per cent alc/vol are absorbed fastest, resulting in a rapid rise in blood alcohol content (BAC), particularly if consumed on an empty stomach. Beverages containing greater than thirty per cent alc/vol are absorbed slowly as they inflame the gastric mucosa, which reduces the emptying ability of the gastrointestinal system. However, they can be absorbed faster if served with a mixer, particularly if the mixer is carbonated.

An alternative pathway called the microsomal ethanol oxidising system (MEOS) also processes a very small amount of alcohol by the way of enzymes in cells changing the chemical structure of the ethanol. The bulk of the alcohol consumed is transported from the gastrointestinal tract, through the hepatic portal system, to the liver where it undergoes a three-step oxidisation process. Oxidisation in medical terms refers to the chemical structure change of a compound by adding oxygen:

- Ethanol is oxidised by alcohol dehydrogenase into acetaldehyde.
- Acetaldehyde is then converted by acetaldehyde dehydrogenase to acetate.
- Acetate is then converted into carbon dioxide and water through peripheral tissues with small amounts of alcohol also lost through sweat and saliva.

The by-production of acetaldehyde in the metabolism of ethanol cannot be avoided, and despite the fact that acetaldehyde is rapidly converted into acetate, which is a harmless compound, acetaldehyde is listed as a Group 1 carcinogen by the International Agency for Research on Cancers (IARC) and is up to thirty times more toxic than ethanol. A Group 1 carcinogen is an agent for which there is sufficient evidence to prove carcinogenicity (cancer causing) to humans. This category includes many other agents, such as asbestos, radiation, and tobacco smoke. If any food or drink contained the level of acetaldehyde the body produces from one SD, it would immediately be banned.

There are at least seven types of cancer to which alcohol is a major contributing factor, and for women, the only known preventable cause of breast cancer is alcohol. There is not conclusive evidence that ethanol itself is carcinogenic. However, as ethanol raises estrogen levels (increasing risk of hormone receptive-positive cancer), impairs the ability of the body to break down other nutrients (decreasing the body's ability to defend against toxic agents) and produces reactive oxygen species (potentially damaging DNA and other molecules), it is regarded as a potentially cancer-promoting compound. Among other factors, such as dehydration and immune imbalances, acetaldehyde is thought to be the primary driver behind the well-known symptoms of a hangover because it can remain at elevated levels hours after consumption. It is estimated that about one in five people do not experience hangovers, and despite there being a number of presumed hangover cures—borage oil, red ginseng and ginger—these have been proven to be no more effective than taking paracetamol or ibuprofen.

Genetic factors also play a role here. For example, at least three-quarters, possibly more, of the Asian (particularly East Asian) population possess alcohol dehydrogenase gene code variants ALDH1B or ALDH1C, meaning that when they drink, the alcohol converts into acetaldehyde very efficiently. This is compounded by the fact that a large proportion of this group also possesses a poorer functional variant of acetaldehyde dehydrogenase (ALDH2, only the cytosolic isoenzyme, not the mitochondrial isoenzyme). As a result, not only does acetaldehyde build up rapidly and efficiently, it is not metabolised into acetate quickly. The build-up and retention of acetaldehyde results in nausea, headaches, a 'flushing' rash, as well as a faster heart rate, and this may explain why many Asian countries, on a population level, have very low total alcohol consumption, and why this condition is associated with much lower rates of alcoholism. In fact, disulfiram, a medication used to treat alcoholism, works in almost an identical way, by inhibiting the acetaldehyde dehydrogenase enzymes and thereby increasing and maintaining high levels of acetaldehyde, producing the hangover effects immediately following alcohol consumption.

In terms of the pharmacodynamics, (how the drug produces its effects), alcohol essentially induces effects through three different mechanisms:

- the upregulation (increasing) of inhibitory neurotransmitters such as GABA
  - Inhibitory neurotransmitters are chemicals that when released in the brain produce feelings of sedation
- the downregulation (decreasing) of stimulatory neurotransmitters such as glutamate

○ Stimulatory neurotransmitters are chemicals that when released in the brain produce feelings of stimulation

- alcohol not oxidised by the liver travels to the heart and reduces both the speed and contraction power of cardiac muscles.

There are approximately eighty neurotransmitters in the brain, all of which have different physiological functions. Neurons can be seen as the hardware and neurotransmitters as the software of the brain. It appears that alcohol's interaction with GABA receptor subunit alpha-1 is responsible for the sedative effects of alcohol, whereas subunit alpha-2 or alpha-3 is responsible for relaxation effects, and subunit alpha-5 is responsible for the memory loss.

Alcohol also interacts with a variety of medications including, but not limited to, antihistamines, non-steroidal anti-inflammatory drugs (NSAIDs), antidepressants and opioids. At low levels, alcohol produces feelings of relaxation, followed by sedation, impaired motor control and respiratory depression. The amount and rate at which alcohol is consumed determines the stages and rapidity of intoxication, and if the level of alcohol consumed exceeds the rate of processing, BAC rises, as do subsequent intoxicating effects.

Possibly the most important molecule in the processing of alcohol is that of nicotinamide adenine dinucleotide (NAD+). NAD+ is a coenzyme, meaning that on its own, it is unable to catalyse a reaction; however, it is utilised by alcohol dehydrogenase and aldehyde dehydrogenase in the oxidisation of alcohol. As the liver, where the majority of alcohol processing occurs, contains a very limited supply of NAD+, the maximum oxidisation rate of alcohol is approximately fifteen grams per hour (just over one Australian SD per hour). This is why we use the rule of thumb in Australia of one SD per hour to keep under the drink-driving limit. However, it is very important to note that a drink served to someone may not necessarily contain one SD, and that fifteen grams per hour is the maximum rate of processing when there can be many factors that impede the rate, such as liver function, gender, and medications.

One of the reasons alcohol possesses much greater toxicity than many of the illegal drugs is because it has a very low safety ratio. The safety ratio quantifies and measures the difference between the effective dose of a drug and the lethal dose of the drug. The safety ratio is extremely important when looking at drugs used for non-medical purposes because the individual using the drug is doing so for its psychoactive effects, but they are rarely aware of how close an effective dose is to a lethal dose. For alcohol, the safety ratio is ten, meaning that the lethal dose is ten times that of an effective dose, for example, two shots of vodka to produce any effect, twenty shots of vodka to kill the individual. This is actually a very low margin, because the effective dose is not the intoxicating dose. The intoxicating dose in this example may be twelve shots (only a few drinks away from rendering the individual unconscious). In fact, an amount of alcohol equivalent to only about seven times the Australian drink-driving limit can be terminal. In fact, it could be even lower. Sixteen year old British boy Jamie Capon died in 2014 after drinking with his friends, and was found dead with a blood alcohol level five times the legal limit. Eighteen year old American student Dalton Debrick died in 2016 from alcohol poisoning at about four times the legal driving limit. Over eighty Australians die each year from acute alcohol poisoning due to the fact that there is very little difference between the amount of alcohol that gets someone drunk, and the amount that kills them. Many of these deaths are young people. According to the poisons standard, ethyl alcohol, the form of alcohol humans consume, was made exempt from scheduling in 1974, due to 'low toxicity'.

Alcohol poisoning kills people acutely through depressing respiration, resulting in starvation of oxygen. In addition, alcohol also stimulates vomiting while blocking the cough reflex, meaning that individuals can choke, or the contents can enter the lungs, leading to acute respiratory failure. A significant proportion of alcohol poisoning deaths occur on celebratory occasions, such as eighteenth birthdays, twenty-first birthdays, end of exams and graduations, which is a tragedy, not only because of the young age of the victim, but particularly if family or friends have bought them drinks and have encouraged them to poison themselves.

Typically, the response from the public and the police in these situations is two pronged: the alcohol could not have been the real killer or the drink must have been spiked. Even though other drugs are rarely found, this is never reported, which means the public are left with the assumption that another factor, such as an underlying medical condition or another drug was the culprit. Anything but alcohol must have killed them. And the same is true for drink spiking. Men and women who are raped while intoxicated and/or unconscious often believe they must have had their drink spiked because they have no memory. The vast majority of drug-related sexual assaults are facilitated through alcohol alone. In the rare case another sedative is used, its effect can be potentiated through alcohol, meaning that the person may not have been rendered unconscious, they may have been able to defend themselves, or they may have remembered the events if the additive drug was not mixed with alcohol.

Personally, I am amazed that hard liquor products, such as vodka, bourbon or tequila, are permitted to be advertised with such abandon, considering most adults would die if they consumed the entire bottle within the space of a few hours. We use alcohol in other products to kill bugs, other organisms and bacteria, so it should come as no surprise that it is fundamentally lethal to humans.

Although covered in Part Two of this book, the above information demonstrates why it is important when educating young people not to jump straight to addressing the harms of harder drugs, such as cocaine, methamphetamine or heroin.

Not only are young people more likely to be harmed or killed by legal drugs such as alcohol, because alcohol is inherently more toxic than many illegal drugs, but beginning the dialogue with illicit drugs as the focus, can, in the process, give young people the impression that alcohol (and tobacco) are not really drugs and that they aren't harmful.

Despite the fact that some people drink and/or smoke in safer ways than others, the concept that there is a safe level of alcohol consumption is a complete myth (see Part Two of this book), and the same goes for tobacco. This is not to say that we dismiss illicit drug education. However, the overemphasis on illicit drugs, which indirectly discounts the harm of alcohol, comes from the fear that children will end up addicted to harder drugs. Parents, teachers and those who work with young people also need to be mindful of their language with regard to separating alcohol from other drugs by using the phrase 'alcohol and drugs'.

I read an article published by conservative commentator, Paul Murray, entitled 'Too many people take drugs, but why do they do it?' and he states 'I smoke, don't drink, and have never taken drugs'. Not only does this dividing language play into the hands of the alcohol industry, but we do not refer to carrots and vegetables, oranges and fruit, cheese and dairy, or tin and metals because that is nonsensical and redundant. One of the organisers of music festival Groovin The Moo stated on television in 2019 'People are choosing to drink less and take drugs instead', when she should have said 'people are taking different drugs'.

The alcohol industry has openly objected to suggestions to change government policies and departments language from referring to 'alcohol and drugs' to 'alcohol and other drugs' or just included in 'drugs', because associating alcohol with other drugs, such as cocaine or heroin, would damage the privileged position and image of alcohol. It would also lead the public to treat alcohol with greater caution and may subject the industry and its products to stricter regulations.

History has proven, however, that the alcohol industry is in no way concerned about the harm that their product causes the community, as their primary aim is to maximise profits. Although the industry aims to sell as much alcohol as possible to maximise profits, the only way to reduce alcohol-related harm is to reduce alcohol consumption. This is why the industry lobbies tirelessly to block any policy or legislative efforts proven to reduce harm as that would reduce profit margins. The alcohol industry has also had the benefit of 'outsider hindsight' in learning from the mistakes that the tobacco industry made by lying about their products. The alcohol industry admits that their product can be harmful. However, it claims that harm is only generated by its abuse, by those who cannot tolerate it or 'enjoy responsibly'. This has allowed the industry to blind the public, governments, politicians and the media to alcohol's harms.

The alcohol industry has now been able to take a step back and let the hospitality industry do some of the heavy lifting. Highly lucrative and influential entities, such as the Australian Hotels Association (AHA) and the Australian Liquor Stores Association (ALSA), have been extremely effective in lobbying governments as well as discrediting evidence on alcohol-related harm. Alcohol marketing also conveys a number of powerful messages that are flawed and misleading:

Individuals should ignore the fact that alcohol is addictive and harmful.

The focus instead is directed towards its origin, craftsmanship and quality. Imagine the public outcry in Australia if we abolished plain packaging on tobacco products and advertised with a focus on the quality characteristics of the tobacco, ignoring the harm it causes. I'm sure that the alcohol industry do not want their products to incorporate a printed warning that alcohol contributes to a significant number of assaults, suicides, homicides and cancers, or that if the average adult consumed an average bottle of spirit in a few hours, it would be highly likely to kill them..

Alcohol-related harms are caused by irresponsible individuals who cannot handle alcohol.

This is quite possibly the most perverse angle that the industry works because without the 'irresponsible' drinkers, the alcohol industry would be out of business. Given that the vast majority of alcohol produced is sold to, and consumed by the heaviest drinkers, the industry directly relies on those people drinking themselves to death to maintain business. They are dream customers for the industry, because, not only do they provide the industry with immediate financial injections, due to the addictive nature of alcohol and the poor prognosis in terms of treating addiction, they are often customers for life. The alcohol industry is able to conveniently shift the blame away from alcohol, onto the individual, effectively distancing itself from any harm caused by the product.

This is an almost identical ploy to the one the National Rifle Association (NRA) trots out in the wake of any mass shooting—'guns don't kill people, people kill people'. This is despite the fact that there are countless examples from all around the world (particularly Australia, in the wake of Port Arthur massacre), proving that gun deaths plummet as soon as regulations that deal with how firearms are obtained and distributed are tightened. Whenever there is an incident that draws the media's attention to products involved in harm, the industry bodies representing the product know that if they can just wait out the outrage, they will fly under the radar, avoiding any hard-hitting changes. The reality is that the alcohol industry does not make money from responsible, casual drinkers—they make it off alcoholics and problematic drinkers. In Australia, the heaviest twenty per cent of drinkers consume approximately seventy-four per cent of all alcohol.

Non-drinkers are not part of culture or are less healthy than those who drink.

Sadly in Australia, not only is alcohol socially acceptable, it is socially expected. Essentially, if you are a non-drinker, you are perceived as antisocial and not part of normal culture. Alcohol advertisements will capture the laughs, leisure, romance and beauty, but ignore the heartache, violence and hangovers that follow all too often. Another recent claim the alcohol industry has attempted to capitalise on is that non-drinkers are less healthy than moderate drinkers, and therefore responsible moderate alcohol consumption is good for your health. Not only is this factually incorrect, but also highly misleading. Although covered in greater detail later in the book, with all levels of consumption, there is a total net harm. The alleged health benefits of alcohol are far outweighed by the harm to the individual at every level of consumption, regardless of age or gender. The claim that those who drink moderately are healthier than those who abstain is true. However, these people may have poorer health for other reasons, not because of their abstinence. Case in point—approximately a year ago, a close acquaintance of mine suffered a handful of symptoms that pointed towards him having an issue with his heart. After his general practitioner referred him to a cardiologist, he was diagnosed with dilated cardiomyopathy (DCM), a condition where the heart is unable to sufficiently pump blood due to the hearts primary pumping chamber (left ventricle) becoming dilated, which means it is enlarged, stretched and weakened. Individuals with DCM may have minor or no symptoms, while DCM in others may deteriorate, increasing the risk of arrhythmias, blood clots, and heart failure. As a result of the diagnosis, this individual was no longer to consume alcohol.

The alcohol industry would use this individual case to support their argument that people who are non-drinkers are less healthy than moderate drinkers. While on face value this seems plausible, abstaining from alcohol is not causing poorer health. This is actually a case of reverse causality. Abstaining from alcohol consumption is not the cause of individual health complications, but the individual health complications are causing the person to abstain from consuming alcohol. The same is true for people who are advised to stop smoking or improve diet. If one individual who smokes and another individual who has a very poor diet are each advised by their doctor to change their habits, and they obey the advice but ultimately suffer a heart attack or a stroke, it does not mean that stopping smoking and improving diet caused these events. The damage may have been done already, or these events may have been caused by another factor. Moderate drinkers may also score higher in terms of health indicators, as this is typically a population who does not smoke, exercises regularly and has a balanced diet, which is the reason for their good health, not their moderate alcohol consumption.

Problems arising from alcohol consumption can only be solved when all parties work together, and education about responsible use is the best method.

While the concept of all parties working together to reduce alcohol-related harm seems reasonable, the reality is that there is never any common ground between submissions made to the government by the alcohol industry and submissions made to the government by health professionals. The alcohol industry submits recommendations that produce little to no effect, require no regulatory changes and are easy to apply, such as increasing education and information, creating partnership approaches and targeting alcoholics. Health committees, on the other hand, recommend targeting entire populations, increasing excise, improving treatment, early and proactive interventions and minimum pricing. Early intervention is crucial, because often, by the time an individual presents to their health practitioner or particularly by the time they present to the hospital with alcoholic-related disease, it is too late.

Education is important, but it is certainly not the only measure, and its effectiveness in reducing population consumption and harm is relatively low. But as the alcohol industry is not interested in reducing consumption or harm, they choose to focus on education because that keeps the focus away from high-impact regulatory changes, such as increasing alcohol excise, restricting advertising and marketing, or raising the legal drinking age, which have been proven to reduce consumption and harm. Alcohol industry representatives immediately become defensive if they believe that proposed measures could threaten industry profits.

Education is also an opportunity for the industry to take initiative and pretend that they are socially responsible in caring about alcohol-related harm. However, through this means, the industry is able to introduce itself to young people under the pretext they are doing something about alcohol harms, while their primary focus is keeping attention away from regulatory changes.

The educational message from the industry is not about drinking less, just drinking differently. Although minimum pricing per unit reduces total population consumption, the most notable reductions are made in three crucial populations:

- Young individuals, particularly under eighteens: This population has a low disposable income and are increasingly priced out of the market. This is why young individuals do not drink Grange Hermitage, Dom Perignon or Johnnie Walker Blue Label and instead typically consume cheap vodka or bourbon with mixers, cask wine or cheap beer.

- Future dependent/addicted individuals: Early consumption of alcohol (eighteen and under) is a very strong predictor of future dependence, and if consumption is lowered in young age groups, heavy consumption in future older age groups is also lowered.

- Current dependent/addicted individuals: Due to the exponential relationship between alcohol consumption and harm, the heaviest drinking cohort is the population that generates the largest costs. Therefore, even if only small reductions are made among the heaviest drinkers, the public health gains are disproportionately higher. If individuals consuming 100 units of alcohol per week (four bottles of spirit or eleven bottles of wine) reduce their consumption by only ten per cent, not only does their risk of death fall by approximately thirty per cent, but crime volumes and hospital admissions would fall by the thousands. Yet if the heaviest drinking ten per cent of the Australian population stopped drinking, total alcohol sales would fall by about fifty-four per cent, which is certainly an outcome that the alcohol industry works to prevent.

Even though France introduced minimum alcohol unit excise and priced much of the young and dependent out of the market, the French alcohol industry has multiplied its profits, because there are greater profit margins in expensive alcoholic products. But despite the proven virtuous circle of wealth and health, it is easy for stakeholders to make money by lying about the harms, perpetuating the myth that alcohol-related problems are best solved by non-legislative means, and not changing their marketing strategy. Key participants within the alcohol industry may also think in the back of their mind that if regulatory changes are introduced, the wheels may be put in motion to open up a wider debate on alcohol control. In a lecture I watched, a UK government medical advisor mentioned that they contacted a major UK alcohol company scientist about potentially introducing a safer alternative to alcohol. The alcohol company scientist admitted that what they were doing was immoral, that people were dying, and they would be interested in an alternative. But, when the scientist proposed this measure to the Chief Executive Officer and marketing executives, he was met with disinterest. Their attitude seemed to have been 'why bother'. It would be a long-term project to develop and launch and market the product and when and if there were any financial returns, they would all be retired or dead, so it wasn't going to make them any money.

Ironically, the same can be said for why politicians play the politically expedient card when it comes to alcohol and other drugs. Before and after serving terms of office, politicians are on record for making statements completely contradicting those made while they are in office. That is because political terms are short, but social change takes time. Being tough on illegal drugs but lax on alcohol is effective for a political campaign for two reasons:

- Most voters drink, but the vast majority do not consider themselves problem drinkers.
- Problem drinkers and problem illicit drug users make up a small portion of the population, but these individuals are frequently

disengaged and disenfranchised from political processes, so no votes are lost from this population.

As a side issue, it is rather concerning to note that a large proportion of drinkers who still function in society are dependent but are unaware of their dependence. They have all been fed the myth that they should not be 'punished' for their responsible drinking. The embedded, accepted and expected culture of alcohol use contributes to the obliviousness and lack of insight that many individuals have into their dependence.

Government advisors would do well to heed Russian novelist and philosopher Fyodor Dostoevsky's dictum: 'A society should not be judged on how it treats its outstanding citizens, but how it treats its criminals'.

Many within government want to maintain the status quo because various systems, companies and jobs depend on alcohol remaining weakly regulated, while other drugs remain prohibited. If select illicit drugs became legal in a regulated fashion, stakeholders within the alcohol industry would lose their jobs, as would customs officers, police officers, civil servants, politicians and prison officers. And it is not inconceivable that within many authorities—the police, the DEA etc.—the drug war is nurtured to ensure job security.

Politicians would also lose many of the kickbacks they receive from the alcohol industry. Many politicians don't even consider alcohol to be a drug, because it is not illegal. This situation also handcuffs individuals to be a part of the system, even if they disagree with it. For example, if a police officer advocated for regulation and taxation instead of prohibition or admitted that kicking someone's door down in a dawn raid to arrest them for cannabis was unnecessary, they might find their career path limited. An entire industry exists that is built on a foundation of unscientific historical glitches where alcohol rules the recreational drug market, while illicit drugs and the people who use them are attacked. It takes the same amount of courage for an alcohol industry representative to admit their product causes damage as it does for a government representative to admit that the system they front causes damage, as both are under pressure to toe the line.

The alcohol industry continues to exercise influence that is comparable with other entities, such as medical associations, when it comes to policy-making decisions, which is absurd. The obvious conflict of interest is that the alcohol industry will block any amendments that reduce consumption and propose amendments that sustain profits. The alcohol industry, particularly in Australia and the UK, has a well-documented track record of keeping on the good side of (and getting in bed with) media and governments to ensure that all parties can work together to keep everyone drinking. The involvement of the alcohol industry in influencing alcohol policy goes back as far as the 1700s in the UK and the 1800s in Australia.

Alcohol marketing is not harmful.

The alcohol industry claims that alcohol marketing does not influence total consumption, only choice of product. Public health experts are in unison that, at the very least, alcohol advertising should be independently regulated (not self-regulated as it is in Australia), significantly clamped down on or, ideally, banned. Independent evidence has shown that every alcohol advertisement viewed by an individual increases total consumption by an average of one per cent. While this does not seem like much, if an individual were to view only one alcohol advertisement every day over the course of a year, they would consume approximately four times as much alcohol as an individual who was not exposed to any advertising. It is logistically impossible to enforce banning advertising to under eighteens. Despite all under eighteens being exposed to alcohol companies' sports team sponsorships; television commercials; and street, news, internet and social media advertisements, the alcohol industry claims that those ads target the adult population. The alcohol industry's rationale reflects statements by tobacco executives: 'If you are really not going to sell to children, you are going to be out of business in thirty years.' (Bennett Leslow, CEO of Brook Group Tobacco Corporation); 'The base of our business is the high school student.' (Curtis Judge, ex-CEO of Newport cigarettes).

Alcohol advertising exists to influence choice of product, however, entities that represent alcohol companies systematically and sophisticatedly campaign to protect the entire industry as a whole. Here are three examples that talk to this point.

In November of 1995 in the UK, an eighteen year old girl named Leah Betts died from acute water poisoning following use of MDMA. After Leah took the ecstasy tablets, she consumed seven litres of water in a short period of time, lapsed into a coma and died five days later in hospital. Leah, like many ecstasy users, was under the mistaken belief that ingesting large amounts of water was an effective antidote to the stimulatory effects of MDMA. Leah's death was reported throughout the UK under the banner of an ecstasy death, even though she would have survived taking the tablets if she had not drunk so much water. When the media discovered that Leah had actually died of water poisoning, not MDMA toxicity, they lost all interest in the case. What also followed after her death was a £1,000,000 anti-ecstasy campaign throughout the UK featuring 1,500 billboards with a picture of her face, and a caption next to it: 'Sorted. Just one ecstasy tablet took Leah Betts'.

'Sorted' was the slang term for an individual being supplied with ecstasy. Around this time, alcohol producers and retailers had experienced falls in sales due to young people substituting alcohol and pubs for stimulants and raves. In the lead up to Leah Betts's death, pub attendance had fallen in the UK by over ten per cent and, at the time, independent market analyst research indicated that pub attendance was projected to fall over twenty per cent by 1997. In the same time period within the UK, illicit drug use among young people had doubled, and over one million young people raved each week. The billboard campaign was funded by three advertising agencies—one listed Lowenbrau as their primary client, and the other two represented energy drink company, Red Bull.

The anti-ecstasy billboard campaign obviously provided potential large commercial benefits for each client through three mechanisms:

- Discouraging individuals away from illicit drugs would indirectly push them towards the legal drug, alcohol.
- Individuals still wanting to consume a stimulant would be able to consume caffeine present in Red Bull.
- Individuals consuming both drugs concurrently would be physiologically able to consume more of both drugs because the intrinsic contrasting effects of each drug reduces subjective intoxication.

In the wake of Leah's death, public concern and media attention was fixated on illicit drugs, creating a smokescreen for alcohol harms, so nobody batted an eyelid when Chancellor Kenneth Clarke chugged whisky on television while informing the public in the same year that, as part of the 1996 budget, alcohol excise would be cut, dropping the cost of booze. However, during the mid-90s the alcohol industry was on a roll anyway. Relaxed regulations allowed supermarkets to sell alcohol, resulting in liver death rates doubling over the next decade, and new legislation was introduced empowering local authorities to close dance clubs if police suspected illicit drugs were being used.

Coupling the intense focus on illicit drugs with liberalising acceptability, accessibility and availability of alcohol (as well as ignoring any harms) is exactly the reason why total alcohol consumption has risen in the UK and why alcohol is now the leading cause of death in men under the age of fifty-five (women are close behind). Alcohol is also the leading cause of death in young Australians, along with suicide, and a significant proportion of the latter is alcohol related.

Any measures that draw attention to and clamp down on illicit drugs only increase the profitability of the entire alcohol industry. The alcohol industry during the 90s was able to counteract the downturn in young people drinking by aggressively marketing ready to drink (RTD)/

pre-mixed/pre-packaged spirits products, which got young individuals into or back into alcohol. RTDs appealed to young people because they were like regular soft drinks in terms of appearance and taste, and many young people do not like the taste of beer, wine or strong spirits. A product that looks like a soft drink, tastes like a soft drink and is not an acquired taste is attractive, and it gently introduces them to alcohol. The sad part is that if the alcohol industry can hook an individual when they are young, that person will almost certainly be a consumer for life.

Another example of how the alcohol industry's marketing exhibits a wider agenda is the financial contributions it makes to the anti-cannabis legalisation in the US. Despite cannabis still being listed as a Schedule 1 drug under federal law, several states of the USA have now legalised or decriminalised cannabis either for recreational purposes and/or for medical purposes. Oregon was the first state to decriminalise personal possession of cannabis in 1973, with California the first state in the USA to allow cannabis for medical purposes in 1996. Since that time, several other states have followed suit, with the majority of the USA now listing cannabis as a legal medicine. Sixteen years later, Colorado and Washington became the first states in the USA to legalise the recreational use of cannabis. Eleven states in the US now list cannabis as legal for recreational purposes. However, up until recently, the recreational drug market was a monopoly, with alcohol being the only available legal drug. Alcohol industry lobbyists are among the most sophisticated activists in the world. Over time they have successfully managed to monopolise the recreational drug market and eliminate any other competition in the form of other drugs previously available such as cocaine, cannabis and opium. They simply do not want to give up their market share.

The pharmaceutical industry, albeit for other reasons, also shows signs of concern over the relaxing of cannabis legislation. This is primarily due to individuals growing their own cannabis and not using prescribed medicine or obtaining cannabis as a medicine on prescription and not needing to use other medications that may have been used previously, such as opioids, where dependence risk is much higher. This is similar to the reason why the pharmaceutical industry is also against psychedelics as medicines: they would replace drugs that individuals are reliant on with something that aids them quickly, with little or no need for re-administration. However, what the alcohol industry and the pharmaceutical industry share in common is that they view cannabis as a threat to their profits.

Working from fear of losing market share, the Beer Distributors Political Action Group (part of the National Beer Wholesalers Association), along with the Arizona Wine and Spirits Wholesale Association and many other alcohol companies, have bankrolled the fight to keep cannabis illegal, at least recreationally, by pouring tens of thousands of dollars into anti-cannabis campaigns and donations to groups opposing legalisation. The beauty and cleverness of this manoeuvre from the alcohol industry is that they are able to put it under the banner of protecting public health, even though protecting profit is the actual reason. If the alcohol industry actually cared about protecting public health, why would they fight so hard to keep alcohol as regulated as little as possible but welcome and promote all efforts to maintain tough control of cannabis?

The anti-cannabis campaign appears altruistic, but it epitomises a double standard. If the alcohol industry was not going to be affected financially, or if it was going to receive commercial kickbacks, they would not bother fighting the cause. One of the anti-cannabis television commercials entitled 'Safe and healthy Massachusetts' (funded by the alcohol industry) claimed that drug-driving fatalities had increased in areas that had relaxed cannabis laws. The truth is that total road fatalities have fallen (particularly for drink-driving). However, there has been a slight increase in the number of fatalities where drivers had trace elements of cannabis in their system. This is primarily due to individuals being prescribed medical cannabis. For those who used the drug recreationally, there was zero evidence from the medical examiner's office that the levels of THC detected would have impaired driving ability. The same double standard exists in this commercial. If the alcohol industry really cared about car accidents, then why not welcome tighter restrictions on alcohol? After all, every day in the USA, almost thirty fatal car accidents that are wholly attributable to alcohol occur. Such campaigns are ploys to divert attention towards illicit drug harms and away from alcohol harms.

Annual financial reports documented by the USA Securities and Exchange Commission (SEC) from heavyweight corporations, such as the Boston Beer Company (Samuel Adams—beer, Twisted Tea—hard ice tea, Angry Orchard—hard cider, Truly Spiked & Sparkling—spiked sparkling water) and Brown-Forman (Jack Daniels, Jägermeister, Chambord, Woodford Reserve, and many other spirits), include advice from senior representatives that investors need to be aware that the legalisation of cannabis may, to a significant extent, affect the demand for their products. The point of tension that underpins all operations within the alcohol industry is whether they will affect profitability for stakeholders.

A further example that reveals how the alcohol industry's primary objective is generating profits for all stakeholders was the response by the industry to alcohol-fuelled violence in Sydney, which gathered widespread media attention from 2011 to 2015. Following a number of serious assaults and deaths (in which alcohol was the main contributory factor) in Kings Cross, one of Sydney's most popular areas for evening entertainment, the NSW government introduced a string of measures to reduce violence in the area and adjacent zones, such as Cockle Bay and The Rocks. The measures included restricting hours of alcohol service, restricting hours at which venues are permitted to allow patrons' entry and creating mandatory sentencing requirements for various drug-related offences.

The measures conveniently did not apply to nearby venue The Star Sydney casino. This could be due to a number of factors, such as the government not wanting to forego the taxation generated from gambling twenty-four hours a day, that the venue includes a hotel and many other facilities serving the more than 11,000,000 visitors per month or that stakeholders are closely enough connected to the media and government officials to avoid restrictions. This is despite the fact that in 2013, according to NSW Bureau of Crime Statistics and Research (BOCSAR), The Star recorded three times as many assaults as the listed most violent venue, the Ivy complex.

The measures introduced were met with enormous opposition from the AHA as well as thousands of other individuals within the hospitality industry. Initially, industry representatives blamed the violence on amphetamines, which was dismissed immediately and treated as the groundless claim that it was. The AHA claimed the laws unfairly punished law-abiding venues and patrons and instead recommended no changes be made to hours of alcohol service and the only change to be made should be that after 3am, venues could only accept patrons who had either booked in advance or were 'existing patrons'—a laughable recommendation, due to its almost complete unenforceability. It appeared to be a ploy to ensure venues can maximise alcohol sales. The AHA also called to repeal legislation which stated that bottle shops within the lockout zone had to cease trading at 10pm. Again, entirely transparent. The pushback gained widespread media attention due to protests and various entities weighing in on the controversial changes. The evidence, however, was clear as day.

The BOCSAR report shows falls in non-domestic assaults within the Kings Cross area by over fifty per cent between 6pm and 1:30am, and almost ninety-five per cent from 3am to 6am. Non-domestic assaults in Sydney CBD entertainment areas fell in total by over thirty per cent, and by over forty per cent when alcohol service stopped at 3am. Hospitality and alcohol industry representatives claimed that the new laws are to blame for the closure of businesses, due to less foot traffic. However, independent research has concluded that the decreased level of foot traffic cited by the hospitality industry is grossly and wilfully exaggerated. One item of evidence that the hospitality and alcohol industry cling to in a bid to resurrect previous legislation is that assault rates in outside areas have increased, and that the laws have simply pushed the problems into other areas. For adjacent and proximate areas, rates of assault after implementing legislative changes did increase by twelve per cent and seventeen per cent respectively, which indicates an increase of about 300 assaults in total. However, the total number of assaults within the lockout zones decreased by approximately 930, which indicates that the decrease in assaults was three times greater than the increase in neighbouring areas. The net result for lockout areas as well as nearby suburbs was a fall of over 600 assaults, primarily due to the disproportional drop within lockout zones.

While an argument could be made that a small percentage of violence may have shifted towards neighbouring areas, the increases are negligible, and a stronger case could be made for extending the restrictions to all areas. This would ensure that the efficacy of the laws for public safety could be applied to all areas, that violence cannot be 'pushed' into other precincts, and that all licensed venues would be treated equally. The alcohol industry does not want more harm, and they are not responsible for alcohol-related violence. However, they are not overly concerned about harm, and they are responsible for blocking measures that unquestionably reduce alcohol-related violence. Essentially, the alcohol industry has a greater desire to protect their profits than government has to reduce alcohol harms. Greater consumption leads to greater harm but greater consumption also leads to greater profits. Although the community wants less harm, the alcohol industry wants more profit, and if harms occur as a side effect of profitability, that collateral damage is considered tolerable by the industry. There is no incentive in the eyes of the industry for societal harms to go up or down, as long as the measures to influence societal harms do not affect alcohol sales. The government, of course, following consistent pressure from the hospitality industry went weak at the knees and decided to relax the legislation, albeit only slightly. The industry also argued that the assaults and deaths that gained widespread media attention, such as those of Thomas Kelly, Daniel Christie and Fady Taiba, did not occur within licensed premises, and occurred earlier in the evening—well before lockout time restrictions would have applied. (This was despite each of the offenders consuming alcohol at licensed premises prior to offending.)

These cases were outliers, as the vast majority of alcohol-related violent incidences occur later in the evening. As the evenings wear on, people drink more, and the numbers of incidences increase. Additionally, partygoers actively seeking or anticipating malice—such as Thomas Kelly's killer, Kieran Loveridge, who stated that evening, 'I swear I am going to bash someone tonight'—are probably going to be most attracted to areas that provide an endless stream of booze all night.

Imagine, however, the industry's reaction if the government responded to this complaint by implementing lockout times based on the cases the industry references and uses as a platform and advised venues that patrons cannot enter after 9pm and that no alcohol will be served after 11pm! There are a lot of contributing factors to alcohol-related violence, such as the pharmacological effects of alcohol, individual characteristics, the environment and societal attitudes. The challenge is tackling the factors we can legislatively change—predominately, the environment—the alcohol industry fights twice as hard to ensure that no hard-hitting measures are implemented.

One of the arguments the industry used to press the government into backpedalling on the legislation was that the laws had forced many businesses to close (including unlicensed venues) due to downturns in revenue. The legislation penalised unlicensed venues as well as licensed venues that had been model businesses in limiting contributing to the harms. However, in order to reach the level of violence that existed prior to legislative changes, patrons of a significant proportion of businesses would have be very intoxicated, indicating a breach of responsible service of alcohol (RSA) laws. Even if people pre-drank and were intoxicated by the time they arrived in the area, they should not have been allowed into venues or allowed to consume more alcohol. As trading and alcohol service hours extend, assault rates increase because individuals become more intoxicated, and until venues learn to rigorously enforce RSA laws, such as not serving drunk patrons, they will continue to face regulations and restrictions.

Other than security, the self-enforcement of RSA laws is extremely poor. I worked for a licensed venue for a short time, and even though this was a high-end venue that occasionally ran RSA-refresher courses, I witnessed from the inside how employees are incentivised to encourage patrons to drink more as well as to serve intoxicated individuals. Venue-sanctioned competitions were run between bartenders as to who could make the most money on an average shift through drink sales, and the winner would receive a few bottles of alcohol. Even though the venue had restrictions on what products they could sell in terms of alcohol content, other products that exceeded the liquor licensing restrictions, such as absinthe (approx. seventy per cent alc/vol.), were frequently sold.

This is one of the reasons the concept of industry self-regulation is absurd. How can regulatory bodies trust venues when such an obvious conflict of interest exists? We owe a great deal to the members of the state police forces who put their lives on the line in overworked and underpaid jobs. However, two police officers strolling through a licensed venue for a few minutes once or twice per night to check that all is above board as the only means of confirming regulatory compliance simply does not cut the mustard.

If alcohol did cause intolerable damage, the media and government would tell us.

It would seem plausible that since one of the primary roles of government is to protect public welfare and one of the primary roles of the media is to generate public awareness of societal issues that both government and media would take steps to ensure the public are informed and protected. However, as both the media and the government receive financial and non-financial kickbacks from the alcohol industry, it is unlikely that they would bite the hand that feeds them.

Leading up to 2011, NSW had been under Australian Labor Party (ALP) rule for sixteen years, and in late March of that year, Barry O'Farrell defeated Kristina Kenneally in a landslide victory to become the forty-third premier of NSW. During the time the ALP was in power under Bob Carr, Morris Iemma, Nathan Rees, and Kristina Kenneally, the relationship between government and the AHA was rather cosy. Premier Carr kicked off the industry-association bond in the 1990s by allowing poker machines into pubs. Then, the tax-free threshold for poker machines was raised to $200,000. During 2017–2018, the AHA donated $1,013,625 to various parties, with the Liberal and National parties raking in over $610,000 and the ALP taking over $345,000.

According to the Australian Electoral Commission, the alcohol industry in its entirety—including other groups, such as Spirits and Cocktails Australia and Lion—donated over $1,800,000 in the same period. Evidence has shown that during policy debates where industry profits are threatened (such as the 2008–2009 alcopop tax) and leading into elections, donations increase exponentially. There is no transparency in the relationship between the AHA and government representatives because, at the federal level, ministerial diaries are not published, and the lobbyist register does not cover peak industry groups.

During Labor's reign, the AHA donated hundreds of thousands of dollars to the ALP, while the Liberal Party received less than one-third of those donations. The relationship soured in late 2010 when the ALP produced a 'name and shame' list of the most violent licensed venues in NSW. The popular incoming premier Barry O'Farrell announced during this time that he would scrap the name and shame list and instead introduce a more watered-down approach. Predictably, the AHA completely reversed the ratio of donations, from over $600,000 to the ALP and less than $200,000 to the Liberal Party, to $35,000 to the ALP and almost $340,000 to the Liberals. Before he announced plans to scrap the name and shame list, however, Barry O'Farrell was wined and dined by the AHA. Malcolm McGuiness, owner of Scruffy Murphy's (one of the state's most violent venues) and member of the AHA, forked out over $70,000 for a dinner with O'Farrell in 2009.

Shortly before this dinner, McGuiness attempted to make a civil claim against Dr Don Weatherburn, Head of BOCSAR, after the

Bureau published research linking violent assaults to proximity of licensed venues. Sally Fielke, who at the time was the CEO of the AHA, supported the move by McGuiness and was in almost complete denial about the venue-violence link. She claimed that shutting down violent licensed venues was not the answer. The proposed measures did not even suggest shutting down venues, and if it was not for the violence, the venues would be allowed to operate almost twenty-four/seven.

Essentially, the industry feared that the 'Newcastle solution' of early closing times and lockouts would spread to other cities. The restrictions on licensed venues in Newcastle brought assault rates down by a third within the space of a year, halved night-time street crime, reduced Emergency Department admissions by about twenty-five per cent, and were used as a blueprint model for Sydney lockout laws. The AHA was not interested in the effectiveness of the Newcastle laws and slammed the regulations in their 2010 annual report. While alcohol-related violence captured the public's attention and solutions to the issue were up in the air, Jason Bartlett, the AHA's communications director, boasted in the annual report that he and Fielke had travelled the state to engage in one-on-one meetings with senior media representatives, and that their contacts had already been paying off.

The bottom line is that journalists and media personnel will write or say whatever the alcohol industry wants, as long as they give them enough to drink over dinner or lunch. In the UK, multinational alcohol company Diageo holds a free drinks party every fortnight that all members of parliament and editors of national newspapers are invited to. A study conducted in the mid-1990s showed that over fifty per cent of UK politicians have direct vested financial interest in the alcohol industry. In fact, in 2014, the *British Medical Journal* (BMJ) revealed that the UK Department of Health had formally met with the alcohol industry on at least 130 occasions over a year in a bid to create a 'U-turn' on minimum pricing, which the alcohol industry considered a sham. From 2005 to 2012, over $1,000,000 was spent by the Global Alcohol Producers Group, now International Centre for Alcohol Policies (ICAP), on lobbying the US federal government to embrace policies diametrically opposed to those put forward by public health experts.

ICAP is wholly funded by the alcohol industry. Lobbying essentially refers to action taken in an effort to influence decisions or policies and it generally targets policymakers and regulatory bodies. Lobbying by pressure groups in Australia has morphed into a multi-billion-dollar industry across various sectors, including retail, property and religion. Lobbyists are effective in enticing legislators as there is almost always some form of mutual benefit. While lobby groups and legislators may benefit from the transaction, often groups in society or society as a whole foots the bill.

The Australian Beverages Council (ABC) consistently rejects objective scientific evidence that links soft drink consumption with any form of health issues because admitting harm equals risking profitability. The ABC also claims that soft drink consumption is declining (which is arbitrary, depending on time period you take) because they can then say we don't need to introduce other measures such as taxing sugar. The primary point of difference with the alcohol lobby compared to other products or sectors is the intrinsic toxicity of the product and the societal damage it wreaks. Legislators are elected and employed to form policy decisions based on what is in the best interest for society, not the best interest for themselves. The irony of the government-industry relationship is that such a large proportion of drug-related debates are fought on moral rather than evidential grounds. If governments really want to represent morality and honour in the drug space, the first step should be to cut ties with the alcohol industry, because the relationship, in itself, speaks volumes to the character of legislators. Donations to political parties from the alcohol industry should be banned so that legislators are not incentivised to put the success of their career ahead of the health of their constituents and the wider population.

Australia is not unique in dancing to the tune of the alcohol industry. Diageo has engaged in bribery, tax schemes and lobbying across various other countries, including India and Thailand, which has likely driven profits in the order of hundreds of millions of dollars. As these schemes spread far and wide and deep, with hefty finance at stake and vested interests going both ways, it is unlikely that the brakes will be applied to the profitability of Big Alcohol any time soon.

6

Darts – Tobacco

Although government campaigns have systematically phased out the availability and reduced the social acceptability of tobacco in Australia over time, about 21,000 Australians still die each year from tobacco-related causes. Tobacco is the leading cause of preventable death in the world, killing approximately 5,000,000 people annually. The practice of tobacco smoking was estimated to have begun approximately 5,000 BC, but it was not until the 1920s that a handful of German scientists began to study the relationship between smoking and lung cancer.

In the 1850s, the concept that smoking was 'dangerous to the lungs' and 'loathsome to the eye', as King James I of England declared in the early 1600s, was debated by medical professionals in *The Lancet*, and the first tobacco-lung cancer risk paper was published in 1912. During the late 1930s and early 1940s, Nazi-affiliated practitioners published scientific studies demonstrating the smoking-lung cancer link that led to the first anti-smoking campaign.

The Nazi anti-tobacco campaign, which was rolled out across Germany, consisted of similar measures to those that are currently adopted throughout Australia and indeed the international community, such as increasing tobacco excise and health education as well as restricting areas of smoking. The campaign was initially considered a failure because smoking rates continued to climb. This was due in part to the inherently addictive nature of smoking, which required time for users to quit, and also due to the enormous pushback of advertising from the tobacco industry. This first anti-smoking campaign ended with the collapse of Nazi Germany. American cigarette companies seized the opportunity, ramping up production, which led to a surge in the popularity of smoking. Almost no research into the health effects of smoking was conducted for approximately a decade.

In the 1960s, the USA Surgeon General began research into the relationship between tobacco and cancer, and in 1964 officially warned the public about the harms of tobacco, particularly its link with lung cancer. Initially, tobacco companies did not aggressively fight the growing body of evidence pointing to the danger of their product, but instead, subtly persuaded the public by using doctors in advertising suggesting that specific products were less harmful or irritating to the lungs and throat than others. In fact, in 1954, the Tobacco Industry Research Committee (TIRC), which was essentially an organisation dedicated to disproving tobacco harms, mailed an eighteen-page booklet to almost a quarter of a million journalists, doctors and politicians. The booklet claimed that tobacco was not hazardous to human health, or at the very least, its harmfulness was unsettled.

Despite almost unanimous support from the medical community to drive down tobacco use, Big Tobacco (all vested parties within the tobacco industry) was able to flex its financial muscles and block almost every effort to reduce tobacco use. It fought relentlessly against all proposed regulations by lobbying, advertising, and denying or obscuring harms based on evidence. The influential power of Big Tobacco was somewhat effective until 1994, when the chief executive officers of the seven largest tobacco corporations were asked to testify under oath in the Waxman hearings (named after USA politician Henry Waxman) on the addictiveness and harm of tobacco.

Every single big tobacco representative lied under oath, denying addictiveness and harms of tobacco, despite mountains of evidence in public documents proving that all companies were fully aware of the harm that tobacco caused. When asked if he smoked the executive president of R.J Reynolds (one of the largest tobacco companies in the USA) responded, 'Are you kidding? We reserve that right for the poor, the young, the black and the stupid.'

Tobacco companies cynically produced a range of innovations, such as filters, light cigarettes and smokeless tobacco, which not only were equally as harmful, but which dissuaded its market from quitting tobacco. It has also been extensively documented that, although on the outside, big tobacco pretended to not target young people, statements by tobacco company executives reveal the opposite was the case:

'The base of our business is the high school student.'

'We must get our share of the youth market.'

'Young people are the only source of replacement smokers.'

'Today's teenager is tomorrow's potential regular customer.'

'Present the cigarette as one of a few initiations into the adult world.'

Science prevailed over time, and because of Big Tobacco's unethical and highly public efforts to protect their profits, they did not have a single leg to stand on. This ultimately led to the downfall of tobacco.

Tobacco and sport enjoyed a lengthy relationship until medical authorities shone a light on the health detriments of tobacco use. Lucrative tobacco companies sponsored large-scale sporting events as well as teams, and many athletes were tobacco users. This was particularly the case with chewing tobacco in USA baseball, where the majority of players chewed tobacco because it allowed them to maintain oral moisture while playing on dusty fields. A number of high-profile baseball players died from diseases related to tobacco use, including the most famous player of all time, George Herman 'Babe' Ruth.

Following the attention drawn to the potential harm of chewing tobacco, players switched from chewing to smoking tobacco but government warnings soon emerged around the potential risks associated with cigarettes, leading to players switching back to smokeless tobacco, in the form of dipping tobacco. The main difference between chewing and dipping tobacco is that chewing tobacco needs to be crushed by the teeth to release the flavour and nicotine, whereas dipping is held between the lip and the gum.

Australia was already ahead of the pack in reducing tobacco use through a range of advertising bans implemented by the Whitlam Labor government during the early 1970s. Since then, Australia has been a public health role model to the rest of the world, bringing tobacco use down from its peak of about fifty to seventy per cent in men (post-WWII to the 1970s), to approximately twelve to thirteen per cent in both genders today (2018).

Throughout history, smoking has been more prevalent in males than females. The closer proximity to major cities, the lower the smoking rates, as approximately one in five Australians smoke in rural areas, one in six smoke in regional areas, and one in eight smoke in major cities. Currently in Australia, a packet of cigarettes costs between twenty dollars and thirty dollars but increases in tobacco excise are expected to bring this figure up to forty dollars per packet. The Australian government makes $17,000,000,000 per year from tobacco excise, excluding GST. With the average smoker in Australia smoking approximately twenty cigarettes per day (about six packets per week), they can expect to pay at least $300,000 in cigarettes over a working lifetime (fifteen to sixty-five years) and, with increases in excise duty, a smoker could easily puff away half a million dollars over their lifetime.

Once other costs to the individual, such as health care or loss of productivity, are factored in, this cost could rise to up to $2,000,000. However, as with all drugs, the financial costs to the individual are only one part of the total harm that the drug causes to both the user and wider society. Deaths are only one measure of harm. As with alcohol, many of the deaths caused by tobacco are not deaths to the user. Second-hand smoke is responsible for the deaths of thousands of non-smokers throughout the world, and for every smoker who dies, about thirty people live with a severe smoking-related illness. Tobacco is also a major cause of stillbirth and sudden infant death syndrome (SIDS). In addition, about fifty per cent of all fires in the world are caused by smokers discarding or leaving still-lit cigarettes, equating to approximately 2,500 fatal burns annually.

Approximately one in three people who try tobacco will be addicted at some point in their life (a thirty per cent capture rate). At least half of all long-term smokers die as a result of their tobacco use and, like alcohol, a person does not have to be addicted to face significant risk of harm. Regulated tobacco products currently make up the vast majority of total tobacco market share (approximately ninety per cent), with a small number of illegally manufactured tobacco products still existing. Increases in tobacco excise have been effective in lowering tobacco use as the majority of smokers take up the habit at a young age when they have low disposable income. However, this deterrence mechanism is a delicate balance; sharp increases in excise can stimulate the illicit tobacco market. Between 2016 and 2017 in Australia, tobacco consumption dropped as it has done for the past few decades, but at the same time, black market tobacco supplies increased.

Although pricing young smokers out of the market is effective, more needs to be done for those who are heavily dependent. As cigarettes are twenty times more harmful to the user overall than e-cigarettes (electronic cigarettes/vaping), the use of e-cigarettes among those dependent should be encouraged. Public Health England has estimated that the cancer risk among e-cigarette users is 99.5 per cent less than smoking. Liquid nicotine is, however, technically illegal in Australia, even though it is safer than smoking, can assist smokers in quitting and is not a gateway for young people into a lifetime of smoking. We shouldn't even be labelling devices that vaporise nicotine as e-cigarettes, because they don't contain tobacco and there is no combustion.

A 2019 study published in the *Journal of the National Cancer Institute*, which was the most comprehensive and definitive study to date, failed to find any evidence that vaping is a gateway to smoking. If anything, evidence demonstrates that vaping is a net gateway out of smoking, because vaping among non-smokers is extremely rare and infrequent, there is no evidence that vaping causes individuals to take up smoking, millions of smokers have been able to cut down or quit smoking because of vaping, and those who smoke and vape tend to have an underlying propensity to use drugs and likely would have smoked anyway. While the ideal is that individuals who are non-smokers and non-vapers never start smoking, established smokers could switch to safer methods rather than face an ultimatum of either quitting or continuing to smoke, particularly considering that almost eighty per cent of smokers have tried to quit and failed. There is evidence that individuals working in tobacco companies are concomitantly involved in illicit tobacco manufacture, primarily to maintain downward pressure on tobacco excise. The *BMJ* released a study in 2000 looking at the response of the Canadian tobacco black market when a three dollar per packet tax was imposed on cigarettes. Illicit cigarettes grew from being a tiny fraction of the market to thirty per cent of all cigarettes sold, which led to the repealing of the tax. The tobacco black market makes up ten per cent of the total tobacco market in Australia, twenty per cent in the UK, between eight per cent and twenty-one per cent in the USA. American states with the highest excise also have the highest tax evasion rates. Drug black markets will always exist, so allowing regulated access is the best means of keeping that market as small as possible.

The drug in tobacco is the stimulant nicotine, and although the stimulant produces increases in alertness and sharpness, paradoxically, nicotine also produces effects such as relaxation and ease of agitation. As inhaling any drug is one of the fast methods of getting it to the brain, nicotine users will experience effects within approximately seven seconds. Each cigarette contains an average of twelve milligrams of nicotine, with the average cigar containing ten to twenty times this amount. For each cigarette smoked, the user absorbs approximately one milligram of nicotine, while as the average cigar user absorbs significantly more nicotine due to the fact that cigars take much longer to smoke. Although the average cigarette smoker smokes approximately a packet per day, the average cigar smoker smokes approximately one or two cigars per day. When tobacco smoke containing nicotine is inhaled, it is able to be rapidly absorbed into the blood due to its ability to transfer across cell membranes, and because the alveoli, which are the tiny air sacs in lung tissue that facilitate gaseous exchange, cover such a large surface area. Peak blood concentrations of nicotine are found at around the cessation of a smoking session. However, the peak concentration of nicotine from oral administration, such as chewing tobacco, is much slower. This is primarily due to gastric fluid in the stomach being acidic, which slows absorption. Nicotine binds to nicotinic acetylcholine receptors, which are expressed throughout the central and peripheral nervous system. Nicotine acts as an agonist, blocking the reuptake of acetylcholine, which increases its extracellular concentration, resulting in stimulatory effects, such as increased alertness and increased heart rate. This, in itself, is not the mechanism for nicotine's addictiveness.

Addiction seems to primarily occur due the release of dopamine following the interaction of nicotine and nicotinic receptor sites. The release of dopamine signals pleasure and is critical for the reinforcing and rewarding effects, which essentially drive drug re-administration. The scientific community, however, is not fully unified with regard to nicotine and the release of dopamine, as alcohol and amphetamines appear to be the only two drugs that release dopamine in a reliable fashion across numerous studies.

One of the reasons nicotine replacement therapies (NRTs), such as transdermal patches, lozenges and gum, do not work for everyone is because the administration and effect onset of nicotine in these methods are quite slow, particularly compared to smoking, and they do not replace the ritual of smoking.

Many people believe that cigar smoking is safer than cigarette smoking because users typically do not inhale the smoke, therefore avoiding risks such as heart disease and cancer. Cigar smokers who do not inhale have lower rates of disease associated with inhaling compared to non-smokers. However, as cigar users draw higher levels of carcinogens, such as nitrosamines, higher levels of tar and other toxins, such as polycyclic aromatic hydrocarbons, as well as higher levels of nicotine, many health experts argue that cigars are more harmful than cigarettes. As nicotine is considered to be the major factor in tobacco addiction, patches or gum that contain the drug are used as treatments to replace the nicotine found in cigarettes but without the harms associated with the inhalation of burnt tobacco. Nicotine can also be absorbed into the body through smokeless tobacco products, such as dipping tobacco or chewing tobacco, as well as through electronic cigarettes. Smokeless tobacco, as well as electronic cigarettes, are not harmless, although they are significantly less harmful than smoking tobacco, as many of the harms that cigarettes, cigars and other products such as tobacco pipes produce are due to the user inhaling a burnt substance. As they also do not produce smoke, they cause significantly less harm to the community due to the absence of second-hand smoke.

The introduction of smoke-free areas has not only created cleaner environments for the community in terms of second-hand smoke, particularly for people with lung conditions, it can help prevent individuals from taking up the habit and help smokers to quit. Even though it is not an active discouragement like an 'every cigarette is doing you damage' advertisement, it creates social isolation for smokers, and removes the visual image of smoking from common areas.

Among other devices used to consume tobacco is the water pipe, or hookah, whose origins lie in the Middle East and South Asia. Hookahs are multi-part instruments used for smoking or vaporising tobacco (which is often flavoured) and sometimes cannabis. Although vaporising tobacco is safer than smoking tobacco, and the tobacco that is either vaporised or smoked passes through water before it is inhaled, water pipe users also face many of the same risks as cigarette and cigar smokers.

Typically, a hookah user inhales approximately the same level of nicotine in a session as a cigarette smoker, 150 to 200 times the amount of smoke as a single cigarette and more carbon monoxide but lower levels of select carcinogens, such as nitrosamines. Hookah users additionally put themselves at risk of contracting disease due to the use of a communal mouthpiece and put others, including unborn babies, at risk through the production of second-hand smoke.

Aside from transdermal patches and lozenges, the safest way to administer nicotine is through an e-cigarette. Other instruments, such as cigarettes, cigars and hookahs, all possess different and unique risks and the evidence is not conclusive as to whether one is more or less harmful than the others. The risks are essentially different. A cigarette smoker may switch to using a cigar or hookah in the belief that it is less harmful but, although they may face less harms in one area, the harms may be greater in another. For example, switching from cigarettes to cigars to avoid inhaling smoke into the lungs may reduce the risk of developing lung cancer, however, the cigar smoker may be at greater risk of oral cancer. Depth of inhalation is likely to be an independent risk factor for lung cancer. If someone switches cigar smoking to using a hookah, the risk of developing oral cancer may be more or less the same. However, there is a greater risk of contracting disease from sharing a mouthpiece.

I have spoken to many people about the risks of hookah use, and the most common response is that it is 'part of culture (or religion)', but cultural attachments in no way diminish the harms of the product, and they are not safe alternatives to smoking. Not only are hookah users far more likely to die of mouth, lung and oesophageal cancer as well as cardiovascular disease than non-smokers, but they also run the risk of contracting serious infections, and those within proximity can inhale the circulating smoke, putting them at risk too. Hookahs have been promoted as being tar and smoke free, but the same can be said for cigarettes and cigars—none of these products produce smoke or tar until they are set on fire. The marketing of hookahs perpetuates the myth that they are safe. Which is why, if you speak to cigarette smokers, they know what they are doing is harmful and that they should quit, but many hookah smokers falsely believe that what they are doing is safe. Even though vaping an e-cigarette is the safest way to inhale nicotine, this practice is not without its critics. These critics make a number of assertions that are not evidence based:

- E-cigarettes are a Trojan horse because they allow tobacco companies access to lucrative advertising and sponsorship contracts, where such agreements for smoking are prohibited.
  - ○ This is a ridiculous assertion—primarily because e-cigarettes did not emerge from the tobacco industry, and because they are either not marketed or are marketed as alternatives to cigarettes, not pathways into smoking.
- Tobacco companies are attempting to portray themselves as campaigners for public health initiatives, when in reality, the production of new nicotine products creates new nicotine markets, which creates greater nicotine addiction. Essentially, the tobacco industry is pretending to be a part of the solution, when they are actually a part of the problem.
  - ○ This suggestion ignores the fact that the inhalation of smoke is the almost sole cause of all tobacco-related harms, not nicotine itself. Although nicotine drives continued use, heating a substance to the point it is vaporised, not burnt, avoids almost all harms caused by smoking.
- E-cigarettes are at least as hazardous to the oral cavity and cardiovascular system as cigarettes.
  - ○ This argument generally comes from those who consider anything that is inhaled to be bad. It is also argued from a non-human evidence base—in vitro, which means outside of the living organism, such as in a test tube. These studies have also generally used acute, concentrated exposures to e-liquid nicotine.
- Nicotine administration through e-cigarettes is detrimental to the developing brain and generates more young addicts.
  - ○ There is no evidence of brain damage or social dysfunction. Smoking rates and the number of people addicted to nicotine (including young people) has declined steadily over the past

fifty years. Nicotine's potential effect on brain development has only ever been demonstrated in animal studies, and you cannot extrapolate from animal or basic science research to make clinical claims.

- E-cigarette users are more likely to go on to smoking than those who have never tried cigarettes.
  ○ This claim is not based on a causal effect, but instead a 'common liability', where whatever reason(s) that inclined an individual to smoke (mental health, peer pressure etc.) also inclines them to vape.
- E-cigarettes constrain the long-term decline in smoking rates by reducing smoking cessation.
  ○ This is not supported by evidence and countries, such as the USA and the UK, have seen an accelerated decline in smoking since the emergence of e-cigarettes.

Apart from various medical communities within Australia, such as the Royal Australian & New Zealand College of Psychiatrists, bodies that support e-cigarettes include:

- US Food and Drug Administration
- American Cancer Society
- Royal College of Physicians
- British Medical Association
- British Lung Foundation
- Public Health England
- Government of Canada
- Cancer Research UK
- Royal Society for Public Health
- Royal College of General Practitioners

The prohibitive approach to vaping is likely to have a number of negative unintended consequences:

- Restrictions on liquid nicotine strength mean that smokers may find it harder to give up because they are unable to receive a satisfactory level of nicotine to meet their withdrawals. This is particularly true during the early stage of vaping.

- Restrictions or bans on flavours can deter smokers from switching permanently as the change in flavour is part of the appeal for vaping. This may also stimulate the nicotine black market into providing flavoured alternatives that are likely to be more harmful.

- Alarmist health warnings that vaping is not a safe alternative to smoking are not only misleading because they do not accurately communicate the relative risk, they downplay the health benefits of switching. This decreases the likelihood of a smoker moving away from smoking.

The reductions in harm that smokeless tobacco products offer is supported by the experience in Sweden, which has both the lowest rate of smoking in Europe and the lowest death rates attributable to tobacco. This is primarily because a large proportion of Swedes use Scandinavian snus, which is a smokeless, powdered tobacco product, as an alternative. The average smoking prevalence in the European Union is about twenty-five per cent, while in Sweden the prevalence is five per cent. The tobacco-related death rate in Sweden is less than half the EU average, with rates of pancreatic and oral cancers the lowest in the EU and lung cancer less than half the EU average.

Similar trends are revealed in Norway. In the space of less than twenty years, daily tobacco use rates for men have fallen from thirty per cent in 2000 to about five per cent in 2017, and for females, daily tobacco-use rates have fallen from about thirty per cent to two to three per cent. It is young Norwegian women (aged sixteen to twenty-four) who have shown the largest decline. In the early 2000s, twenty-five to thirty per cent of young women smoked, but by 2017 this was down to one per cent. In the same period of time, male consumption of snus increased from seven to eight per cent of the population to about twenty-five per cent, and female consumption of snus increased from one per cent to about sixteen per cent. Tobacco-related deaths are still high in Norway (more than 6,000 deaths per year in a population of about 5,300,000), and this due not only to high historical smoking prevalence (seventy per cent in males, thirty per cent in females in the 1970s), but also a weaker commitment to tobacco control. This is illustrated by far fewer tobacco packaging warnings, an absence of plain packaging and a lower excise duty in comparison to other countries.

As long-term, chronic use of tobacco drives almost all tobacco-related deaths, the recent increases in snus consumption and decreases in tobacco consumption are expected to have a delayed effect in terms of reducing deaths. It was not until 2000 that smoking rates for men and women dipped below thirty per cent. Despite smoking rates dramatically declining and snus consumption increasing since 2000, reducing the measurable harms of smoking, such as deaths or hospitalisations, is a long-term process, because the risks and damage caused by a lifetime of smoking take many years to erase. Snus is effectively banned everywhere else in Europe and is prohibitively expensive in Australia. Sweden—without banning smoking or snus—is well on its way to be the first smoke-free country in the world by taking the rational approach of allowing its population access to safer alternatives.

Tobacco use causes a myriad of health detriments to both the user and the wider community through a number of mechanisms. The principal health complications from either direct or second-hand smoke are diseases of the head, neck, heart and lungs. Although the drug in tobacco is nicotine, which drives users to continue smoking, nicotine itself is a fairly benign compound compared to the other chemicals present in tobacco. While nicotine can increase blood pressure and heart rate, there is limited and conflicting evidence that moderate doses of nicotine produce any significant health harms. In animal studies, nicotine has been shown to inhibit apoptosis, which suggests that it may be a tumour promoter, however, this is yet to be categorically proven. Nicotine itself can cause serious harm including death if a large amount is ingested in a short period of time (as seen in the film *Thank You For Smoking*) but this typically occurs when nicotine products (particularly liquid nicotine) are swallowed, because processing the drug in the gastrointestinal system means the effects of the drug are delayed. If three toddlers were to each accidently eat a cigarette, it is highly likely that one of them would die. It is possible to administer a fatal amount of nicotine through rapid constant smoking, but because smoking induces almost immediate effects, users are able to regulate their intake with ease. The safety ratio for nicotine is approximately thirty (possibly higher), as about one to two milligrams of nicotine are needed to produce an effective dose, while sixty milligrams is considered a lethal dose to an average adult. Death from tobacco use never occurs (with a tiny fraction of exceptions) as a result of acute exposure. However, if someone experiments with smoking, there is about a thirty per cent chance they will become dependent, and if they do become dependent, there is a very strong chance they will die from their smoking. There is a large number of other highly toxic molecules found in tobacco smoke, and although these chemicals are only found in very small quantities, the average smoker is exposed to these chemicals at least once every hour. As a result of the frequency of administration, as well as the longevity of a smokers' career, the bulk of harm is concentrated towards chronic harm not acute harm.

One of the major chronic health harms caused by tobacco is cancer, particularly in areas that come into contact with tobacco smoke, such as the mouth, oesophagus and lungs. The more a person smokes, the more their body is exposed to carcinogens found in tobacco smoke, meaning the greater their body is impeded in defending and responding to biological malfunctions.

Under normal conditions, genes that are present in cells have the ability to respond to malfunctions by undergoing a process called apoptosis (otherwise known as programmed cell death or cell suicide). Cells may perform programmed cell death (PCD) to prevent mutated cell division and growth, or cells may self-repair and, if unsuccessful, undergo PCD. Either way, the cell will either repair and continue in a normal cell cycle or perform PCD. Carcinogens change the functionality of cells by mutating specific characteristics that are intricate features of PCD. If these mechanisms, which ensure PCD proceeds systematically, are altered, cells may begin to divide in an uncontrolled manner; this is known as carcinogenesis (the formative stage of cancer). There are a number of different types of mutations, and mutations are present in other disorders, such as sickle-cell disease. In rare cases, mutations can even be beneficial, such as in the case of a person who possesses a specific base pair deletion mutation. This significantly delays the onset of AIDS after HIV is contracted.

Although there are a number of different specific mechanisms, two processes that link tobacco smoke and cancer are K-RAS and P21/P53 gene mutations. The P21 and P53 genes arrest cells early in their cycle if a fault occurs, and if so, perform PCD. Because of this unique function, these genes are essential in tumour suppression. Carcinogens found in tobacco smoke damage these genes, and P53 genetic mutations exist in eighty-five per cent of lung cancers, eighty per cent of neck/cranium cancers as well as more than fifty per cent of all cancers.

There are trillions of cells in the body, and researchers are aware of approximately fifty different types of proto-oncogenes present in human cells. Proto-oncogenes are genes that ensure the growth, division and deaths of cells occur in a regulated and orderly fashion. K-RAS is a proto-oncogene, and smoking is strongly linked with K-RAS mutations. The mutation of proto-oncogenes leads to severe problems:

- a poorer and slower rate at which cells recognise genetic alterations
- unregulated cell division
- a diminished rate of cell death.

Approximately one in three lung cancer cases, one in three colon cancer cases, and approximately ninety per cent of pancreatic cancer cases involve K-RAS mutations. What this means is that chemicals found in tobacco smoke disrupt, diminish and inhibit biological processes in the body that function in protecting, identifying and rectifying genetic malfunctions that lead to cancer.

Other peripheral and respiratory problems that arise from tobacco use include stroke, peripheral arterial disease, coronary artery disease, COPD, and other respiratory illnesses. The major cause of COPD is smoking, where the inhaled contents gradually become deposited and trapped within the lungs, restricting airflow, inflaming the lung tissue and damaging lung tissue. The patient is then unable to properly inhale and exhale, hence 'shortness of breath' and reduction in blood oxygen levels, which can ultimately lead to vasoconstriction (narrowing of vessels). At least half of all long-term smokers will develop COPD. After watching my grandparents (both of whom smoked) increasingly struggle for air in the latter stages of their life, I can assure you that COPD is a distressing and painful way to die. There is no cure and no treatment to reverse damage. Steroids and other drugs that dilate the bronchioles offer some aid in reducing airflow resistance, but lung transplants are often needed, despite the fact that organ donations are seriously limited, and transplants carry major potential risks and complications. Apart from a clinical diagnosis of COPD, smoking causes general heavy breathing, making it difficult to exercise, increasing the risk of obesity, which adds to the risk of intrinsically toxic tobacco smoke. It is estimated that every cigarette shaves off about ten minutes of life expectancy.

Other respiratory and cerebrovascular diseases caused by smoking often occur through atherosclerosis, which refers to the inner narrowing of arteries due to the accumulation of degenerative material on the blood vessel wall. Arteriosclerosis refers to the stiffening of arteries; however, atherosclerosis specifically refers to the stiffening of arteries through lipid (fatty) plaque deposits. In medicine, 'athero' refers to arteries, and 'sclerosis' refers to the stiffening of a particular structure—so osteosclerosis is abnormal stiffening of bones structure; lichen sclerosus is a stiffening of connective tissue typically around the genital area; and with multiple sclerosis, muscles become stiff due to spasticity. With atherosclerosis, blood flow becomes restricted with the build-up of plaque in the vessel wall, and this is the overwhelming cause of respiratory and cerebrovascular diseases, particularly among smokers.

Although the mechanisms through which tobacco causes atherosclerosis are unclear, it is believed that tobacco smoke impairs vascular function through a number of ways. Firstly, tobacco impairs the production of nitric oxide (NO), which is a vasodilator. 'Vaso' refers to vessels, and 'dilator' refers to an agent that causes dilation, so a vasodilator is an agent that dilates the blood vessels, causing them to widen and, with the reduction of NO as a vasodilator, the arteries become constricted, placing greater stress on all areas of the cardiovascular system.

NO also plays a role in regulating the anti-adhesive properties of the vessel wall, and with a reduction of NO due to smoke inhalation, there appears to be an increase in a number of intracellular adhesive molecules. This means that vessels are positioned and activated to 'grab' passing cells, leading to a gradual build-up of material on the cell wall, restricting blood flow and increasing pressure on the cardiovascular system. Smoking also oxidises low-density lipoprotein (LDL), and as this continuously stimulates intimal cells (cells within the blood vessel membrane wall), atherosclerosis progresses.

Smoking further contributes to atherosclerosis by increasing the concentration of plasma fibrinogen, a molecule responsible for blood clotting. When blood vessels are damaged, fibrinogen responds to the inflammation by clotting the area, and as smokers have much higher levels of fibrinogen, they are much more likely to suffer strokes, heart attacks and peripheral artery disease as the increased levels of fibrinogen put them at a much greater risk of blood clotting. All of these risks, albeit to a lesser extent, are also evident in passive smoking.

Despite the various harms that smoking causes to both the user as well as wider society, smoking does provide a number of health benefits. Smokers have a slightly lower risk of developing ulcerative colitis (an inflammatory bowel disease), Parkinson's disease (PD), endometrial cancer, pre-eclampsia (pregnancy-related hypertension disorder) and obesity. To believe these reported studies on their face value, however, is to be misled, because each benefit is a double-edged sword. Smokers have a lower risk of developing ulcerative colitis but have a higher risk of developing Crohn's disease, which is another type of inflammatory bowel disease. Smokers have a lower risk of developing Parkinson's disease; however, they have a higher risk of developing Alzheimer's disease, which is another neurological disorder. Smokers have a lower risk of developing endometrial cancer but a higher risk of developing other cancers, such as oral, oesophageal, lung, bladder and pancreatic cancer. Smokers have a lower risk of developing pre-eclampsia; however, one of the acute effects of nicotine is increasing blood pressure, and smoking causes hypertension with long-term use. Smokers also have a lower risk of developing obesity and yet some of the primary health concerns related to obesity are cancers and cardiovascular disease, for which smoking is a major contributing factor. So, despite the somewhat trivial protective health benefits of tobacco, overall, there is a significant health risk.

For the 21,000 tobacco-related deaths, there are about 200 smokers 'saved' by the habit, which equates to one life saved every 100 deaths. So, for anyone reading this who is a current smoker, it is almost certain that you will die as a result of your smoking before you can reap any health benefit from it. Reducing your risk of getting Alzheimer's disease at the age of eighty isn't much good if you die of a heart attack in your mid-sixties.

7

MARY JANE – CANNABIS

Cannabis, the most widely used illicit drug in the Western World, is one of the oldest medicines in the world, and in 1971, was the first product to be purchased on the internet. Approximately one in three Australians have reported using cannabis at least once in their lifetime. Hundreds of millions of people use cannabis every year, and within the drug space, the drug's legal status generates enormous political and societal tension.

There is evidence of cannabis use in Egypt as long ago as 4,000 BC, Indian pharmacopoeias have physically documented the medical utility of cannabis 2,000 years BC, and the drug became popularised in the UK in the 1840s. Some suggest that cannabis dates back even further, as archaeological evidence on broken Chinese pottery dating back 10,000 BC shows rope imprints of hemp, which is a variety of cannabis plant containing a very low level of THC (0.3 per cent). Chinese emperor Shennong, who was known as the father of Chinese medicine, is said to be one of the first people to document the medical benefits of cannabis around approximately 2700 BC. It was widely used throughout China for clothing and medicines up until 500 BC when it was banned because of its psychological effects.

Cannabis refers to a family of flowering plants, however the species that are of primary focus are *Cannabis sativa* and *Cannabis indica*. Cannabis is a highly complex compound containing hundreds of different chemicals, many of which are found on the trichomes (external appendages/growths on the cannabis). The trichomes exist as an evolutionary response by the plant to protect itself against agents that could damage the plant, such as insects, wind, and ultraviolet rays.

Although the public perception of cannabis is that of a drug that intoxicates its users, there are a myriad of other products, such as hemp oil, that are cannabis based. Hemp oil or hemp seed oil is extracted from specific varieties of the *Cannabis sativa* plant that are predominately THC free. Cleaning then pressing hemp seeds produce hemp oil. It is very high in essential fatty acids (EFAs), which are often used in an effort to improve immunity and skin and cardiovascular health. Other sources of EFAs include fish and shellfish, flaxseed oil, walnuts and sunflower seeds.

Cannabis is typically smoked through either a joint (cigarette type mechanism) or bong (multi-component utensil usually comprising of at least a mouthpiece, glass or plastic chamber partially filled with water, stem and socket for holding the drug). Cannabis can also be consumed through vaping or eating edibles. Traditional cannabis contains a fairly even mixture of THC and CBD, with THC being the psychoactive (stoning) component, and CBD actually counteracting some of the acute negative side effects of THC, particularly the paranoia and anxiety. Some hybrid strains of cannabis such as Skunk, Durban Poison and Sour Diesel contain particularly high levels of THC, and these exist due to private growers attempting to produce cannabis products that offer the most 'bang for your buck'.

Although cannabis poses some level of risk to its users, the risks are relatively low, particularly when compared to other drugs. In terms of deaths, cannabis has produced not a single overdose in history. In mid-June 2017, a handful of physicians in Colorado reported that an eleven month old boy had died from a cannabis overdose two years earlier.

It was later revealed that the boy had a very rare condition known as myocarditis (inflammation of the heart muscle), and although the boy did have cannabis in his system, this does not mean that the cannabis he consumed *caused* his death. It is also reported that he may have eaten the cannabis. To put this in context, a healthy child of the same age would have a reasonably high risk of dying if they were to eat a tobacco cigarette. His death may be attributable to another factor, such as an allergy. This is a perfect example of where much of the confusion surrounding cannabis comes from. For the average adult to overdose on cannabis, they would have to consume in excess of 620 kg in fifteen minutes. Although theoretically this is possible, in reality, it is impossible. I have however met many young people who appear to be keen on taking on this challenge! This does not mean, however, that there are no acute harms from cannabis.

Cannabis is a depressant, and cannabis users who smoke or vape often experience initial effects within a few minutes. However, some users report feeling effects during their first exhalation although this is typically if they are using a high potency strain. The 'high' that a user experiences generally lasts for a few hours, but it can last for significantly longer if the user consumes THC-infused edibles instead. This is due to the fact that when a substance is inhaled, the entry into, and the exit out of the brain occurs at a much faster rate than that of oral administration. Additionally, smoking cannabis delivers THC to the brain quickly via the lungs, however edibles are processed by the liver, and because the liver converts THC into a by-product called 11-hydroxy-THC—which is four to five times as potent as tetrahydrocannabinol—edibles can produce longer lasting and more powerful effects.

The effects of cannabis are distinct from many other drugs in that they are triphasic (three distinct effect phases). Relaxation is the initial effect of cannabis, typically followed by introspection, often coupled with some level of anxiety, then followed by hunger, hence the term 'the munchies'. There can be some residual irritation following cannabis use; however, the 'set' and 'setting' play a vital role in regulating the user's experience (although somewhat more relevant for psychedelic drugs) in terms of whether it be positive or negative.

The set is what a person brings to the experience: their state of mind, their physiology, their expectations, thoughts and experiences. The setting is the environment in which they consume the drug: the number of people; which people; topics of conversation; and physical safety, such as proximity to roads, balconies, pools and emergency services.

The psychoactive ingredient, THC, produces the 'stoning' effects by binding to a number of cannabinoid receptors. THC is an agonist meaning that when it binds to a receptor, it produces a biological response, whereas an antagonist binds to a receptor but blocks a response. An example of this is naltrexone, which is an opioid antagonist, blocking the effects of opioid drugs such as heroin or morphine. As cannabinoid receptors are involved in many biological functions, such as appetite and mood regulation, the effects a user experiences can be multi-faceted. It is hypothesised that cannabis affects appetite through three main mechanisms:

- Cannabinoids affect and increase odour detection within the olfactory bulb, the part of the brain that processes information about smells.

- Cannabis administration appears to release ghrelin, which is a hormone naturally released by the stomach to look for food when it is empty.

- Cannabinoids appear to alter the functioning of a protein known as proopiomelanocortin (POMC). When someone eats food, POMC naturally releases alpha-melanocyte stimulating hormone (α-MSH), which promotes feelings of satiety (being full). With administration of cannabinoids, POMC instead of releasing α-MSH, releases beta-endorphins (β-endorphin), which when administered have been proven to stimulate appetite.

Genetic mutations of POMC are therefore not surprisingly associated with early-onset obesity.

❧

Despite the fact that there is little to no causal evidence, there is a common belief in the community that cannabis causes psychosis, schizophrenia and brain damage. In fact, this misplaced fixation on the mental health effects of cannabis can detract from potentially legitimate harms, such as the deleterious effects on the cardiovascular system and the potentially increased risk of heart attacks associated with smoking the drug.

Despite the fact that cannabis had been used as a medicine for thousands of years, with solid efficacy and very few side effects, in 1934 the League of Nations decided that cannabis had no medical use, primarily because it was politically expedient to be tough on drugs. The League of Nations illegalised the trafficking of cannabis resin in 1925, following the suggestion from Egyptian representatives that cannabis was a drug used by the lower classes, and its prohibition would be a stride towards civilising and disciplining the lower classes, therefore benefitting wider society.

It was also around the same period of time, that cannabis facilitated the birth of jazz music. Many musicians used cannabis, however, being stoned makes it difficult to play in time. Therefore, while under the influence of cannabis, musicians syncopated, instead of playing with precise rhythm. Jazz music thankfully survived, notwithstanding efforts by the US government to arrest users such as Louis Armstrong. Along with the black jazz movement, the fear of Mexican immigration was a key motivator in some of the first anti-drug laws in the USA. Cannabis was banned virtually internationally in 1961 under the UN Single Convention on Narcotic Drugs.

Seventy years after the demise of the League of Nations, the World Health Organisation (WHO) still classifies cannabis as a Schedule 1 drug, alongside cocaine, heroin, remifentanil (more than 100 times more potent than morphine). WHO bases its stance on a League of Nations cannabis report, which is over eighty years old and cannot be cited or found anywhere. In Australia, cannabis is listed as a Schedule 8 or 9 drug, depending on the preparation. The United Nations (UN), which replaced the League of Nations, continued the ban on cannabis, and following consistent US pressure over the years, cannabis was essentially illegalised internationally. It remains illegal today because of Egyptian politics in the early 1900s, the misprescribing of cannabis in the UK in the 1960s (when the offending doctors should have been banned, instead of the actual drug) as well as consistent US pressure to terminate hemp cultivation.

Various areas around the world such as the Netherlands and select states of the USA have allowed regulated access to cannabis. However, internationally, cannabis is still primarily considered an 'illegal' drug.

Every time a country has swum against the tide of US prohibition, they have been criticised and threatened, such as in 2001, when the Jamaican government proposed decriminalising the possession of cannabis. The US responded by threatening to decertify the country in terms of non-compliance with their drug policy priorities. The US has openly criticised the Netherlands for their regulated cannabis market, as well as other European nations for harm-reduction programs, such as needle exchange to prevent the spread of HIV. US consular representatives forbade Canada in 2003 from opening up the first safe injecting site, and during the 1990s when heroin trials were taking place in Switzerland, the US attacked this research because it did not align with their agenda.

The primary reason why the ACT heroin trials were scrapped in 1997 was because the US threatened to withdraw support for opium production in Tasmania. The trial was also scrapped because, although Prime Minister John Howard had initially supported the program, the newly appointed head of the Australian National Council on Drugs, Major Brian Watters, an avid prohibitionist, advised against it, despite the trial having bipartisan support, as well as support from the Australian Federal Health Minister and five states.

Some would argue that countries outside the US, such as Australia, have never had a war on drugs. However, the enormous influence that the USA has had in dictating government policies through their bilateral agreements and multilateral agreements as well as in the UN, in putting punishment above harm reduction, has meant that other nations have either followed suit, or they have been criticised or threatened. American drug policy pressure dates back to when immigrants brought drugs across the border into the USA, and the government thought that if they could extend prohibition to other countries, that all drugs would disappear. US anti-drug campaigns have been translated throughout the world, even though they have no relevance for the intended populations.

One of the most important moments in the history of cannabis was in 2014, when President Barack Obama announced that cannabis was no more harmful than alcohol. The statement blew a hole in the US federal drug policy as cannabis was still illegal under federal law. In addition, with multiple states rejecting the federal law by legalising cannabis and thereby rescinding the federal government's autonomy, the USA government no longer had authority to dictate international drug prohibition.

Essentially, the foundations of the war on cannabis were beginning to crumble, because the USA could not control their own backyard, rendering them unable to control anyone else's. Leading up to this, however, the DEA had performed over 250 medical marijuana raids in the first four years of the Obama administration—more raids and greater spending than the entire decade under President George Bush. This was despite Obama promising during his campaign '[to] not have the Justice Department prosecuting and raiding medical marijuana users—It's not a good use of our resources'.

This was largely due to President Obama appointing Michele M. Leonhart as the administrator of the DEA in 2010. Ms Leonhart had previously worked in law enforcement and was unarguably a die-hard prohibitionist. This was made patently clear when, under Ms Leonhart, prescription opioid deaths continued to rise rapidly, yet action taken against pharmaceutical companies declined at an equally rapid pace. She openly criticised President Obama's statement that cannabis was not as harmful as alcohol, and stated that 'the unfortunate level of violence is a sign of success in the fight against drugs', in a response to being informed that in 2009 over 1,100 children had been killed in drug-related violence.

The deaths of over a thousand children is a very cynical index to cite when declaring success. It is important to keep in mind, however, that this is not an exclusive opinion. The former executive director of the United Nations Office on Drugs and Crime (UNODC), Antonio Maria Costa, stated, 'Many countries have the drug problem they deserve'.

The drug war in parts of the world like Mexico and South America has resulted in hundreds of thousands of deaths, and tens of thousands of missing persons in the past decade alone. Between 5,000 and 10,000 drug-related murders occur every year in Mexico, where the collective armed power of drug cartels exceeds the power of the military. It has also led to the partial funding of several terrorist groups, such as the Revolutionary Armed Forces of Columbia (now known as FARC dissidents), Al Qaeda and other groups, such as Hezbollah.

On the streets, children are kidnapped for ransom, murdered or used as watchmen for law enforcement, and innocent bystanders caught up and killed in cartel tensions. At the same time, citizens lose out on infrastructure, healthcare and education because their government blows billions of dollars trying to destroy supply and politicians are corrupted by drug money. Children get drawn in to selling drugs because becoming a blinged-up dealer is more attractive than getting an education and slugging out a forty-hour week.

Of course, more affluent, developed countries are far from immune to serious corruption. In Australia in late 2011, Mark Standen, then assistant director of the NSW Crime Commission, was found guilty for his role in importing 300 kilograms of pseudoephedrine (with a street value of more than $100,000,000), which is a precursor for amphetamine. He received a twenty-two-year sentence, a non-parole period of sixteen years and his appeal was rejected in 2015.

The last thing that illegal drug manufacturers and cartels want is a regulated market, because that immediately dries up their funding. Why did President Obama, a democratic and progressive leader, pick Michele Leonhart, who could not be further to the right of politics? Because getting tough on drugs would make him appear more moderate and increase his chances of winning in the 2012 election—a disappointing political strategy, devoid of any public service motive.

When a drug does not contribute to mortality, and its harm pales in comparison to tobacco and alcohol, governments find it difficult to justify its illegal status. The vast majority of the reasons governments put forward to defend their decision to keep cannabis illegal are exaggerated (often wilfully) or false:

- Cannabis is a gateway drug: using it increases the likelihood of moving on to other drugs, particularly more harmful ones.
- Cannabis causes psychosis and schizophrenia: using cannabis will make someone psychotic or cause them to become schizophrenic (or at the very least, cannabis is correlated with types of mental illness).
- Cannabis causes brain damage.
- Cannabis causes traffic accidents: using cannabis before driving, or while driving, increases your risk of a traffic accident.
- Cannabis is much stronger now than years ago: there is more THC in cannabis than in previous years.
- Cannabis has no medicinal value, and we already have cannabis-based medicines.

Claims that cannabis is a gateway or stepping-stone drug (escalation/progression hypothesis) have become standard justification for keeping the drug banned. The claim is that using cannabis increases the chances that you will move on to other more harmful drugs, such as ecstasy or cocaine. During the time I worked in drug rehabilitation, I made it a personal assignment to ask each person what the first drug they used was. Every one of them said cannabis, and many of them went on to use more harmful drugs. I realise that my sample size is not enormous—we are talking about maybe fifty people. After each of these people reported cannabis, I then asked, were you drinking before that? Every single person said yes. So even if you believe in the concept of a drug having a gateway characteristic, the gateway drug is unquestionably alcohol. That is almost always the first drug that a person uses for psychoactive effects. Additionally, alcohol is rather unique in terms of its ability to disinhibit judgement—it's really the only drug that intoxicates someone in such a way that they are more likely to use another drug than if they were sober. As Paul Dillon, the Director of Drug and Alcohol Research and Training Australia (DARTA), stated in a presentation I attended, 'If we get the alcohol part right, the rest of the illicit drugs will follow'.

Cannabis is almost never the first drug that someone uses. Even if someone does use a more harmful drug after they have used cannabis, or they use cannabis alongside other drugs, that does not mean that their use of cannabis has *caused* use of other drugs.

If someone does 'A', and ends up with 'B', that does not mean that A caused B; there are twenty-four other letters in the alphabet that may be the cause. Correlations are not causations. For example, there is a ninety-five per cent correlation between annual cheese consumption per capita, and annual deaths caused by being tangled in bed sheets in the United States. The same correlation applies to US crude oil imports from Norway and drivers killed in railway collisions. There is, however, no causal relationship, and these events obviously have nothing to do with each other. People who drink a few cups of coffee throughout the day live longer and have lower mortality rates than people who do not drink coffee. However, those who drink this amount of coffee may also exercise more, eat healthier or have higher incomes, allowing access to better healthcare—all of which could contribute to longer, healthier lives. This does not necessarily mean that coffee has no effect, it just means we haven't demonstrated it, and we cannot assume it to be the cause just because it precedes an outcome.

The gateway concept for illicit drugs may be the person who supplies the illicit drugs to the user. There have been many cases where a person contacts their dealer for a drug, and the dealer supplies the user with the drug they are after but also supplies them with another drug or encourages that person to try a new, often more harmful substance. A recent tragic case in the UK highlights this point. An eighteen year old man, Robert Fraser, died after he went to his dealer with some friends to get cannabis. He was sold the cannabis but additionally given what he was told to be something similar to MDMA (ecstasy). Robert was unaware that he actually had been given was fentanyl, and he died of a fentanyl overdose, as it is significantly more potent that other depressants, such as morphine or heroin.

If you want to stop dealers walking their clients through a 'gateway' to more harmful drugs, then allowing regulated access to cannabis is the most effective way to achieve this. This will not be a perfect solution, as we see with the illicit alcohol and tobacco trade; however, it would certainly be a step in the right direction. Judge Roger Dive of Sydney's Parramatta Drug Court has explicitly stated that he has 'never met a heroin addict who didn't start on alcohol and cannabis'.

While it is true that the vast majority of people who use other illicit drugs, such as cocaine or heroin, have tried cannabis (and alcohol) in the past, the vast majority of cannabis users never go on to use other substances. There is zero evidence of a biological gateway. In fact, there is even evidence to support the use of cannabis in protecting individuals from progressing to harder drugs, because often those who use alcohol or opioids (which are much more harmful) swap these substances for cannabis.

A 2013 Canadian study of almost 500 individuals who had been prescribed medical cannabis showed that almost ninety per cent of patients substituted alcohol, other prescriptions or illicit drugs (fifty-two per cent substituted alcohol, eighty per cent other prescriptions and thirty-three per cent illicit drugs). Those who do go on to use harder drugs after using cannabis have an underlying propensity to use drugs—not any one specific drug. It may well be that the opportunity to use cannabis simply arrives earlier than the opportunity to use harder drugs. (More on this in Part Two of this book.)

Cannabis as a cause of brain damage has also been used as a justification to maintain its illegality. The term 'brain damage' is, however, an unspecific term. It may refer to either the actual structure of the brain, suggesting that cannabis shrinks or alters the size of the brain or that cannabis impairs the functioning of the brain—or both. In regard to the physical size of the brain, cannabis does not cause brain atrophy. However, certain sub-parts of the brain appear to be slightly altered. This may not be caused by cannabis itself, as there are various other confounding factors, such as lower socio-economic status, higher rates of other drug usage, poorer nutrition and higher exposure to stress, all of which could contribute to differences in brain structure.

The main areas of the brain that are possibly physically affected are the right ventral striatum, hippocampus and the amygdala. These changes, however, have not been proven to be negative, and may simply indicate a trivial network re-wiring, rather than an actual diminishment of either size or capacity in terms of brain morphology. A 2014 study showed that, although long-term cannabis use might result in a very small volume reduction in the orbitofrontal cortex (OFC), at the same time, cannabis increases the neural connectivity in the OFC. Some would argue that the reduction inhibits decision making, others argue that the interconnectivity increases creativity. Virtually all published research into the effects of cannabis on the brain, however, is biased towards finding negative effects. There is very little evidence to support the fact that the hippocampus is affected neuroanatomically, even among heavy cannabis users, and any evidence demonstrating changes has also shown that changes restore after abstinence. It should also be noted that even if cannabis has a detrimental effect on the brain, the effect is trivial when compared to alcohol. A study was released in 2008 showing amygdala and hippocampal reductions (seven per cent and twelve per cent respectively) among males who are long-term, heavy cannabis users. The study was, however, a snapshot in time, containing fifteen participants. Other confounding factors could have caused the shrinkage, the cannabis use may have followed the atrophied brain regions, and the sample size is too small to draw conclusions.

Although these studies should give pause, they certainly don't warrant alarmist headlines claiming that cannabis definitively causes brain damage. An article in *The Washington Post* entitled 'Even casually smoking marijuana can change your brain, study says' is a testament to the scaremongering around the effects of cannabis on the brain. The article and related reports are based on a 2014 study by Gilman et al. in the *Journal of Neuroscience*, which utilised only twenty people, and the majority were consuming over ten joints per week, with one participant smoking more than thirty per week. The sample size was too small to draw any conclusions; the participants—for the vast majority—were not 'recreational' users; there was no significant correlation between use and brain volume; and there were a range of other methodical flaws in the study, such as reporting uncorrected p-values and not using multiple MRI scans. Additionally, those within the study who were recreational users—smoking one to two joints per week—experienced zero deleterious effects.

There is certainly a concern within the community that cannabis damages one's cognitive capability. Many people hold the stereotypical image of a cannabis user as a stoner who lacks motivation as well as intelligence and is going nowhere in life. While there are unquestionably individuals who fit these criteria, the majority of cannabis users function well within society, and there are many highly intelligent, as well as successful, cannabis users. This may beg the question though. How intelligent or successful could these people have been if they did not use cannabis? Are they limiting their full potential?

On average, regular cannabis users from early in life do score lower on intelligence tests, have lower levels of education and have slightly poorer memories. Cannabis may slow the development of child brain to an adult brain and, as cannabis can interfere with memory, this may explain why regular cannabis users score lower on intelligence and memory testing. This is, however, highly dependent on genetics, age of initiation, frequency of use, environmental factors and the content of the drug, such as whether the person is consuming high THC compounds. Higher THC compounds/low CBD compounds have greater addiction propensity and may be more damaging to cognition. Once an individual's brain is fully developed, it is unlikely that initiating cannabis usage at that point will damage their intelligence. In fact, there is very little evidence to prove that cannabis use after the age of twenty-five causes any significant physiological damage. If someone is going to smoke cannabis, like drinking alcohol, they should delay their initiation as long as possible.

Being addicted to cannabis, like many other drugs, can make it difficult to succeed in various areas of life, even if the drug is not harming the brain at all and is simply taking up time that the person may have spent engaging in other activities, such as training or studying. Perpetuating negative stereotypes can be counterproductive as this can instil negative self-views. This is due to what is known as stereotype threat, where an individual is conscious a behaviour in which they are engaging conforms them to a particular, and most likely inferior, social group. When stereotype threat exists, those individuals belonging to undesirable stereotyped groups score poorer on performance tests.

An example of this would be an elderly person forgetting where they left their keys. The stereotype here is that elderly individuals are forgetful. As the elderly person seeks their keys, they become increasingly aware of the fact that they are an example of the negatively stereotyped group. This is despite the fact that people of all ages misplace personal items from time to time. It is also despite the fact that there may be another reason for the keys not being able to be found such as the keys having fallen out of their pocket or having been stolen, or their partner is using them. Ironically, as the person becomes increasingly focused on the fact that they are epitomising the negative stereotype, it may cause them to become anxious and distract their attention from finding the keys, which then confirms the negative stereotype.

There have been a large number of individuals with shrill voices in the media, such as USA political commentator and columnist Ann Coulter, who continue to aggressively perpetuate the underachieving stoner stereotype with baseless unscientific justifications. In multiple interviews, Ms Coulter has claimed that people who use cannabis are 'incapable of following simple instructions and getting a job done', that 'they can't perform daily functions', that cannabis makes people 'retarded' (even though the last three USA presidents used cannabis) and that 'there is a difference between drugs and alcohol'. (Apparently alcohol is not a drug!) Keep in mind, however, that this is coming from a woman who wants people to smoke tobacco, so they work hard, die young and save the social security system money. Ms Coulter also states that alcohol is good for you, while cannabis is bad, and claims that the scientific community supports this position, although the scientific community maintains the completely opposite position, so she is biasing science to support her moral position.

As a woman apparently consumed by self-interest ('Potheads are going to be on my tax bill... At least they would save me money if they just go ahead and die'), she should at least consider alcohol-related harms, as alcohol is involved in the majority of domestic violence and sexual assault cases. When asked about the Netherlands' pragmatic and successful cannabis policy, her response was that the Netherlands was 'not an economic powerhouse' and that 'they are a mediocre country'. The Netherlands is in the top twenty largest economies in the world, the top ten for gross domestic product (GDP) per capita, has the same unemployment rate as the USA, is the third most innovative country in the world, has a higher life expectancy than the USA and has been independently rated to have the best health care system in Europe and a better health care system than the USA, Canada, New Zealand or Australia.

One of the problems with individuals like Ms Coulter is that, because their arguments are put forward with such passion and aggression, they drown out any contradictory arguments from the dialogue, and people who hear this penetrating noise often mistakenly believe that people like Ms Coulter actually have a strong evidence-based argument. An example of this was during *Hannity* ('Stoned America' special edition), a USA political talk show, averaging over 3,000,000 viewers per month, hosted by Sean Hannity. A particular episode, which was originally aired in 2014, consisted of approximately twenty panellists discussing and debating whether cannabis legislation should change.

Even before broadcasting the episode, Fox News had already made their anti-cannabis position clear with a snippet preview of the show on *Foxnews.com,* entitling the episode 'Stoned America: Shattering the myth that pot is safe'. However, during the show, the only panellist to inject a credible contribution was Dr Anne Williams, who only got the chance to speak for approximately thirty seconds, because other panellists mistakenly thought their opinions took precedence. Bo Dietl, a former New York detective, jumped in to state that 'It's fact—every individual who smoked pot is brain-dead' and their brains are 'defunkitated', while Todd Starnes (Fox News Radio) claimed that legalising cannabis would result in a 'rising body count and more people dying'.

There are no words to describe this level of scaremongering, particularly considering individuals have to consume over half a tonne of cannabis in a short period of time to produce a potential overdose, and out of the last four USA presidents, three have used cannabis—you cannot have a brain that is 'dead' or 'defunkitated' and run the largest economy in the world at the same time. In an earlier episode of *Hannity* 'Spring Break Exposed', viewers were enthusiastically shown how to shotgun a beer (not how to consume alcohol responsibly). It is strange that a program would take such as biased and scientifically contradictory stance, considering that every year during spring break at least one or two students die from acute alcohol poisoning, almost ten per cent of students meet the criteria for alcohol poisoning, there is a nine per cent increase in traffic accident deaths under the age of twenty-five and alcohol facilitates countless sexual assaults on young women.

Bo Dietl also mocked the THC-infused edibles as 'candy that seven year olds would eat', despite the fact that the edibles are arguably safer than smoking cannabis and that cannabis accessibility is age restricted to over twenty-one. Dr Williams was one of three doctors on the panel and the only physician against prohibition. One of the other doctors was Dr Mark Siegel, a Fox News medical correspondent—being objective is difficult when it might mean that you bite the hand that feeds you. The other was Dr Eric Braverman, who has had his practicing license suspended for continually misdiagnosing and mistreating patients. All of the claims that Dr Braverman made in this episode are nothing short of ridiculous. Dr Braverman has also been charged with larceny as well as sexual assault, and his wife does not want her children near him, as he uses his medical authority to inappropriately medicate them.

Clearly *Hannity* is scraping the barrel to find experts willing to get in front of a camera and lie about cannabis. Some of the more progressive voices in the room didn't help their cause either. An author, Gavin McInness, 'wants all drugs legal, because he trusts people to use their own moderation' and 'doesn't want the state to regulate his morality'. Comedian Sherrod Small stated that 'everyone in the room had smoked pot before'. McInness and Small are successful comedians, and while they inject another perspective as well as some humour into topic, these are not legitimate reasons when forming public policy, because most people don't use cannabis, and health policy should be based on science not morality.

Two common arguments put forward by progressives are that it is nobody else's business what someone puts into their body if they are not harming anyone else and that because of the medical utility of the drug, it should be available for recreational use. However, it is a myth to consider yourself an entirely autonomous person not affecting anyone else, as your freedom to put cannabis into your body before you get behind the wheel of a car directly infringes on the safety of other drivers and pedestrians. Your freedom to use any drug that damages your health affects your employment and destroys your relationships. It affects the taxpayer that funds the public health system, the unemployment benefits that you will call upon and your family and friends who become cut off from your life.

Claiming medical value to justify recreational use is misplaced. Not only could that case be made for almost any drug, but using this argument actually undermines valid medical evidence. Prohibitionists can then claim individuals use medical cannabis as a red herring or Trojan horse to give the drug a good name and to subtly promote legalisation, when in reality, any medical research has been silenced, because the drug has been subjected to blanket prohibition. Many people who originally advocated against the prohibition of recreational cannabis use have conceded that fight but today simply want society to be able to benefit from its medical properties.

The media is incredibly important here because it has played a large role in shaping the way the world looks at drugs as well as how drugs have been regulated. Since it has been such a powerful force in getting drugs banned, it may prove to be equally as powerful in applying a more pragmatic approach.

In regard to cannabis, research shows that if individuals begin using the drug at a young age and continue into adulthood, the average drop in IQ is approximately eight points. More recent researchers, however, have criticised older studies into the relationship between cannabis and IQ on the basis that previous studies did not account for other confounding factors that may explain the drop in IQ. When data is restricted to control for other factors, such as only looking at individuals from middle-class backgrounds or twins, there is no change in results. Previous studies of a similar nature have also yielded results that have attracted significant controversy, such as comparing IQ between different racial groups or different genders.

The reality is that we are all aware (including those who use cannabis) of the stoner stereotype that exists. However, data that links cannabis users with lower IQ scores does not address the existence of stereotype threat, which in this situation, may be how those who use cannabis have been educated or how they have been treated by teachers, parents or employers. This is more likely to be the reason for their fall in IQ, not their use of cannabis. This is not to say categorically that cannabis does not play a role in cognitive decline, but it is to say that cannabis highly unlikely to cause cognitive decline or, at the very least, produce a very small effect and is one of many factors involved.

Drivers in many parts of the world, including Australia, are now subject to mobile drug testing (MDT), which is very similar to random breath testing (RBT), however in Australia, we allow drivers who hold an unrestricted licence a limited amount of alcohol in their system. With cannabis, as well as other illicit drugs tested in MDTs such as amphetamines, the law does not allow any margins. You either test positive or negative. The only possible margin would be that the drugs are eliminated out of the driver's system before time of testing. Drivers subjected to RBTs are penalised according to the level of alcohol present. However, with MDTs, drivers are penalised if they return a positive sample, even if they had used the drug some time earlier and are in no way affected by the drug during time of testing. There is also the possibility that a person may return a positive MDT and be prosecuted due to the presence of trace elements. Another person may avoid prosecution in an RBT due to their results being under the limit, even though the person affected by the alcohol may pose a much greater risk to themselves and others.

The argument that cannabis should remain illegal because cannabis use is a risk factor in traffic accidents is contentious. The evidence regarding cannabis's contribution to motor vehicle crash risk indicates that if a person drives stoned, the risk of having a car accident is 1.25 to two times greater. However, if a person drives drunk, their risk is approximately eight-fold (about four times as risky as driving stoned). If a person drives drunk and stoned, the risk is over ten-fold. To put it in perspective, it is inadvisable to drive under the influence of cannabis. However, it is extremely inadvisable to drive under the influence of alcohol, or a cannabis-alcohol combination. The jury is still out on recently released research from the US as to whether the existence of THC (chemical in cannabis) alone, actually increases accident risk at all. A 2013 meta-analysis of sixty-six studies looking into the risks of cannabis and accidents did not find a causal relationship. In Australia, if an individual returns a positive drug test (for THC), they are subject to the same penalty as repeat low to mid-range drink-driving offenders.

～～

In an interview on 3AW Radio, in March 2018, Dr Alex Wodak AM, former Director of St Vincent's Hospital Alcohol and Drug Service and former President of the International Harm Reduction Association commented:

> If it is decided that cannabis does contribute to road crash death, the contribution is much smaller than the contribution from drugs like opiates, antihistamines, antidepressants, a range of therapeutic drugs, which certainly do contribute to an increase risk of road crash... It's not a question as to whether I'm saying it or not saying it—it's a question as to what the evidence shows... The Department of Transportation in America did a big analysis of all this data—and it's them who I'm actually quoting—that the jury is still out on this.

Drivers in Australia are permitted to drive with up to 0.05 blood alcohol content (BAC), which at least doubles the risk of an accident, and in the UK, drivers are allowed up to 0.08, which increases the risk three to fourfold. The message here is not that it is safe to drive under the influence of cannabis, but the law should be consistent in reflecting the relative risks that drugs pose both to the user and greater society. If you believe in the cannabis-car accident risk as sufficient evidence in banning cannabis, why would you not ban other drugs that pose equal or greater risk?

There is very strong evidence to show that other prescribed drugs pose a greater risk than cannabis or the allowed alcohol limit, particularly narcotic analgesics and sedatives. Drivers under the influence of alcohol are approximately eighteen times more likely to cause a fatal car accident, whereas drivers under the influence of cannabis are approximately 1.65 times (less than double) more likely to cause a fatal car accident. In fact, a study conducted by the Centre for Automotive Safety Research, as part of the University of Adelaide, showed that having alcohol alone in your system poses the greatest risk for driver accident culpability than any other drug category.

Victoria was the first jurisdiction in the world to introduce random roadside drug testing. However, the drugs that are tested for—THC, methamphetamine, cocaine and MDMA—barely contribute to total road crashes. These just happen to be the drugs that are hated by authorities and the media. Put simply, the drug-driving laws are not based on evidence. Senior Australian National Party member Andrew Gee stated, 'It does not matter if they (the driver) appear to be affected by the drugs. The mere presence of the drug establishes the offence... A driver can be charged—no matter how high or low (in terms of the THC reading).' By this logic, Mr Gee deems it acceptable to severely penalise people when they aren't endangering themselves or anyone else. That is exactly why the public loses respect for the government, the law and those who represent it. People can see through the transparency of this law—it is entirely evidence free, has nothing to do with protecting the public and everything to do with looking down on cannabis and cannabis users. It is also at complete odds with the policy regarding alcohol and driving because there is no penalty for keeping under 0.05 BAC (which is about two SDs), yet penalties increase incrementally in terms of fines and incarceration above this limit with regard to the prescribed content of alcohol.

This is a very rational policy, which is consistent with the base of evidence. It would be irrational to punish drivers who had traces of alcohol in their system from past consumption but were no longer affected. The USA actually has a more rational approach to this:

- Police officers must be given reasonable suspicion of the driver being impaired.
- The driver must fail a standardised field sobriety test.
- Officers must be given a reasonable suspicion of drug impairment.
- Officers then perform the drug test.

∽✦∼

A student once asked me how long cannabis can stay in your system after you use it in terms of testing positive roadside test. A police officer had told him that it can stay in your system for up to three months. Occasional users of cannabis may test positive up to three days after using, chronic users, up to about two weeks, and heavy chronic users (multiple times per day) may test positive up to one month if using urine, blood or saliva testing. There have been reports of people testing positive for trace elements of THC in hair follicles up to three months, however, this is exceedingly rare, and hair follicles are not tested for drug-driving. Drug-driving laws are not based on evidence and are merely an extended representation of how we attack select drugs. These attacks on drugs however are inevitably and ultimately attacks on drug users.

It is unarguable that there must be hundreds, possibly thousands of individuals who now have criminal record for drug-driving, when they were not impaired and not a risk to others. It is absurd that the police need only to prove the drug's presence in the person's sample. There is no burden of proof on the police to prove that the drivers driving ability was impaired. The cost of enforcing MDTs also significantly outweighs the penalties recuperated. A study in 2019 at the University of Sydney looking into the efficacy of MDTs found the false negative rate to be nine to sixteen per cent and the false positive rate between five and ten per cent, meaning that of the 10,000 drug driving prosecutions in NSW in 2016, up to 1,000 could be innocent, while thousands of impaired drivers are let go.

As stated, the accident risk is an argument often used to maintain the illegality of cannabis. However, if you applied this logic for all drugs, there would be many more drugs that would be illegalised. We don't ban opioids, antihistamines, benzodiazepines and antidepressants even though their use poses a greater risk of causing crashes than all four illicit drugs tested for. We don't even ban alcohol because some people drive under the influence. Instead, we introduce appropriate measures in an attempt to deter people, such as RBTs and warnings on medical packaging.

During the time a very close family member of mine was prescribed diazepam (Valium), not only did her psychiatrist advise her she was not allowed to drive, there were also warnings on the drug packaging. We do not ban Valium because a small group of people disregard these messages, just as we do not ban alcohol because some people drink drive.

This will be covered later, but it is interesting to note that when the public are allowed access to safer drugs, many people switch to achieve similar effects minus the harms. In areas of the US that have introduced medical access to cannabis, the number of fatal car accidents has fallen (approximately nine to ten per cent).

This may be due to the fact that a significant proportion of drivers choose to smoke cannabis instead of drink alcohol, that people who smoke pot don't drive or that the link between cannabis and serious car accidents is very weak. According to research conducted by the University of Colorado and the National Highway Traffic Safety Administration, 'the percentage of drivers with non-zero blood-alcohol levels has decreased'. In the ten years leading up to Colorado's legalisation of cannabis in 2012, the number of traffic fatalities averaged about forty per month, yet in both 2013 and 2014, the average per month was about thirty-five. According to the Colorado Division of Criminal Justice Office of Research and Statistics, from 2014 to 2017, DUI cases decreased fifteen per cent and from 2016 to 2017, the percent of drivers in fatal crashes who tested positive to delta-9-THC decreased from 11.6 per cent to 7.5 per cent. A further study by Santaella-Tenorio et al. in 2017 in the *American Journal of Public Health* concluded that, from 1985–2014, medical marijuana laws and dispensaries were associated with reductions in traffic fatalities, particularly in those aged twenty-four to forty-four. Another study in the *American Journal of Public Health,* published 2017, concluded that there was no statistically significant change in crash fatalities post-legalisation in Colorado and Washington—the two states to first legalise recreational cannabis—compared to states without legal cannabis. It is repeated ad nauseum that fatalities increased in Colorado post legalisation; however, the raw number of fatalities was higher decades prior to legalisation, the increase began before legalisation, and the rise in fatalities has risen in almost perfect correlation with the rise in vehicle miles travelled. In fact, there is an almost perfectly inverse relationship between cannabis use and overall road fatalities in the USA.

Lifetime cannabis use in the USA and Australia from the late 1960s to late 2010s has increased by over 2,000 per cent. Yet despite massive motorisation, road fatalities in the same period of time have dropped from 250 per million to 100 per million in the USA, and from 250 per million to forty per million in Australia.

When someone has smoked cannabis, they typically do not feel like driving, and if they do drive, they tend to drive very slowly and cautiously, as opposed to if they were drunk, where they would likely consider themselves race car drivers.

There are many people who have refuted this by stating that since cannabis has been made available, the number of people testing positive for any cannabinoid while driving, as well as those involved in fatal car accidents has increased. While true on face value, given the fall in positive tests for the psychoactive ingredient, this is likely to be driven by increased non-psychoactive medical cannabis prescriptions. Even if we erred on the side of caution and claimed that road fatalities were falling anyway and cannabis use has prevented the fall from being as pronounced as what it would have been if legalisation did not occur, we can very safely say that, overall, cannabis's contribution to traffic accidents is extremely small.

⁓

The existing, very limited use of cannabis in medicine, coupled with the idea that its effectiveness as a medicine is poor, is another argument frequently used as justification to maintain its illegal status. One extremely important issue here is that, due to stringent regulations, it is almost impossible to conduct research into drugs that are illegal. This in itself makes it difficult to prove any medical benefits because proving the benefits requires research, and if the research is constrained due to regulatory issues such as cost, ethics and politics, no medical benefits can be proven. This problem is, of course, magnified when the only time the drug gains attention is when it has been used illegally. As a result, the public see a drug with no medical benefits (because the medical community logistically and financially are handcuffed by red tape to demonstrate benefits), and then the drug appears on the evening news where a member of the community has ended up in the emergency department for using an illegal version of the drug. This vicious cycle not only creates a moral panic but embeds ill-informed views among the community, which makes it extremely difficult to study certain drugs. When asked about anabolic steroids, in the documentary *Bigger, Stronger, Faster,* Professor of Medical Ethics, at the University of Wisconsin-Madison, Norman Fost responded:

> *I'm not denying that there aren't some serious adverse effects from anabolic steroids, it's just that we have not been able to demonstrate any of them. Maybe that's because we don't study them. One of the problems with the ban on steroids is that it is impossible to do the research that would answer some of these questions.*

And prohibitionists don't want to allow illegal drugs any legitimate air, because they fear that will indirectly condone recreational use.

Cannabis does, however, exist to a very limited extent in Australian medicine, where nabiximols (brand name Sativex), dronabinol (brand name Marinol) and nabilone are available to a very small group of the population, in theory. Marinol and nabilone can only be obtained through import, by way of a special access order from a practitioner and must be approved by the Secretary of Commonwealth Department of Health. The use of Sativex is only approved for patients with spasticity due to multiple sclerosis. Nabiximols is the only cannabis-based medicine listed on the Australian Register of Therapeutic Goods (ARTG). It is extremely difficult both for a patient to get approval for the drug as therapy and for a practitioner to obtain the drug from Novartis Pharmaceuticals Australia. The approval is time limited, meaning that both the patient and practitioner must re-apply after the time has lapsed. The cost of Sativex is $745 for a six to eight-week supply (about $100 per week and not subsidised by the pharmaceutical benefits scheme), which is significant, bearing in mind that this is typically administered to a group of the population who are already likely to be financially stretched. Some have to pay three to four times as much, which means they suffer, go broke, exhaust all of their disability payments, resort to the black market or grow their own—the last two both attracting attention from the law.

Available in theory, unavailable in reality—this means that, even if it does hold medical utility, the vast majority who need it are forced to use cannabis as a medicine illegally. There are only a limited number of practitioners in Australia registered to prescribe cannabis, and patients are unable to simply search for a doctor licensed to prescribe due to privacy laws. It should be noted that this is true at the time of writing—cannabis laws are subject to change in the future.

New South Wales was the first state in Australia to obtain Commonwealth approval to run a medical cannabis trial in 2019; however, the trial is essentially re-running research, which we already have extensive evidence on from all throughout the world. There is simply no reason or justification for doubling and tripling down on answers we already know, particularly when the entire process involves ludicrous protocols such as testing in a secret location with very high security.

Cannabis is treated like a nuclear weapon, when other drugs that are far more dangerous by any metric are dispensed without anyone batting an eyelid, and it's the same in other countries. Despite there being over 160 hospitals in all of the UK, only four have a licence to hold cannabis. This research does nothing for those who suffer today and tomorrow, which is exactly the reason why over 100,000 Australians turn to black market cannabis for medicine. The government buys time, changes nothing and waits for the outrage to pass—meanwhile thousands suffer.

The most remarkable discovery in the history of the treatment of epilepsy is that of the case of Charlotte Figi, a young American girl who was effectively dying from Dravet syndrome. Dravet syndrome is a severe form of infant epilepsy, where the child suffers febrile seizures (seizures related to high body temperatures) multiple times throughout each day and, in Charlotte's case, a violent seizure every thirty minutes (over 300 per week).

Charlotte made headlines throughout the world at five years of age, when her parents and physicians made public that after unsuccessfully treating her with all conventional anti-epileptic drugs, Charlotte was administered with a cannabis strain known at the time as 'Hippies' Disappointment'. This strain had very high CBD and very low THC, therefore producing negligible psychoactive effects. Charlotte's seizure frequency reduced 99.8 per cent, from over 1200 per month to approximately two per month. She transitioned from being increasingly severely disabled and terminally ill to being able to go to school and leading a predominately normal life. Her case had been so perilous that her parents had prayed for her to pass away, as it was too painful to watch their child seize and convulse every thirty minutes, never knowing which seizure would kill her.

To achieve one of the most extraordinary recoveries in medicine, her parents reportedly had to break the law and move out of state to treat their child.

This is similar to the case of an NSW Blue Mountains father, Stephen Taylor, who gained widespread media attention in 2018 for treating his two daughters who suffered from Crohn's disease with a cannabis extract. Stephen grew the plants in his house before it was raided in early December 2017. His two daughters were repeatedly hospitalised, had severe reactions to pharmaceuticals and on several occasions almost died. Stephen's youngest daughter carries a stoma bag attached to her small intestine, and his eldest daughter had to have her colon removed. He remembers carrying his younger twenty-one year old daughter into the hospital weighing just above thirty kilograms. Stephen faced imprisonment because doctors were too afraid to take on the TGA. Two young women, with their entire lives ahead of them, denied access to the only medicine that would save their life or, at the very least, pull them out of severe disability, purely because the drug is banned due to historical anomalies and political expediency.

For an individual and their family to be dragged through the criminal justice system and to face prison time because he is providing the only medicine to their family that would keep them alive is grossly inhumane. Australia is not unique, however, when it comes to the government deciding that medicines are not medicines. In the UK, a mother named Charlotte Caldwell journeyed to Canada in early June of 2018 to purchase cannabis oil for her son, Billy, who suffered up to 100 seizures per day, any of which could be fatal.

Up until this time, Billy had been prescribed cannabis oil by his doctor, however, the Home Office ordered the doctor to cease prescribing the medicine because it is a Schedule 1 drug (no medical value). When Charlotte returned from Canada, the oil was immediately confiscated. Shortly after, Billy was back in intensive care. Any mother would rather have their son or daughter illegally alive than legally dead.

As Dr Alex Wodak from Australian Drug Law Reform has stated, 'often bad policy is good politics'. It is inconceivable that any pharmaceutical company in the world would have had the courage or ability to discover this. The first trial in the UK using LSD to treat people with depression was held in 2018 and, for twenty volunteers, the trial cost exceeded £300,000 (over AUD $500,000 or AUD $25,000 per volunteer). Just obtaining a licence to hold the drug costs approximately AUD $10,000. The cost of trialling illicit drugs, such as cannabis, can easily exceed several million dollars, and few pharmaceutical companies in the world would want to take this risk.

A more recent study has estimated that the costs to launch a new drug can exceed $2,550,000,000. Expecting a drug to generate a minimum $2,000,000,000—just to break even—is a massive risk. Because of this, the pharmaceutical industry is conservative and tends to work on variations of existing drugs, rather than producing entirely new products. It is rare for hospitals to hold illicit drugs, and universities are seldom allowed to research. This is despite the fact that hospitals are allowed to hold drugs such as morphine or heroin—drugs with substantially greater potential for harm.

In the UK, it takes thirteen years to bring a psychiatric drug to the market, making innovation extremely slow. Even if pharmaceutical companies have the financial power, all that is needed is one person to have an adverse reaction through illicit use, and the medical utility of the drug is automatically dismissed. This is another reason why it is critical that the police, politicians, and general media allow scientific processes to take place when reporting drug-related stories, rather than assume specific drugs played a role; generating panic and polluting evidence with scaremongering based on hearsay provides no benefit to the public.

In terms of treatment utility, across ninety-one randomised controlled trials, cannabis-based medicines were favourable in eighty-two (ninety per cent), which is better than many medicines we don't blink at dispensing. Leaving aside the cost effectiveness, randomised controlled trials have resulted in cannabinoids demonstrating seventy-five per cent favourable outcomes in disseminated (multiple) sclerosis, 97.5 per cent favourable outcomes in chemotherapy-induced nausea, 100 per cent favourable outcomes in HIV/AIDS cachexia (appetite loss and subsequent atrophy), 100 per cent favourable outcomes in cancer-related cachexia, eighty-three per cent favourable outcomes in neuropathic pain, and eighty-eight per cent favourable outcomes in other chronic pain. Patients are also not administered cannabis via smoking a joint, just like diamorphine is not delivered through smoking opium. Some of the medical compounds in cannabis include THC, cannabidiol, cannabinol, carophyllene and cannabigerol, which, on top of the evidence above, have been shown to hold anticonvulsant, antianxiety, antipsychotic, anticancer and antibacterial utility, as well as efficacy in treating PTSD and intraocular pressure.

There is also evidence to support the use of cannabis for obstructive sleep apnoea (OSA), a disorder characterised by episodes of suspended breathing during sleep, leading to low blood oxygen levels and other health issues, such as high blood pressure. Sufferers of OSA can also suffer fatigue during the day, which increases dangers if operating machinery or driving a motor vehicle. Sufferers of OSA typically are treated with surgery to remove any obstructive anatomy, or with respirators, which regulates oxygen supply while sleeping. Surgery poses potential risks and complications and may not fix the underlying problems. Respirators do not fix the underlying problem, and patient compliance is poor as respirators are uncomfortable to wear.

Sedative medications, such as zolpidem, zaleplon, eszopiclone, as well as benzodiazepines, which are often used to treat sleep-related disorders, cannot be used for OSA as they suppress respiration. As OSA is very difficult to treat, cannabinoids may provide sufferers with an answer, due to their ability to stabilise erratic respiration patterns during sleep. Evidence also supports the use of cannabinoids in the treatment of social anxiety disorder (SAD), and as with many of the other illnesses mentioned, patients with SAD are often resistant to conventional treatments. A further key medical benefit that cannabis/cannabinoids may be able to provide is allowing patients to be weaned off corticosteroids. Corticosteroids are steroids with anti-inflammatory properties used in the treatment of various conditions, including allergies, leukaemia, brain tumours, vasculitis, arthritis and Crohn's disease. Corticosteroids, however, particularly if used long term, have very damaging side effects, such as weakening the immune system, osteoporosis, hypertension, stomach ulcers, muscle wasting and diabetes. There have been many cases where patients have died as a result of corticosteroid use, not the underlying condition, and therefore if cannabis-based medicines have the potential to ween people off of corticosteroids, more research should be done to maximise this potential utility of cannabis.

Recent evidence from the USA has also shown that the states that have regulated access to cannabis have seen major falls in opioid prescriptions and opioid deaths. For many of the conditions involving pain for which cannabis may provide relief, the current medications used are far more harmful. Initial pain treatment typically involves paracetamol, codeine or aspirin; however, none of these are particularly strong. If pain is more severe, oxycodone (endone/oxycontin) or stronger opioids, such as morphine or fentanyl, may be prescribed. In terms of toxicity, however, there is a large gap between initial medications used and the stronger opioids. Cannabis would, however, fill this gap because it may be more effective for pain relief, and there is no risk of overdose. Cannabis also has a very low addiction potential, whereas addiction risk to strong opioids is quite high.

The American opioid crisis is covered in great detail in Part Two of this book. However, opioid deaths began to mount in the USA during the later 1990s, followed by a steady increase during the 2000s, to a peak in 2017, when there were more than 70,000 drug overdoses. Sixty-five per cent of these deaths were opioid related, with heroin and synthetic opioids (such as fentanyl, fentanyl analogues, tramadol, etc.) showing the biggest increases. This massive rise in deaths is largely attributable to continuous law enforcement attacks on opium production, resistance to harm reduction initiatives and the over-prescription of pharmaceutical opioids. Fentanyl is much less likely to be detected in trafficking as it is extremely potent and therefore often smuggled in small amounts, and the street value is up to 400 times greater than original product cost, so it is more attractive to criminal networks than other drugs. It is also attractive to criminal networks because, unless the drug is in the form of a transdermal patch or lollipop/lozenge, the short duration of effects means that users need to re-dose faster, increasing risks of dependence.

Concerns surrounding fentanyl patches have been raised due to the risk to young children of accidental exposure if the patches have not been discarded responsibly. One of the major concerns with the spread of fentanyl is that, due to the fact that some of the fentanyl analogues, such as lofentanil, carfentanil, and ohmefentanyl, are so incredibly potent (several hundred to several thousand times as potent as heroin), they are impossible to weigh out in any kind of reliable fashion, even on digital scales.

Recent evidence has also emerged showing the potential of THC in treating Alzheimer's disease. Alzheimer's is a neurodegenerative disease, most common in individuals over the age of sixty-five, and accounts for the majority of dementia cases. It is generally accepted that the major causes of Alzheimer's disease are amyloid protein mutations and amyloid protein misfoldings, which essentially means that the proteins do not change into their normal structure and instead 'fold' into being inactive or toxic (beta-amyloid proteins) in terms of their functionality. These inactive proteins build up to create plaque deposits that damage connections between nerve cells, leading to degeneration in brain function. Numerous studies have now replicated cannabis protecting against and delaying beta-amyloid production. Other studies have also shown that cannabis may be helpful in addressing some of the behavioural aspects of dementia. To quote Dr Lester Grinspoon, Emeritus Professor of Psychiatry at Harvard University Medical School, 'People who say that there is no established medical use of marijuana simply do not know what they are talking about. It's the most non-toxic medicine I have ever encountered.' There are many other indications for which cannabis may be used as a medicine.

The argument that cannabis is stronger or higher in THC now than previous years has some credibility; however, this is rather misleading. The chemical composition of herbal cannabis has not changed; however, high potency strains now exist, fundamentally as a result of cannabis prohibition. Traditional herbal cannabis contains a fairly even mixture of THC and CBD, and as CBD can counteract the negative aspects of THC, particularly the paranoia, some of the stronger high-THC strains of cannabis can produce very unpleasant effects, partially due to the fact that with increases in THC come decreases in CBD. Cannabis typically contains approximately five per cent THC, while resin cannabis contains slightly higher levels of THC. As previously mentioned, there are increasing numbers of high potency cannabis strains, such as Skunk (approximately fifteen per cent THC), White Widow (approx. fifteen per cent THC) as well as Dabs, which are concentrated butane hash oil (BHO) products, otherwise known as distilled cannabis. Comparing the strength of traditional cannabis to high-THC strains (excluding distilled cannabis) is similar to comparing full-strength beer to sherry (five per cent alc/vol versus fifteen to twenty per cent alc/vol). Dabs are reported to contain up to eighty to ninety-nine per cent THC and are produced by extracting THC among other cannabinoids through the use of heat and various solvents such as butane, propane or carbon dioxide. It is worth noting that the manufacture of BHO does not always eliminate some of the toxic and flammable chemicals used in production. A number of people have suffered severe burns from fires and explosions when attempting to make BHO in their home.

Home-grown, high potency cannabis hybrids of either bush (grown in soil) or hydroponic (non-soil and grown in a water-mineral solution) nature are manufactured in an attempt to maximise profit margins for black market sellers. These hybrids are often created through cross-breeding, the use of grow lights, as well as spraying the cannabis with other chemicals. Hybrid cannabis contains very erratic levels of THC,

erratic levels of CBD, as well as other by-products that have been created, added or not removed in the manufacturing process. High-potency
THC strains are often sold in much smaller quantities for equal or higher
price, as they are supposed to offer the consumer equal or greater value
and effects in much smaller quantities. Manufacturers of high-potency
THC strains also incur significant costs, such as the purchase of additional chemicals and copious amounts of electricity. Names such as 'The
Pure' or 'The Clear' have been coined for some extremely high-potency
THC strains due their alleged almost 100 per cent THC content, free
from any impurities. On the one hand, compounds can be more harmful
if they contain low purity because this inevitably indicates higher levels
of adulterants, impurities, by-products or other added chemicals, but on
the flip side, high purity compounds can produce much more powerful
effects, which are often undesired.

Although high-purity strains produce generally predictable effects
because the main variable is the level of THC, synthetic cannabinoids
(SCs), such as Spice, K2, and Kronic, have a very different chemical
composition. SCs are pro-psychotic, pro-convulsant and contain an
abnormal mixture of compounds, which interact with the same receptors as traditional cannabis. However, as the THC in traditional cannabis is only a partial agonist, it cannot produce effects nearly as extreme
as SCs, as they are full agonists, and so produce a much more powerful
response. The weakest SCs are double the potency of cannabis, while
some of the more powerful compounds are up to 100 times as potent.
Over the space of thirty years, Emeritus Professor of Organic Chemistry
at Clemson University, John William Huffman, synthesised over 400
SC compounds—not because he was searching for a psychoactive, but
because he was searching for a non-steroidal anti-inflammatory.

SCs are a much greater public health concern than herbal and resin
cannabis or high-THC cannabis because the effects of SCs are entirely
unpredictable, frequently produce enormously severe adverse effects,
such as coma and seizures, and are relatively inexpensive. Numerous SC outbreaks throughout the world have resulted in thousands of

hospitalisations and hundreds of deaths. In the early 2000s, there were virtually no seizures resulting from use of SCs reported throughout Europe. However, from 2013, the European Monitoring Centre for Drug and Drug Addiction (EMCDDA) reported an average of 25,000 to 30,000 SC seizures every year. SC products are difficult to test for, despite claims made by testing companies, whereas carrying or transporting traditional cannabis on the other hand is risky because it is often bulky, with a discernible odour, and difficult to dispose of hastily. As manufacturing and supplying traditional cannabis produces smaller profit margins, higher risks of detection for users, dealers and suppliers, and less powerful effects, it is not surprising that the SC market continues to grow. High-strength THC products and SCs are products of prohibition. Yes, there is a small group of users who want to get maximally stoned, but the vast majority of cannabis users do not want super strength cannabis, just as the vast majority of drinkers don't want to drink straight vodka, absinthe or liqueur essence. As criminal penalties have gradually increased, so too has the THC level as a means of offsetting the risk for those manufacturing, dealing and trafficking in cannabis related products.

The use of SCs has not only grown among the general public, but also among prisoners attempting to evade testing positive to cannabis. This has led to serious adverse health consequences in prisons as well as corrupting prison staff. Despite the fact that authorities have failed to keep the government's most tightly controlled facilities free from illicit drugs, creating serious adverse health consequences for prisoners, we continue to bow at the altar of prohibition, because it fits our mantra of putting punishment above health.

Drug-Free Australia (DFA), a prevention-focused organisation that has openly criticised all harm-reduction policies, recommends that possession of cannabis should be dealt with five year spent conviction, which essentially means that if the user can provide drug-free blood or urine tests over a five-year period, their criminal record is expunged. Some believe that spent convictions do not need to be declared to anyone, which is false. Spent convictions have a number of exclusions, including working with children as well as with any law enforcement agency. This is not only highly unlikely to act as a deterrent, but is also a completely disproportionate punishment, particularly when compared to other penalties for far more dangerous behaviour. For example, offences, such as speeding through a red light, where there is a chance someone will be injured or killed are met with a monetary penalty notice, not a criminal conviction. Aside from disproportionality, what happens if the convicted individual relapses because of trauma, withdrawals or other hardships? Demanding that addicts stay drug free is not realistic or pragmatic in all circumstances, and in the case of some drugs, it is even dangerous. There are many people who, for physiological or psychological reasons, are not ready to stop immediately. Some argue that criminalisation provides a mechanism to be led towards treatment; however, the main reason many problematic drug users do not get help is because of the stigma attached to criminality. Being incentivised or led towards treatment is fine, but the criminality needs to be removed, because even if the user does seek help—and in a best-case scenario, gets clean—their criminal record will endure and continue to affect their life.

DFA has, however, had a history of manipulating data to support their prohibitive ideological agenda, which is at complete odds with the scientific/medical consensus. Expert independent entities have consistently rejected DFA's attempts to discredit rigorous peer-reviewed literature that has the support of entities such as Australian Medical Association (AMA), Australasian College of Addiction Medicine, Australasian College of Emergency Medicine, Alcohol and other Drugs Council of Australia, Royal Australasian College of Physicians, Australasian Professional Society for Alcohol and other Drugs, and the Royal Australian College of General Practitioners. DFA is certainly not going to achieve a society free from drugs. Their methods are, however, free of compassion and evidence, and worse, their views are inhumane. In 2019 during a television special on cannabis, a DFA representative responded when asked about the medical efficacy of cannabis with 'power of placebo'. Individuals are not entitled to discount or invalidate the objective improvements in the health of others when their underpinning arguments are void of evidence and fundamentally exist to supress recreational use as a means of achieving some kind of moral superiority. DFA oppose needle syringe programs, injection centres, pharmacotherapy, vaping, drug checking, harm reduction education and any initiative that resembles a position that has backed down from prohibition.

Governments, particularly in Western culture, continue to preach that banning drugs is the way to keep society safe, a position they justify by stating that individuals fail to listen to the warnings and continue to take risks. It takes political courage and leadership to admit that perhaps the wrong message is being preached.

The law also cannot keep up with the ever-growing number of SCs, and as SCs are reported to be significantly more addictive than traditional cannabis, they are of greater interest to manufacturers and sellers due to the higher chance of repeat business. The SCs, however, are not new to the medical research community. Many of these chemicals were synthesised and tested decades ago, primarily as a means of building on cannabis as a treatment. Due to the serious adverse effects these drugs had on volunteers, they were all principally dismissed as therapies. SCs, such as JWH-018, AMB-FUBINACA and HU-210, have since made a resurgence due to cannabis being illegal, and this is quite possibly the most concerning outcome of banning cannabis as well as other drugs. As certain drugs get banned, more harmful compounds take their place. When JWH-018 was banned, AM-2201 and AM-2203 took its place— both were untested and later proven to be highly toxic.

One of the arguments put forward as a means of eliminating the criminal market is legalisation or decriminalisation. These terms get thrown around; however, it is important to note that between full prohibition with no recognised utility and full legalisation with no regulations, there are many stages of regulation. It is often difficult to have a rational debate about drug law reform, because those who advocate for anything other than full prohibition are often accused of being 'pro-drugs' and wanting illegal drugs to be advertised and sold in supermarkets, which is not true and an absurdly reductive reasoning tactic. Every single drug, including freely available drugs such as caffeine, paracetamol and ibuprofen, is subject to regulations. On one end of the spectrum, we have full prohibition, with no utility (no medical use, no recreational use and almost impossible to research, such as MDMA or LSD), and then at the other end of the spectrum we have drugs that have a limited number of regulations such as limitations on the total number of servings/doses and limitations on the amount of the drug in each serving/dose. One step down from full prohibition is decriminalisation, which can be either in the form of *de jure* or *de facto*. In Latin, *de jure* refers to legal recognition, whereas *de facto* refers to the practice of enforcement. Decriminalisation does not mean legalisation, as there is no means to legally obtain the drug under this policy. *De jure* decriminalisation essentially means that criminal conviction is removed from legislation and instead may be replaced with civil penalties. *De facto* decriminalisation refers to non-enforcement of the law, where police may use discretion in not prosecuting offenders or refer offenders to education or treatment instead of the criminal justice system.

There is also depenalisation, which refers to reducing severity of punishment, such as lowering prison sentence length or lowering monetary penalty. It is a false dichotomy to claim that governments must choose between full free market legalisation or complete prohibition, because there are many options in between. Black and white thinking conceals the fact that there are more effective approaches; Part Two of this book covers this topic in greater detail.

It is important to note that originally, prohibition was seen as a progressive concept, particularly in the 1800s and early 1900s when areas of the USA temporarily banned alcohol. Although prohibition was seen as a way of progressing society in a more positive direction, at the time, Americans did not have todays evidence or hindsight to see that prohibitive policies arguably cause more harm than good.

There are, however, approximately twenty-five countries throughout the world that have implemented decriminalisation as well as about a dozen states in the USA. A handful of these countries also have legal regulated access to cannabis, as well as other drugs, such as psilocybin in the Netherlands, Brazil and Jamaica, and DMT in Peru. In Australia, all states provide some form of cannabis decriminalisation (for personal use), with the principal form being de facto. States other than NSW and QLD also have de facto decriminalisation for personal use of other drugs. However, no state has removed criminal penalties for all illicit drugs, which is why many individuals are still prosecuted and imprisoned for being in possession of small quantities. If the apprehended individual does not meet eligibility requirements, such as being a first-time offender, they will be processed by the court system (this includes for non-compliance). Legalisation on the other hand is a very vague term as all drugs are subject to some form of regulation—be it alcohol content, restrictions on where people can smoke or level of caffeine in energy drinks—so there is no such thing as a 100 per cent legally unregulated drug. If we are discussing law reform in regard to cannabis, like many other drugs, the term 'legalisation' should be changed 're-legalisation' or 're-regulation', as these were once upon a time legal in a regulated fashion.

～⁓

So, does this mean that cannabis is a safe drug? As previously stated, there is no such thing as a safe drug. The only way to be sure that you avoid all harms is to not take any drug. Although best practice for any drug is abstention, and this should always be on the table, millions of Australians consume drugs for non-medical purposes every year. If that message fails, we need to have measures and messages in place to reduce harm at all ends of the spectrum—from telling a young person to delay their first alcoholic beverage for as long as possible and to consume in a safe environment, to encouraging cannabis users to take t-breaks (tolerance breaks) and teaching heroin addicts that if they can't stop injecting, they need to ensure they rotate injection sites or at least don't inject into hazardous areas.

Because the drug is illegal, the harm that cannabis causes to the Australian community is primarily economic, as half of illicit drug arrests, half of illicit drug seizures and almost a third of illicit drug seizures by weight are cannabis. This is primarily due to the fact that cannabis is the most widely used illicit drug, and it is also a drug that is difficult to dispose of swiftly. If someone is carrying an illicit drug in pill or powder form, they can easily ingest the substance and avoid arrest as it is not illegal to have taken an illicit drug (unless operating a motor vehicle), but it is illegal to be in possession of an illegal drug. It is difficult, however, to swallow an entire joint, and cannabis has a discernible odour. Decriminalising recreational use of cannabis and allowing its medical use does not mean that all harms disappear. As Peter Hitchens in his book, *The War We Never Fought,* states, 'less law, less crime forgets that crime has unpleasant effects on victims.'

One of the major hurdles advocates for progressive drug policies face is convincing the public that we cannot live in a free society and a drug-free society at the same time. There has never been a drug-free society. Diverse cultures throughout the world have discovered that if they consume plants or fruits that have been fermented, that can change the way they feel. Drugs have existed for thousands of years, are derived from nature, and the desire of humans to use drugs to produce physiological changes is innate. Efforts to ban and restrict drugs arrived thousands of years later, so the onus is on those who preach these policies to prove that they are worth implementing. The desire to change one's state of consciousness is universal, and anyone who claims that a drug-free society is possible is delusional. Deep down, even supporters of prohibition know this. Therefore, if we cannot make substantial headway in reducing use, we should adopt policies that have been efficacious in reducing harm.

The entire debate around cannabis and other drug law reform is contentious, because having any environment other than prohibition taps into people's fear—fear that drug use will rise, fear that addictions will increase, fear that people will start dying, fear that the streets will become less safe, and fear that it will put increased strain on the health care system. In fact, most of the resistance to any drug reform is rooted in fears that are unsubstantiated by evidence and that have not eventuated in countries that have introduced such reform.

Cannabis does cause some harm to the community outside of policing resources, however. One of the primary reasons users of cannabis report suffering from psychosis is not because they are actually psychotic, but because the acute 'stoning' effects of the drug is the closest sensation that they will experience to having a psychotic experience. You would not diagnose someone as an insomniac if one evening they struggled sleeping after drinking too much coffee late in the day, and you would not diagnose someone with vertigo if they feel like the room is spinning after they have consumed a significant amount of alcohol. These are the acute effects of the drug, not long-term persistent medical conditions. As the acute effects can include perceived distortions or detachment from reality, users are at a higher risk of injuring themselves, such as when cooking, operating machinery, falling from heights or walking in front of a car. About thirty people die each year in Australia from cannabis-related causes including injury, polydrug use and cardiovascular conditions. This is across approximately 3,5000,000 Australians who report using cannabis in the past year.

Unfortunately, most people who use cannabis do so in the most harmful way, that is, smoking cannabis mixed with tobacco without a filter. Outside of the drug's pharmacology, one of the reasons why cannabis causes significantly less harm than virtually all other illicit drugs, such as amphetamines, cocaine, heroin, or other opioids like fentanyl, is because you cannot inject it. Therefore, cannabis users do not face injection risks, such as collapsed veins, contracting and spreading disease or overdosing. Cannabis smokers may have a slightly higher risk of developing bronchitis or head, neck or lung cancers than non-smokers due to the possible carcinogenicity and irritant nature of inhaling burnt particles. Not all studies have shown this. Some show the complete opposite, and those who use a vaporiser (not containing tocopheryl acetate) are at even less risk. Approximately one in ten adults and one in six children who use cannabis will become dependent at some point. However, if the cannabis is cut with tobacco (a drug where approximately one in three users become addicted), this can facilitate entry into tobacco addiction, an expensive habit that is difficult to break and that has a fifty per cent mortality rate.

Those in favour of winding back restrictions on cannabis do not help their case when they talk in absolute terms, such as 'cannabis doesn't addict', or 'cannabis doesn't kill'. Even though overdosing from smoking half a ton of cannabis in fifteen minutes is logistically impossible, and of the ten per cent of cannabis users who become dependent, only a fraction become addicted, people have died in cannabis-related accidents, and cannabis addicts do exist. Such sweeping statements are both incorrect and damaging to the credibility of other legitimate harms. It is much more effective to state that these risks are possible, but highly improbable.

In users who are predisposed to mental health disorders, such as psychosis, anxiety and depression, cannabis may bring on the predisposed illness earlier or it may aggravate the symptoms. However, the acute effects of cannabis can mimic many psychiatric disorders and many people use cannabis after they have developed a psychiatric disorder, which is a case of reverse causality. A 2016 systematic analysis of twenty-two studies found only preliminary evidence that exposure to substances (including cannabis) increases the risk of bipolar disorder. The mechanisms and evidence of cannabis and mental health issues including the relationship to violence is discussed in detail in Part Two of this book. Mixing cannabis with other drugs can increase or change potential harms. An example of this is greening out where alcohol and cannabis are consumed within close time proximity together, and the user experiences negative side effects, such as nausea and dizziness. Cannabis's antiemetic properties make it an effective treatment for nausea, such as when induced by chemotherapy; however, one of the ways the human body rids itself of toxins is through vomiting. As one of the common effects of drinking too much alcohol is vomiting, cannabis, if used alongside, can not only increase risk of choking if the person does vomit but can possibly increase the risk of succumbing to alcohol poisoning because the body is unable to empty the stomach contents. This is different to cannabis hyperemesis syndrome (CHS)—a relatively newly recognised illness that occurs in a very small number of chronic cannabis users, characterised by recurrent nausea, abdominal pain and vomiting, that can be alleviated by hot baths or showers. Antiemetics, benzodiazepines and antipsychotics show mixed results as treatments, and CHS only definitively stops by quitting cannabis. The mechanisms of CHS are unknown. Repeated vomiting can lead to severe kidney injury as well as tears in the oesophagus. Although more research is needed to provide certainty, using cannabis while pregnant may increase chances of low birth weight. An extensive 2017 literature review by Orsolini et al. concluded that 'although cannabis use may be considered a risk factor for the occurrence of pregnancy-related morbidity issues, many studies relied on self-reports and showed inconsistent results when controlling for potential confounders, including tobacco use.' The use of synthetic cannabinoids among pregnant women, however, is strongly recommended against.

Many people argue that introducing a fourth legal psychoactive drug (alongside caffeine, tobacco and alcohol), will simply add to current total harms if more people take up smoking cannabis. Some also argue that re-illegalising a drug is very difficult after it has become legal, when actually the opposite is true. History is littered with examples of drugs with proven medical efficacy and much greater safety than alcohol or tobacco becoming banned, primarily due to media focus, political expediency, and/or social concern, and efforts to repeal these mistakes have been predominately unsuccessful.

One of the plausible explanations as to why cannabis use is low and/or falling in areas of the world that have allowed regulated access is because removing the illegal status of a drug may also remove some of the cachet attached to it. We know that when a drug is illegalised, it (cannabis) becomes a lot more interesting to young people. Stripping back the mystique of drugs shows that they are just a few elementary molecules. In the 1990s, the Dutch former Health Minister, Eddy Engelsman, stated, 'We have succeeded at making pot boring'.

It is almost impossible to quantify or measure whether the illegalisation of cannabis results in curbing usage. However, even if you are to believe some of the reports claiming that it does, the other harms that are generated by illegalisation far outweigh the potential trivial falls in usage. As emergency medicine and toxicology specialist Dr David Caldicott at Calvary Hospital in Canberra stated in one of his seminars, 'Do you want people to use less drugs, or do you want people to get less hurt? Because you probably cannot have both'.

There is some evidence—particularly from the USA—to support that it is easier for young people to be directly supplied cannabis than alcohol, because there is no incentive for cannabis dealers to deny supplying a person under the age of eighteen or twenty-one, whereas alcohol retailers can lose their license or face huge penalties. Some people refute this by stating that if cannabis were easier to purchase, then why is alcohol more of a problem with young people? That's pretty simple— we have regulated alcohol badly over a very long period of time, and as a society, we have downplayed the harm that alcohol causes because most adults consume alcohol and don't want to face their own drinking.

Sean Hannity claimed in one of his episodes that Dutch marijuana use rose 250 per cent from 1984 to 1992. However, that does not coincide with the Netherlands' liberalisation of their drug policy in the 1970s, and the prevalence of cannabis use in the Netherlands is significantly less than the USA, particularly among young people.

One claim consistently asserted by those in favour of maintaining cannabis illegality is that removing the barrier of illegality will lead to increases in use and that increases in use lead to increases in harm. There is basically no evidence to back up this fear-driven concept and, more importantly, the notion that increased usage leads to increased harm is overly simplistic and certainly not true of all drugs, particularly cannabis. Countries such as Australia, the US and the UK that have historically taken a punitive approach towards cannabis have seen a proportion of cannabis users switch to SC instead, which are a much more harmful group of compounds.

SCs are entirely products of prohibition, and if cannabis were available in a regulated fashion, the synthetics would not exist. This is why there is no market for synthetics in the Netherlands. This is also true for other drugs, such as Paramethoxyamphetamine (PMA)/paramethoxymethamphetamine (PMMA) replacing MDMA, the NBOMes replacing LSD, crack cocaine replacing powdered cocaine, heroin replacing opium, desomorphine replacing heroin, fentanyl replacing desomorphine, methanol replacing alcohol or camfetamine and methiopropamine replacing fencamfamine—the relative former of each pair being significantly more toxic. Not only has the level environment failed in deterring use, it has also encouraged the manufacture of more toxic substances. Criminal manufacturers do not begin distributing milk and cookies when it gets difficult to make smack or pingers; they just substitute for another precursor or an alternative product. This is not a problem of the drugs themselves, but a problem of how we have dealt with them.

In 2019, the NSW Premier, Gladys Berejiklian, parroted what many politicians have said in the past 'there is no safe way to take illicit drugs'. To be fair, there isn't a safe way to take any drug. However, it is unarguable that all drugs are less safe when they are provided by the black market as opposed to being provided by the white market.

The reason why use does not explode following legalisation, particularly in the long term, is because those who are really keen on blazing up are already doing so, regardless of illegality. And what is equally important is that even if the law has deterred some curious people, a significant proportion of this group are responsible users who will not cause measurable harm to themselves or others. Those smoking cannabis who are harming themselves and/or others are already prepared to break the law. Therefore, if these people who have been abstaining because of prohibition are able now enjoy the substance legally and responsibly—without harming themselves or others—that is an unquestionable benefit, because this is use that should be allowed. This is precisely the reason why relaxed cannabis laws have not manifested into explosions in harms, because firstly, true increases are undetermined, and even if there are any increases, it is from those who are responsible users, not problematic users. Reported increased use does not indicate actual increased use; some individuals will only admit to using a drug if it is legal. Therefore, any surveys taken post-legalisation/decriminalisation, indicating increases in use, cannot be interpreted as true increases. The surveys have often just provided more accurate, representative data, instead of actual real changes. Even if use has truly increased, the fact that cannabis harms have not materialised alongside, suggests that the drug is probably much less harmful than it has been made out to be.

The argument of adding to existing harm assumes that the law provides some barrier to people smoking cannabis, an idea with almost no evidence and some evidence to the contrary. Just because there are international examples where strict drug laws, harsh penalties and low drug crime rates exist does not mean that the severe laws and punishments are the cause of low crime. There are other regions that have identical laws and punishments in terms of severity but have very high drug crime, which points towards another factor being the explanation for usage patterns.

In Australia, we prohibit and enforce against many activities, not because they cause harm to the individual engaging in the activity, but because the activity to some level causes harm to greater society. However, serious crimes are still committed. The majority of society does not commit crime for several reasons: personal reasons (moral, familial, cultural, health etc.), perception of risk or certain punishment. Although, there very little evidence that increasing the severity of punishment deters crime, there is evidence to support deterrence if punishment is certain, and if laws are seen to be legitimately just. In regards to drug laws, all of the evidence from around the world suggests that the legal environment makes little to no difference to consumption levels. Evidence from the RAND (Research and Development) Corporation, the EMCDDA, the CATO Institute, as well as various other organisations and think tanks has exhaustively disproved the harsh laws-low drug use theory.

The chance of getting arrested for cannabis is approximately one in 10,000–12,000 joints smoked. The more someone smokes, the greater their chances of getting caught and, like all other drugs, this inevitably targets those who are dependent—who need help, not handcuffs.

In the US, there are approximately 800,000 arrests per year for cannabis possession. Even though many are given a simple ticket and asked to appear before a judge at a later date, the entire ordeal is more about punishment and sending a message because the entire procedure costs more than the actual fine. Punishment should be swift, certain, but modest, as opposed to what it is currently—delayed, uncertain and severe. Telling someone that there is a five per cent chance that in nine months' time, they will be arrested and go to prison is a hollow threat.

When nine Australians (Bali Nine) attempted to smuggle eight kilograms of heroin out of Indonesia in early 2005, each trafficker was fully aware that they might face the firing squad (death penalty) if caught. Despite the potential severity of the punishment, the corrupt and ineffective nature of Indonesian law enforcement did not indicate punishment was certain. Even in developed nations, unless you multiply the police force, place police on every corner, skyrocket taxes, and ignore more serious crimes, creating certainty for the vast majority of drug-related offences (mostly possession) is logistically impossible. The cost and effort are entirely disproportionate to the harm the drug causes.

Law enforcement certainly has a role, but it is not the primary role. Unfortunately, it is almost impossible to find evidence that highlights any benefit of banning cannabis, although it is very easy to find evidence of serious harm being caused.

If cannabis law reform did take place, we can assume one of five possible outcomes:

1. Drinkers and smokers would continue drinking and/or smoking, and they would use cannabis additionally.
2. Drinkers and/or smokers would substitute cigarettes and/or alcohol for cannabis.
3. Cannabis consumption would remain unchanged among drinkers and smokers.
4. Non-drinkers and non-smokers would take up cannabis.
5. Non-drinkers and non-smokers would not take up cannabis

If outcomes 3 and 5 occurred, no change among drinkers, non-drinkers, smokers, and non-smokers, society would benefit because a huge amount of financial effort across various bodies involved in the policing of illegal cannabis would no longer be required. This would free up funds to be redirected in a constructive way, such education, healthcare or even the reduction of the harms of some of these drugs.

In response to outcome 1, it is not desirable for anyone to take up smoking cannabis on top of his or her current alcohol or tobacco use, as this would add to total harm. This outcome is, however, theoretical as it has not been the experience in areas of the world that have allowed regulated access to cannabis. Instead, these areas have seen falls not only in cannabis use, but in other more harmful drug use as well. This is possibly due to the fact that as it is no longer illegal, the drug may lose some of its allure. Evidence suggests that while cannabis use may rise slightly immediately after reform, over time, this settles and drops.

In the event of outcome 2, it is unlikely that cannabis would have any impact on tobacco smoking patterns, as it would not reduce nicotine withdrawals. Smokers, however, are a minority within the population, whereas consumers of alcohol are the majority. Evidence suggesting that increases in cannabis use results in increases in tobacco use is largely due to the fact that most cannabis is cut with tobacco, which facilitates the steps towards tobacco use. If drinkers, particularly heavy and/or hazardous drinkers, switched to smoking cannabis instead, it would unquestionably be a positive step forward in terms of population public health.

When talking about liberalising access to cannabis in Scotland, David Nutt, Professor of Neuropsychopharmacology at Imperial College London, and previously UK Chief Scientist during the Edinburgh International Science Festival, commented, 'You could go from drinking buckie beer or buckie wine (fortified drink with caffeine) and kicking people's faces in, to keeping calm and smoking weed and having coffee shops.'

This is obviously a simplistic statement; however, the argument is accurate and plausible, given the enormous cost that alcohol bleeds out of the community. Alcohol sales have fallen by approximately fifteen per cent in the areas of the US that have allowed regulated access to medical cannabis.

In the event of outcome 4 transpiring, where non-drinkers and non-smokers take up cannabis, although this is undesirable, non-drinkers represent a very small fraction of the community. This group primarily chooses not to use alcohol for health reasons, and because of this stance (not because of cannabis's illegality), they are *extremely* unlikely to take up cannabis. The same is true for non-smokers.

I am a non-drinker and non-smoker, and I have made these choices for the benefit of my health. The illegality of cannabis to me is irrelevant, because illegally acquiring cannabis would be relatively easy, and it is unlikely I would get caught, so there is no penal deterrence. It makes no difference to these groups whether there is a legislative barrier to cannabis use or not because they have already imposed a personal barrier on themselves. In essence, allowing a regulated market is likely to benefit society in the long term (as seen in the areas that have taken this approach), and the negative outcomes that are fear driven, not evidence driven, are highly unlikely and substantially outweighed by the benefits.

Some people also argue that if cannabis is decriminalised, it will be a slippery slope, leading indirectly to the gradual decriminalisation of other drugs (which, in the case of possession, many public health experts are already advocating). If anything, allowing access to cannabis is actually taking a step towards less harm, because it enables people to use a safer product. What is more concerning is not the slippery slope of decriminalising other drugs, but the slippery slope of incarceration and criminal records.

If cannabis causes less public health harm than alcohol or tobacco, then why would decriminalising cannabis somehow facilitate the decriminalisation of other more harmful illegal drugs when we are moving down the ladder of harm? If anything, the public should be more concerned about continued alcohol and tobacco use and, particularly, the lax approach to alcohol regulation that unquestionably causes greater harm.

If we were in a situation where cannabis was legal, but both alcohol and tobacco were illegal, you could argue that legalising alcohol and/or tobacco would represent a breakdown in public health policy because society would be tolerating more harmful drugs.

If we had never prohibited cannabis, but instead established stronger regulations for tobacco and alcohol, perhaps we would not be facing the current public health predicament, where the only drugs that people can consume (except caffeine) are drugs that cause enormous mortality and morbidity. And if an individual wishes to use a safer drug such as cannabis, they face arrest. Knowing what we know now, if we had our time again, we could do things very differently.

From a political standpoint, one of the challenges facing the decriminalisation of cannabis is that the only political party that appears to be talking sense about the drug is the Australian Greens. Although it has existed as a party since the early 1990s, the Greens have only had three leaders. Its policies are based on the ideological framework of social justice, environmentalism and nonviolence. Historically considered a fringe political party, with little public support due to the perception of its policies being radical or unbalanced, the Greens have more recently gained significant traction among the Australian public. Some would argue that this is a result of disillusionment with the two major political parties.

The current Australian Greens leader, Richard Di Natale, quite possibly has more authority than any other individual in parliament to put forward an opinion on a public health issue, as he is a physician and public health expert. Dr Di Natale has argued that his party's plan to allow the public regulated access to cannabis, both as a medicine and recreationally, would be highly beneficial, as the current approach does little, if anything, to deter individuals from using the drug, denies patients access to treatment and adds to the harms that the drug causes to the community (all of which is correct).

However, evidence based and beneficial the Greens' proposal may be, previous policies put forward by the Greens have polarised the community to such an extent that any rational policies are frequently dismissed out of hand. To put it bluntly, the public as a whole pay only a small amount of attention to the Greens, and often their policies are not taken seriously, regardless of how meritorious they may be. Around the same time that the Greens announced their proposal for legislative changes to cannabis, they also had on the table a proposal to ban all petrol and diesel cars by 2030 (within twelve years) for environmental purposes. While a couple of countries throughout the world, such as Norway and the Netherlands, are moving in this direction, and the principal aim of the policy has merit, political opponents and critics instantly blew holes in the planned policy, resulting in widespread public dismissal.

When the Greens announced their plan for changing cannabis legislation, the vast majority of news sources equated the rationality of this proposition to the proposed ban on petrol/diesel cars, despite the two policies being entirely different in their purpose, logistical application and projected outcomes. The press was able to equate this proposal with previous Greens' policies to claim that this was just another 'stupid idea', or as Bill Shorten called it, 'political clickbait'. This example is reflective of a wider issue where individual policies are often not treated on their individual merit but, instead, assumed to hold equal standing with other policies. Unfortunately, many constituents do not even bother reading past the headline—policies regarding drugs or public health in general do not belong in headlines and should not be decided on a political platform. If one of the major parties had put forward this proposal, the media and the public would certainly not have treated it with the levity they did. For policies to be unheard or not taken seriously simply because the representative party holds less public traction is unfair on the party as well as the community who could benefit from such policies.

One of the other major hurdles that society faces in adopting a more pragmatic approach to cannabis is the shrill noise generated by those in opposition, particularly from the right. In late May 2018, Australian conservative columnist Miranda Devine interviewed Tony Wood, a staunch campaigner and advocate for zero tolerance of cannabis after the death of his daughter Anna in 1995. During the interview, Tony Wood said 'We're going to decriminalise cannabis and make medical marijuana, which is a ridiculous thing to do'. This is similar to the comments made during an anti-cannabis medicine advertisement in 1998 by American former first lady, Barbara Bush, 'Now is not the time to send the message to our young people that marijuana is medicine. It is not. It is a dangerous, illegal drug'.

Firstly, blocking extremely sick or terminally ill patients from access to the only treatment that improves their quality of life (and that is safer than current treatments, such as opioids or benzodiazepines) is the ridiculous notion, not making medical marijuana, as Tony Wood insisted. As author Howard Bloom puts it better, 'Is it legitimate for any human on the face of planet earth to deny another human being the thing that will remove them from that infinite torture chamber? No, it is not acceptable. It is utterly and completely immoral.'

People will die unless they are provided medical cannabis. Several thousand children die every year from epilepsy because of which they suffer hundreds of seizures per day, and many of these children could be saved by medical cannabis. In the years it takes for governments to deliberate on the potential harms versus utility of cannabis, more children will die. This is the price we pay for denial. Morally and scientifically, it's not even worth debating. If medical cannabis were the only drug that could have saved the life of Tony Woods's daughter, would he be against it? How far would you go to save the life of your child or a loved one? Because there are thousands, possibly millions of parents throughout the world who are watching their children die and being denied access to the only drug that could save that child's life.

Cannabis is not perfectly safe but it is far less damaging than other medical interventions that we allow patients to elect, such as chemotherapy, which can damage the liver, kidneys, heart or cause secondary cancers later in life. We allow the elderly to undergo serious surgery, even though up to fifteen per cent die after surgery. Some argue against the use of cannabis as a medicine on the basis that cannabis-based medicines are not first-line treatments for any medical condition. However, this is a non-argument because practitioners are so hamstrung and restricted by regulations regarding cannabis-based prescriptions that virtually all other options are explored before cannabis is even considered.

Secondly, even if it is not a first-line treatment, that does not invalidate its efficacy for patients who may be resistant to first-line treatments, for patients who have terrible allergic reactions or if it is used as an adjunct treatment. We don't deny patients levofloxacin or moxifloxacin if they have tuberculosis and are resistant to rifampicin (unless there are contraindications), just as we don't deny nanoliposomal irinotecan in pancreatic cancer patients if they are resistant to gemcitabine or paclitaxel, or electroconvulsive therapy (ECT) or tricyclic antidepressants if depressed patients fail to respond to other medications, or macrolide to patients resistant to benzylpenicillin.

Even in cases where symptoms become 'partial', which is where symptoms improve with medications but not to a level of remission, we do not deny them further options. Harm minimisation in medicine is realistic in terms of weighing risks from both sides—the risks of taking the drug and the risks of not taking the drug. Taking an antidepressant can produce side effects, such as insomnia and temporary increases in anxiety or restlessness. However, if not treated, the individual's life may be destroyed by not being able to leave the house, talk to anyone, engage with any activity and, in some tragic cases, the patient may choose to end their life. Chemotherapy can have enormously detrimental effects on the body, but without it, the patient could die. All drugs have downsides, but unfortunately the downside of not taking a drug can be greater than the downside of taking it.

In *Leaving Early,* which looks at the issue of youth suicide, Tony Wood said that nineteen out of the twenty cases used in the book were marijuana users. The implication clearly is that cannabis caused, or at the very least, made a significant contribution to the deaths. While this is possible, the individuals may have used cannabis once five years ago or used cannabis because it helped their depressive state—both entirely plausible reasons that would match the definition of cannabis users, without cannabis having contributed in any way to their deaths.

If a car breaks down half an hour after filling up with petrol at a service station that does not mean that the petrol at the station caused the breakdown. In an earlier interview on the Channel 7's Sunrise program in May 2012, Tony Wood said, 'We need to get back to zero tolerance'. He backed this up by claiming that when asked to assist in drug testing an American cruise ship of 300 people, with a zero-tolerance policy, less than one per cent of the results returned positive. What if the passengers are all middle class and over the age of sixty, where illicit drug use among this age group is less than one per cent anyway? A causal relationship cannot be proven merely by the existence of two events being present in proximity to each other. Ms Devine responds that there is 'unequivocal evidence out there that long-term, large-scale studies show you have a much higher risk of psychosis and mental illness if you smoke marijuana'.

The evidence is anything but unequivocal, and the twenty-fold increase in cannabis use in Australia since the 1960s has not resulted in any population increase in rates of psychosis. In fact, psychosis prevalence in Australia is slightly declining. Ms Devine also claims that cannabis brings on early Alzheimer's disease, but there is little to no evidence to support this and stronger evidence to support the use of cannabis in protecting against alcohol-related dementia and in improving the quality of life of patients with dementia.

Tony Wood continues on the anti-cannabis march by stating that 'Cannabis is seventy per cent more carcinogenic than tobacco', and that 'Every mass murder (including Martin Bryant) in Australia has been marijuana involved'. If you want to raise awareness about Alzheimer's disease, then perhaps you should mention the fact that the disease actually starts in the brain three to five decades before symptoms show, and that alcohol actually initiates the inflammatory response that leads to brain atrophy.

While carcinogenic compounds are found in cannabis, and cannabis smoke has been implicated in respiratory dysfunction and cellular damage—inhaling any burnt particulates will irritate the mouth, throat and lungs—cannabis has not been causally linked with any tobacco-related cancers. Multiple studies have shown that compounds in cannabis destroy a variety of cancer cells, including lung, leukaemia, lymphoma, prostate, skin and pheochromocytoma (a rare tumour of adrenal gland tissue). Cannabis has been shown to reduce carcinogenic pathways, reduce free radical production and inhibit tumour angiogenesis, whereas tobacco smoke produces completely contrasting effects. Both tobacco and cannabis contain carcinogens, however they are nowhere near equally carcinogenic because of the different chemical makeup and because cannabis burns at a lower temperature than tobacco.

Some authorities have been partially responsible for sensationalising cannabis harms. In June 2012, the British Lung Foundation claimed that a joint of cannabis was as carcinogenic as twenty cigarettes. A misleading assertion, considering that multiple studies have demonstrated the potential anti-tumour effects of cannabis, and a study out of the university of California showed that even smoking 20,000 cannabis joints does not increase lung cancer risk. Although cannabis users often inhale deeper and hold their breath for longer, thereby increasing oral, throat and lung tissue exposure to smoke, there is no strong evidence to causally link cannabis use with cancer. While cannabis is often packed more loosely than tobacco, meaning there is less filtration and greater inhalation of particulate matter per breath, cannabis is intrinsically less carcinogenic. Less total particulate matter is inhaled, those dependant on tobacco smoke much more often than those dependant on cannabis, and a tobacco smoker's career is typically much longer than a cannabis user's career, because nicotine has a greater propensity for dependence and its effects are shorter lasting.

While I have great respect for Tony Wood, and I feel deeply sorry for his loss, scaremongering is not educative. It does not assist the public in making safer choices, particularly when this comparison also makes tobacco look safer. It is much better for the public to be smart than scared, because not only do scare tactics not reduce consumption, but they also insult the intelligence of the public.

As for cannabis being involved in every mass murder in Australia, this assertion is entirely baseless. There was one report of Martin Bryant possibly purchasing cannabis once. However, the forensic psychiatrist who analysed Martin Bryant said that he explicitly reported no illicit drug use, including opioids, cannabis and amphetamines.

One commonly cited study to support the assertion that cannabis causes violence is 'Cannabis use and violence in patients with severe mental illness: a meta-analytical investigation' in *Psychiatry Research*. The concluding sentences are clear:

> *These findings are clinically relevant for violence prevention/management and highlight the necessity of further investigations with methodologically sound studies. Longitudinal studies adjusting for important confounding factors (i.e., psychopathic traits and stimulant use) are warranted.*

The insightful reader would realise that this study in no way claims to make either a conclusive or causal link between cannabis and violence.

Not to mention that subjects of concern are those with *severe mental illness*, which excludes ninety-seven per cent of the Australian public.

Towards the end of the interview, the interviewer, Miranda, and Tony Wood agree that the only answer is to be 'tough on drugs and kind on rehab'. However, being kind on rehab is irreconcilable with being tough on drugs and having zero tolerance. A handful of high-profile media personnel have attempted to blame numerous terrorist attacks and other murders on cannabis as the offenders may have used the drug in the past, but this is basically a stab in the dark. Although this is covered at greater length in Part Two of this book, if cannabis caused violence, then why has the twenty-fold increase in cannabis use over the past fifty years coincided with falls in overall violent crime? This is certainly not to say that cannabis reduces violent crime, however the two are largely unrelated. Even if some of these individuals had used cannabis previously, it does not mean that the drug had anything to do with their crime. Some of the terrorists may have used cannabis in the past; however, all of the terrorists where it was alleged that cannabis was related to their crime, were also men with dark complexions. We don't claim that men with dark skin are likely to be terrorists, because there is no causal relationship. There are many individuals who are quick to blame something like cannabis, because that either reinforces their prejudice against the drug or it provides an explanation when they are trying to understand why such atrocities occur.

∼⁀∽

In May 2018, conservative commentator Steve Price interviewed Dr Andrew Laming, the Federal Member for Bowman, on the topic of pill testing at music festivals. During the interview, Mr Price said, 'It seems we are on the edge of a very slippery slope… Everyone runs around going what you're doing, law enforcement doesn't work, so let's give up on that and let people take whatever they want'. This was exactly the same comment he had made when interviewing Australian Conservatives leader,

Cory Bernardi, in mid-2017 on the topic of decriminalising cannabis. This all or nothing response is part of the problem when attempting to engage in a rational discussion, and it almost resembles a toddler throwing all of their toys out of the pram because they don't get their way.

Individuals advocating for drug law reform do not want more drug use, more drug users or more drug harm, even though this is what they are accused of. As soon as drug law reformists modestly profess that past and current approaches are not working and we need to re-think our strategy, they are accused of wanting to have heroin or crack cocaine advertised to the public and available in supermarket aisles. I certainly do not want anyone to use any illicit drug, particularly while they are illegal, because aside from legal ramifications, any drug is always going to be more dangerous when it isn't regulated.

I have heard countless drug policy advocates claim that they would love to live in a world where law enforcement reduced use, users and harms, but at least they appreciate that perfect solutions in public health policies simply do not exist. Both prohibitionists and progressives are trying to achieve the same outcome—less drug harm. The only thing that separates the two groups is the way to achieve that goal. It is very challenging to make headway when individuals come into the space ready to fight because they are so adamant that zero tolerance is the only approach. Before any evidence is presented and even after evidence is presented, they have already decided they don't like drugs or drug users, and that position clouds any rational judgements.

Steve Price also claims that state endorsement to run drug testing will market the festival to drug dealers. Festivals are already naturally marketed to dealers. Pill testing actually puts pressure on those who sell drugs to provide safer products. Studies from overseas have also proven that many users dispose of the drugs and warn their friends off if the test comes back positive, resulting in less drug users, less drug use and less drug mixing (pill testing is covered in greater detail in Part Two of this book). But when you have already taken a moral position, evidence doesn't matter. Dr Laming astonishingly responds to these findings by claiming 'Some people have a frontal lobe so small that they decide to use drugs there'.

He should appreciate that basically every single one of those individuals who uses illicit drugs at festivals will go on to obtain jobs, pay tax and support their families, and many will go on to be highly successful, outstanding contributors to society. All of that is threatened however if they ingest something entirely unknown as well as if they are handed a criminal record for possessing drugs. This comment by Dr Laming just affirms that he looks down on drug users. One of the fundamental principal precepts in medical ethics is *primum non nocere*, which translated is 'first, do no harm'. Why would we not apply the same to the law?

Another well-known proponent for cannabis prohibition is UK journalist and author Peter Hitchens, who debated with former UK government advisor Professor David Nutt on the topic of drug law reform. The discussion was held in 2010 after Professor Nutt, along with approximately thirty medical experts, produced a study assessing the relative harms of twenty different drugs to UK society. The objective of the study was to comparatively scale the twenty drugs according to over a dozen different parameters of harm to both users and others, and then based on findings, provide the government with suggestions on how to improve drug policy in reducing the harms of drugs.

After Professor Nutt explained this to Peter Hitchens and to the host, Hitchens's opening comments aimed at discrediting the study:

> *The report is barely written in recognisable English, and seems to me to be a heap of pseudoscience, in which for instance, stomach ulcers, deforestation, the reputation of the community, mood disorders, and the littering of the streets with used syringes are all lumped together as factors. How anyone can produce an objective classification on the dangers of drugs on the basis of this I don't know... You tell me what peer-reviewed means; I think on this occasion it has to be treated with a certain amount of suspicion. It doesn't look to me like objective science.*

To claim the report is written in barely recognisable English is simply admitting that the study is too complex for him to understand. To claim the study is pseudoscience is absurd, as the study utilised a technique known as multiple-criteria decision analysis (MCDA), which is not only a highly complex and sophisticated analytical method for evaluating criteria, but was the most advanced system in assessing the harms of drugs to date. The harms to which Hitchens refers are all authentic and appropriate, and to disregard the validity of the study by questioning the legitimacy of it being peer reviewed is to disregard the fact that the study is published in one of the most prestigious medical journals in the world and assessed by various outside experts working in the field.

Hitchens also claims in the interview that he would be able to produce a better study, referring to the chart as 'silly', which is an insult to the doctor and his team of experts. He went on to say:

> If these drugs (particularly cannabis) were legalised, or as these people now euphemistically say, decriminalised or regulated, their harms would be far greater than those of alcohol.

Decriminalisation is not a euphemism for legalisation. They are two entirely different types of regulations. Evidence from all around the world has proved that the latter part of Hitchens's predictions is incorrect. Alcohol is an intrinsically more toxic drug than cannabis, and countries with liberal cannabis laws have seen falls in alcohol consumption.

David Nutt has been criticised for having a conflict of interest due to his plans to produce a 'synthetic alcohol'. However, his appreciation of alcohol-related harm and criticism of the alcohol industry came years before the suggestion of developing a synthetic alternative.

Throughout the interview, Hitchens continued to shout down Professor Nutt and ends with his assertion that Nutt is attempting to 'blur the line between the legal and illegal drugs'. This is inaccurate given that the principle aim of the study is to objectively quantify drug harms based on science, regardless of morality or legality. Much drug harm is caused by the legal status of the drug at both ends of the spectrum. Alcohol harms are significant, because the drug is widely available, whereas many heroin-related harms stem from the fact that users don't have it on prescription, which encourages unclean needle exchange and unsafe injecting environments.

When Hitchens was asked back to provide some further comments regarding the interview, he explicitly stated that drug law reform 'is not fundamentally a scientific argument, it's a moral and legal argument'. While he can take a moral position, public health issues cannot be shaped by morals, because morals are subjective, meaning that we could be having the same conversation one hundred years from now. It is also wrong to present a case utilising hypotheticals or distorted evidence to suit your position. Additionally, all drugs must be regulated according to their individual scientific characteristics, not historical legal anomalies, as regulations have proven to be unscientifically based and therefore not in the best interest of public health. Hitchens again states that the study should be questioned and that it was not scientifically perfect. This is true to *some* extent in certain aspects:

- The study only scaled drugs individually, while many drug users are poly drug users.
- The study did not take into account drug benefits such as taxation generated by tobacco sales.
- The objective parameters utilised could arguably be subjective, for example, death from a heroin overdose and death from COPD are objectively two deaths. Yet while heroin overdoses are often painless with the person dying while unconscious, dying from COPD could mean that the person—for weeks or months—becomes forcibly sedentary, only able to breathe via mechanical ventilation as they struggle for their last breaths.

With this in mind, the study was executed with the best scientific methodology we have to date on the harms of drugs. When someone is morally opposed to drugs, this is frequently at the cost of science, or at the very least, only the studies supporting that person's moral position are considered. Professor Nutt was sacked from his role as government advisor because he presented objective scientific evidence that was not convenient to hear and did not indulge the prejudicial views held by the Brown Labour government. This completely defeats the purpose of enlisting independent scientific advice.

In early 2017, Hitchens published an article in his *Daily Mail* blog entitled 'Stupid arguments for drug legalisation examined and refuted'. The first argument that he refutes is that marijuana use is a victimless crime, an argument I would never espouse, because there is no such thing as a safe drug and all drugs can be harmful to the user and others. Anyone who uses this as a pillar in their argument for allowing access to cannabis is ignoring any externalities. Illegalising cannabis does, however, create more victims than a regulated market, and it is almost impossible to enforce against chiefly victimless crimes unless aggressive measures that invade civil liberties, such as raids, sniffer dogs and strip searches, are implemented.

The second argument that Mr Hitchens refutes is that correlation is not causation. He infers that although correlation may not necessarily mean causation, it may not necessarily mean that it is not causation. Correlated events may be direct or indirect causations. However, he fails to acknowledge common causality, other confounding factors that may explain the correlative relationship, or reverse causality such as in the cases of those people who take up cannabis after they become psychotic, because it actually aids their symptoms. Correlations or associations are not causations.

Hitchens cites the 2012 Dunedin study, the 1969 Swedish Conscript study as well as the works of Scottish psychiatrist Sir Robin Murray. The Dunedin study failed to account for other confounding factors that could have caused the drop in reported IQ. As the study was a snapshot in time, this is a chicken-egg scenario. Various other long-term studies have shown that when other factors such as environment are controlled, there is no relationship between cannabis use and IQ decline. The other cited study is the Swedish Conscript study, which looks at the evidence surrounding cannabis and schizophrenia (Refer to 'Will cannabis make me lose my mind?' chapter in Part Two of this book). Hitchens also cites the work of Professor Sir Robin Murray, Professor of Psychiatric Research at Kings College London. However, studies produced by Kings College are typically looking at high-THC strains of cannabis such as skunk, as well as young, heavy or long-term users, not from single or rare use, which is the majority of people who have ever tried cannabis.

While some of the research out of Kings College points towards the possibility of cannabis harms being slightly more serious than other studies have shown, Professor Murray himself considers criminalisation foolish, is a strong supporter of decriminalisation and is undecided on full legalisation, which does not align with Hitchens' position. It can, however, be difficult for individuals to accept a different position when they have dedicated a significant portion of their career to proving the harms of cannabis. Hitchens goes on to say that legalisation will be irreversible, as we have seen with the cultural intractability of alcohol and tobacco. These are, however, the only drugs that have actually survived from illegality, as every other drug has been banned. Prior to widespread prohibition, a wide variety of drugs were available, such as cocaine in Coca-Cola, cannabis in tincture as well as opium. For the most part, these drugs have been systematically illegalised. The struggle to re-introduce cannabis in a regulated fashion is testament to the fact that it is actually harder for drugs to stay in the good books of society and government and remain legal.

With new substances, Australia's response is consistent with the rest of the world (for example, the UK with the *Psychoactive Substances Act 2016*, which banned any new psychoactive substance, and according to the government's own report in 2018 was an extensive failure). As soon as we can identify what the product is, we ban it without any reference to harm, even if it could make people healthier or more intelligent.

Hitchens also states that it is impossible to do proper research on the medical utility of cannabis as the test group will be aware, due to its psychoactive effects, and the control group receiving the placebo will know they have been provided something of a non-drug nature. Despite there being several hundred chemicals in cannabis, one of the primary compounds is CBD, which is non-psychoactive, so both the control group and CBD group would experience nil psychoactive effects. The other compound is THC, which is psychoactive. In this case, the control group could be given an alternative drug with similar psychoactive effects, resulting in participants from both groups experiencing comparable effects.

What is absurd is that in the US, which has dictated international drug policy for at least fifty years, the National Institute on Drug Abuse (NIDA) is solely focused on proving harms of cannabis. NIDA governs and controls all research into cannabis throughout the US, however, there are no provisions for studying the medical utility of the drug; research conducted only looked into the harms. It has been claimed that between 2007 and 2011, the US National Institute of Health provided over $14,000,000 to cannabinoid research, which continued into 2016–2017. It was only in the last year or so that the NIH allowed research into the benefits of cannabis. Additionally, the USA government now allocates approximately $100,000,000 towards cannabis-related research each year. However, if you read the fine print, the budgetary allocations are firmly committed towards researching drug abuse, not therapeutic use. About eighty per cent of 'cannabis research' funding is injected into studying 'cannabis abuse disorders', and only 16.5 per cent of NIDA's spending goes towards the therapeutic properties of cannabis, with much of this money directed towards cannabis abuse. And despite the DEA providing manufacturing licenses to other privately funded laboratories to study all other Schedule 1 drugs (heroin etc.), cannabis is the only Schedule 1 drug that is prohibited from being researched in such a manner. The University of Mississippi is the only federally approved facility to undertake such study, but because researchers must obtain the plant from a NIDA-contracted entity, which is not mandated to study medical use, the research conducted is disproportionately biased towards finding negative health effects.

The DEA revealed a new policy in 2016, designed to expand the number of entities allowed to research cannabis. Since this time, the DEA has received countless applications, but have been effectually blocked by the Department of Justice from taking any action. The downstream implication of this is that there is no formal acceptance of cannabis's medical utility because it is not FDA approved, and simultaneously, the very research needed for FDA approval is obstructed.

Similarly, the media focuses on any findings that support their harm-only bias, while remaining sceptical and resistant to the mountain of available evidence documenting the medical benefits.

This is not however the case with other drugs that do not carry the same kind of baggage that cannabis does. If we were talking about how scientists have tweaked carbamazepine (a drug commonly prescribed for childhood epilepsy), and the new compound was shown to drop seizure rates like a stone, the media would pick this story up and run with it in the hope it could transform the lives of the children who suffered from the illness as well as their families. If we replaced the word 'carbamazepine' with 'cannabis', it would be considered dangerous and reckless, even if the efficacy and side effects were identical.

Hitchens goes on to make a handful of other arguments against law reform, such as attempting to refute the idea that reform would lead to a shift in market share away from criminals to regulated enterprises and arguing that even if the drug was regulated, that would not mean that consumption would be safe. Nobody is claiming that regulated markets protect against all harms, and Hitchens accepts that illicit drug use will still take place regardless of legislation. However, when the illegal trade occupies 100 per cent of market share, there is zero production and distribution control. If you accept that illicit drug trades will always exist (e.g. alcohol and tobacco), a tightly regulated market is the most effective way of keeping the illicit trade market share as small as possible. We do not ban alcohol or tobacco, and rational individuals are not advocating for this. In Australia, as in many other parts of the world, we have been able to significantly drop tobacco use and harm without attaching criminality to it.

Like many others, Mr Hitchens also attempts to refute the argument against prohibition that we do not illegalise other dangerous (and arguably more dangerous) activities, such as mountain climbing or riding motorbikes. Some people regard the rule of law—not harm—as paramount, and often defend this position by stating that legal activities involving risk, such as rock/mountain climbing, horse riding, are not fair comparisons to illicit drugs because these activities improve the individual's life, the individual can take necessary precautions to protect themselves, and you can learn these activities from a young age. However, exactly the same can be said about drugs. These are all simply unnecessary behaviours that expose an individual to unnecessary risk. People take drugs because they feel it is providing their life with some benefit (for example, coping, self-discovery, pain reduction), there are many harm reduction measures one can take with any drug to reduce risk (safer ROA, safer dosing, safer setting) and often it is the young who are at greatest risk because they are naïve about risk factors such as dosing, environment, mixing drugs, etc.

There are justifiable reasons as to why people engage in dangerous legal activities, just like there are justifiable reasons as to why people take illicit drugs. And even though some legal activities are more dangerous than taking many illegal drugs, banning them would magnify the existing risks—banning motorbike riding, for example, would not stop everyone riding, and those who do, ride on unregulated, dangerous roads on bikes that have not have safety checks.

With regard to cannabis, you can easily take harm reduction measures, such as vaporising or using edibles instead of smoking cannabis to administer the drug at slower rate, not holding your breath or drawing deep while using cannabis to protect the lungs, inhaling only small amounts to begin with so dosage can be titrated, taking tolerance breaks or avoiding alcohol beforehand to minimise risk of greening out.

One of Hitchens's last arguments is refuting the success of Portugal and the Netherlands in decriminalising cannabis (refer to 'Portugal' in Part Two of this book). He is a strong advocate for the rule of law and for prosecuting cannabis users although he admits to using cannabis in his teens. He claims that it did not harm him and that he regrets the experience. I would certainly not have been in favour of criminalising Hitchens at a young age for smoking cannabis, because that would have very likely impeded him from progressing onto studying at City of Oxford College and the University of York and becoming the outstandingly successful journalist and foreign correspondent that he is—unquestionably a much worse outcome than the health effects of dabbling in cannabis.

In terms of moving forward, this article does bring two very important issues to light. One is that it is almost impossible to debate morals against science, because morals are subjective, whereas science is objective. As Kanye West stated in his most prolific moment 'the only facts we have now are feelings'. So we have to ask ourselves whether we having a moral debate or a scientific debate. Is it more important to punish people or reduce harm? How quantifiably harmful does a drug have to be before it is banned, and what are the appropriate parameters/comparators? What are proportionate punishments? Many will argue that abstention is best practice because all drug use is harmful, even if the harm is arguably trivial. However, those who push this argument need to accept that there are millions of individuals throughout the world who use drugs and function perfectly well in society, and some are even more functional than non-drug users. And if 'zero risk' were the standard we used to allow the public regulated access to any drug, there would not be a *single drug* available.

Considering that drug topics and attitudes are dominated by morality, is it even possible to have neutrality when discoursing in the drug space? British philosopher John Stuart Mill stated that 'the only justification for a government to exercise power or force over a citizen against his or her will is to prevent harm to others. Preventing harm to oneself is not sufficient justification'. In terms of drug use, there will always be some degree of harm to others—it may be insignificant, but at what point do we deem the behaviour harmful enough to warrant government intervention, and when do the harms of government intervention outweigh the harms of that behaviour to others without intervention?

The issue of confirmation bias or the backfire effect, which essentially means that the individual becomes more steadfast by searching for information to support their belief and disregarding evidence contrary to their belief, makes having a rational argument almost impossible. Presenting any evidence or argument that contradicts the individual's standing results in the person digging their heels in deeper. But being open to other voices and ideas is critical for progress.

Given the harms that both alcohol and tobacco cause to the community, and if we can rationally accept that we will never rid the community entirely of these drugs, then how is it not immoral to deny the community safer alternatives? Despite the Australian government claiming that efforts are being made to lower or eliminate tobacco- and alcohol-related harm, the government obviously considers these harms tolerable, as both are legal, and in the case of alcohol, actively promoted. Since the real governmental agenda with alcohol and tobacco is apparently just to 'manage the damage' (as all policy decisions are made in a vacuum), officials should be explicit about that and admit that they are perfectly happy to allow more than 25,000 Australians to die annually, while they deny access to and continually focus on drugs like cannabis, which cause next to no public health harms. The government essentially needs to be explicit about the fact that for both legal and illegal drug policies, evidence is not the driving force.

The truth is that both society and government want to reduce alcohol and tobacco harms, because the hard data is so chillingly and undeniably clear, however, governments are pressured by various entities to inhibit change. This means that, despite representatives' claims to the contrary, policy is not based on evidence or science. They are taking a moral position. Even if the government's position on cannabis were transparent, the policy is flawed from both a moral and evidence-based approach. It is ethically wrong to disallow access to safer alternatives and insist that society only consumes alcohol, which we know causes significant damage. That would be like banning cars, and only allowing people to ride motorcycles, even though the risk of death is almost forty times higher riding a motorcycle than a car. Apart from immorality, it is also unhelpful from a public health point of view to deny society a safer product. Regulated access to safer drugs, such as cannabis, incentivises people to use these drugs instead of more harmful drugs, such as alcohol, tobacco and SCs.

Additionally, if the policy decisions are to be based on evidence (which they aren't), that does not mean cherry picking out one piece of evidence that vaguely or barely supports the policy, while ignoring the mountain of objective evidence that disproves the policy. It also does not mean using weak anecdotal evidence or beliefs to justify the policy, such as in 2012 when US presidential candidate Mitt Romney stated 'It's my belief that cannabis is a gateway drug'. Before this comment, Romney was asked whether marijuana should be legalised for medical purposes, and he responded, 'Aren't there issues of significance you would like to talk about?' Romney should have placed himself in the shoes of the thousands, possibly millions of his constituents who would have watched this interview while in pain, or in a wheelchair, or in the middle of a seizure, or watching their child have hundreds of seizures per day, or while feeling nauseous from chemotherapy (just to name a few), who felt completely ignored, or according to Romney, that they were just of no 'significance'. Mitt Romney may have had better political traction if he didn't view medical cannabis as an insignificant issue.

Government should create policies that are based on evidence, not create evidence that is based on policies. Essentially, there needs to be a shift from policy-based evidence, to evidence-based policy. It takes a great deal of courage for government ministers to not toe the line and to stand up against the laws that they are supposed to represent and defend, particularly in the face of overwhelming contradictory evidence. Words are easy and many, while great deeds are difficult and rare. Additionally, governments should not pretend that policies are based on evidence, when they are actually based on morality and then use invalid, manipulated or sensationalised evidence to support their position. Negating anecdotal evidence when shaping public policy does not mean that the individual presenting the anecdote is denied their belief or experience. However, due to anecdotes being subjective, uncontrolled for other factors, not being wholly representative, and utilising small sample sizes, they are largely disregarded based on their logistical invalidity. This is not just true for those in favour of prohibitive measures, but also progressive measures, as the inadequacy of anecdotes goes both ways. Individuals who claim to know others who use drugs and function perfectly well are standing on an equally weak foundation for their argument as individuals who claim to know others that have used drugs and ruined their lives. Anecdotes can make for powerful stories and can be the catalyst for going deeper down the rabbit hole, but are largely irrelevant for issues concerning public policy. Anecdotes are also only suitable for hypothesis testing, not for hypothesis confirmation.

Cannabis, like every drug, is not 100 per cent harmless. As with all public health issues, there is no perfect solution. Although most of the world has taken a prohibitive approach, based on the evidence, this is much less perfect solution than a rational decriminalised approach. As Denzel Washington's character says in *The Equaliser*, 'Progress, not perfection'.

Having a balanced and logical conversation around cannabis is challenging because often both prohibitionists and progressives are so quick to dig their heels in and defend their position, polarising the entire issue into two camps: 'cannabis is a medicine' and 'cannabis is a harmful drug'. The plausibility of these arguments depends on who uses the drug, how often, for what reason, in what environment and the type of drug they take. Cynics may argue that the push to decriminalise cannabis is largely fuelled by 'big dope' or 'big weed' (a collection of wealthy individuals who wish to manufacture and distribute the product for their own financial gain). This is largely a myth.

The primary group advocating for decriminalisation are public health experts and medical practitioners who have no financial incentive to encourage this movement. While there are certainly people who will attempt to gain a financial advantage from the deregulation of cannabis (I've seen Dan Bilzerian's *Ignite Cannabis* Instagram posts, and I am aware of George Soros's financial backing of Drug Policy Alliance), the individuals who are going to generate the most influence and traction in terms of policy change are medical and public health experts. If cannabis were legalised and private companies were in charge of manufacture and distribution, albeit within the constraints of regulations, then it would be possible for private companies to wield political influence. This does not have to be the case. We have had decades of experience in dealing with both the tobacco and alcohol industry and could learn from the mistakes that have been made.

When it comes to controversial drug-related issues, such as cannabis law reform, politicians tend to go where the wind (public opinion) blows, which can actually be a good thing. Thanks to the internet and other technological advancements, the public have become much more aware that the way we have been dealing with cannabis for at least fifty years has been wrong. Policy makers are clued into the tidal shift of public knowledge and opinion. What was considered politically expedient a decade or two ago is no longer blindly accepted.

8

Molly – Ecstasy

Ecstasy, pingers, molly, pills, X, E, XTC, and caps are all street slang for any product containing the drug MDMA (methylene-dioxymethamphetamine). Ecstasy comes in three different forms: MDMA powder (drug in loose powder form), capsules/caps (capsules containing pure MDMA powder), and pills (pressed tablets containing MDMA although purity varies as the MDMA may have been cut with other substances). Ecstasy is the second most widely consumed drug in Australia, and on a global scale, Australia is among the highest users of ecstasy per capita. Despite this, the vast majority of Australians have never tried ecstasy. Approximately one in ten Australians aged fourteen and over have tried ecstasy at some point, meaning that ninety per cent have never experimented with ecstasy.

MDMA is a Schedule 9 drug in Australia, and a Schedule 1 drug in the 1971 UN Convention on Psychotropic Substances (UNCPS). The UNCPS supplemented the 1961 UN Single Convention on Drugs, as the scope of the former treaty was limited to regulating substances such as opioids, cocaine and cannabis. It was not until after the 1961 convention that drugs such as LSD, MDMA and other amphetamines became widely available. These treaties, however, are not self-executing, meaning that signed nations (such as Australia) must implement the provisions into domestic legislation to ensure compliance. Today, three UN treaties dictate international drug law:

- Single Convention on Narcotic Drugs, 1961
- Convention on Psychotropic Substance, 1971
- Convention against Illicit Traffic in Narcotic Drugs and Psychotropic Substances, 1988

~⁓~

MDMA is a stimulatory entactogen. Stimulants are agents that increase central nervous system (CNS) activity, and entactogens are agents that produce feelings of social connectedness. All forms of ecstasy contain inconsistent levels of MDMA, the average dose falls somewhere between sixty milligrams and 120 mg, with the average cost per pill ranging between ten dollars and twenty-five dollars. Users in Australia who wish to purchase pure MDMA powder pay a premium price of several hundred dollars per gram. Dealers also increase the price if selling inside dance music events (where ecstasy is often taken) to compensate for the increased risk of detection by authorities.

The safety ratio of MDMA is sixteen, which is higher than heroin, morphine, cocaine or alcohol. As there is a large margin between an effective dose of MDMA and a lethal dose, ecstasy-related deaths are very rare, and when they do occur, it is not generally MDMA that has caused the death. MDMA dependence is very rare, with only one in fifty users becoming dependent at some point (a capture rate of two per cent). The initial onset effects of MDMA occur approximately thirty to forty-five minutes post ingestion, reach a peak at approximately ninety to 150 minutes post ingestion, and the half-life of MDMA is approximately eight hours. The half-life is the time it takes for the body to clear half of the existing blood plasma concentration of a substance. All drugs have different half-lives, ranging from minutes to months. The half-life of a drug is particularly important for anyone who drives a motor vehicle or operates machinery, as one- or two-night's sleep may not be enough time for the drug to be cleared from the body. It takes eight hours for half of the initial MDMA dose to be cleared from the body, sixteen hours for three-quarters to be cleared from the body and forty hours for over ninety-five per cent of the drug to be cleared from the body.

MDMA typically has four distinct phases: the come up, the peak, the comedown, and the day(s) following. During the come up (thirty to ninety minutes post-ingestion), users typically experience improvements in hedonic tone (happiness and positivity) as well as an increase in feelings of closeness to others. During the peak, which can last for several hours post-ingestion, users experience floating sensations, euphoria, happiness, excitement and a more intensified feeling of closeness to others. When an individual is 'rolling' (under the effects of MDMA), they can also experience negative effects, such as nausea, bruxism (jaw clenching/teeth grinding), dehydration and increased perspiration, heart rate and blood pressure. During the comedown, which can last for several hours, individuals can experience fatigue, flatness, irritability, anxiety, and insomnia.

The days following ecstasy use are critical because as the saying goes, what goes up must come down. The main side effects in the days following ecstasy use are restlessness and insomnia and depressive emotions are also reported, which is where the term 'suicide Tuesday' or 'black Tuesday' originates. Ecstasy is typically consumed at the end of the week or on weekends, and due to the fact that MDMA releases serotonin, dopamine and noradrenaline (chemicals in the brain involved in various biological functions), early in the following week, these chemicals are in temporary depletion. MDMA releases a number of neurotransmitters (chemicals that communicate signals from one neuron to another in the brain) that, along with other functions such as regulating heart rate and blood pressure, provide feelings of pleasure. Neurons are the primary component of the central nervous system (CNS) and are involved in all biological functions to some extent. The brain is comprised of over

80,000,000,000 neurons, and over a lifetime, brains undergo trillions of synapses (communications between neurons). The structures and communications between neurons make up the neural network.

When an individual consumes MDMA, a large amount of serotonin (as well as other chemicals), is released from neurons, providing the user with an intense pleasure among other effects. The biological response from this surge in serotonin is to downregulate the activity of serotonin receptors, which means that they are temporarily inactive. As the neurons are in a depleted state of serotonin and the receptors that are involved in the releasing of serotonin are temporarily inactive, there is a very low level of the chemical in the brain. Low levels of chemicals, such as serotonin, dopamine and noradrenaline, contribute significantly to depressive emotions, and as a result, in the days following ingestion of MDMA, there can be increases in suicidal tendencies. Although rare, very high doses of MDMA can cause excessive release of serotonin, potentially resulting in serotonin syndrome, where negative symptoms can range from mild to life threatening. As serotonin is a regulator of body temperature, high doses of MDMA resulting in serotonin syndrome can raise body temperatures to dangerously high levels, which can lead to cramping, vomiting, muscle weakness, collapsing and seizures.

Serotonin syndrome can also occur with use of other drugs, such as cocaine, other amphetamines and antidepressants, including selective serotonin reuptake inhibitors (SSRIs), serotonin noradrenaline reuptake inhibitors (SNRIs), serotonin dopamine reuptake inhibitors (SDRIs), tricyclics (TCAs) (which work on three neurotransmitters: serotonin, noradrenaline and dopamine), monoamine oxidase inhibitors, (MAOIs) and serotonin antagonists. SSRIs block serotonin reuptake in nerve terminals, which slowly increases the level of serotonin in the brain, however, initial increases can cause unpleasant symptoms such as insomnia. The concomitant use of multiple serotonergic drugs greatly increases the risk of serotonin syndrome and is of particular concern among individuals who have substance-use disorders as well as

other mental health issues. Medications, such as moclobemide or venlafaxine, used to treat illness such as depression or social anxiety, as well as
drugs used recreationally, like cocaine or MDMA, both separately result
in greater concentrations of extracellular serotonin, increasing the risk
of serotonin syndrome.

Possibly the most dangerous aspect of ecstasy use is that MDMA
is often substituted with another chemical, paramethoxyamphetamine
(PMA) or paramethoxymethamphetamine (PMMA), which are far more
toxic than MDMA. Some say that American chemist Alexander Shulgin
was the first person so have synthesised PMA in the 1960s, while others
argue Gordon Alles got there first in the 1930s. Although PMA/PMMA
are technically amphetamines, the mechanisms and effects are extremely
different to MDMA. MDMA takes about thirty to forty-five minutes to
kick in, whereas PMA/PMMA can take up to 1.5 to two hours, and
while MDMA produces stimulatory effects, PMA/PMMA produce
almost sedative-type effects. PMA/PMMA are up to ten times as potent
as MDMA, because they cause considerable surges of serotonin in the
brain, block the reuptake of serotonin, and inhibit monoamine oxidase
A (MAO-A), which metabolises serotonin. This accentuates the level of
serotonin, drastically increasing the risk of serotonin syndrome. Users
often ingest PMA/PMMA under the misapprehension that they have
taken MDMA, and when there are delayed or dull effects—or they wear
off quickly—users often mistake this as having taken a weak pill, which
encourages them to double-drop (re-dose). Another chemical found in
ecstasy tablets, 4-MTA (4-methylthioamphetamine), otherwise known
as a 'flatliner', also has a slow onset. If an ecstasy user is accustomed
to taking a pill containing the average dose of MDMA, which may be
around ninety milligrams, and they actually get a pill with ninety milligrams of PMA/PMMA instead, they can take the average equivalent of
ten ecstasy tablets. If they do not feel any effects for an hour or so, they
may re-dose themselves, which means they will have taken the equivalent of approximately twenty ecstasy tablets within an hour. By the time
the user begins to feel the effects, it is too late.

If an individual experiences slow or delayed effects, that does not mean that what they have ingested is weak, and the solution is certainly not to re-dose. Half a pill from one batch may contain the equivalent pharmacological strength to five pills from a different batch, so there is no such thing as a small, low or weak dose when you are ingesting something unknown. The vast majority of ecstasy-related deaths are caused by six major factors:

- mixed drug toxicity (alcohol, opioids, other amphetamines, novel psychoactives etc.) or ingesting PMA/PMMA, other adulterants such as methylenedioxyprovalerone (MDPV), NBOMe analogues, n-ethylpentylone, MDA (as seen in Europe in 1992), 4-MTA or other unknown substances
- underlying or undiagnosed individual physiological condition. Unfortunately, there will always be a group of people who will suffer severe reactions for reasons that we do not understand or could have never predicted.
- drinking too much water following ecstasy use resulting in water poisoning
- heatstroke from dancing vigorously in the hot sun or in unventilated nightclubs
- suicide in days following ecstasy use
- *not MDMA*. MDMA overdoses have occurred, but they are very rare and only occur in non-clinical settings when high doses of MDMA have been used.

We must keep in mind, that leading up to the 1980s, prior to when MDMA was used in recreational settings and subsequently banned—when it was used in therapeutic settings—there was zero evidence of adverse health events and certainly no deaths. The 2009 paper by Kaye et al. found that of the eighty-two ecstasy-related deaths in Australia between 2000 and 2005, less than a quarter were caused by MDMA alone. The 2020 paper by Roxburgh and Lappin found that of the 392 MDMA-related deaths in Australia between 2000 and 2018, only four-teen per cent were caused by MDMA alone. So statistically, both of these papers found that in Australia, about three people die each year from MDMA toxicity, and that is across 750,000 annual users of ecstasy and millions of doses taken.

The question is why does PMA/PMMA exist? The base product of MDMA is safrole, which is synthesised from sassafras oil, harvested pri-marily from the sassafras tree. Safrole acts as a natural insecticide for the more than 360 tree species from which it is derived. Using mechani-cal string, trimmers and grinders, safrole is distilled by shredding the roots, bark, branches and leaves, then suspending the material over heated water in a large steel cauldron. A connected outlet pipe funnels the safrole-abundant steam into a condensing chamber. Although the sassafras tree is native to parts of the US, the majority of sassafras oil is harvested from tropical parts of Asia. There are a number of precursor routes to MDMA, such as MDP-2-P, beta-nitroisosafrole and piperonal. However, the essential oil safrole is the preferred synthesising precursor because it requires fewer steps and generates greater yield.

Although safrole is used in various legitimate products, such as fla-vourings and fragrances, it is a well-known prohibited precursor to MDMA, which means that purchasing in bulk immediately places you on the radar of policing authorities. Near its origin, safrole oil sells for approximately fifty dollars per litre, and one litre can produce thousands of ecstasy tablets, depending on purity. In response to the use of saf-role as a precursor in the manufacturing of MDMA, the UN introduced stringent controls in the late 1990s regulating the supply of safrole and sassafras oil. Safrole is now a Schedule 10 substance in Australia. Following the restrictions, enforcement authorities around the world made several large seizures, resulting in a substantial decline in safrole availability. There was a fifty-tonne seizure made in Thailand in 2007, a thirty-three-tonne seizure of safrole made in 2008 in Cambodia, and a 300-litre seizure made in Indonesia in 2013. All of the seized safrole was destroyed. Around the same time, a major MDMA bust took place in Australia uncovering 15,000,000 pills that had been trafficked from Naples to Melbourne in tomato cans.

Collectively, these seizures starved the ecstasy market of hundreds of millions of pills. Although production of MDMA was made difficult by the controls on safrole, demand for ecstasy was undeterred and continued to drive supply; this is where PMA/PMMA came in. Criminal manufacturers of ecstasy looked for a substitute for MDMA and quickly discovered that if anethole instead of safrole, synthesised from anise oil (instead of sassafras oil), underwent similar a chemical processing as sassafras oil, the result was another amphetamine (PMA or PMMA, depending on the chemical reaction used in manufacturing). The beauty of anethole for criminal manufacturers was that due to the fact that it is widely used for its fragrance utility in perfumes, foods and soaps, it cannot be controlled without destroying multiple industries. *Pimpinella anisum* (aniseed) and *Illicium verum* (star anise) both contain up to ninety per cent anethole.

PMA/PMMA existed in criminal networks before controls on safrole were introduced, but they were used for their hallucinogenic properties as substitutes for LSD. PMA/PMMA were originally studied for their potentially beneficial effects on mood. However, as the drugs provided no clear benefit, they were discarded and illegalised in the UN conventions. As MDMA grew in popularity throughout the 1970s and 1980s, PMA/PMMA deaths stopped and did not return for almost twenty years. Due to the fact that MDMA was significantly lower in toxicity, as well as providing users with rapid and euphoric effects, PMA/PMMA only returned to the illicit market due to the crackdown on MDMA's precursor.

PMA/PMMA is slow, unpleasant and toxic; however, it exists simply because authorities have tried to stop individuals using MDMA. Illicit drug manufacturers no longer need to go through the process of extracting sassafras oil and turning it into safrole anymore, as they soon figured out that it would be much more efficient to just artificially produce safrole. And now due to this underground enlightenment, there are copious amounts of safrole, which is why MDMA purity has sky-rocketed over the past few years. On top of PMA/PMMA pills, we now have super strength MDMA pills. In the US between 1999 and 2016, the number of novel psychoactive substance (NPS) deaths where PMA/PMMA was a significant factor increased by over 800 per cent, while in the UK, NPS deaths rose from three in 1999, to over 120 in 2016.

The NPS trade was able to flourish through the development of the dark web, and for some time, sellers were able to evade drug, food and medicine legislation by labelling compounds 'not for human consumption' as room deodoriser, plant food or bath salts. When they were sold for human consumption, they were often labelled health supplements, and they were imported from unsuspecting countries. In 2005, the EMCDDA early warning system made approximately 1,000 NPS seizures. By 2010 this had risen to 20,000, and in 2015, about 75,000 seizures were made.

❧

The other reason for ecstasy-related fatalities is acute water poisoning (also known as water intoxication), which typically occurs when users of ecstasy presume that drinking copious amounts of water will stave off the negative effects of MDMA, such as overheating and dehydration. Cases of water poisoning have also been reported in other circumstances, such as water drinking competitions. Overheating and dehydration can occur as a result of MDMA administration. However, this is typically if a very high dose is ingested, if the person is exercising or dancing energetically or if the drug is taken in hot environments. As MDMA is a scheduled drug with no approved medical usage, it exists only as an illegal substance with no regulatory control, and therefore, users are unaware whether they are taking a high dose or not.

Users often assume that if they drink a large amount of water, this will keep them in the safe zone, particularly if they have taken a large dose. Although water consumption may to some extent keep the users hydrated, this is a big catch 22. Not only does MDMA secrete antidiuretic hormone (reduce kidneys ability to rid excess water), but it also interferes with nerves on the bladder, meaning that individuals are unable, or feel no sensation to urinate.

The combination of rapid, high water intake, perspiration from using MDMA, and/or dancing leads to a significant drop in sodium (salt) levels in the body, leading to a condition caused hyponatremia. Hypo = low, natr = prefix for sodium, emia = blood-related, so hyponatremia indicates low levels of sodium in the blood. The first stages of hyponatremia include dizziness, confusion, nausea and headaches, possibly progressing to severe symptoms, such as seizures, unconsciousness and death. Hyponatremia occurs due to homeostatic imbalances in plasma osmolality (this means that there are dangerous electrolyte imbalances). Under normal conditions, extracellular (outside cells/bloodstream) fluid is evenly balanced with intracellular (inside cells) fluid in terms of water and sodium concentration. Sodium levels are higher in the bloodstream than within intracellular fluid, as water may pass from the bloodstream to intracellular fluid unreservedly. Sodium, however, does not enter the cell freely and must pass through ion channels. With rapid voluminous water consumption, the extracellular concentration of sodium falls due to being flooded with water and becomes disproportionately low compared to intracellular sodium levels. The body attempts to correct this imbalance by drawing water into the intracellular fluid, therefore increasing its water content and achieving a homeostatic equilibrium between the intracellular fluid and extracellular fluid in terms of water/electrolyte concentrations.

As water is drawn into the intracellular fluid, the cells expand in size. When cells in the brain expand, this causes the brain to expand in actual size. As the brain is spatially constrained by a fixed, bony structure (the skull), it has no room to expand. Brain function of patients becomes significantly compromised and can ultimately lead to cerebral oedema or a brain herniation, which is very likely to either kill the patient or leave them significantly disabled. This is due to increased pressure on areas of the brain that control key bodily functions, such as respiration. If respiration is arrested and the brain is starved of oxygen (cerebral hypoxia), the brain will begin to die after a few minutes.

Treatment of patients with hyponatremia depends on underlying cause and severity. Mild hyponatremia may be treated with fluid restriction, adequate sodium and protein intake, and aquaretic drugs, such as conivaptan and tolvaptan. With severe cases involving cerebral oedema, the priority in terms of treatment is surgery to relieve intracranial pressure.

Although it is understandable why an individual would consume large amounts of water following MDMA use due to the stimulatory effects of the drug, this was facilitated by licensed venue legislation, for example, the *Liquor Control Act 1988 (WA)*, *Liquor Licencing Act 1997 (SA)*, and *Liquor Act 2007 (NSW)*. Although licensed venues in each Australian state are regulated by different legislation, all licensed venues throughout the country must make available free drinking water for patrons at all times. This was enacted to curb excessive alcohol consumption, but also, particularly in nightclubs, to stop ecstasy-related deaths. The early ecstasy-related deaths, which had occurred in nightclubs (which were often poorly ventilated), were a result of dehydration and hyperthermia/hyperpyrexia. Ecstasy itself did not play a primary role in these deaths.

While many ecstasy users are not strangers to the nightclub scene, and the use of the drug may have heightened their experience or made them more likely to dance vigorously, the drug itself was not the cause of dehydration and hyperthermia. The excessive dancing, often associated with ecstasy use, was the primary cause of dehydration/hyperthermia deaths, not the actual drug, and the euphoric effects of MDMA can mask dehydration. Nightclubs also provided other measures in an attempt to reduce harm to illicit drug users, such as cool, quiet rooms. In fact, the notion of 'chilling out' originates from early ecstasy use in the jazz era, where those under the influence of the drug would either return home or retreat to back rooms of clubs and cool down.

The measures taken were a step in the right direction, however as previously stated, there is no such thing as a perfect solution in public health issues. Even widely accepted public health measures, such as RBTs are not without flaws. While it can be argued that many lives have been saved on the roads due to falling drink-driving rates, some have argued that this has given rise to a surge in binge drinking. It is suggested that since drinkers are deterred from consuming a handful of drinks before they drive due to RBTs, they either ask someone else (often their partner or a friend) to drive, so they can consume an enormous amount of alcohol. Additionally, instead of spreading their drinks across the entire week (which was the trend some years ago, when all you had to worry about was walking in a straight line in the unlikely event of being pulled over by the police), drinkers now abstain for a period of time and then consume a truckload of alcohol in one night. However, even though the rise in binge drinking may be a side effect of RBTs, this would not serve as a sufficient justification for discontinuing RBTs. Despite not being a perfect solution, the enormous fall in road fatalities resulted in a net benefit to the community.

Patrons who used ecstasy misunderstood the measures implemented. They assumed that water intake was an antidote to the negative effects of ecstasy, and consumed copious amounts of water. So, when ecstasy-related dehydration/hyperthermia deaths fell, they were replaced by hyponatremia deaths. Ecstasy users effectively drowned their brains under the misapprehension that water intake would save them, just as it would have (supposedly) saved past deaths.

Another major issue for the venues was that while patrons were provided with some measures aimed at increasing safety, those who popped a few ecstasy pills before heading out to go clubbing were in no need of additional drugs to enjoy their night, because the MDMA would last at least a few hours. This means that those who were using ecstasy were rarely drinking alcohol. Since many of the venues operated in expensive areas with very high running costs, it was necessary that they sell as much alcohol as possible. The use of ecstasy in licensed venues, however, attracted drug dealers, who attracted police (and sniffer dogs), which deterred patron attendance and lead to the closure of many clubs. There have been many venues throughout the world, such as Fabric in London (later reopened) and the Phoenician Club in Sydney, that were forced to close their doors after hosting events where patrons died after using illegal drugs, even though the venues had no causative role in the deaths.

∿

The final key risk with the use of MDMA outside of PMA and water poisoning is suicide in the days following use. Although some studies show that in the days following MDMA use, individuals experience depressive symptoms, other studies show that depressed individuals are more likely to use MDMA, so this may be a case of reverse causality. In exceedingly rare cases, MDMA has also been associated with deaths involving liver or kidney failure, heart attacks, brain haemorrhages and uncontrolled bleeding, as serotonin is involved in blood clot regulation. It is highly likely that genetic predispositions have played a major role in these cases, like peanuts triggering fatal allergic anaphylaxis. In pure statistical terms, taking an ecstasy tablet is as risky as riding a motorcycle for ten kilometres or a pushbike for thirty kilometres.

∿

So, if ecstasy deaths are extremely rare, and the ecstasy-related deaths are almost never caused by MDMA, why was MDMA banned in the first place? MDMA has existed for over 100 years, but it has only been of interest to the public for approximately thirty years. MDMA was accidently discovered by German scientist Dr Anton Köllisch at Merck as an intermediary precursor, while attempting to synthesise the blood-clotting agent hydrastinine. At the time, the plant used to derive hydrastinine, *Hydrastis canadensis*, was difficult to cultivate, so another German chemist, Dr Hermann Decker, created a synthetic synthesis route and sold it to the pharmaceutical company Bayer. Merck attempted to circumvent the synthetic route described in the patent, and in the process, Dr Köllisch synthesised MDMA.

At the time, it was customary for companies to patent every chemical on the synthesis route to eliminate competition. However, because this was an accidental discovery, and it was hydrastinine that was attempting to be synthesised, MDMA was left alone. Between 1920 and the 1950s, a number of researchers—most notably Dr Max Oberlin, Dr Albert Van Schoor and Dr Wolfgang Fruhstorfer—studied MDMA for a range of reasons, including its relative toxicity similarity to other stimulants such as ephedrine. Because MDMA was the first drug synthesised in circumvention of the law, it is widely regarded as the first designer drug.

In 1952 at the New York State Psychiatric Institute, MDMA and seven other drugs were studied in humans, and one subject was accidently given an overdose of the drug MDA (methylenedioxyamphetamine). MDA was originally tested as an anorectic drug (appetite suppressant) and became popular in the hippie culture of San Francisco's Haight Ashbury during the 1960s, before MDMA began to be used recreationally. It was known as the 'hug drug'—similar to MDMA but trippier and faster. MDA did not take off like MDMA because of its powerful hallucinogenic effects, and it did not generate nearly as much yield from precursors as MDMA did.

The first published studies of MDMA appeared in the late 1970s and 1980s, and due to the praise that chemists Alexander Shulgin, Dave Nichols and George Greer gave the drug, its use in clinical settings spread. MDMA was originally given the name 'Adam', as it supposedly produced effects of primal innocence, however, the name was later changed to 'Empathy'. It is suggested that MDMA missionary, Michael Clegg, coined the name 'ecstasy' after his personal experience with the drug in Mexico in 1978.

He later wrote, 'The night I took my first hit on the beach in Mexico, I said to myself—my mission in life is to get this to the entire world.' At the time, there was only one source of MDMA, a legion of underground chemists named 'the Boston Group' who produced and distributed the drug exclusively for therapeutic use. It was used in couples therapy to allow troubled partners to open up and talk with one another. It assisted chronically or terminally ill patients in facing their fate and communicating with their family without resentment over their diagnosis, and it was used to help victims of rape, incest or child abuse to come to terms with their past trauma.

Because the *Controlled Substances Act 1970* had already banned human research on psychedelic drugs, advocates attempted to keep MDMA under wraps and strictly for clinical use in the fear that it too would be prohibited for any purpose. However, by the mid-1980s, a conglomeration of manufacturers called 'the Texas Group' were able to popularise the name of the drug on a mass scale—selling half a million tablets each month in that state alone.

Originally, Shulgin was a consultant for the DEA, holding pharmacology seminars and serving as an expert witness. However, in 1994 after the DEA raided his lab, confiscated his chemicals and fined him $25,000 for violating the terms of his Schedule 1 license, he published his entire body of work in two pivotal psychedelic chemistry books— *PIHKAL (Phenethylamines I Have Known and Loved): A Chemical Love Story* and *TIHKAL (Tryptamines I Have Known and Loved)*.

Like the majority of drugs that we prohibit, before the 1980s MDMA existed as a medicine, although it was used by therapists in a somewhat underground fashion. Recreational use of MDMA began in the USA in the early 1980s, and moved into the European club scene in the late 1980s. When profits declined in nightclubs due to falls in alcohol sales, event organisers looked for large, open areas to hire, where the volume of entrants was huge and largely unrestricted, and they could charge for entry—this was the birth of large-scale dance music festivals. These events posed a legitimate threat to public health—thousands of people dancing, far away from hospitals, while on multiple drugs. At music festivals, there is also an increased likelihood that dealers will sell a toxic or counterfeit product, because dealers can easily blend in and get lost among thousands of people.

During this time, the media generated concern, which prompted politicians to begin the international illegalisation of MDMA. Once the USA banned the drug, the rest of the world would follow suit. As described by Mike Power in *Drugs 2.0*, the rise of nightclubs and the global dance scene during the 1980s and 1990s generated what could be described as the 'principal model of illegal youth culture in most of the world'.

The Texas Group was the primary manufacturer of ecstasy at this time, and when it became public knowledge that the DEA had plans to Schedule the drug, the group ramped up production to distribute as much ecstasy as possible. In the couple of months leading up to the scheduling, the amount of MDMA produced was almost equal to the total amount produced during the entire duration of business operation, and it is estimated that the Texas Group produced in excess of 2,000,000 ecstasy pills. By this time, MDMA was already illegal in the UK under a Modification Order made in 1977 to the *Misuse of Drugs Act*. This primarily occurred because a clandestine Shulgin-copycat chemist had been caught manufacturing MDMA, and because the Modification Order specified the mechanisms of ring substitution, many substances in Shulgin's books were banned before publication. The USA did not have as such broad legislation and, instead, relied on the *Federal Analogue Act*, a section of the *United States Controlled Substances Act* passed in 1986, which attempted to enforce against substances that were similar to already banned drugs.

The DEA filed their first intent to ban MDMA in 1984 after Texas Senator Lloyd Bentsen formally pleaded for its ban in 1983. In the initial 1984 hearings, leading psychiatrists, pharmacologists and therapists testified that the drug had medical applications, that it was different to other stimulants and hallucinogens, and that more research was needed, which would be made impossible if the drug was placed in Schedule 1. The DEA were so desperate to ban MDMA that an appeal for emergency scheduling was made, which was granted, and the drug was temporarily placed in Schedule 1 in 1985. Throughout May and June of 1986, John C. Lawn, who was Administrator of the DEA, ignored the recommendations of their own judge, Francis Young, who presided over the schedule hearing, to place MDMA in Schedule 3. Because Young was an administrative judge, he had no legal authority in dictating or overruling the DEA's decision. This would have allowed the drug to be used in medical settings, and sale without prescription would be illegal, without blanket prohibition. The medical community overwhelmingly objected to the anti-scientific scheduling by the DEA, however, virtually all efforts were ignored. Since this time, some practitioners have administered it illegally, but the vast majority were afraid of being prosecuted or losing their licences. *At the time, MDMA was the only drug to have ever been emergency scheduled in this fashion.*

After years of fiery debate and hearings, MDMA was re-legalised in late January 1988 thanks to a successful appeal made by Harvard Professor Lester Grinspoon. However, going against the entire medical, scientific and legal community, the DEA decided on 23 March in that same year that MDMA was to be permanently placed in Schedule 1. In order for the drug to be granted emergency scheduling, evidence of imminent threat to public safety had to be proven.

There were three arguments that the DEA put forward to justify their position on illegalising MDMA urgently:

- The drug causes brain damage.
- The drug causes Parkinson's disease.
- The drug has no medical utility.

The concept that the drug is a cause of brain damage originated from evidence presented by Dr Lewis Seiden, Professor of Neuropharmacology at the University of Chicago. Seiden presented research that was conducted looking at the effects of MDMA on brain cells. Although there were no problems with the research in terms of the methodology or findings, four major flaws were present, given that the research was used as a foundation for the DEA's proposition to ban MDMA.

The first flaw was that the research was conducted on rodents, not on humans, and therefore it could not be assumed that the effect produced in the rodents would be comparable to the effects in humans. The second flaw was that the rodents were administered with the drug through an injection, however, humans ingest the drug orally. Administration through injection is exponentially more risky than oral ingestion. The third flaw was that MDA was the drug used, not MDMA, and even though the two drugs come from the same class, they are very different in terms of effect type and duration. The fourth flaw was that the research conducted revealed that intravenous MDA administration resulted in changes in neuronal axon terminals, which are sections of neurons that facilitate electrical impulses. These changes, however, were not deemed to be necessarily negative, and certainly did not result in brain damage.

In essence, the study conducted is irrelevant when looking at MDMA control because the research was not on humans, was with a different drug, with a different ROA, and did not result in significant negative findings.

However, while there are many who favour prohibition on the basis that these drugs have demonstrated adverse outcomes in animals, MDMA enthusiasts must be very careful not to do the same. I have met some very keen ecstasy users who have claimed that taking supplements, such as alpha-lipoid acid, sildenafil, carnitine or various other vitamins/minerals, offer a range of physiological protective aspects. However, these too are based on animal studies. Therefore, those who discredit the evidence of MDMA toxicity must treat the evidence regarding supplements that reverse any potential harms with equal validity; it is hypocritical to claim that animal evidence demonstrating harm is not good enough, but claim that animal evidence demonstrating benefit is good enough.

A further paper was released in 2002 by Johns Hopkins University researcher, Dr George Ricaurte, entitled 'Severe dopaminergic neurotoxicity in primates after a common recreational dose regimen of MDMA'. The study was published in *Science,* and was widely reported throughout the media, and cited by authorities, such as the director of NIDA, who claimed 'This says that even a single evening's use is playing Russian roulette with your brain'. The study was later retracted because the vials used in the study contained methamphetamine, not MDMA.

The media were not interested in the retraction, and the public were left with the idea that MDMA caused brain damage, which is incorrect and portrays the drug as more harmful than what it is. If a study or claim is retracted or refuted by fresh evidence, it needs to be given at least the same amount of airtime as the original suggestion. The public should either be not alarmed in the first place or, at the very least, wrongs should be righted.

The same goes for drug-related deaths reported by the media. The vast majority of ecstasy-related deaths have proven not to be caused by MDMA. However, inevitably, they are immediately claimed to be 'ecstasy overdoses' before toxicological reports could possibly have taken place. Not only does this inaccurately portray MDMA being much more harmful than it actually is, but it also drastically reduces the ability for these drugs to be studied for their treatment utility—or even contemplated by the public as possible medicines—and it sends a message to ecstasy users that if they just take a low dose, they will be safe.

Strong evidence has recently emerged from brain imaging studies suggesting that changes in brain sections affected by MDMA are not long term. Any cognitive impairment tends to be mild and reversible upon cessation. Studies looking into individuals who have used only ecstasy and no other drugs (including alcohol) have found no differences in cognitive functioning compared to those who have taken no drugs. MDMA has been shown to damage 5-HT nerve terminals in the brains of rats and monkeys. However, studies in humans have never yielded comparable results. Toxicity to animals does not mean toxicity to humans and vice versa—for example, chocolate to cats and dogs.

Studies attempting to link MDMA use to brain damage have also often not accounted for confounding factors, such as prior drug use, polydrug use or that users may have taken ecstasy that does not actually contain MDMA. There is also the issue of publication bias, where the conclusions that authors come to are often exaggerated or at odds with the data produced in the study. An example of this was the 2007 paper 'Cognition in novice ecstasy users with minimal exposure to other drugs: A prospective cohort study', where the authors concluded that 'even a first low cumulative dose of ecstasy is associated with a decline in verbal memory'. However, if you look at the data in the study, cognitive tests were completely normal, and there was no decline in memory. The entire claim was based on the finding that there was no increase in memory.

The second case put forward was that MDMA is a cause of Parkinson's disease. Around the same time that MDMA entered the public spotlight (early 1980s) in terms of its potential ban, a handful of intravenous heroin users in California made headlines when they unintentionally administered themselves with a substance known as MPTP (1-methyl-4-phenyl-1,2,3,6-tetrahydropyridine).

MPTP is a prodrug, meaning that it is not a pharmacologically active compound until it is metabolised in the body. It is essentially a precursor to a drug, until biological bodily functions transform the prodrug into an active compound. Prodrugs are used in medicine because they may be less toxic, be more efficient in terms of metabolism or target specific areas or functions more effectively. Two common examples of prodrugs are aspirin, which is converted in salicylate, and valaciclovir, which is converted into acyclovir. Aspirin is commonly used to treat conditions, such as pain and inflammation, whereas valaciclovir is used to treat herpes.

In regards to MPTP as a prodrug, an enzyme in the brain converts this substance into another chemical called MPP+ (1-methyl-4-phenyl-pyridinium). The '+' symbol at the end of the acronym indicates that the molecule is a cation, meaning it is a positively charged ion. MPP+ is neurotoxic, meaning that it is injurious to neurons in nerve tissue, which are the primary component of both the central and peripheral nervous system, which essentially govern as well as regulate all bodily functions. MPP+ affects neurons by damaging the mitochondria, which is a subunit of cells that play a key role in generating and controlling cellular energy, signalling, cycle, and death. One of the primary roles of the mitochondria is to produce adenosine triphosphate (ATP, which is a source of chemical energy that is used to undertake various biological functions). When the mitochondrion becomes damaged, depletion of ATP ensues, and with a depletion of ATP, cells begin to die prematurely. MPP+ is pumped from the extracellular fluid to dopamine nerve terminals by the dopamine transporter. As the majority of dopamine is produced in the dopaminergic neurons within the substantia nigra pars compacta, this is the area of the brain that is detrimentally affected by MPP+. Deterioration in motor control, among other symptoms of Parkinson's disease, is a result of cell death in the substantia nigra pars compacta.

MPTP, which is converted to the toxin MPP+, was produced as an accidental by-product in the attempted synthesis of an illicit heroin substitute known as MPPP (1-methyl-4-proprionoxypiperidine). In one particular case in California, at least seven heroin users developed Parkinson's disease following injection of what they thought was heroin or synthetic heroin, but instead contained MPTP. This was far from an isolated event; however, this particular case was highly publicised, and many television broadcasts that were documenting the use of MDMA began documenting the use of MPTP.

MPPP and MPP+ are completely unrelated to MDMA by almost every metric. However, as each of these substances are illegal, began with the same letter, and was represented by a four-letter acronym, the synchronicity lead to the public tarring all compounds with the same brush. The harmfulness of MPTP, MPPP and MPP+ is entirely irrelevant for almost any discussion regarding regulation of MDMA, and yet evidence surrounding these chemicals was used as a justification to illegalise MDMA.

The third main argument is that the drug has no medical benefits. Unfortunately, by the time MDMA had entered the public eye, no clinical trials had been undertaken. Despite the fact that the medical community protested against the banning of MDMA, as they were certain it would end its use as a therapy, the evidence surrounding MDMA's use as an adjunct treatment in psychotherapy at this stage was almost entirely anecdotal. There was a mountain of evidence from pharmacologists, psychologists, psychiatrists, chemists, psychotherapists and patients, but as none of the evidence was in the form of clinical trials, the drug was dismissed as a therapy. There were virtually no reports from therapists of adverse effects and certainly no deaths.

It is only now that MDMA has been studied in a very limited fashion as a treatment for PTSD, alcoholism and depression. It is thought that the medical utility of MDMA in treating PTSD is caused by the drug's ability to allow patients to confront past trauma in terms of the factual events without the emotion. In the early days of MDMA-assisted therapy and prior to its prohibition, therapists said that the drug allowed patients to find solutions to their problems by enabling them to open up and engage in objective analysis. MDMA also increases empathy, meaning that patients are also more likely to stay in the room and engage with the therapist for longer. It is extremely difficult for individuals who have been traumatised to talk about and re-live past trauma without getting overwhelmed with the emotion attached to it. With the increasing numbers of military personnel being involved in armed combat throughout the world, the prevalence of PTSD is going to rise, and those affected will demand an effective treatment.

A 2012 study by Mithoefer et al. showed that MDMA-assisted psychotherapy resulted in significant reductions in symptom severity at two months post treatment, and greater reductions were shown at four years post treatment. There have now been four separate trials of treating PTSD with MDMA-assisted psychotherapy, all of which have shown great promise—approximately sixty to seventy-five per cent of participants met criteria for being PTSD-free. Many sufferers of PTSD also drink alcohol excessively to suppress traumatic memories, meaning that MDMA may hold utility to stop people drinking. However, using an illegal drug that carries a lot of baggage to treat problems associated with a socially accepted legal drug is an extremely challenging concept for the public to grasp. It's much easier for the government to assert that disorders, such as alcoholism, are moral weaknesses for three reasons.

Firstly, it means that the message can be reduced to a simplistic 'just get over it'. Secondly, it means that funding doesn't need to be allocated towards the issue. Thirdly, it appeases the alcohol industry, who wants to protect profits by thriving on the concept that people with alcohol-related problems cannot 'enjoy responsibly'.

~⁂~

Even if we erred on the side of caution and concluded that at the time, MDMA had no clinically proven benefits, what the prohibition of MDMA did achieve was the silencing of any anecdotal evidence and the elimination of the possibility of any future research. It's like putting an innocent person in jail, not giving them a trial, and then throwing away the key. Government-funded medical research, after all, has made it possible for society to be provided with countless medicines, such as penicillin, the polio vaccine and chemotherapy drugs. As simple as it is for the government to make researching drugs possible, it is just as simple, as in the case of MDMA, to make the research impossible, even if it means stopping active research.

An example of this occurred in the UK, where a group of researchers began working on a series of MDMA analogues to treat PD and dyskinesia—both of which are neurological disorders. Around the same time, 'head shops' began selling products of a similar nature for recreational use. Head shops are outlets that specialise in selling tobacco products as well as other drug paraphernalia and are perfectly legal as long as they do not sell illicit products. Following the media hysteria over the retail of these products, the UK government decided to impose a blanket ban on MDMA analogues. However, due to the broad nature of the ban, this included the compounds that were being researched, meaning that researchers needed Schedule 1 licences to continue. The research ceased because such licences are out of financial reach to the groups conducting the research. So now, the development of new drugs to treat these debilitating illnesses is severely restrained because of cost and regulatory hurdles, as well as investors regarding any work with illegal drugs as an indirect message of condoning drug use. Placebos can also be controlled drugs, such as cannabis placebos in the UK, meaning special import/export licenses are needed, and licenses only last for short periods of time, meaning they can expire before suppliers can sort out all contractual/compliance documents, restarting the entire process. It is a legal requirement that research personnel be trained in how to handle and dispose of such substances, the substances have to be locked in an official fridge, cabinet or safe, and there has to be security surveillance—all of which adds to cost. Given that the majority of researchers do not have the time, money, patience or energy to work through the convoluted regulations, it's not surprising that researching the medical utility of illicit drugs has occurred at a snail's pace.

This resistance to study safer alternatives to alcohol or treatments for alcoholism exists even amongst people who would benefit, such as UK MP Jim Dobbin, who died in late 2014 of acute alcohol poisoning. Dobbin died in Poland after drinking a series of shots during a meal, which elevated his blood alcohol level to about 0.4, which is eight times the legal Australian driving limit or five times the UK legal driving limit. He mentioned feeling unwell at the end of the meal, was advised to sleep it off, and when his wife checked on him that night, she was unable to wake him. Dobbin was found to have food in his lungs, meaning he would have choked to death while unconscious.

Prior to his death, Dobbin had attacked numerous senior British scientists for studying the therapeutic utility of illegal drugs, and using his parliamentary privilege, he attempted to revoke the licenses of several researchers. This is despite the fact that very scientists and science he was trying to censor could have developed a safer alternative to alcohol or a treatment for alcoholism that may have perhaps saved his life.

In the period of time from its prohibition to today, it is unquestionable that thousands, possibly millions of people would have benefitted from the use of MDMA in therapy. Given that the cost of mental illness to the Australian community is approximately $60,000,000,000 and that the cost to Europe and the USA is in the trillions for each, it is absurd to deny patients access to treatment simply on the basis of invalid historical abnormalities. One of the reasons the cost of mental illness is so high is because many patients are treatment resistant, meaning that they are ill for longer (if they ever go onto remission or recover), which adds to the medical, individual and social costs both directly and indirectly.

It was also purported that MDMA puts holes in the brain, which is entirely unfounded, and that MDMA drains spinal fluid, which is also untrue—this most likely originating from the fact that those pinging on MDMA had been dancing for hours, causing them to have a stiff back afterwards. In the 1980s, research on ecstasy users involved spinal taps (lumbar punctures—procedures that do drain spinal fluid), and in 1994, further research was conducted into the spinal fluid of ecstasy users. The research simply looked at the broken-down products or serotonin in cerebrospinal fluid. MDMA does not damage the spine.

MDMA became popular among young people for a number of reasons:

- There was a new drug to take, new music to listen to and lots of fun to be had.
- The oral ROA was convenient, and the appearance of the pills was similar to pharmaceuticals.
- The fear of snorting or injecting something foreign that could result in addiction, diseases or overdose was removed.
- The fear of losing control through hallucinations caused by psychedelic-type drugs was removed.

- Ecstasy seemed like almost a healthy alternative to alcohol; everyone was happy, healthy and dressed in bright colours, as opposed to being drunk, violent, offensive or passed out in the gutter.

These non-arguments have been fuelled by a number of hysterical comments made by high profile individuals in the press, such as director of the Drug Abuse Research Centre at the University of Chicago, Dr Charles Schuster, who stated that MDMA can 'poison the nervous system, possibly irreversibly'. Or worse, when Richard Fiano, the DEA chief of operations, stated in a 2000 press conference, 'what is happening over the next couple of days after taking ecstasy their brain cells are actually being programmed to die'.

In 2001, the USA Sentencing Commission quadrupled the mandatory minimum for possessing 200 grams of MDMA from fifteen months to five years prison, and tripled the mandatory minimum for possessing two kilograms of MDMA (equivalent to 8,000 pills) from three years to ten years prison.

～✺～

I rarely, if ever, initiate a conversation on the topic of drugs with people, as I am fully aware that my interest in drugs may exceed theirs, causing them to be subjected to a seemingly never-ending lecture. However, one comment or question that is always mentioned in regards to ecstasy is you can always get a bad pill and what happens if you get a bad pill? While this is true, this is a statement or question directed towards ecstasy, not MDMA. Ecstasy is a slang street name for the drug MDMA, just as bootleg or moonshine is a street name for illegal alcohol. You can get bad ecstasy, but you cannot get bad MDMA. You can get bad moonshine, but you cannot get bad ethanol. Despite the repeal of alcohol prohibition in the USA not fully eliminating the production and distribution of illicit alcohol, individuals today who purchase alcohol from licensed premises know what they are consuming and to what level. Imagine purchasing bootleg beer, and being sold a product that is forty per cent alc/vol. instead of four to five per cent alc/vol. If the taste did not warn of the content, consuming an amount that would constitute 'a few beers' with something that is forty per cent alc/vol. is likely to place the drinker into a lethal coma.

～✿～

Those who support allowing recreational, regulated access to select illicit drugs, such as cannabis or MDMA, are consistently criticised for proposing a regime that sanctions less control or lets drugs off the chain, when they are advocating for the complete opposite. As Peter Reynolds from CLEAR Cannabis Law Reform stated in a debate at Southampton Debating Union when discussing the topic of whether cannabis should be decriminalised, 'We are not advocating for less control, we are actually advocating for more control'. Many people fear legalisation or decriminalisation because they view it as a loss of control. However, this mistakenly presumes that law enforcement does control the illicit trade, when, in fact, it is prohibition that is the abdication of control.

As he states in regards to cannabis, the fact that the drug is not subject to regulations that the pharmaceutical, alcohol, tobacco and food industries must comply with, means that there is zero control on illicit products sold. Allowing regulated access does not imply indirect endorsement or encouragement, but it does mean the product can be available in controlled, low and consistent doses, as opposed to being available in unregulated, potent and erratic doses.

The efforts by the DEA to supress MDMA use have been a complete failure. USA customs seized 750,000 pills in 1998, 3,500,000 in 1999 and 9,300,000 in 2000. Now, between 20,000,000 and 25,000,000 Americans have used ecstasy at least once in their lifetime, and about 1,000,000 are monthly users.

We know that MDMA is not a perfectly safe drug, but practically every ecstasy-related death could have been avoided if people knew what they were ingesting and were given appropriate harm-reduction advice. You do not get bad paracetamol, bad caffeine, bad alcohol, bad tobacco or bad codeine in Australia, because every single one of these drugs is subjected to rigorous testing before it is made available. In Indonesia, a form of moonshine known as arrack can contain methanol, which causes vomiting, blindness, organ failure and death, because it is illegally manufactured. You can get a bad hit of acid (NBOMe/N-Bomb analogues, which cause seizures, serotonin syndrome, hyperthermia and clonus at sub-milligram doses) as Henry Kwan and Nick Mitchell did in Australia in 2013, because it is illegally manufactured. The media reported these cases to be deaths caused by synthetic LSD, even though the two boys took an entirely different drug. You can get bad pot (synthetic cannabinoids, which cause acute psychosis, seizures, convulsions and heart attacks), just as you can get bad pills that may contain PMA/PMMA or other amphetamine-type drugs, which are much more toxic or potent than MDMA, because they are both illegally manufactured.

While drugs like MDMA that are used recreationally are not safe, the result of disallowing regulated access is the circulation of products that are erratic in both potency and contents, leading to bad batches and bad pills. Although we cannot predict with perfect accuracy how someone will respond to any product, this argument can be made for anything humans consume—after all, many people die every year after having allergic reactions to food or pharmaceutical drugs.

We need to be honest and objective about drug harms—if someone negates the harm of a drug because it is blown up or fictitious, and then that person gets criticised for implicitly encouraging use, that is most likely because that person is beginning to unravel all of the untruths they have been told throughout their life.

One of the arguments against allowing the public regulated access to drugs that are currently illegal is that you are playing Russian roulette with your life, or you could get the 'empty chamber'. This is actually an argument against an unregulated market because regulated markets subject the compounds to rigorous testing and keep the risk as small as possible. Drug checking is covered in greater detail in Part Two of this book. The inherent harm of the drug itself is small compared to the harms generated by its prohibition.

Australia has now taken the prohibitive approach to MDMA use a step further, by not only enforcing against the actual possession of MDMA, but also against the suspected possession and past possession of MDMA. In early June 2018, NSW Police announced that at a large music event in Sydney, they would exclude entry to patrons if sniffer dogs sat down next to a person, which would indicate the presence of drugs. This is despite the fact that the person could have used the drug in the past (which you cannot prosecute for), that the person could have been in the presence of someone using the drug (which you cannot prosecute for) and that sniffer dogs get it wrong (both false positives and false negatives) up to seventy-five per cent of the time.

This overreaching move from the police force is an example of how zero tolerance is the main focus of authorities, even though this approach cannot be described in any other way other than gross infringement on personal freedoms, particularly considering police could deny entry even if no drugs were found, rendering individuals guilty by association. It can also be an unpleasant and traumatic experience for individuals who are incorrectly identified. At the end of 2016, NSW Police boasted about not only seizing a myriad of drug paraphernalia, but also, half a dozen ecstasy testing kits, which were perfectly legal to possess. NSW Police uploaded a picture on their Facebook page until criticised for not having grounds to confiscate the legal kits, after which the post was deleted. This was an operation for media/social media purposes, designed to send a symbolic message that the police are 'tough on drugs'. Individual police officers, however, should not be held to account for these actions. They swear an oath to uphold the law, regardless of whether they hate busting people for smoking a joint or taking a pill. That's not what they want to do. It is sad that many retired police officers reject legislation that they used to enforce, yet were unable to speak out at the time, because that would have undermined their role and the entire system they represented.

If it were concluded that the prohibition of certain drugs actually led to net increases in harms, at what point should the line be drawn to allow access to other drugs? One drug that would be very difficult to advocate for regulated access is methamphetamine.

9

POOKIE – METHAMPHETAMINE

I f you were an alien reading any Australian newspaper over the past few years, you could be forgiven for thinking that Australia had been completely frozen over by an ice age. Ice is slang for the drug methamphetamine, a stimulant drug within the amphetamine class. Methamphetamine typically goes under the name of speed (powder form), ice (crystallised form) or base (liquid form). Approximately six to seven per cent of Australians have used the drug, with approximately one to two per cent having used the drug in the past year.

Despite the fact that ice use has increased in Australia, it is important to note that total amphetamine use (including other forms, such as speed and base) has remained largely stable. This is due to the fact that many methamphetamine users have moved away from less potent forms towards ice, which is pure methamphetamine hydrochloride. The drug is called ice because the final product resembles shards of glass or frozen water. Methamphetamine is a potent stimulant that provides users with feelings of increased confidence and energy. Users also experience increased sex drive, which increases the risk of unplanned pregnancy, sexually transmitted disease, as well as sexual assault, due to the drug potentially producing additional effects of agitation and aggression.

As with all drugs, the use of methamphetamine is a zero-sum game. Due to the fact that the effects of methamphetamine can last for several days, the initial energy provided results in a massive crash, and the extensive comedown from the drug results in insomnia, delusions, restlessness and extreme tiredness. It is very rare for someone to die from an amphetamine overdose, but it does happen and is usually the result of a stroke or heart attack as the drug raises blood pressure and heart rate and constricts blood vessels. Long-term use of amphetamines causes damage to the heart and may result in arrhythmia, which can cause light headedness, chest pain, shortness of breath, and, if serious, can put the user at increased risk of heart failure or stroke. The effects of administering amphetamine orally kick in after around thirty minutes, with effects from snorting experienced after a few minutes and effects from injecting experienced almost instantly. The typical cost and dose of amphetamine varies as it depends on purity and ROA. Oral dosage of methamphetamine ranges from five to 100 mg, which can last up to twelve hours, compared to intravenous doses that range from five to forty milligrams and last six to seven hours.

Pure pharmaceutical grade methamphetamine consists of equal amounts of levo-methamphetamine and dextro-methamphetamine. The safety ratio of methamphetamine is ten, which is equivalent to alcohol, and between ecstasy and heroin.

Methamphetamine users may also experience 'meth mouth' (oral cavity damage, particularly tooth decay). This is likely to be caused by a combination of methamphetamine-induced causes, such as dry mouth and bruxism, as well as non-methamphetamine-induced causes, such as consumption of acidic or high-sugar carbonated drinks, poor oral hygiene and concomitant tobacco smoking. Amphetamine, and particularly methamphetamine, is considered to be a drug with a high propensity for addiction, and the damaging effects of addiction often outweigh the biological harm caused to the individual. Approximately one in three individuals who use methamphetamine will become dependent at some point (capture rate of approximately thirty per

cent), and about ten per cent of individuals who have used methamphetamine will become addicted. Long-term use of amphetamine can
destroy quality of life for users by causing anhedonia, a condition characterised by failing to get any pleasure out of life without the existence
of the drug. Anhedonia can remain for extended periods of time after
users quit. There is evidence that use of amphetamine causes changes
in brain structure, and use of methamphetamine (particularly repeated
administration) is toxic to dopamine neurons in the substantia nigra,
which is why methamphetamine use is linked to an increased risk of
Parkinson's disease.

～⁓

The common public perception of methamphetamine users is similar
to that of heroin users: derelicts or junkies who are a blight on society.
However, many people use amphetamines for reasons other than feeding an addiction.

Amphetamines have been around for over 100 years, with benzedrine being the first pharmaceutical product to contain amphetamines.
Methamphetamine is used as a second-line treatment for narcolepsy and
ADHD, which is interesting as the effects of amphetamines are almost
diagnostic of ADHD. Adderall (amphetamine/dextroamphetamine),
Ritalin and Concerta (methylphenidate) are the most commonly used
amphetamine-type drugs, used to treat narcolepsy and ADHD. These
drugs are often taken in the morning because this allows the individuals
to stay focused during the day for school or work. When the drugs wear
off later in the day resulting in fatigue, the individual can sleep better
and improve their sleep cycle. Some practitioners are sceptical of the
classification of ADHD as a mental disorder and do not prescribe medication, which can lead to students not engaging with education, which
can result in a poor start in life. I am not denying that some children
could do with some serious discipline or other intervention, such as
alternative teaching techniques or using technology or computer games

to aid their brain instead of drugs, but prescribing medication to some students at least gives them an opportunity to succeed at school.

University and college students typically use amphetamines to keep themselves awake so they can study for longer or as a stimulatory measure so they can 'peak' for exams. In medicine, this is known as 'diversion', where an individual uses a drug outside of guidelines, not for medical reasons and without medical advice. Using an 'upper', such as modafinil, to maintain alertness or study for longer can be counterproductive and lead to poorer results in school or exam performance due to the crash when the drug has worn off. The user may be deprived of sleep, and even though they may have studied for longer, memory of material may not be maintained. Using an upper to peak for an exam can also be problematic, as it may overstimulate the user, causing them to make mistakes such as answering the same questions twice, missing sections, not reading question correctly or producing confusing answers.

As mentioned, benzedrine was the first available medication that contained amphetamine and was marketed initially as a decongestant inhaler by the pharmaceutical company Smith, Kline & French, which exists today as GlaxoSmithKline (GSK), one of the largest pharmaceutical companies in the world. Benzedrine was replaced by Benzedrex (propylhexedrine) when amphetamine became a controlled substance and is sold today by BF Ascher Company Incorporated.

Methamphetamine was first synthesised in Japan in 1893 by Nagai Nagayoshi, and methamphetamine hydrochloride (acid salt version) was synthesised by another Japanese chemist Akira Ogata in 1919. Amphetamines were widely prescribed by doctors for fatigue from 1930 to around 1950, and the use of amphetamines became popular during World War II, particularly with go/no-go pills used by the armed forces. A 'go pill' contains a stimulant used for fatigue management, while a 'no-go pill' contains a sedative, such as temazepam or diazepam, used to provide rest as part of recovery.

The USA Air Force banned the use of amphetamines in the military after the 2002 Tarnak Farm friendly-fire incident. After a ten-hour night patrol in Afghanistan, two USA fighter jet pilots mistakenly bombed a group of Canadian allies, killing four and injuring eight. The pilots had taken 'go-pills' containing amphetamines as part of their patrol, and despite the controller from airborne early warning and control advising the pilots to hold fire, the pilots did not wait for confirmation. Approximately thirty seconds after the pilots had called 'bombs away', they were advised that on the ground were Canadian allies. The pilots blamed amphetamines for their poor judgement and decision made in haste.

Amphetamines were banned in most western countries during the 1960s. Like most drugs that were originally developed for good purposes, such as spiritual or medical use, once amphetamines leaked outside of regulated networks to recreational markets, they became increasingly demonised. Two of the precursor chemicals used to synthesise methamphetamine are ephedrine (Schedule 4 in Australia) and pseudoephedrine (Schedule 3 or 4, depending on amount). Ephedrine is synthesised from ephedra, which is extracted from the ephedra plant species. Ephedra has been used in traditional Chinese medicine for thousands of years, however, it is banned in Australia. In 2006, regulations on pseudoephedrine were tightened with availability only through prescription or a pharmacist after identification is produced and logged through the computer program *Project STOP*. Over the counter medications originally containing pseudoephedrine have now been replaced with phenylephrine in an effort to stop the manufacture of methamphetamine.

Methamphetamine has been the drug that has gathered the most attention in Australia over recent times, with newspaper front page headlines reading 'Ice epidemic', 'Ice age', 'A generation on ice', 'Ice avalanche', 'Ice hits school' and 'On ice, aged 10'. Not only are these headlines largely fictitious, they generate an enormous moral and social panic that misleads the public into believing that Australia is in the midst of an apocalyptic methamphetamine crisis, which is far from true.

The Examiner headline 'ice avalanche' refers to a story covering a small area of Tasmania, which reported a tenfold increase in amphetamine drug seizures for the 2014 year. This is despite the fact that this is more than double the rate for all of Tasmania, fifteen times greater than South Australia as well as ACT, forty-five times greater than the national average, 100 times greater than the NT and 350 times greater than NSW. The report also failed to mention that the actual weight of amphetamine seized fell by over twenty-five per cent. There was also no mention of the fact that the following year in Tasmania, amphetamine drug seizures fell by twenty-four per cent, amphetamine seizure by weight fell by thirty-three per cent and national amphetamine seizures by weight fell by twenty-seven per cent.

More recent data from the Australian Institute of Health and Welfare actually shows that the total number of Australians who use amphetamines is declining. Cherry picking statistics by not only mentioning a specific area of a state that has the highest seizure increase (despite the amount of the drug seized actually falling, as it did in three other states), but also ignoring subsequent falls in the same area and across the nation, paints a completely unrepresentative picture to the public.

The story 'Ice hits schools' from the *Herald Sun* suggests that ice has infiltrated the school system, with students either turning up to school affected by ice, in possession of ice, selling ice at school or manufacturing ice at school. If the story had provided some evidence that any of these suggestions existed, it may have had some credibility. The story actually begins with an attempt to persuade the reader into believing that it is a bad thing that 'the numbers of young people seeking treatment to wean themselves off methamphetamines, including the killer ice, have increased fourfold over five years'. But if it is a bad thing, then why not put equal weight of the story on the fact that in the same time (as reported in the article), treatment for heroin (which is a more harmful drug) use almost halved? Why wasn't 'Heroin use down and treatment is up' the headline? Additionally, since the total use of methamphetamine has remained largely unchanged, then wouldn't a greater proportion of people actually getting treatment be a good thing? While I am aware that there are school-aged individuals of who have either had contact with or have used the drug, there is no mention of any evidence or incidences of ice entering schools. Unfortunately, the vast majority of people who see this headline, either through purchasing the paper or simply seeing it in a newsagency, in a petrol station, in a café or while sitting opposite someone reading it in a bus or train, will not read past the headline, and they will assume that methamphetamine is within the school system.

Australia has seen headlines, such as 'A generation on ice', 'Meth addiction destroying next generation of Australians' and 'Ice nation', and we have witnessed high-profile Australians saying that we are going to lose an entire generation to ice. The news story published in 2015 by news.com. au entitled 'The country town being overtaken by ice' is another story that portrays Australia as a nation with as many ice users as coffee drinkers. Three paragraphs of this story contain messages that simply do not match evidence. One local businessman commented he had seen '"good kids" fall foul of the drug and believes society would lose a generation to ice', yet this is entirely inaccurate given that only six to seven per cent of Australians have *ever* used the drug meaning that over ninety per cent of Australia have *never* used the drug. With one to two per cent of Australians having used the drug in the past year, this means that approximately ninety-eight to ninety-nine per cent of Australians have not used the drug in the past year. A *60 Minutes* report in April 2018 recycled the same inflammatory language, with journalist Tom Steinfort claiming there is a 'fear we are losing generations to an ice epidemic that's out of control'.

The vast majority of methamphetamine users are not school age, and despite it being reported that Australia has the highest methamphetamine dependence rates in the world, only 0.4 per cent of Australians are dependent on methamphetamine. So, with over ninety-nine per cent of society not being dependent on methamphetamine, we are certainly not going to lose a generation to ice.

Dependence also does not necessarily mean that the person is addicted. An individual who is dependent may still function well in all areas of their life, and their dependence may be able to be controlled or minimised. When a person is addicted, however, they continue to use the drug despite negative consequences to their life. So, with over ninety-nine per cent of Australia not being dependent on methamphetamine and some individuals who are dependent on methamphetamine still functioning well, such as maintaining relationships and employment, stating that it will wipe out a generation or we are a nation on ice is nothing but scaremongering.

A local businessman on the program commented, 'Once upon a time at parties, there would be three or four people in the corner doing drugs... Now there are three or four people in the corner who are not doing drugs.' This ignores the fact that the vast majority of society do the right thing and steer away from illicit drugs, but we never acknowledge that group.

Whenever I ask a group of students, how many people they think use illicit drugs as a percentage of the population, almost invariably 100 per cent of the room think that the vast majority of Australia have used an illicit drug at some point in their life. That is because there is a relentless focus on the small group of users, while we ignore the majority. This has the effect of making those kids who feel like they are 'missing out' feel even more isolated, because they (like the rest of the community) are led to believe that they are in the minority, when actually they are the majority. Why do we continue to perpetuate the myth that most people have tried it or are doing it, when that is completely inaccurate, entirely unhelpful and reinforces to young people that they are missing out?

The media needs to realise that when you sell the 'drugs are everywhere' slogan and instil the belief in a non-drug-using young person that they are somehow an oddity or not part of the big group, that makes the conversation a parent has with their child extremely difficult. Saying no to your child drinking or using another drug is difficult enough, but it is made even more difficult when the child believes that they are one of the only kids who aren't participating. Editors and producers know that hysteria sells papers and generates ratings by sucking in curious audiences and concerned parents. Since this reportage is not likely to change, it's up to us to dispel the myth that everyone does drugs.

This is compounded by the fact that the individuals who have used drugs are inevitably making the most noise about their behaviour. This is known in psychology as availability heuristic, where an individual makes a judgement of an event or occurrence not because it is common or likely to happen, but because it comes to mind easily. An example would be the fear of a shark attack, where the individual has much more chance of drowning or dying in a car accident on the way to the beach. On the very rare occasion that someone gets taken by a shark, the story ends up as major news, accompanied by graphic footage or photos, which figuratively tattoos the event into the person's mind. Individuals who use or have used illicit drugs stand out in our minds, while those who never do fade into the background.

Police Inspector Rob Wallace, in the same news story on the ice epidemic in Sale, stated, 'It [ice] is right across all ages', which implies that the vast majority of people across all ages are at the very least in contact with the drug or its effects. That statement is not based on any evidence and achieves nothing other than alarming the public on a false premise.

In May 2018, Australian columnist Miranda Devine kicked off an interview with NSW Minister for Police, Troy Grant, on the topic of pill testing by stating that drug use in Australia was at an all-time high and that the fifteen to twenty-four year old bracket was the fastest growing. Both comments are incorrect. Creating social concern and panic is purposeless when the issue is not supported by hard data, and particularly when there are more pressing matters on the agenda when it comes to the drug space.

While methamphetamine does cause harm to its users and their families, portraying the drug as something that will wipe out generations achieves nothing and can only be described as scaremongering.

Research shows that stigmatising the people who are harmful users of amphetamine by using alarmist claims, such as 'Australia suffering more carnage and casualties than any other country', reduces the chance that those people would seek healthcare or treatment. However, the fact that amphetamine users are branded in a disapproving and judgemental manner, in turn decreasing the likelihood of them actually getting better, is probably not of great concern to the journalists who are reporting. It is also interesting to note that, when it comes to drugs, the media give ample airtime to law enforcement representatives, such as police officers, commissioners, judges etc. while experts in the field of public health or drugs, such as physicians or toxicologists, either barely have a voice or are shouted down.

The 2014 *Courier* headline 'On ice, aged 10', with the subheading 'Children as young as ten using ice in Ballarat' is another story riddled with sensationalist claims. There is no mention anywhere in this article of any individual aged ten using methamphetamine. A nurse from a withdrawal service in Ballarat stated in the article 'it was common for young people to use ice as their first experience'.

It is *not* common for anyone, let alone young people to use ice at any stage, and not only is alcohol the legal drug that people almost always use first (aside from medication), the initial illicit drug overwhelmingly used first is cannabis. There is actually a picture in the article of a lunchbox containing a sandwich, apple as well as bags of white powder (assumingly methamphetamine) with a meth pipe next to the lunch box. I cannot confirm this with any evidence, however, I highly doubt that any parent is conscientiously packing their child's lunch box with healthy options, such as sandwich and an apple, as well as some meth in case the child needs a 'pick me up' during the day.

Headlines referring to an ice epidemic, pandemic, plague or scourge have been across every newspaper source and are misleading for a number of reasons. Without being too politically correct, both words 'epidemic' and 'pandemic' refer to infectious diseases, such as influenza, cholera or HIV/AIDS, and therefore cannot be applied to rates of methamphetamine because a person using methamphetamine cannot cause another person to use the drug through infectious means. Epidemics and pandemics also refer to the infection spreading to a lot of people over a short period of time.

Although users of methamphetamine may have switched to the more potent form that is ice, there is no evidence to support the notion that methamphetamine is spreading in a short period of time to large numbers of non-users. A pandemic refers to a global epidemic, which is not the case with methamphetamine. A 'plague' refers to specific forms of infectious disease, of which the most well-known was the Black Plague, which killed upwards of 50,000,000 people in a short period of time.

❧

We need to put harms into context, and not forget that hundreds, if not thousands of times more people have had their lives torn apart by drugs that society tolerates, such as alcohol. While I do not deny lived experiences and the reality of ice damaging users, families and communities, when you stack all amphetamines against other drugs such as opioids, alcohol and tobacco in terms of harm, as the President of the AMA, Dr Michael Gannon, stated, 'Ice pales into insignificance'.

Globally, tobacco kills 900 people per hour, alcohol kills about 340 people per hour, and illicit drugs kill twenty to thirty people per hour. Even though many more people drink and/or smoke tobacco than take illicit drugs, the illicit drugs certainly do not cause the same level of societal damage and, in many cases, are much less deadly.

The media also continually focuses on *use*, rather than *harm*, and when focusing on use, attention is given to drugs that are increasing in prevalence. Every year in Australia, school students are surveyed about drug usage patterns, ranging from what they have used, to how much and how recently. From 1996 to 2011, hallucinogens, amphetamines, cocaine and ecstasy use among young people in the past year fell and were the lowest on record. However, cannabis use increased by one per cent, and that was the drug the media chose to report on. Ignore the drops in use for significantly more harmful drugs, because those trends don't align with the voice of doom.

Harm is also rarely the main focus, possibly because only a small fraction of users develop harm that is explicitly reported, such as in deaths or acute hospital admissions. If use was the primary concern, then why don't we talk about the fact that millions of Australians use paracetamol or ibuprofen on a weekly basis? About 8,000 Australians are hospitalised every year for paracetamol poisoning. Or about the fact that almost all Australians use caffeine on a daily basis, and many struggle to get through a day's work at a productive level without it? It is because publishing a story on legal drugs, where both usage and harms are significantly higher (which inevitably contextualises the harms compared to illicit drugs), does not fit the narrative that legal drugs are safe and illegal drugs are unsafe.

It is also interesting to note that not only are the general media fixated on current illicit drug-related events, there is a common pattern of rehashing past illicit drug events. Not only does this keep the illicit drug at the forefront of the public mind, it also creates a situation where attention is given to illicit drugs, justifying or obscuring the fact that nothing is being done about the sixty to seventy Australians who die every day from either tobacco or alcohol. It is a common ploy—draw the public focus away from topics that need attention to non-issues, then fill those non-issues with hot air, and the public will soon forget the issue that needed attention.

⁓

Towards the end of 2017, on my drive home from a hospitality establishment in the eastern suburbs of Sydney, I recall hearing on the radio that a Sydney man had been charged in relation to a methamphetamine-linked incident, which occurred three years earlier. I kept my finger on the pulse for weeks after this report, not because I was interested in the particular case, but because of what happened before I got in my car that evening. As this was towards Christmas time, the venue was busy and festive. During dinner with some close friends of mine, I noticed a group of drunk and disorderly young men being ejected from the venue. Another group of men was already outside, and obviously due to prior tensions, the two groups of men, as well as security, became embroiled in an enormous brawl out the front of the venue (where dozens of families were eating dinner inside). It was violent with punches and glasses thrown, with some men covered in blood. Very quickly a dozen police cars arrived as well as an ambulance. The street was closed off, one man was taken off to hospital and about fifteen men handcuffed, arrested and charged. It was a horrible and costly event, which would have terrified many onlookers, particularly children.

The point is, however, that no report exists to this day about this event, and that is a reflection of a much wider problem. The media's conscious choice to unremittingly maintain focus on illicit drugs fuels the ethos within the community that we have a war on our hands with drugs, such as methamphetamine, but that any problems that occur as a result of alcohol are tolerable. How can society possibly be aware of alcohol-related issues if they are rarely reported, and they stand in the shadow of all attention drawn to illicit drugs?

It is unquestionable that drugs, such as ice, cause major problems, but the biased and sensationalist attitude the media has towards illegal drugs appears to be a deliberate ploy to avoid confronting objective realities. I find it worrying that when I ask young people what they think the most harmful drug is, ice is mentioned ninety-nine per cent of the time, when almost none of those students will come into contact with the drug, but out of a year group of students, a handful will certainly die as a direct result of their alcohol and/or tobacco use.

One has to ask the question, are there vested interests in perpetuating the ice epidemic? Why is there almost a competition among media sources to cite the area with the worst ice problem? Obviously generating hysteria is a recipe for good ratings. However, as the vast majority of government spending for drugs is geared towards law enforcement, all entities involved in the criminal justice system serve to benefit when the scale of methamphetamine-related problems is amplified. The press should treat objectivity, proportionality and truthfulness with equal importance as arriving first on the scene. Being first on the scene first is irrelevant if what is then broadcasted to the public does not match reality. Being pressed by a short deadline is not an excuse to fabricate or blow up an issue. While we do not need to make comparisons on the relative harms with all drug-related stories, at the same time we should not lose sight of the fact that legal drugs—which we choose not to talk about—cause a great deal more harm than all illegal drugs.

10

LUCY – PSYCHEDELICS

The term psychedelic was first coined in the 1950s by British psychiatrist Humphry Osmond and British philosopher and psychonaut Aldous Huxley. The word combines two Greek words 'psyche' meaning 'mind or soul' and 'delos' meaning 'to reveal', resulting in the foundation meaning of psychedelic being to 'reveal the mind or soul'.

Aldous Huxley described the psychedelic effects of mescaline in his 1954 book *The Doors of Perception*, yet despite Huxley being one of the most pre-eminent intellectuals of the 1900s, his death attracted almost zero attention. This was primarily due to the fact that his death occurred about five hours after the assassination of US President John F. Kennedy on 22 November 1963.

Before Huxley, UK physician Havelock Ellis wrote about the subjective effects of mescaline in his paper 'Mescal, a New Artificial Paradise', which was released in 1898—one year after mescaline was first synthesised.

The first documented psychedelic experience occurred approximately 2700 BC, when Chinese Emperor Shennong recounted the hallucinogenic effects of cannabis. For several hundred years, the ergot fungus was known to have special properties and was used by women to control bleeding during menstruation and in the prevention of excessive bleeding after a woman had given birth. Ergot, like psilocybin, is a type of fungus. However, ergot grows on rye, whereas psilocybin mushrooms grow in woods and meadows, hence the term 'shrooming the countryside'.

Psychedelics refer to a category of drugs that alter how an individual perceives reality in terms of time, sound and vision. Psychedelic drugs have historically been synonymous with other related activities, such as psychedelic rock and psychedelic therapy. These activities and experiences were a part of larger social change (psychedelic era), evolving throughout the 1960s in the Western world, particularly in the USA due to the Vietnam War. The counterculture that developed throughout the 1960s consisted of many emerging groups, such as the Civil Rights Movement, Free Speech Movement, and Anti-War Movement.

The counterculture movement essentially referred to a movement that challenged and opposed conventional beliefs and systems. Although some critics argue that aspects of the counterculture movement exist today in a somewhat misrepresented form, many of the progressive movements gave rise to positive social changes, such as equal rights, regardless of gender, race or sexual orientation. These changes were reflected in politics, such as new left wing movements, in art, with the emergence of psychedelic-influenced music from bands, such as the Beatles, the Rolling Stones, the Beach Boys and Pink Floyd, in civil rights, such as Martin Luther King's 'I Have a Dream' speech, and also with drugs, with the popularisation of psychedelic drugs.

What each of these facets of the counterculture movement had in common was that they challenged conventional systems and were a method of viewing the world from a different perspective in the hope of bringing change. Psychedelic drugs were pivotal to the progressive movements of this era. Not only were they a means by which individuals could alter their perception of reality, but the use of psychedelic drugs was symbolic of a culture that was rejecting the Vietnam War. Drugs, such as psychedelics and cannabis, were viewed by many as the holy grail for those involved in the counterculture and an example of a wider societal movement towards individualism. Despite acts such as passing a joint or dropping acid being seen by some as a selfish pleasure, these rituals were symbolic of collective rebellion against conventionalism.

The Vietnam War occurred due to the fear held by the US government about the spread of communism to the wider world, but the majority of the population did not understand this concept, and by the end of the 1960s, the vast majority of Americans considered the military involvement to be a mistake. The counterculture was not exclusive to the USA, however, with the UK, Australia and other parts of the Western world slowly moving in an anti-war direction.

Although society had a conceptual understanding of the violence involved in war, this was the first televised war, the first war in people's living rooms. Even though the footage was not live, it was uncensored, confronting and consistent, which led Americans to question why their husbands, fathers and sons were being forced to travel to a foreign country that they knew nothing about to kill or be killed for a concept that was not understood. This gave rise to the societal movement away from war, towards peace, which is where the use of mind-altering drugs stepped in.

The increased use of psychedelic drugs epitomised the cultural shift towards anti-establishment (anti-government) and progressive ideas. Instead of subscribing to the notion of fighting communism, young men and women increasingly decided to migrate to hotspots, such as San Francisco and Washington DC, and intensify the anti-establishment movement. The mood of the times has been depicted in movies, such as *Forrest Gump* and *Born on the Fourth of July,* as well as in contemporary music, such as Scott McKenzie's *San Francisco* and John Lennon's *Give Peace a Chance.* Among anti-war slogans, such as 'Make love, not war' and 'Save our sons', were slogans such as 'Marijuana is wholesome' and 'Drop acid, not bombs'.

Acid (lysergic acid diethylamide or LSD) was first synthesised by Swiss scientist Albert Hofmann in the late 1930s, while he was working for the pharmaceutical company Sandoz (now part of Novartis). Hoffman resynthesised the compound again in April 1943, alongside other compounds linked to the ergot fungus, some of which had been used to restrict blood loss in childbirth.

It was not until the late 1940s/early 1950s that LSD was used in psychiatric therapy. By the time the drug was illegalised in the late 1960s, over 1,000 peer-reviewed clinical papers covering over 40,000 patients had been published. Of these, about 130 studies were funded by the US government. LSD was banned in the UK in 1966, in Australia about the same time, and in 1968 in the USA under the Staggers-Dodd Bill (an amendment to the *Food, Drug and Cosmetic Act 1938*).

LSD was the first synthetic psychedelic. The overall results from its clinical use were overwhelmingly positive. In fact, in the six studies between 1955 and 1965 looking into treating alcoholism with LSD, the effect size was approximately fifty per cent, which is greater than any current therapy. Even the founder of Alcoholics Anonymous, Bill Wilson, was able to overcome his addiction through the use of psychedelics.

Over 80,000 Americans die every year from excessive alcohol consumption (an average of 88,000 annually between 2006 and 2010, and 95,000 between 2011 and 2015), which means that since the ban of LSD, at least 4,000,000 Americans have potentially died as a result of excessive alcohol consumption. Even if LSD had saved a quarter of these people, that would calculate to over 1,000,000 lives saved, and that is just America. Conservative estimates of premature lives lost internationally due to alcoholism since the ban of LSD sit at around 100,000,000 people. Years of potential life lost (YPLL) for alcoholism averages at least fifteen years. None of these people have had access to LSD to treat their alcoholism. However, if they did and it saved a quarter of these people (very conservative estimate), 25,000,000 lives and at least 375,000,000 YPLL would have been saved.

Due to the fact that government policy has tunnel vision and is so blinkered in favour of prohibition, legislators ignore any wider agenda, such as research or treatment. In almost all developed countries, the number of people who die from tobacco is greater than the number of people who die from alcohol. However, the YPLL is greater for alcohol because alcohol kills many young people. Even if it could be proved that a prohibitive drug policy actually reduces use, it would not serve as adequate justification for immobilising research. The medical utility of psychedelics, however, should not be used as an endorsement of their use recreationally or outside of a supervised medical setting. These drugs must be given the respect they deserve. This can be challenging, as many people who have taken psychedelic drugs, particularly in medical settings, regard the experience as one of, if not the most, profound experience of their lives, comparable with the birth of a child or falling in love.

Select scientists in the past have been partially to blame for giving certain drugs a bad name, such as psychologist Timothy Leary during the 1960s. Despite being one of the pioneers of psychedelic research, Dr Leary popularised the use of psychedelic drugs, which had a negative effect on legitimate scientific research. He was even regarded by President Nixon, as the 'most dangerous man in America'. Leary was not the most dangerous man in the US, but he was one of the biggest dangers to the government's attack on psychedelics.

Not only does drug policy treat research as unimportant, it also deters individuals from calling for help because of fear of prosecution and fails to provide responsive strategies when things go wrong in drug-related situations. But then again, prohibition advocates would respond to this by stating that individuals wouldn't need to call an ambulance or utilise any reactive strategies if they were responsible and didn't use the drug in the first place. This is a perverse and simplistic attitude. A significant portion of drug-related deaths would be avoided if those involved weren't scared of calling for help or if they had been rationally advised that although drug use poses risks and we don't want individuals using drugs, this is how you respond in the event that someone chooses to use.

Fifteen year old Sydney school student Anna Wood, who was the most publicised illicit drug-related death in Australia, died in late

October 1995 from water poisoning, three days after taking ecstasy. Anna would have survived if she had just taken ecstasy and did not subsequently drink copious amounts of water or if her friends had not been too afraid to call for help. The message to 'Just Say No' and 'Don't Do Drugs' failed to stop Anna from using ecstasy, it failed to go further in providing her friends with any strategies to save her, and it failed to protect Anna because her friends were scared to get help fast enough.

This is just one of thousands of drug-related deaths where the simplistic and unrealistic message of 'Say No to Drugs' falls far too short in protecting individuals who have stepped over the line of prohibition. Many adults are so afraid to provide young people with any harm reduction advice because they fear it sends the wrong message. Yet this is despite the fact that we take a harm reduction approach to many other risky activities—some of which are even illegal (seatbelts and speeding for example), and this kind of advice in many situations could prevent their children or students from dying. As a side but extremely important note, in the same week that Anna Wood died, six young people in Sydney died from the acute effects of alcohol, yet nobody has heard of any of these people.

◦◦◦

The scheduling and classifying of LSD in the US, Australia, the UK and almost all parts of the western world as an illegal drug with no medical utility is a complete lie and an injustice to those who may have benefitted from the use of the drug. LSD was banned due to the collusion between government authorities (particularly the DEA and the Central Intelligence Agency (CIA)) and the media, resulting in unsubstantiated scare stories, leading to public concern about the drug. Research on LSD stopped because it was illegalised, because the drug's patent had expired, and due to the discovery in the early 1960s that another drug, thalidomide, caused birth defects and child deaths, resulting in tighter research regulations. Social concern is all you need to get a drug banned, not evidence of harm. The moral panic that inevitably followed the media reports was enough ammunition for the government to outlaw the drug. Even one of the most powerful men in the world, US Attorney-General, Robert Kennedy—who would have probably been president if he wasn't assassinated—disagreed with the prohibitive approach to LSD:

> *Why if [clinical LSD projects] were worthwhile six months ago, why aren't they worthwhile now? I think we have given too much emphasis and so much attention to the fact that it can be dangerous and that it can hurt an individual who uses it that perhaps to some extent we have lost sight of the fact that it can be very, very helpful in our society if used properly.*

Even though the underlying reason for the illegalisation of LSD was that society was gradually seen to be behaving in a way that was non-conformist to what the government desired, it was hidden under the banner of front page headlines such as 'Girls Gives Birth To A Frog—Doctors Blame LSD' (*The Examiner*, US, 1968), 'Man Knifes Best Friend 87 Times In LSD Frenzy' (*The Bulletin*, US, 1970), and 'LSD Made Me A Prostitute' (*The National Tattler*, US, 1967). As 2GB commentator Ray Hadley has stated on various occasions, 'The one thing I do know about law and order is that people need to feel safe'.

Throughout history, political parties have almost been in a race among themselves as to who can ban the most drugs fastest because that appeases the anti-drug community, and it makes them appear they are in control. The US government clothed its underlying beliefs and intentions in the admirable and politically expedient robes of patriotism and national safety, when the banning of LSD was simply a manoeuvre to ensure society obeyed the establishment. The risks associated with the use of LSD are almost entirely a result of the actions of the users while they are under the influence of the drug (falls, running onto the road etc.), as nobody has ever overdosed on LSD due to the safety ratio being approximately 1000.

Despite the fact that users can become attached to the profound experiences LSD produces, it is not considered an addictive drug because LSD does not produce withdrawals or compulsive drug-seeking behaviour found with other drugs like cocaine or heroin. It takes time for the brain to lower its resistance to psychedelic drugs after usage, so subsequent doses in the following days produce little or no effect, therefore there is no incentive to re-dose.

Due to the drug not being pharmacologically addictive and the high safety ratio, tolerance is not a major concern because users are not driven to seek out the drug, and an overdose is practically impossible. Users of LSD do run the risk of experiencing a 'bad trip', which is categorised as an unpleasant, disturbing or frightening hallucinogenic experience. These negative experiences can range from mild to severe. However, many people who experience a negative trip through the use of LSD or another psychedelic do not regret their choice to use the drug, as they benefitted from the experience by gaining insight into themselves, their lives and problems from a different perspective. Other than a very small group of individuals who are predisposed to psychosis, people who have taken psychedelics overall have much better mental health.

Researchers at Harvard Medical School affiliated hospital, McLean Hospital in Massachusetts, published a study in 2005 showing that not only did individuals who regularly used peyote not have any cognitive deficits, they actually scored better across multiple measures of mental health. A 2007 study by Santos et al. in the *Journal of Ethnopharmacology* found that users of ayahuasca scored better on measures of panic/anxiety-like states as well as hopelessness. Some people consider the psychedelic experience to be one of the most significant events in their life. Through an altered state of consciousness and an improvement of being able to think outside the box, users often gain clarity and understanding into issues that normal consciousness can only comprehend from limited viewpoints.

Although very rare, individuals who have used LSD can develop a condition known as HPPD (Hallucinogen Persisting Perception

Disorder), which is characterised by recurrent sensory disturbances, comparable to the individual reliving the experience of a previous hallucinogenic drug experience, for example, visual hallucinations like halos or trailing objects. HPPD is dissimilar to flashbacks, which are transient and are not characterised by someone reliving the experience.

Bad trips and disturbing HPPD experiences are more likely to occur if the individual has a history or family history of mental health issues, such as anxiety, or if they have taken the drug when in a negative or fearful state of mind. There have been reported cases where individuals have committed suicide, attempted suicide or self-harmed. However, this again is most likely to occur with individuals with prior mental health issues. In the days following LSD use, individuals may feel worn out due to the draining psychological and physical nature of the psychedelic experience. Users may even encounter 'echoes' of the experience, but this primarily surfaces if other drugs are used.

⁓

One of the major risks of taking LSD, like any illicit drug, is that there is no guarantee that the individual using the drug is actually taking LSD, how much LSD exists on their blotter, or if another drug is present instead of LSD or present alongside it. Two drugs that have been used as substitutes for or present alongside LSD are DOB (dimethoxybromoamphetamine), and analogues of NBOMe. DOB is a hallucinogenic stimulant that has been known to be present on LSD blotters because it can create similar effects to LSD. DOB, however, can take several hours to produce an effect, and so, like PMA/PMMA instead of MDMA, users mistake this as being a weak or inactive dose and subsequently may re-dose themselves in a short space of time.

The safety ratio of DOB is also significantly lower than LSD, making it an intrinsically riskier drug in terms of overdose. Both DOB and the NBOMe analogues have been used as LSD substitutes because they fit easily onto a sheet of blotter paper. Some argue that the emergence of

NBOMe analogues has been a result of the global crackdown on LSD, encouraging criminal manufacturers to look for alternatives, which are inevitably more harmful.

Some of the NBOMe analogues are of particular concern such as 25I-NBOMe, which induces not only powerful hallucinogenic experiences, but is also pharmacologically toxic at low doses, particularly if mixed with other drugs or administered through other means than buccally (in the cheek) or sublingually (under the tongue). Another less common substitute is 2C-P (2,5-dimethoxy-4-propylphenethyl-amine)—another Shulgin compound—which can take four to five hours until onset of effects and last for twenty hours.

Another hallucinogenic concoction is ayahuasca, which is a plant-based brew. Used in traditional medicine, religious, spiritual or healing ceremonies, ayahuasca typically contains two plant ingredients: *Banisteriopsis caapi* and *Psychotria viridis.* Although the latter contains the hallucinogenic drug DMT (dimethyltryptamine), it is not active when ingested alone orally. If taken concomitantly, however, the alkaloids harmine, harmaline and tetrahydroharmine present in *Banisteriopsis caapi* allow DMT to enter the blood stream, cross the blood-brain barrier and produce effects. The blood-brain barrier protects the central nervous system from potentially injurious foreign substances. Molecules that are large, non-fat soluble or highly electrically charged are either inhibited from entering the brain or pass at a very slow rate.

Despite DMT being a Schedule 9 drug in Australia, like other psychedelic drugs, it has seen a resurgence in popularity due to an increased interest in its therapeutic utility, particularly for illnesses that are difficult to treat, such as drug dependence. Despite the apparent increased popularity in ayahuasca retreats, there is little evidence on the number of Australians who have actually tried the drug. Compounds in the *Banisteriopsis caapi* vine act as monoamine oxidase inhibitors (MAOIs), which are a class of drugs that possess antidepressant properties. MAOIs are typically reserved as a last line of therapy when other antidepressant drugs have failed, due to the relative ease with which consumption of particular drugs or foods alongside use of MAOIs can produce toxic and potentially lethal interactions. MAOIs, like other antidepressants, may also produce withdrawals, which can be controlled if dosage is gradually lowered over an extended period of time and not discontinued abruptly.

The brewed infusion of the two plants, *Banisteriopsis caapi* and *Psychotria viridis,* over several hours produces a bitter-tasting tea, which is then drunk. Initial hallucinogenic effects of ayahuasca begin thirty minutes to one hour following ingestion and can last for several hours. Adverse effects from using ayahuasca include nausea, anxiety, paranoia, sweating, vomiting as well as some reported cases of psychosis. Ayahuasca, like any illicit concoction, produces effects based on individual variables, such as gender, weight, experience with the drug and whether other drugs have been taken in proximate time. With ayahuasca, however, the mixture is often brewed and consumed in 'natural' settings, such as in rainforests, meaning that the mixture is dependent on the contents of what is directly harvested from its primitive origin. The ingredients are highly unlikely to be uniform with every session/ceremony, and the brew is not prepared in a laboratory. Not only are the final contents of the brew dependent on what the natural settings provide, but ayahuasca is often consumed with little or no medical supervision and far from medical help if something does go wrong.

Twenty-four year old New Zealand man, Matthew Dawson-Clarke, died in 2015 in Iquitos, Peru, after attending an ayahuasca ceremony, not only because he went into cardiac arrest in the hours following ingesting the drug, but because the retreat was deep in the rainforest, far from medical care, and because shamans and helpers were entirely unqualified to respond. Nineteen year old British student, Henry Miller, died the previous year in the middle of the Columbian rainforest under similar circumstances after he consumed the concoction for the second time in two days after feeling no effects the first day. In both situations, these deaths can be attributed to the fact that the men consumed a brew of entirely unknown strength and contents, there was incompetent medical care, and there was no access to proper medical care in the vicinity.

This is another example demonstrating that where and how the drug is consumed can be contributing factors to the harm outcome, not the drug itself.

This is the key reason Sydney's Medically Supervised Injecting Centre (MSIC) in Kings Cross has handled thousands of overdoses without a single fatality—because of where and how the drug is consumed. If those same people shot up in dark back alley streets, with no medical supervision, in secret and alone, it is unarguable that some of those people would have died, even though they are consuming the same drug. Not only have thousands of overdoses in the MSIC occurred without a single fatality, the hundred or so other drug consumption facilities (also known as shooting galleries or fix rooms) throughout the world have also experienced thousands of overdoses, without one single fatality. In the Canadian state of Alberta, since 2016, over 300,000 people have visited the six supervised consumption centres where over 4,300 overdoses have occurred; 100 per cent have been reversed.

The primary reasons for individuals seeking ayahuasca retreats are either medical, in situations where they have been resistant to other treatments, or spiritual, where individuals seek enlightenment or awakening. Ayahuasca appears to not only dull areas of the brain that are overactive in illnesses, such as depression or addiction, but also to disrupt locked patterns of thinking, which are regulated by the brain's control centre.

These findings are similar to those on the effects of other psychedelic drugs, such as LSD and psilocybin. It is this unlocking of inflexible brain patterns where individuals experience epiphanies, see life or themselves from different angles, and/or feel more connected and accepting of their situation or existence. The effects of psychedelics on the brain have been described as 'taking the conductor out of the orchestra'. Another perspective may be that a psychedelic trip is like climbing a tall tree after you have been battling through the undergrowth of life, allowing you to get a different perspective and get some bearings. Further research is needed in this area as the findings have utilised small groups and are yet to be published in a peer-reviewed journal.

Numerous scientists, designers, engineers, entrepreneurs and pioneers across various fields, including Bill Gates, Francis Crick, Kary Mullis, Steve Jobs and John C. Lilly, have credited LSD as the facilitator in their imaginative breakthroughs and moments of inspiration. Individuals who wish to undertake spiritual awakenings without drugs may, however, be able to achieve this by travelling to parts of the world that are culturally or geographically inspiring.

∿

Psychedelic mushrooms, which contain the prodrug psilocybin (which the body converts into psilocin, the psychoactive compound), are yet another group of psychedelic drugs. There are approximately 200 different varieties of psilocybin-containing mushrooms. These are commonly referred to as magic mushrooms due to users reporting magical or spiritual experiences while under the influence of the drug. Psilocin interacts with the same receptor as other psychedelic drugs (serotonin 5ht2a receptor), however, psilocybin is not as potent as LSD. LSD has a much higher affinity with this receptor, meaning that the drug is very 'sticky' to the receptor, and psilocybin is relatively selective in terms of specifically targeting the serotonin system, whereas LSD interacts with various receptor sites.

Psychedelic mushrooms gained widespread attention in Western culture during the late 1950s, and despite psychedelic mushrooms being native to Australia, they are a Schedule 9 drug, and the cultivation, manufacture, possession and supply of the drug is illegal.

Mushrooms are typically sold in their dried or natural form, both of which have pros and cons. While natural mushrooms may be proportionally weaker in potency than dried mushrooms due to much of the weight of the mushroom being water, natural mushrooms can contain mould, which may upset the stomach. Occasionally, mushrooms are sold in a processed form, where the mushrooms are coated in another substance, but this can be risky due to an increased chance of getting the dosage wrong as well as the coating containing harmful adulterants. One of the largest risks evident with the use of psychedelic mushrooms is that their physical appearance is similar to other mushrooms, many of which are highly poisonous to humans.

Blue meanies (*Panaeolus cyanescens*), straw mushrooms (*Volvariella volvacea*), and death caps (*Amanita phalloides*) all look very similar. However, blue meanies are psychedelic mushrooms; straw mushrooms are edible mushrooms found in supermarkets; and death caps are fatally poisonous mushrooms. Initially, consumers may experience little to no acute symptoms. At twenty-four hours, side effects such as diarrhoea and cramping can ensue, yet because these often pass relatively quickly, consumers and consulting physicians can make a judgement call that the worst is behind them. After this 'hiatus', the serious signs of liver failure may not show up until 100 hours post ingestion, with death usually occurring at around 170 hours (about a week) post ingestion, particularly if the patient is unable to receive a liver transplant.

Death caps have also been reported to taste pleasant, and this, coupled with the delay in symptoms of poisoning, makes the process particularly dangerous. Additionally, if users mistake a poisonous mushroom for a psychedelic mushroom and anticipate hallucinogenic effects, they may be prompted to take large amounts after not feeling any effects, which means they are likely to ingest a large amount of the amatoxins and phallotoxins, the substances that cause liver failure and death. There are about eighty mushrooms classified as fatally poisonous. Only a small amount (half a cap) needs to be consumed to cause liver failure.

Some people choose to dry the mushrooms out and then add to a brew of tea instead of picking and eating them. While boiling some mushroom types, such as the fly agaric, can reduce and break down toxins, this is certainly not the case with most poisonous mushrooms. Amatoxins present in poisonous mushrooms are heat resistant, meaning that exposing the mushrooms to heat through boiling or other cooking does not reduce their lethality.

Apart from picking the wrong mushrooms, the largest risk associated with the use of psychedelic mushrooms is the consumer's distorted or detached perception of reality, which increases the risk of injury. Individuals who consume magic mushrooms typically experience altered thought processing, as well as changes to their visual and auditory perceptions, which can range from very mild to overwhelmingly powerful. Users can also experience distortions in their perception of time, typically feeling as though minutes last for hours. In fact, the father of psychedelics, Albert Hofmann, ingested LSD in a laboratory before his bicycle trip home in April 1943 and recounts that his trip home seemed to have taken hours despite it being a very short ride. April 19 is now known as Bicycle Day, and this first classical psychedelic trip began the psychedelic era.

LSD is incredibly potent—being active at approximately 0.1 milligrams—meaning that one single gram could send 10,000 people on a trip. Typical doses of psilocybin will last four to five hours. However, after the drug has worn off, users may experience residual effects, which can be accompanied by nausea, dilated pupils and fatigue.

Like LSD, it is extremely difficult to ingest an amount of psilocybin that would be toxic to the body or brain as only a small amount is needed to induce hallucinogenic effect, and the safety ratio of psilocybin is well into the hundreds, possibly as high as 1000. Due to the enormous gap between effective and toxic doses of psilocybin, physiologically they are without question one of the safest drug groups in the world, because the risk of overdose is essentially non-existent. The drug is not without harm, however, and users of psilocybin should ensure that while tripping they are nowhere near roads, cliffs, balconies or anywhere that could be hazardous. This obviously includes getting behind the wheel of a car or operating any machinery.

Set and setting are crucial when it comes to psychedelics. Even though the set and setting are generally referred to in the context of recreational use, their relevance has been evident in medical studies, such as the 1950s Saskatchewan LSD trial, where patients were screened, prepared, placed in calm environments and offered support afterwards, leading to very positive experiences. This study was conducted in Canada, yet when another hospital in Canada ran LSD trials, they tied patients down while they were under the effects of the drug, leading to very negative experiences.

Bad trips do happen, but this is almost always due to factors outside of the drug itself, such as taking the drug at a party with dark rooms and loud music, surrounded by strangers. Bad trips in clinical settings can be reversed with risperidone, as this blocks the receptor site that psychedelics, such as LSD and psilocybin, work on.

Although a low risk, psychedelic mushrooms may trigger mental health conditions in genetically predisposed individuals, or they may exacerbate pre-existing conditions such as anxiety. Individuals who use psychedelic mushrooms run the risk of HPPD; however, the risk is very low, it is more common in users of LSD and individuals often recover in a few weeks. Like with any other drug, individuals who use psychedelic mushrooms are strongly advised to avoid using any other drugs in conjunction due to potential drug-drug interactions, particularly psychiatric medications.

Psilocybin is illegal in most areas of the world except for a handful of countries, such as Brazil and Jamaica. Although psilocybin is legal in truffles in the Netherlands, fresh mushrooms were banned in December 2008, following the death of a young French girl who jumped to her death from a bridge while on a school trip. It is reported, however, that this poor girl suffered from severe psychiatric problems prior to the event. Psilocybin was illegalised just for good measure by the USA during the period of time that illegal drugs were considered by President Nixon to be public enemy number one.

꧁꧂

Like LSD, psilocybin holds medical utility for a number of difficult-to-treat disorders, such as cluster headaches, depression, cancer-related depression, OCD, tobacco addiction and alcohol addiction. However due to red tape, they are almost impossible to research, both from a logistical and financial perspective. It is actually easier for practitioners and researchers to work with drugs such as heroin or morphine, even though they are incomparably more dangerous at every level. It can take several years for a pharmaceutical company to satisfy ethics and safety approvals, and even if this is achieved, each dose of psilocybin is likely to cost thousands of dollars due to all of the regulations to be complied with. In the meantime, however, millions of people throughout the world are suffering from disorders that may be able to be cured.

Preliminary studies have shown that the effect size of psilocybin for treatment-resistant depression is larger than current antidepressants or psychotherapy. There is also the challenge that, due to the fact that psychedelics such as LSD and psilocybin often heal patients in a single dose or a few doses, the drug has to be made very expensive for the public in order for pharmaceutical companies to consider the investment worth the initial cost. Unless entirely altruistic, why would a drug company invest in a drug trial that is both horrendously expensive and publicly controversial? Even if the drug gets to the shelf, it will not generate repeat business and has to be within financial reach to consumers. Cheap products must be sold in high volumes to be financially viable for manufacturers, which is highly unlikely for psychedelic drugs because of their ability to treat sufferers rapidly.

There is a reason no new antibiotic class has been discovered since 1987. In any given year, most people don't need antibiotics, and even if they do, it's only for a short period of time. In contrast, there are a lot of people who have diabetes, high cholesterol or high blood pressure, and these people will need medication every day for the rest of their life. Encouraging pharmaceutical companies to produce drugs for conditions that are not needed en masse and/or for a very lengthy period of time is incredibly difficult, because there is no financial incentive.

The only other treatment similar in nature in terms of being rapid and requiring limited repeated doses is ECT, which many people find scary because of potential risks, including memory loss. Drug companies

favour treatments such as antidepressants, antipsychotics and benzodiazepines over psychedelic drugs, because it is often extremely difficult
for individuals to ween off or discontinue using these drugs. In contrast, psychedelic drugs do not cause dependence, often work quickly,
and subsequent doses are seldom needed. For researchers to study these
drugs, however, is next to impossible for logistical and financial reasons.

The Medical Research Council (MRC) in the UK funded a study in
2012 looking at whether psilocybin would be a beneficial treatment for
individuals with treatment-resistant depression. The study, however,
took several years to get off the ground, and the cost equated to AUD
$3,000 per dose. Many countries simply are disallowed from studying
drugs like LSD because of the Goods Manufacturing Practice (GMP)
production compliance bureaucracy.

Psilocybin shows promise in treating depression, as current antidepressants work by dampening down areas of the brain that are overactive in depression, and psilocybin appears to exhibit the same results,
albeit with a greater effect size. And since the effectiveness of psilocybin
treatment can last for months, sometimes years, the benefits cannot be
attributable to the intoxicating effects of the drug. Brain imaging usually
involves either MEG (magnetoencephalography) or fMRI (functional
magnetic resonance imaging) scanning, which both measure brain
activity. Brain imaging is incredibly important, although it is probably
highly underutilised. Cardiologists use cardiac computed tomography
scans; obstetricians use ultrasounds; neurosurgeons and orthopaedics
use MRIs and X-rays. However, psychiatrists often have to rely on what
the patient tells them, rather than actually scanning their brain.

To trial any illegal drug is a huge risk, not because of scientific reasons, but because of how the drug is viewed by government and society, and psychedelics have an unjustifiably bad rep. It came as a surprise
that the MRC study actually gained funding. However, it is likely it did
because depression is now the leading cause of disability throughout the
world. Several hundred million are affected, up to half of patients do
not respond to antidepressants, and approximately twenty per cent of

patients fail to respond to any treatment. Essentially, the treatment gap is enormous.

A hospital in Melbourne, Australia, was set to run a very small trial of psilocybin in treating anxiety brought on by a terminal diagnosis in early 2019. However, some people who are vehemently opposed to this notion, view psilocybin as nothing other than an illegal drug that can't be used in such a situation, because dying is not technically a diagnosis.

Psilocybin shows huge promise as current treatments, such as benzodiazepines and antidepressants, are much more toxic to the body, interact with many other drugs, are not responded to by everyone and don't actually get to the route of the anxiety. The biggest hurdle that drugs like psilocybin and LSD face in being used as therapies is their attached political baggage. Instead, patients are provided with drugs that constipate, confuse, addict, weaken and waste them away, because governments would rather block their ears and not listen to evidence demonstrating that banned drugs—contrary to the stereotype—may hold medical utility.

❧

Two other drugs that fall into the psychedelic class are mescaline and salvia, both of which are derived from plant material, and grow naturally in Mexico. German pharmacologist Arthur Heffter was the first person to synthesise mescaline from the peyote cactus in 1897, and approximately twenty years later, the drug was synthesised again by Austrian scientist Ernst Spath. Although considered psychedelics, the effects of salvia and mescaline are somewhat dissimilar to other psychedelics, as salvia often induces strange psychological and dissociative states, while mescaline is reported to produce very different visuals, such as recurring patterns. The onset of salvia is fast and short lasting, particularly if smoked, whereas the onset of mescaline may take slightly longer and effects dissipate at a slower rate. There is little to no evidence to show that salvia is physiologically toxic to the body or brain, and the safety ratio of mescaline is higher than other drugs, such as MDMA, cocaine or alcohol. Both mescaline and salvia can be chewed, brewed as part of a drink or, in the case of salvia, smoked. Salvia may cause users to become totally unaware of their surroundings and detached from reality, increasing their risk of injury. In the case of salvia, mescaline and indeed all psychedelics, factors other than the drug itself play the largest role in regulating both safety and the nature of the experience.

I would personally argue that the most crucial safety factor in an individual's psychedelic experience is the presence of a trip sitter, a sober person who takes care of the individual while they are under the influence. An experienced sitter would have the ability to eliminate most harms and risks by using grounding techniques, keeping the individual away from hazards; ensuring the environment is positive and calm; ensuring the individual does not take risks, such as using other drugs while under the influence; and, if anything does go wrong, calling for medical help.

Numerous external factors can be modified to ensure safety for individuals who consume drugs that are inherently safer drugs from a physiological standpoint, such as psychedelics. Harms from other more dangerous drugs, such as GHB or heroin, can also be minimised by external factors, such as changing the ROA and providing drug consumption rooms. However, due to the fact that some of these drugs pose major physiological risks based purely on their pharmacology (for example, respiratory depression from heroin or fentanyl, seizures from synthetic cannabis), some harm is unavoidable, regardless of how the external environment is managed. However, a small improvement on an external factor, such as swapping a used syringe for a clean syringe or using a drug with medical supervision instead of in isolation, may be the difference between life and death.

One of the reasons psychedelic drugs cause very little harm to both the user and to wider society, is because they pose minor risks to the individual at a biological level, and any non-drug risk can be managed with simple steps.

11

SMACK – HEROIN

Heroin is the original trademark name for diamorphine, an opioid drug used in medicine for pain relief, albeit its medical prescription is not as common nowadays. While attempting to synthesise a chemical that could wean morphine addicts off the drug, chemist Charles Romley Alder Wright synthesised diamorphine in 1874 in London. Before aspirin, penicillin or other drugs were invented, opioids were used to slow down the bowel in cases of diarrhoea caused by poor water sanitation. When prescribed to patients, the most common side effect is constipation, and this can be managed quite effectively.

The average post-operative patient in hospital receiving pharmaceutical pain relief does not match the public's typical image of a heroin user. The stereotypical image conjured up of a heroin user is that of a homeless addict shooting up in a gutter down a dark alleyway. Only a very small percentage of the Australian population (one to 1.5 per cent) have used heroin at some point in their lifetime, but due to the pharmacological qualities of the drug, a high proportion of these users are dependent and addicted. This coupled with the very high capture rate (approximately twenty-five per cent), the very high relapse rate (at least fifty per cent, but possibly closer to ninety per cent), the extremely low safety ratio (six) and the chronicity of use among users means that heroin, despite not being used by the wider population, poses *a signifi-cant public health issue.*

Individuals who are dependent on heroin (or alcohol, methamphet-amine or other opioids) can develop anhedonia, and although the condi-tion can gradually reduce in severity, it is a strong predictor of relapse.

Although intrinsically dangerous, a significant proportion of the heroin-related harms are caused by individuals not accessing the drug through regulated means. Of the Australians who use heroin at least once, one in four will become dependent, and very quickly their lives can spiral out of control in a biological, economic and social sense. Women often turn to sex work, while men turn to property crime. Individuals who are dependent on heroin can easily spend several hundred dollars per day to fund their habit, as withdrawals for heavy heroin users can begin within hours of previous use. Although withdrawals from opioids such as heroin are not typically considered life threatening, they can be extremely powerful.

Heroin is typically injected (intravenously), as this produces the fast-est and most pronounced rush, more so than smoking through a glass pipe, snorting or smoking off a sheet of aluminium foil, which is other-wise known as 'chasing the dragon'. Despite inhalation of heroin fumes being potentially detrimental to the mouth, oesophagus and lungs, as well as the brain in the case of spongiform leukoencephalopathy, it is considered safer than injecting, due to the avoidance of blood-borne/viral/bacterial/fungal disease transmission, overdose risk, risk of inject-ing other products such as anthrax, vein damage and abscesses. Indi-viduals who smoke heroin are also able to inhale small initial amounts to estimate the purity, which then allows them to titrate dosage depend-ing on strength. Street heroin is erratic in purity as well as adulterants, greatly increasing the risk of poisoning from additives as well as over-dose, due to individuals mistakenly injecting potentially fatal amounts of higher purity heroin. Titrating dosage is extremely difficult when injecting, particularly if the user has gained tolerance and requires higher doses to achieve similar effects, meaning that they are getting ever closer to an overdose. Illicit heroin is erratic in purity as well as adulterants, and like all drugs, increased purity does not indicate increased safety.

Heroin induces an acute, intense rush, accompanied by euphoria, relaxation and sedation, which is similar to other opioids like morphine; however, it is reported that heroin induces a much more intense transcendent-like experience. The primary acute concern with heroin use is respiratory depression, leading to lack of oxygen, which can be fatal. If an overdose occurs, individuals are treated with an opioid antagonist, such as naloxone, which is a drug that binds to opioid receptors and blocks the pharmacological effects of opioid drugs.

For opioid dependence, the drugs most commonly used are naltrexone (blocks effects of on-top heroin use, so the incentive to use heroin diminishes), buprenorphine (blocks on-top heroin use and controls withdrawals), and methadone (similar to buprenorphine). While naltrexone is effective, patient compliance is low. Methadone comes in the form of a liquid or tablet that can be ingested orally, therefore eliminating injection-related risks. The effects of methadone last a lot longer than heroin (four to six hours, compared to twenty-four to forty-eight hours), meaning that the individual does not need consistently repeated dosage. One regulated dose every day or two is much safer than three to four unregulated doses daily. Injection opioid users are four times more likely to die if they do not receive regulated access to methadone or if they are discharged from substitution services. The safety ratio of methadone is twenty, which is about three times as high as heroin, meaning there is a much greater margin of safety in terms of overdosing. Although effects of on-top heroin use are blocked by buprenorphine and methadone, if an individual uses heroin as well as methadone or buprenorphine or other sedative drugs such as alcohol or benzodiazepines, the risk of overdose is much greater as each of these drugs potentiate the biological effects of one another. As heroin suppresses respiration, which in high doses may arrest breathing, users risk choking on vomit while unconscious, particularly if the user has ingested another drug, such as alcohol.

Pharmacological opioid substitutions therapy essentially comprises five categories (extracted from *Drugs Without the Hot Air* by David Nutt, pages 183-184):

- full agonists: agents that bind to the same receptors in identical fashion, but are safer because the ROA is less risky, the dose is regulated, and the high is long lasting
- partial/mixed agonists: agents that bind to the same receptors enough to avoid withdrawal but produce less of a high
- antagonists: agents that entirely block drug effects, so there is no incentive to use
- pseudo-antagonists: agents that block positive effects and produce the negative effects of the drug
- disorder-modifying agents: agents that can prevent relapse by controlling aspects of addiction.

This type of opioid substitute therapy is often criticised by prohibitionists, who claim that the individual is just switching to stay on a different drug without any plan of exit. From a withdrawal and relapse standpoint, it is actually highly unadvisable for users to stop abruptly; however, the ultimate goal of opioid maintenance therapy is cessation. One of the reasons people are against this type of therapy is because they have been sold the idea of abstinence-based therapy. While abstinence may work for some, it is negligent to insist or force this type of treatment, because those who are not ready are highly likely to relapse, which makes them very likely to die.

Critics have also been quick to point out that this type of harm-reduction therapy is fundamentally opposed to the successful policy of reducing tobacco use, headlined by the seemingly abstention-focused 'quit' campaign. While quitting smoking is the ultimate goal, steps towards cessation such as cutting down, switching to vaping, smokeless or other non-combustible tobacco, using patches or gum (because both still administer the drug), and taking tolerance breaks are all part of that policy, just like switching to a safer drug, a safer route of administration and a safer supply are steps towards opioid cessation. Abstention can also be the principal focus for tobacco policy because the acute risks are very small, whereas for opioids the acute risks are very high, particularly when taken through unregulated means.

In 2006, almost 200 UK prisoners sued the Home Office for denying them methadone while they were incarcerated. Each prisoner was awarded £6,000 in damages for being forced to go through withdrawals. This was a highly controversial case because much of the research highlighting the efficacy of methadone treatment had been conducted among those within a community or therapeutic environment, which is very different to a custodial setting. However, research within Australia, as well as mounting international research, suggests that prison methadone maintenance is efficacious in terms of reducing the number of injections, as well as the level of syringe sharing.

Opioid substitute therapy appreciates that cessation is the ultimate goal, however, the journey to that end may be extremely difficult, and the individual involved is treated as having a health problem, rather than viewed as making a lifestyle choice. Before cessation, there are many other issues that often need to be sorted out, such as mental health, debt, unemployment and familial problems. Not only does regulated pharmacotherapy reduce the risk of overdose and infections and provide long-lasting doses that block on-top opioid use, but crucially, it stabilises the individual so they can engage with facilities, groups and professionals to assist them in steering their life in a more positive direction. Not only from a relapse perspective is abrupt cessation not advised, but additionally, some people who have undergone trauma are at higher risk of suicide when they are sober, because those past experiences can be vividly brought to the surface, which they are often not ready to face.

Comprehensive programs are much more effective than drugs alone or counselling or groups alone, because pharmacotherapy alone fails to address the holes in the individual's life that has led them to use drugs, and counselling alone fails to address the physiological issues driving continued drug use. Sydney facilities, such as Clinic 16, Clinic 36, Clinic 180, as well as the Medically Supervised Injecting Centres (MSIC) in Sydney and Melbourne are examples of comprehensive treatment facility services. Although these are not flawless solutions, they are certainly a step in the right direction. People can become addicted to the drugs used in opioid substitute therapy, which is why more research needs to be done into non-addictive alternatives.

Drug consumption rooms, such as MSIC, are not only beneficial for the user, but they also benefit society in a number of indirect ways:

- creating safer streets by both reducing the number of discarded needles as well as the number of intoxicated individuals
- reducing the spread of disease to the non-drug using population
- improving public access to emergency services
- improving the ability of drug users in integrating back into the community through employment, education and other training programs, which are economically beneficial.

The idea of 'retoxing' inmates has also been floated. This is where opioid addicts are re-introduced to methadone or heroin in a minimal, regulated fashion to reduce their risk of overdosing on relapse. It is very controversial, however, because many argue that this defeats the purpose of 'drying out' in prison and that prisoners should not have the right to use drugs when incarcerated, particularly if they have passed the stage of withdrawals.

Critics of methadone treatment often claim that evidence for getting people drug free is poor, and suggestions are often made that the way we stop getting people dependent on opioids is prevention. While true in principle, this is an idealistic, non-pragmatic concept that does nothing for the thousands of people who are currently dependent.

~~~

Heroin use was exceedingly rare until the early 1900s, when laws restricting the importation, distribution and use of opium were introduced, encouraging individuals to substitute opium for heroin. Prior to Federation, opium was readily available in Australia with warning labels as the primary means of protecting users. The first drug law in Australia was the *Opium Duties Act 1857*, where an import duty was placed on opium. As opium had been used recreationally in China for hundreds of years, the legislation was primarily enacted to discourage Chinese people entering Australia. The Australian indigenous population was prohibited from using opium under the *Aboriginals Protection and Restriction on the Sale of Opium Act 1897*, and the entire population of Australia was prohibited from using opium in 1908. In the same year, the UK amended the *Pharmacy Act of 1868* to regulate pharmaceutical opium, as a means of reducing suicides and poisonings.

The control of opium and cocaine in the UK was extended in 1916 under the *Defence of the Realm Act*, which essentially meant that the Home Office controlled both drugs. And in 1920, the *Dangerous Drugs Act* in the UK built on this existing regulation by restricting the production, importation and distribution of morphine, cocaine and opium to licensed entities. Heroin was still legally available on prescription until the early 1950s, and as with all other drugs, Australia did not have a problem with heroin until it became prohibited. Heroin overdose deaths in Australia increased from six in 1965 to over 1,100 in the late 1990s, which represents an over one-hundred-fold increase when adjusted for population.

Some may argue that global efforts to prohibit drugs began when the USA convened the International Opium Commission in 1909 in Shanghai, China. During this thirteen-nation gathering, the USA put forward recommendations to restrict and prohibit the trade of opium, cocaine and their related products (morphine, diamorphine, crack cocaine). In 1912, following the International Opium Convention, opium was prohibited on an international scale. When opium was banned in Australia, people switched to using heroin, and when heroin was banned, people switched to injecting with contaminated needles.

Although both heroin and opium are harvested from the opium poppy, heroin is several times more potent than opium, and heroin is predominantly injected, while opium was mainly smoked. Are you noticing a pattern yet? Banning one drug leads to the manufacture of more harmful drugs, and in the case of heroin, a much riskier ROA. It's like a game of musical chairs, and every time one drug gets up, a stronger one sits down in its place.

Additionally, and in a broader sense, pushing down on certain behaviours by banning them leads to increases in other harms, so that if we banned alcohol, not only would that probably lead to the production of methanol and bootleg alcohol, but also an increase in harms related to stress. It's a balancing act. You would think that the world would have learnt by this time.

Now, with crackdowns on heroin, fentanyl and related analogues have stepped in and raised the bar in terms of threatening public health. In fact, some countries have such absurdly tight controls on drugs like heroin and morphine that patients with serious illnesses are left to die in agony. Eighty per cent of the world's population does not have access to opioid pain management because countries blindly follow the UN.

In 1961, UK medical authorities lobbied the government successfully to reject the UN's recommendation to globally ban heroin, which meant that patients in the UK have been able to receive adequate pain relief, whereas in other nations, patients spend the rest of their lives suffering.

With the drying up of opium availability, heroin use continued to grow in Australia, and was further popularised during the Vietnam War era. During this time, US troops visited major Australian cities including Sydney while on R&R, and through multiple organised crime syndicates, USA troops were provided access to various street drugs, such as heroin. Heroin was exported to US troops in Vietnam from Chinese laboratories situated along the Thai–Burmese border, and at one stage, over thirty per cent of US troops were using heroin.

During the 1960s and 1970s, government and police had little success in suppressing organised drug crime, particularly due to the fact that corruption within politics and law enforcement was rife. Criminal entrepreneurs expanded into other markets, such as prostitution as well as gambling, and by the mid-1970s, there were over a dozen illegal gambling casinos in Sydney. Due to extended periods of corruption and the inability of the police to make any substantial dent in organised crime, which was spread over multiple industries, the heroin market shifted from small dealing to large-scale trades. The Kings Cross precinct in Sydney achieved major notoriety during this era for being a hub where drugs and sex were bought and sold in abundance.

Although Kings Cross had the reputation, the area was simply a reflection of the wider counterculture movement taking place in society, which included exploring altered states of consciousness as well as the anti-war movement. Much of the public distaste towards the war was directed to the then US President, Richard Nixon and his administration. Despite the overwhelming majority of US citizens disagreeing with the military involvement, Nixon preached that the majority of the USA supported the war (the silent majority), and that those involved in public anti-war protests were the shrill minority. Richard Nixon defeated Lyndon Johnson in the 1969 presidential election, and in 1972, Nixon faced candidate George McGovern. However, with such public tension over the war, the Nixon administration needed to cultivate public support.

They knew that if they could enlist the same supporters from the 1969 election, they had an exceptionally strong chance of winning the 1972 election. Richard Nixon's top advisor was John Ehrlichman, who later became known for his co-conspiring in the Watergate scandal. John Ehrlichman was interviewed by Wall Street Journalist Dan Baum, who at the time was in the process of writing the book *Smoke and Mirrors: The War on Drugs and the Politics of Failure,* a book tracing the war on drugs back to its roots. Ehrlichman had spent time in prison and the public considered him a disgrace by the time he was interviewed by Baum, so he had nothing to lose when recounting the real motive behind the Nixon campaign:

The Nixon campaign in 1968, and the Nixon White House after that, had two enemies: the anti-war left and black people. You understand what I'm saying? We knew we couldn't make it illegal to be either against the war or black, but by getting the public to associate the hippies with marijuana and blacks with heroin, and then criminalising both heavily, we could disrupt those communities. We could arrest their leaders, raid their homes, break up their meetings, and vilify them night after night on the evening news. Did we know we were lying about the drugs? Of course we did.

Even though the Nixon administration was entirely self-focused in the sense of retaining office, they were probably unaware at the time that they were about to plant a seed that would later grow to become the war on drugs. Through attacking drugs and their users, Richard Nixon won forty-nine out of fifty states in the 1972 election, making him the most powerful man in the world. The landslide victory sent shockwaves throughout the entire world because it let politicians know how beneficial it would be to their political careers if they were as tough on drugs as possible. President Nixon's campaign against drugs was a testament to how drugs had been viewed up until that time—that marginalised groups, such as indigenous communities (Native Americans, Aborigines), gay individuals and poor people, were not model citizens, lacked moral fibre and were more likely to use drugs and become addicted. Therefore, the moral basis and divisive underpinnings of the campaign were fundamentally about maintaining social hierarchy.

Nixon appointed Richard Kleindienst as Deputy Attorney-General, and during the presidential campaign, Kleindienst stated that the Nixon administration knew that drug treatment worked and incarceration did not; however, the political payoff was too difficult to refuse, so they elected for the criminalisation route. The motives behind the Nixon campaign were entirely void of any desire to actually address drug-related problems within the community. Since this period, the global status quo when it comes to politics and drugs (except in a handful of countries) has been to simply increase all prohibitive efforts, which has been increasingly driven by the US.

The term 'war on drugs' was coined by Richard Nixon in 1971 and was followed by Nancy Reagan's 'Just Say No' campaign in the following decade. Within two years of being in office, Ronald Reagan's administration tripled spending on drug law enforcement. Reagan's administration considered cannabis to be the most dangerous drug in America. President Lyndon Johnson was the first person to declare a war on an issue with the war on poverty. This was followed by the war on drugs, and then the war on terror. Some have argued that the war on drugs is a war on nature, since many of the drugs attacked by government are plant derivatives. This adds to the existing difficulty in enforcing against these drugs, and it also makes the prohibitive efforts harder to justify rationally.

Towards the late 1980s, it appeared that Australia might have been turning a corner when the Federal government altered its drug policy framework. The principle of 'harm minimisation', however, was a sham to appear compassionate to drug users, as still today, almost three-quarters of drug-related funding is allocated to arresting our way out of the problem. Harm minimisation was introduced in 1985, very shortly after Australia learnt that Rosslyn Dillon, the daughter of the then Australian Prime Minister Bob Hawke, and her husband were both heroin addicts.

Despite the world folding to consistent pressure from the US to pursue the war on drugs, harm minimisation seemed to address drug-related problems humanely. It is sad that Australia needed to wait until someone from a family in the public arena succumbed to drug addiction before adopting a more compassionate approach.

Harm minimisation is characterised by three pillars:

- supply reduction: reducing availability and accessibility to drugs
- demand reduction: reducing desire and demand for drugs
- harm reduction: reducing harmful outcomes of drugs.

Whether the pillar of supply reduction through enforcement measures, such as raids, seizures and police saturation, actually reduces supply in the long term is open to debate. Sustained seizure rates of sixty to eighty per cent are needed to successfully put a drug trafficker out of business, however these rates have never been achieved. Evidence from the UK has demonstrated that across all drugs, authorities seize between 0.5 per cent and 4.6 per cent of the total availability. This figure is a testament to the futility of prohibition and a wake-up call to every politician, policeman and authority representative who clings to the notion that being tough on drugs is the answer. This is particularly the case when what is seized is of low purity—authorities can report seizing fifty kilograms of brown powder to be sold as heroin, but when they find out later the substance is only ten per cent pure (five kilograms of actual heroin), it doesn't get the same attention. Seizure rates need to be maintained at a high level because illicit drug enterprises are incredibly resilient and lucrative, and this is primarily due to danger money, i.e. premium price for risks of detection and prosecution. Although these figures are subject to change depending on drug, source country and destination country, by the time a drug has been distributed from source country to destination country, the mark up can be anywhere from 150 per cent to 7000 per cent.

Profit margins are extremely high in the illicit drug trade, but they need to be to offset the risk and labour and time intensive nature of the work. Many deals are done in areas such as motel and hotel rooms, which means the room has to be bug-checked for listening and monitoring devices; the area has to be scoped thoroughly to see if anyone has trailed them or is watching; smoke alarms have to be disabled if cooking; watchmen are placed in outside areas; and a getaway plan, as well as a dump site, is often needed.

Apart from the evidence, I have spoken to countless police officers who claim that with every house they raid, another one surfaces immediately. Knocking out one supply source just creates the opportunity for someone else, which often leads to tension and violence among gangs, which the community becomes drawn into. Not only does denting the drug market lead to increased violence as criminal networks fight for new territory, but reducing drug supply leads manufacturers to finding substitutes or diluting the drugs with adulterants, both of which are generally more harmful. It also leads to more overdoses if purity levels increase, because the user population loses tolerance. Additionally, overdoses can also increase illicit drug syndicate profits, particularly in the heroin and cocaine market, because the word will get out that you have the most potent, 'bang for your buck' product.

Although the use of illicit drugs may not be overt in public, research shows that individuals who use illicit drugs report that getting access to the drugs is easy. Approximately sixty to seventy per cent of government drug-related spending is directed towards supply reduction (policing etc.), while demand reduction receives a smaller amount, and less than two per cent of spending is directed towards harm reduction.

It is thought that the concept of harm reduction originated from the UK Rolleston Committee Report in 1926, where the suggestion was made that doctors should provide heroin to those who had failed treatment and were unable to stop or reduce use. The real catalyst for initiating harm reduction in the UK came in 1988, when the Advisory Council on the Misuse of Drugs (ACMD) stated 'the spread of HIV is a greater danger to individual and public health than drug misuse'. In 2009, the International Harm Reduction Association explicitly characterised harm reduction as being about reducing the harms as a result of drug use, not necessarily reducing consumption.

Drug-related spending is highest in the areas for which there is little to no evidence of effectiveness, and lowest in the areas that pay disproportionate dividends to the community (harm reduction). This quite simply means that the policy is not evidence based. So, what then drives this dishonesty?

Shortly after Australia announced harm minimisation as the official drug policy, the government were put to the test to reveal whether their motives aligned with the new framework. In the early 1980s, leading up to harm minimisation, several thousand individuals in Sydney who injected drugs (predominately heroin) became infected with HIV. Due to the fact that many individuals with early stage HIV are asymptomatic or have mild symptoms, or the individuals are given false negatives (type II error in statistics), individuals with HIV can unconsciously spread the disease rapidly.

As recently as 2018 in Australia, ten to fifteen per cent of individuals with HIV are unaware they are infected. In the early 1980s, several thousand men, who were injection drug users and/or homosexual, presented over an extended period of time to St Vincent's Hospital, close to Sydney's central business district and the infamous Kings Cross precinct. Although HIV affects women and heterosexual men, the group most severely affected is men who have sex with other men. This is due to the fact that HIV is transmitted more easily through anal sex than vaginal sex as the risk of condom tearing is much higher—the insertive partner can contract the infection through penile abrasions or the urethra, and the receptive partner can contract infection due to semen coming into contact with the rectum, which is thin in its lining.

Apart from drug use, HIV is also significantly more prevalent among homosexual men than heterosexual men because the group pool size is much smaller, meaning that those within the pool are at a greater risk of engaging with an infected individual. There are also other factors at play, such as numbers of sexual partners, sexual activity in prison (as prisons are segregated by gender), as well as the stigma attached to HIV that discourages individuals from getting tested. Some argue that stigma can be effective at deterring the community from risk-taking behaviour. However, stigma also creates a sense of shame and guilt, which inhibit those engaging in the behaviour from seeking help. Drug stigma also occurs at different levels. In Australia, alcohol has less stigma than tobacco, tobacco has less stigma than cannabis, cannabis has less stigma than ecstasy, ecstasy has less stigma than cocaine, cocaine hydrochloride has less stigma than crack cocaine and crack has less stigma than heroin.

HIV is thought to have originated in non-human primates and spread to humans in the early twentieth century. Like rabies and bird flu, it is a zoonotic disease, meaning an infectious disease that can be transmitted from animals to humans and then among humans. The US Centres for Disease and Control and Prevention (CDC) are partially to blame for the stigma attached to HIV. Even though the first group of individuals affected were injection drug users and gay men, the CDC labelled the disease '4H' (homosexuals, heroin users, haemophiliacs and Haitians). It is also unconstructive to solely associate HIV with homosexual men, because ignoring women who are HIV positive has created the notion that infected women must be part of the sex trade, highly promiscuous or drug users.

Because the men in Australia diagnosed with HIV were drug users and sexually active, the medical community at St Vincent's Hospital knew that it was highly likely that many more individuals had been unknowingly infected, and that the city may have been on the brink of a HIV epidemic. If this situation were not treated quickly and effectively, HIV would spread from the drug-using population to the non-drug-using population, which would result in a widespread health disaster. Unlike the Australian 'ice epidemic', a generation could have been lost due to drug-related reasons because HIV is a communicable terminal illness.

At the time, the head of the Alcohol and Drug Service at St Vincent's was Dr. Alex Wodak, who, along with his colleagues, recognised the rapid increase in HIV cases and took the law into their own hands by initiating the first needle syringe programme (NSP). Clean needles were made freely available, although by doing so, the medical team running this initiative were breaking the law.

If the government had accepted just one of the thirteen submissions made by Dr Wodak and his colleagues proposing an NSP prior to this, they would not have had to act illegally. Dr Wodak and his team were summoned by the NSW Department of Health and the police to explain their actions, and after much deliberation, the police decided not to press charges because Dr. Wodak and his colleagues provided bullet-proof evidence supporting that their actions protected the community. Since the police were not willing to enforce the law, the government had to give way, and fast-forward to today in Australia where all states have implemented legal NSPs.

Since the implementation of the first NSP, annual HIV diagnoses fell from approximately 2,500 in the late 1980s to less than 700 in the 2000s, and among injection drug users, rates of HIV have been kept very low at around one per cent. This is despite a national population increase since the 1980s of almost 10,000,000 people, which represents about a sixty-five per cent increase.

Countries that ignored these harm-reduction programs have lived to regret it. Thailand's HIV rates increased from 300,000 in 1990 to over 700,000 in the space of five or six years, with over 100,000 new HIV cases being reported each year between 1989 and 1994. Across Europe, HIV prevalence averages about 4.7 cases per million. There are exceptions to this such as Latvia, which has about sixty cases per million. Russia has one of the highest rates, with almost 100,000 new HIV cases each year, with 40,000 of these being directly attributable to intravenous drug use.

Denying healthcare leads to other major health problems such as TB-HIV, where individuals develop tuberculosis on top of HIV because they have lived for a long time in poverty and been consistently denied treatment. In 2016 alone, approximately 375,000 people died from TB-HIV, the majority being in Africa and South East Asia.

The Australian government was so keen to stick to its prohibitive guns, but it did not have a leg to stand on in the face of objective scientific evidence. Incredibly, the Thatcher government in the UK faced exactly the same predicament. Margaret Thatcher was heavily criticised by her own supporters for her implementation of needle exchange in 1986, as this progressive policy was considered inconsistent with her no-nonsense conservative stance. The Thatcher government, like the

Hawke government in Australia, had to decide whether they wanted their legacy to be protecting the community with needle exchange, or whether they would be remembered for prohibition and the spread of HIV/AIDS.

Throughout the world today, there are over 100 medically supervised injection centres, none of which have suffered a single fatality, and which have all been crucial in suppressing the spread of diseases like HIV. A study conducted by MacDonald et al. in the *International Journal of Drug Policy* (2003) looked at ninety-nine cities throughout the world that have implemented NSPs to see whether the programs had an effect on HIV. The prevalence of HIV in cities that implemented these programs fell on average by almost nineteen per cent per annum, and the prevalence of HIV in cities that never implemented needle and syringe programs increased on average by approximately eight per cent per annum.

This is yet just another example where political ideologies need to step aside when it comes to public health issues. Rates of AIDS diagnoses in Australia have plummeted since the late 1980s/early 1990s, and even though HIV among drug users has increased slightly since the early 2000s, this is thought to be attributable to complacency surrounding HIV awareness following Australia's quick initial response as well as reductions in condom use.

Although difficult to measure, NSPs and other harm-reduction-related programs were very likely to provide a substantial buffer against heroin-related harms during the early 1990s in Australia. Cheap, high-grade heroin entered Australia during this time and became readily available, leading to increases in usage and subsequently surges in over-doses and individuals seeking treatment. In 1999, over 1,100 Australians between the ages of fifteen and fifty-four died from opioid overdoses, with one in eight of all deaths between the ages of fifteen and twenty-four attributable to opioid overdoses in the same year. From the early 1990s to 2000, the number of individuals on methadone programs in

Victoria increased by 500 per cent, while in NSW the number of individuals on methadone programs increased by 300 per cent.

~∾~

In the lead up to the early 1990s, Southeast Asian trafficking groups
concentrated heavily on the USA east coast, however, trafficking was
heavily disrupted due to a joint Thai-US DEA operation in 1994, leading to a huge hole in the USA heroin market. Increases in opium cultivation and heroin manufacture in Columbia during this time allowed
for Columbian traffickers to fill the supply void on the USA east coast,
so the Southeast Asian traffickers switched their focus towards the Australian market.

Due to Southeast Asian distributors holding very close links with
increasingly powerful members of criminal syndicates dominating the
Australian market share, cheap, high quality heroin was readily available. While the number of opioid overdoses dropped after 2000, the
number of individuals on methadone programs continued to increase,
primarily due to the lengthy nature of opioid substitute therapy and the
data reflected a delay in which individuals using heroin during the 1990s
would engage in treatment.

Australia did experience a sharp decrease in heroin availability and
purity, as well as an increase in price in the late 1990s/early 2000s.
There are a number of plausible explanations, including changes among
producers, such as moving away from heroin and towards methamphetamines; changes among traffickers, such as reducing availability to
increase profits (scarcity creates value); source country changes because
of bans or restrictions in opium production; as well as changes in law
enforcement, such as numerous international interdictions. The drop in
heroin availability is most likely to have occurred due to a combination
of these factors as well as additional confounding variables.

Many proponents of prohibition claim that the zero-tolerance
approach by the Howard government of the time was the principal and

unequivocal cause of the heroin shortage, illustrating a victory for supply reduction. However, using this potentially minor correlation as evidence in adding weight to the argument of prohibition is a stretch. This is particularly so, considering that, since 1996, heroin production had fallen by eighty per cent in Myanmar (the Southeast Asian region that supplied the majority of heroin trafficked to Australia) and that other source regions had to some extent replaced heroin production with methamphetamine production. Myanmar was also the primary heroin supplier to Canada and Hong Kong, countries that all experienced significant declines in heroin availability within the same period.

In the 1990s, consumption of heroin also increased tenfold in China and, as heroin trafficked from Myanmar to Australia travelled via China, it is possible that much of the heroin on the way to Australia entered the Chinese market before it was able to reach Australia. And there are often drug trends that we cannot explain—these are not opportunities for people to fill in the gaps with explanations that align with their agenda or belief systems.

Furthermore, despite the Howard government marketing themselves as prohibitionists (primarily to appease its conservative constituency), the discreet funding for needle syringe programs, the $200,000,000 funding allocated to diverting drug users away from the criminal justice system towards treatment and support of international harm-reduction policies reflected a government in favour of harm reduction as public health strategy and zero tolerance as a political strategy. Mr Howard, who would be considered one of the most conservative politicians in Australia's history—which some would argue would naturally align him in favour of zero tolerance—actually maintained harm reduction as a paramount pillar in government drug policy.

To speak of the heroin 'drought', however, is slightly misleading, as the abundant heroin availability prior to this time in no way reflected a normal heroin market and should not be used as a benchmark against which to compare fluctuations, other than to state that this period of time during the 1990s was a heroin surplus.

High-level law enforcement operations are likely to have played a contributory role in reducing supply, for example, the Australian Federal Police (AFP), Customs and other international agencies working together in seizing over 1000 kilograms of heroin in 2000. However, proving a causal relationship is challenging, and even if you are generous to the relationship, it was only one of many influential factors. It is unarguable however, that the harm-reduction approaches funded by the government from the late 1980s to 2000 were extremely effective at reducing HIV rates.

Independent research has concluded that from the initiation of NSPs to the end of the heroin surplus, at least 25,000 cases of HIV were prevented, and at least 20,000 cases of hepatitis C were prevented. The cost of the NSPs during this time was approximately $130,000,000, however, health care and treatment savings in the same timeframe are estimated to have been between $2,400,000,000 and $7,700,000,000, which means that even at the lowest and most conservative end, for every one dollar spent on the initiative, over eighteen dollars on health care and treatment was saved. Higher end estimates would put the savings as over three times as much. The Commonwealth Department of Health commissioned an independent study into the NSPs that concluded that between 2000 and 2009, 33,000 HIV infections and 100,000 cases of hepatitis C were prevented, saving over $2,400,000,000 at a cost of $200,000,000 to the public purse.

One of the contributing factors to the large number of overdose deaths during this period was that police would usually turn up alongside ambulance staff in the case of an overdose. Individuals who anticipated police attendance would be scared of calling for help for fear of prosecution. Now in every jurisdiction throughout Australia, following a major push from the National Drug and Alcohol Research Centre (NDARC), police only attend overdoses where serious crimes have been committed, or if another factor such as a threat to ambulance staff is evident. Unfortunately, delays in calling for help for fear of police attendance and subsequent consequences still exist today to some extent in emergency situations, particularly among young people.

Although heroin use has not evaporated entirely, the majority of opioid-related deaths in Australia now result from prescription opioids, such as oxycodone, hydrocodone, codeine, and to a lesser extent fentanyl. Each year in Australia, 15,000,000 opioid prescriptions are written. Opioid-related deaths, of which there are three per day in Australia, come from a mixture of using the drugs outside of prescribed guidelines and illicit use. There are a number of reasons why prescribed opioid deaths have risen in Australia:

- Opioids create withdrawals, making discontinuation difficult.
- Individuals prescribed the drug consider it to be safe because it has come from a practitioner and associate increased consumption with increased effectiveness.
- Opioids interact significantly with other drugs, particularly alcohol.

We have also sadly become a society that demands a drug for every health concern. Even for minor ailments, such as headaches, the first point of call should not be to reach for an opioid to numb the pain, when a glass of water, a cold compress or lying down for a short time may be beneficial. There has also become an increasing pressure on practitioners to alleviate pain or discomfort in patients quickly.

In early 2018, the Australian government tightened regulations on codeine, classifying it as a prescription-only medication, in an attempt to both curb codeine abuse as well as reduce individuals stepping up to more potent opioids. Whether this lowers harms in the long term, time will tell. What public health experts fear in the coming years is the replacement of heroin by fentanyl, which has a high potency, attractive to criminal syndicates, because trafficking a very small amount of fentanyl yields the same profit margins as a huge amount of heroin, with less risk of detection.

12

Tootski – Cocaine

C ocaine is a stimulant drug that is extracted from the coca leaf (*Erythroxylon coca* plant) growing in South America. Apart from its stimulant qualities, cocaine also produces an anaesthetic effect. However, due to the coca leaf and its extracts being largely prohibited internationally, cocaine is seldom used in medicine. The first Westerners to discover coca were Spanish conquistadors in during the 1500s. The Catholic Church subsequently declared that all coca should be destroyed because it had 'satanic' powers. However, indigenous people were allowed to work while chewing the coca leaves because they were far more productive with the stimulant aid. The coca leaf is classified as a Schedule 1 drug under the UN Single Convention on Narcotic Drugs and as a Schedule 9 drug in Australia. As a result, synthetic drugs, such as procaine, lidocaine and tetracaine, are used for anaesthetic purposes in place of cocaine. Cocaine is a naturally occurring compound in the coca plant that has evolved as a protective measure against insects. The plant has survived by producing an insecticide that deters and kills insects by overpowering their nervous system.

Individuals living in the Andean region (mountains of Columbia, Ecuador, Peru, Venezuela etc.) traditionally consume cocaine by chewing coca leaves or brewing the leaves in tea to reduce fatigue at high altitudes. Both these methods are safe ways to administer the drug as there is no smoking risk to the head, neck and lungs; no intravenous risks to the skin or veins; and no risks to the nasal cavity from snorting. The drug is administered in a less potent form and administered at a slower rate.

In terms of contemporary cocaine use, a small minority of users inject cocaine, and this carries the greatest risk of harm, including contracting infections and damage to the veins. The risk of overdose is particularly high with intravenous administration as users experience a fast and intense rush. However, the effects diminish quickly, often prompting users to re-inject within a short period of time.

One of the forms that cocaine comes in is hydrochloride, which is an acidic powdered solution of cocaine. The other form is crack, which is a crude form of cocaine. Cocaine also comes in freebase form, which, although visually similar to hydrochloride, is less pure than hydrochloride. Powdered cocaine is snorted or injected but does not burn well like crack, which is typically smoked. Powdered cocaine can also be rubbed into the gums or added to drinks. The name 'crack' cocaine comes from the popping or cracking sound that the drug makes when it is smoked in a glass pipe, as crack cocaine is cocaine mixed with baking soda and water. Powdered cocaine on the other hand is typically snorted, and this carries its own distinctive harms, including damage to nasal cavity, resulting in nosebleeds, particularly if small particles get trapped within the nostril.

Cocaine is erratic in purity. The 2015–2016 Australian Criminal Intelligence Commission (ACIC) found the median purity ranged from 31.5 per cent in the Australian Capital Territory (ACT) to 62.2 per cent in South Australia (SA). Although seizures have recovered cocaine with purity levels of 100 per cent, this is rare, and individuals who use cocaine typically consume a product that is fifty to seventy-five per cent pure.

Some of the adulterants or fillers are less harmful or harmless, such as sugar, caffeine or flour, while others are comparably harmful, such as other amphetamines. On occasion, some of the adulterants can be more harmful than cocaine itself and have included finely crushed glass, boric acid and levamisole, which is used to de-worm livestock. It is thought that the concomitant use of levamisole increases the stimulatory effects of cocaine. However, levamisole has been withdrawn from human medical use and is largely only used in veterinary medicine, as consuming the drug causes significant damage to various parts of the human body, including facial necrosis (tissue death).

Women who are pregnant should not use cocaine, as the drug can cause a range of problems for the foetus as well as an almost ten times greater risk of Sudden Infant Death Syndrome (SIDS).

Other chemicals that produce anaesthetic or analgesic effects such as lidocaine or, to a lesser extent, paracetamol have also been found to give users the impression that the cocaine is of high purity. Cocaine use is spread across all socio-economic classes; however, crack cocaine is associated with disadvantaged populations. This is thought to be due to the fact that snorting powdered cocaine takes five to ten minutes to produce effects, whereas smoking crack cocaine induces effects immediately, yet dissipates rapidly. This increases the desire to take more, which increases the risk of addiction. This is particularly the case for the users who inject crack cocaine after dissolving it into an acid base. In terms of toxicity, the safety ratio of cocaine from intranasal administration is fifteen, which is slightly lower than MDMA, but not as low as heroin, alcohol or methamphetamine. Although the capture rate for cocaine is somewhat debated, currently it is thought that somewhere between fifteen and thirty per cent of individuals who try cocaine will become dependent at some point. The acute effects of cocaine include increased alertness, confidence, happiness and psychological acuity. Cocaine increases body temperature, blood pressure, breathing and heart rate.

Although increases in sexual desire occur with cocaine use, so does anaesthesia, meaning that those engaging in sex can find it more difficult to achieve orgasm, leading to more vigorous sex and an increased risk of condoms tearing. This is also the case with other drugs such as

MDMA. Some people do experience increases in sexual desire, others do not, and as cocaine can also increase assertiveness or aggressiveness, those who have increased sexual desire as well as increased aggression may be more likely to force an individual into unwanted sexual activity.

Cocaine is sometimes taken in conjunction with alcohol, which is exceptionally risky, as the presence of these two compounds in the body produce a new chemical called cocaethylene, which is cardiotoxic (weakens heart muscle leading to electrophysiological dysfunction)— it is much more harmful than alcohol, cocaine as well as the sum of both and has a much lower lethal dose. The presence of cocaethylene appears to lengthen the effects, which increases the time in which the heart is under strain. Alcohol may also allow more cocaine to get into the blood stream, and as some of the intoxicating effects of alcohol may be masked by the stimulant properties of cocaine, individuals may drink more. Individuals who use cocaine are also at greater risk of serotonin syndrome if they are using other medications alongside, such as escitalopram, moclobemide or venlafaxine, all of which are medications used to treat depression and anxiety.

Hospital admissions and deaths where cocaine is the primary cause are relatively low in Australia, with only a few hundred admissions each year and approximately twenty-five deaths. However, as the harms from cocaine may not show up until later in life, this figure of a few hundred is likely to substantially underestimate cocaine's contribution to hospital admissions. In Australia from 2012 to 2017, annual hospital admissions for cocaine increased from approximately 440 to approximately 820. Many of these admissions involve alcohol as well, and individuals often present with significant chest pain. Cocaine also reduces seizure threshold, making it more likely for an individual to experience a seizure through overheating, particularly if the individual suffers from epilepsy, or is using other medication that reduces seizure threshold, such as bupropion or tramadol.

Although splitting a bag of coke and bingeing over a night or weekend may result in acute harms, long-term use of cocaine also produces noteworthy physiological changes. Bingeing on cocaine often deprives individuals of sleep and proper nutrition, and this can result in psychotic episodes. Following bingeing, users can feel restless, agitated and fatigued, and withdrawals can begin within a day or two, lasting for approximately two months, with the first week or so being the most challenging. Long-term use of cocaine may result in the development of arrhythmias, structural changes to the heart including cardiac fibrosis (enlarged heart valves) as well as stiffening of blood vessels (atherosclerosis). The risk is compounded if the individual smokes, is obese, has diabetes or has high blood pressure, as these factors can also cause atherosclerosis. These factors increase an individual's risk of cardiovascular-related death and are compounded if there is a family history of sudden cardiac deaths or if the individual engages in physical activity while under the influence of cocaine, including dancing or sex.

A handful of studies looking at autopsies of chronic cocaine users who have died of sudden cardiac death have shown that those chronic users typically have heart sizes ten to fifteen per cent larger than predicted for the individual's physical body size. Heart size increase is an independent risk factor for sudden cardiac death due to a number of reasons:

- Heart size increase leads to QT dispersion. The QT interval is a measure of time between two specific points (Q wave and T wave) in the hearts electrical cycle. Greater spatial dispersal between the Q wave and the T wave leads to premature action potentials, which leads to arrhythmias, which can cause ventricular fibrillation (VF). VF is where the heart quivers erratically, rather than pumping systematically. This ultimately causes cardiac arrest, for which survival rates are quite poor, particularly if outside of a hospital setting.

- In a hypertrophied heart (enlarged heart), the endocardium, which is the innermost layer of protective tissue lining the chambers of the heart, does not get adequate blood supply. This increases pressure on the heart and also increases the risk of a fatal arrhythmia. An arrhythmia is an abnormal heart rate, which can be too fast (tachycardia) or too slow (bradycardia).

- Heart enlargement leads to stiffening of the heart wall, which impedes blood flow and heart valve function. Often enlarged hearts are asymptomatic, however when the heart fails to pump blood properly, heart failure can ensue, where shortness of breath, difficulty breathing, chest pain and dizziness are common symptoms.

The risk of cardiovascular-related death is likely to be higher in individuals who smoke cocaine rather than snort, as the burnt particles will irritate the mouth, throat and lungs. Furthermore, burning the cocaine base in a glass pipe also creates other harmful chemicals, such as methylecgonidine. Apart from the route of administration dictating many of the harms associated with cocaine use, even in its purest form, cocaine causes significant physiological damage, particularly to repeated or chronic users. One of the particular areas of concern regarding cocaine use is its effect on the heart and cardiovascular system. Users of powdered cocaine are often middle to high income earners, who appear physically healthy and function well in terms of their employment, family and social life, which makes drawing attention to and acknowledging the underlying physiological damage much more difficult.

Cocaine possesses a unique ability to interact with sodium channels, which is how the drug creates anaesthetic effects, risk of seizures and changes in heart function. Sodium channels are proteins that form ion channels within cells that play a role in regulating action potentials, which are central to cellular communication. Cocaine interacts with protein Nav1.1 and Nav1.5, which are proteins involved in body temperature, heart function and the CNS. Mutations in protein Nav1.1 have been shown to cause febrile seizures, which are seizures associated with high body temperature. Interactions with protein Nav1.1 as well as other proteins have been shown to block pain sensations, and changes to protein Nav1.1 as well as Nav1.5 have been implicated in heart dysfunction because these two proteins are expressed in cardiac myocytes (cardiac muscle cells). Other diseases relating to disturbances in ion channels fall under the banner of channelopathies.

The majority of cocaine-related overdoses have occurred when the drug is used in conjunction with another drug, such as alcohol, or when an individual is smuggling drugs internally and the packaging ruptures in their intestines. The bulk of all cocaine deaths occur, however, in chronic cocaine users because heart function is compromised over time. In terms of acute psychoactive mechanisms, cocaine releases adrenaline from the adrenal glands as well as blocking the reuptake of serotonin, noradrenaline and dopamine. Release of adrenaline causes increases in heart output and increases in blood flow to muscles. Blocking the reuptake of these neurotransmitters means that there is a temporary increase in the extracellular level of these neurotransmitters in the brain, because the *postsynaptic* neuron (receiving the electrical message) does not absorb the neurotransmitters and the *presynaptic* neuron (delivering the electrical message) is blocked from allowing the neurotransmitters to re-enter. Higher extracellular concentrations of these neurotransmitters stimulate many circuits in the brain, including the reward circuit, which regulates craving for pleasure.

The drug was first isolated from coca leaves by German scientist Albert Niemann in 1859, and the findings were published in his PhD dissertation the following year. Throughout the mid-nineteenth century, European researchers showed significant interest in the compounds, mechanisms and effects of coca leaves, which had been used extensively throughout Latin America for at least 1000 years without any reported cases of the consumption of toxic amounts of cocaine. This is due to the slow administration of the drug through the act of chewing, as well as the physical effort needed to chew a large enough number of leaves. It would take many leaves, chewed vigorously, over a substantial period of time to administer a toxic dose.

During the mid to late nineteenth century, wine that contained cocaine (coca wine) was sold widely throughout Europe, with products such as Vin Mariani containing approximately ten to fifteen per cent alcohol and each glass of wine containing approximately twenty-five milligrams of cocaine. The small amount of cocaine present in commercial wine would produce minimal, if any, effects, which may explain why there were no reports of cocaine toxicity during this period.

In the late 1890s, Austrian ophthalmologist Karl Koller began using cocaine as a local anaesthetic in eye surgery. Before this, Sigmund Freud was aware of the analgesic (pain killing) properties of cocaine, however, was unaware of its anaesthetic properties. Although both analgesics and anaesthetics are similar, the mechanisms of action are different. Analgesics reduce pain, while anaesthetics block all sensations, including pain. Freud published a research paper in 1884 praising cocaine as a highly valuable drug, which, combined with Koller's pioneering use of the drug in surgery and his findings being demonstrated at the Heidelberg Ophthalmology Congress, led to the pharmaceutical company Merck stepping up production. Although at the time, despite being the primary European producers of cocaine, in 1883, Merck produced less than one pound of cocaine. In 1884, output increased to approximately 3,180 pounds, and two years later in 1886, approximately 158,350 pounds were produced.

The increases were driven by demand as well as the development of moderately refined cocaine, which allowed the drug to be incorporated into drops, inhalants and beverages. One of the limitations for cocaine supply at the time was the fact that coca leaves travelled poorly, and by the time the leaves reached the destination, much of the cocaine from the coca leaves was lost. However, once transportation became easier, drugs such as cocaine were able to spread around the world.

During this time, Merck's strongest competitor was US pharmaceutical company Parke-Davis, which is now a subsidiary of Pfizer. In 1885 a chemist working for Parke-Davis devised a way of producing semi-refined cocaine on site. This revolutionised the drug's production and trade by simplifying storage and shipping, leading to increases in supply as well as falls in price. As the cost of cocaine fell precipitously, patent drug manufacturers increased the level of cocaine in their products exponentially more than had existed in products, such as Vin Mariani, previously. This soon led to many cases of toxicity, some of which were fatal, and the adverse health outcomes as a result of the cocaine surplus were further amplified by the introduction of hypodermic syringes, with information around safe injecting still in its infancy. With the rise in cocaine-related harms and death from recreational use, a strong anti-cocaine push emerged, resulting in dwindling acceptance for its medical use.

During the early 1900s, cocaine was attacked and increasingly prohibited. Other drugs, such as novocaine and lidocaine, replaced its use in medicine. Following the prohibitive attempts to get rid of cocaine, came not only the decline in medical use and the suppression of research, but also the advent of crack cocaine in the early 1980s because border controls skyrocketed the price of cocaine, leading producers to develop cheaper alternatives.

The fact that crack cocaine was smoked brought insights into cocaine's addictive nature. Smoking crack results in greater concentrations of the drug in the brain than snorting and it enters and exits the brain faster, incentivising users to re-dose and increasing risk of addiction. The entry of crack cocaine into the market created a definitive schism between higher class 'cocaine' users and lower class 'crack' users. Crack cocaine was not only attractive to exporters because smaller quantities with similar profit margins could be exported with less risk of detection, but also to dealers, because profit margins were high and the individuals using crack became easily addicted, meaning repeat business.

During the 1980s, cocaine-related hospital admissions began to rise quickly. For example, in 1985 in the United States, cocaine-related hospital admissions rose by approximately ten per cent, the following year they doubled, and in 1987, doubled again to almost 100,000 admissions. It is argued that cocaine was possibly the first 'modern' global drug due to its spread via the rapid expansion of the international economy during the early 1900s. However, as it was only early days in terms of attempts to reduce drug-related harms through policy and prohibition, little was known about how effective the policies would be. As the principal aim was to reduce cocaine use, it seemed fitting to take a 'draining of the marshes approach' and push the majority of efforts into disrupting the manufacture and distribution of cocaine.

At the time, the public perception of cocaine was that it damaged individuals and the wider community as well as having an association with poorer marginalised groups. The medical utility of cocaine had been permanently sidelined; the world, including the United States, were unaware of the safer versions of the drug, and no one understood the negative outcomes of prohibition.

During this time, crack cocaine had also made its way into South American countries, such as Peru. However, instead of locking up crack addicts, they were treated with coca tea, which lead to relapse rates falling by seventy-five per cent and days of abstinence increasing seven-fold. In North America, however, not only was there a division between middle-class cocaine users and lower-class crack users, but also a division between the black community and the white community. Black males in particular were more likely to use crack than powdered cocaine, and in the late 1980s, the US government introduced legislation in which the possession and trafficking of crack cocaine attracted the same penalty as trafficking one hundred times the amount of powdered cocaine. In essence, the same penalty applied to an individual in possession or trafficking ten grams of crack cocaine, as an individual trafficking 1000 grams of powdered cocaine. Also, those in possession of five grams or more of crack cocaine faced a mandatory minimum sentence of five years in federal prison.

Today, less than twenty per cent of the USA population is black, and during the surge in cocaine use in the USA during the 1980s and 1990s, the black population was an even smaller minority. They were, however, as a result of the sentencing disparities, significantly over-represented in incarceration rates. This pushed the black community even deeper into an underclass situation, where crime increased dramatically, including a doubling in homicide rates in black males between ages fourteen and twenty-four. This has added to the existing racial tension between government and the black community, following a long history of explicit and overt discrimination, privileging whites over blacks. The black community felt as though legislation and policing patterns were racially motivated.

In terms of usage and distribution patterns, black individuals were only marginally more likely than white individuals to be users and distributors of illicit drugs. However, of all illicit drug and crack cocaine users, the majority were white individuals. This is due to the fact that the majority of the population was white, therefore white individuals made up much higher total users, but lower proportional users. In regards to cocaine use disparities, white individuals were more likely to use the powdered version, while black individuals were more likely to use crack. Both drugs were the same price per unit, but powdered cocaine tended to be slightly more expensive as it was sold in grams, therefore associated with affluence. At the time, a unit of crack only cost a few dollars.

Crack cocaine was used by black individuals to self-medicate the consequences of generational oppression, such as poverty, trauma and violence. Treatment was almost non-existent and because many lived in poverty or broken homes, there were no supportive networks to protect and respond to addiction. In 2014, approximately 350,000 black Americans were arrested on drug-related charges, compared to 830,000 white Americans. However, because the black population was a minority, black individuals were approximately three times more likely to be arrested on a drug-related charge than whites.

The 2010 *Fair Sentencing Act* reduced the crack cocaine weight sentencing disparity from 100:1 to 18:1. Even though the gap had shortened, the combination of several factors kept the disparity thoroughly entrenched:

- Black individuals were only slightly higher statistically than white individuals to use or distribute illicit drugs.

- Black individuals were statistically higher users of crack cocaine, while white individuals were higher users of powdered cocaine.

- Black individuals were more likely to become addicted and become trapped in addiction due to environment and intrinsic addictiveness of crack.

- Black individuals were more likely to be arrested.

- Black individuals, particularly men, were five to ten times more likely to go to prison than white individuals.

The US and wider world have taken significant steps towards racial equality. However, due to the fact that major social changes take time and the actual movement towards equality is recent when stacked against the timeline of historical institutionalised racism, we still have a way to go. While among older generations, black individuals are more likely to have used crack cocaine than white individuals, the level of crack cocaine use by black individuals since the 'crack epidemic' has been on a downward trend, and incarceration rates for black individuals have also declined. It would appear that inherently being a person of colour would predispose you to arrest and imprisonment, however, does this mean that the laws actually target colour, or are people of colour indirectly targeted?

Controlling for all other factors, crack cocaine is more harmful than powdered cocaine, however, the 18:1 sentencing disparity in US legislation is excessive. The strongest correlate for arrest and imprisonment is not colour or minority status, but being on a low income. When controlled for other socio-economic variables, such as education or employment, there is no racial disparity. However, one of the primary reasons black individuals are more likely to get caught and therefore more likely to be imprisoned, which the data cannot explicitly quantify, is the way in which the laws are policed. Although it is possible that racism does still exist to an extent among law enforcement officers, the discriminatory arrest and imprisonment rates can certainly exist without individual officers actually holding prejudicial views. It has been suggested that police departments are inclined to focus efforts in urban areas, with low income and outdoor, street drug markets, where it is more likely the offenders will be black. It is also suggested that simple frisk searches are more likely to disproportionately target black individuals.

The 2000 UK Runciman Report found that police were given discretionary powers when it came to enforcing drug laws, which allowed individual officers to pursue other agendas, which may have been disproportionately prosecuting individuals from ethnic minorities. Sadly, research also shows that many white individuals subconsciously associate black individuals with criminality and favour harsh punishments as a means of correction, whereas favour rehabilitation as a means of correction for white criminals. Not only can imprisonment exacerbate the problem, as many continue to use in prison, are introduced to harder drugs, or overdose upon release due to a reset in tolerance, but also, individuals who are imprisoned are unable to be treated for their addiction.

For this reason, crack cocaine is still today considered a 'black' drug or a drug used by the socioeconomically disadvantaged, and this label in itself often deters those users from seeking help. At the other end of the spectrum, powdered cocaine users are often high functioning individuals. This combined with the fact that biological damage from cocaine use is often asymptomatic until too late makes the behaviour of this group particularly difficult to disrupt.

13

GEAR – STEROIDS & SUPPLEMENTS

Despite the term 'steroids' being stereotypically associated with anabolic steroids, they are only one of the two main types of steroid classes. The other group of steroids are corticosteroids, which are typically used for their anti-inflammatory properties. Anabolic steroids, also known as anabolic androgenic steroids (AAS), are synthetic performance-enhancing drugs, which replicate the effects of the male sex hormone, testosterone. Testosterone is a central factor in the development of male sexual characteristics, both primary and secondary. Primary sexual characteristics refer to sexual reproductive organs, while secondary sexual characteristics are non-reproductive differentiations of sex within a species, such as facial hair and Adam's apples in males and breast development and wider hips in females.

Both corticosteroids and AAS are used in medicine for very different purposes and despite corticosteroids causing substantial health damage if used long term, AAS are the steroids that get the bad rep. As with many drugs, this is because of the drug's usage outside of a prescribed medical setting, where they are typically used for the following purposes:

- stimulating protein synthesis, which results in increased muscle mass in a shorter period of time

- increasing blood volume and haemoglobin concentration, which increases oxygen availability therefore raising levels of endurance
- increasing bone mineral density and strength, decreasing risk of fractures or osteoporosis
- increasing recovery rate from fatigue and injury, allowing for greater total workload
- potentially increasing genetic ceiling (natural limit)
- increasing pain tolerance, allowing for greater total workload/ intensity
- decreasing body fat, increasing muscle definition and power- weight ratio
- increasing reflex response, improving reaction speed.

Using drugs for performance purposes has existed since the 1800s, with the use of laudanum (tincture of opium) for sleep, so endurance runners could maintain alertness during events, and by the end of the 1800s, cyclists were using nitroglycerin to stay awake during lengthy events.

Although anabolic steroids are not considered psychoactive drugs, like all chemicals that produce physiological changes in the body, there are risks with every benefit. Although increased recovery rate and pain tolerance may benefit the athlete from a performance standpoint, the athlete may increase their risks of serious injury or illness. Masking pain may allow an individual to push through and continue exercising, but the individual may be at greater risk of further or serious injury if they ignore early warning signs. This is also the case with using psychoactive drugs for performance purposes, such as in the case of British cyclist Tom Simpson, whose heart failed from heat exhaustion during the thir- teenth stage of the 1967 Tour De France.

Before the race, Simpson had taken alcohol to keep his heart rate low, and amphetamines to allow him to push further on. Chances are the drug combination did not improve his performance, but they masked the effects of heat exhaustion. If he had not taken the drugs, the early warning signs, such as extreme fatigue and dehydration, would very likely have encouraged him to slow down or stop, which would have saved his life.

Further, while adaptions in skeletal muscle capacity occur alongside increases in mechanical loading, adaptions in tendon strength occur at a much slower rate. Thus, rapid progression in mechanical loading puts the athlete at risk of tendon rupture because the tendon has not yet adapted. AAS may also cause dysplasia of collagen fibrils and changes to tendon crimp morphology (arrangement of longitudinally aligned collagen fibrils), leading to poorer tensile strength, and capacity to withstand loads (either under stretch or contraction). Other additional trade-offs with steroids exist, such as the stimulation of protein synthesis, increasing muscle mass and power output; however, it is important to remember that the heart is also a muscle. While it may be desirable to enlarge visible muscles, it is not desirable to end up with DCM from heart enlargement, as it can increase an individual's risk of heart failure. In terms of cardiovascular disease, including heart failure, the risk appears to be greatest in strength and power athletes who then begin using AAS, as this particular group appears to, irrespective of AAS use, have a higher incidence of cardiovascular deficits. This is likely to be caused not by the nature of power training, but the absence of cardiovascular training.

One of the real challenges when it comes to informing people, particularly young people, about drugs is that due to a history of dishonest and sensationalist claims made about drug harms, not only can it be difficult to determine fact from fiction, but when forewarnings are legitimate, they are often disregarded or treated with suspicion because of credit prejudice. For example, why would the public listen to the warnings from the media regarding the rise and harms of fentanyl or synthetic cannabis, when for years they have sensationalised the harms of countless other drugs? Credibility can be very fragile, and unless we are honest and transparent about drugs, we risk becoming the boy who cried wolf; this is particularly true with steroids.

Many individuals who use steroids have a particularly negative view of the medical community and often do not disclose their drug use to their practitioners. This is despite the fact that a practitioner may be able to advise the individual how to use the drugs in a safer and more efficient way. Over half the individuals who use AAS do not advise any practitioner, and almost fifty per cent of steroid users have the same level of trust in the quality of information provided by their dealer as they have in that provided by medical practitioners they have consulted.

Some of the AAS users' scepticism towards the medical community may be attributed to the 2003 edition of the *Physicians' Desk Reference* (PDR), a book published primarily for physicians to use as a reference and information point when prescribing medication. Although the book is updated annually and is a legally mandated document, it is partially funded by pharmaceutical companies, which has given rise to questions surrounding the impartiality of the advice and information contained in the book. Leaving that aside, in the 2003 edition, the PDR section on AAS explicitly stated 'anabolic steroids have not been shown to enhance athletic ability'. This has been proven incorrect countless times, across various measures of athleticism. The same AAS section within this book also detailed proven risks associated with AAS use. Even though the risks were valid, the entire AAS section was discredited when the lack of benefits were proven to be of unsound standing.

Essentially, the risks were tarred with the same brush as the benefits in terms of credibility. It is far better to state uncertainty and conclude that further research is needed, than make assertions that later prove to be incorrect. Like many examples in life, credibility is easy to lose and very difficult to regain. Not only do many AAS users conceal their drug use from their physicians, but these individuals often fit the criteria of very healthy individuals on standard metric tests due to the fact that they are diligent in their exercise routine. They may not smoke or drink alcohol; they eat healthily, train exceptionally hard, and function well in other areas of life, such as employment and relationships, which lead them to believe that using AAS is not actually causing any significant harm.

Apart from heart-related risks and hypertension, use of AAS may also create lipid profile changes, which are essentially changes in cholesterol and triglyceride levels. Acne, male pattern baldness, gynecomastia (swelling under breast tissue in men) and testicular atrophy, leading to decreased sperm count and transient infertility, are all additional adverse side effects of hormonal imbalances arising from AAS use. These side effects tend to dissipate after cessation. Some studies have shown an association between AAS use and liver damage, including liver tumours. However other studies have concluded that while the liver is the primary site of steroid clearance, the claimed risks may be overstated or dose-dependent and may be more prevalent among individuals with other or pre-existing diseases, such as hepatitis, cancer or Fanconi's syndrome.

Liver damage may be asymptomatic in some individuals, while serious liver problems potentially arising from AAS use, such as liver tumours, cholestasis (impediment of bile flow from the liver) or peliosis hepatitis (development of random, enlarged blood-filled cavities or cysts in the liver), can produce symptoms, such as pain in the upper right abdomen, jaundice, very dark urine, nausea or pale stools. Specifically, 17α-alkylated AAS, such as oxymetholone and stanozolol, appear to present the greatest risk to both the liver and the heart. It is hypothesised that 17α-alkylated AAS poses the greatest risk to the heart due to increasing production of thromboxane A2 (a hormone that stimulates platelet aggregation by vasoconstriction, resulting in blood clots), while decreasing platelet production of prostaglandin I2 (a compound that is a vasodilator, which increases blood flow). The increase of thromboxane and decrease of prostaglandin can result in the blood forming a hypercoagulable state, which essentially means that blood progresses from being a liquid to a gel, resulting in blood clots.

Many AAS users also 'stack' different steroids, which often involves starting a cycle on a particular steroid and then adding further steroids as the individual progresses through training blocks as intensity changes or increases. The risks of stacking are dependent on the drugs taken. However, using multiple steroids at the one time, particularly over an extended period of time, holds much greater risk than using specific steroids in isolation.

❧

A further potential side effect of steroid use is psychological and behavioural changes and, more specifically, increases in arousal, aggressiveness and irritability. The relationship between AAS use and adverse psychological effects was first analysed in 1972, where approximately ninety prison inmates in the US were tested for testosterone levels in a single sample. The study found that approximately nine in ten inmates who had the highest level of testosterone were violent offenders and nine in ten inmates who were non-violent offenders had the lowest levels of testosterone. Several other studies using comparable methodologies have reported similar results. However, these findings should be treated with caution due to the unnatural environment within prison; the relatively small sample sizes; and other confounding factors, such as how the individuals have been raised or treated by others. One study in 1994 and another in 1995 showed that, on average, six out of ten users of AAS experienced increases in antagonism and irritability. However, a further randomised controlled study in 2000 showed less uniform results in terms of the aggression-testosterone association, as most of the subjects showed no significant changes in aggression and only a handful showed pronounced effects. The positive relationships between testosterone and aggression has only been established in animal studies, and a meta-analysis in 2001 covering forty-five human studies found a weak and inconsistent relationship.

If higher testosterone did increase aggression, this may benefit some athletes involved in competitive sports, as a higher rate of aggression may facilitate improved sharpness during competition. Evidence suggests that adverse psychological and/or behavioural effects in individuals who have used AAS tend to subside with discontinuation.

The media have attempted to link a number of high-profile athletes involved in crime to their steroid use, such as professional wrestler, Chris Benoit. In 2007, Benoit murdered his wife and son before hanging himself. Benoit showed slightly higher than average levels of testosterone, most likely due to his prescribed testosterone replacement therapy. However, despite Benoit committing suicide before confirming a motive, doctors have concluded that chronic traumatic brain damage from wrestling along with alcohol abuse were the primary causes.

Due to continuous injury, Benoit's brain structure and function had significantly deteriorated, causing severe behavioural problems, comparable to an eighty-five year old with Alzheimer's disease. Crime scene evidence also shows that the murders were premeditated and executed in a deliberate, calm manner, suggesting the crime was not an act of rage or aggression. The victims were murdered one day apart, with a copy of the bible left beside each body. They were asphyxiated or suffocated rather than beaten, and the son was heavily sedated with alprazolam and was possibly even unconscious when killed. This was one of the many cases where 'roid rage' was brought to the public forefront. However, a clear-cut cause and effect relationship between testosterone and aggressiveness is unfortunately yet to be established.

One of the ongoing debates within the sporting community is what constitutes performance enhancement? Are larger swimsuits that create less body-water friction or beta-blockers to reduce anxiety or cortisone injections that reduce inflammation considered performance enhancements? Is having laser eye surgery to obtain better than perfect vision or sleeping in an altitude chamber to increase red blood cell count considered performance enhancements? Or, if your parents have the financial means to send you to private lessons every day and fly you all around the country to compete, is that performance enhancement? Floyd Landis, who won the 2006 Tour de France, slept in his altitude chamber, which was not against the rules unlike blood doping and taking erythropoietin

(EPO), yet all three measures result in a higher concentration of red blood cells.

There is also controversy surrounding the politics and fairness of drug testing, where numerous athletes have been labelled as drug cheaters because they have been caught, even though their competitors were also using performance enhancers. High-profile athletes, such as Barry Bonds, Ben Johnson and Lance Armstrong, have, after investigation, admitted to some or multiple forms of illegal performance enhancement, but they have justified their actions by claiming that out of all the athletes who were using the drugs, they were just the ones who were caught and that all athletes should be held to equal accountability. Often it is highly successful athletes who have been singled out and made examples of, and this may explain why the phrase 'on steroids' has passed into the vernacular and come to mean a bigger, stronger, more impressive version of something it is similar to.

There is a degree of underlying tension between many athletes who use performance enhancers and athletes who do not, particularly in sports involving muscular speed, power or size, such as sprinting, weightlifting or bodybuilding. Expressions from natural athletes in reference to unnatural athletes such as 'they are on gear though' indicate that often those who do not use performance enhancers consider those who do cheaters. Many individuals who use AAS refute this by claiming that they can be used safely, that 'everyone is doing it' and that steroid users train much harder than those people who are natural. One aspect of this entire issue that I find particularly frustrating is athletes either denying or refusing to admit to the use of AAS, even though the elephant is standing in the room. Like many individuals, I do not judge those who use AAS and compete either against themselves or in a non-drug-tested field, as long as the individual does not lie about it and conceal it from fellow competitors and testing authorities.

When it comes to safe use, there is no such thing as a perfectly safe drug, and higher doses lead to increased risks and more pronounced side effects. However, the benefits of AAS can outweigh the risks if used under medical supervision. The notion that everyone, or many people, use these substances is simply untrue, as the vast majority of people who exercise non-competitively, exercise competitively and even compete in sports with the highest failed drug test rates are not using AAS. Sure, if we pick a sport that has a high failed drug test rate and then select the competitive federation that does not drug test and take the top athletes from that pool, then you might find that the majority are using AAS. But that is not representative of any sport or sport in general. It's a cherry-picked example to support an argument.

Many AAS users also claim that after using AAS for an extended period of time, they are healthy and have no health ailments and therefore deem the drugs to be relatively safe. There are also many smokers who never get lung cancer as well as many obese individuals who do not develop heart issues, but exceptions to the rule cannot be applied on a population or large-scale basis.

To say that those who use AAS train much harder is a non-argument, because the use of AAS allows the athlete to trainer harder. If a natural athlete trains vigorously, but then, despite natural recovery measures, such as hot/cold therapy, massage or sleep, is not able to train efficiently for twenty-four hours, then how is it fair to be compared to other athletes who utilise these therapies but additionally use AAS, which may shorten recovery time to eight to twelve hours? Both athletes are working to capacity; however, the total training load capacity is higher among AAS users compared to non-AAS users, just as the training load capacity is higher among those who utilise natural recovery methods compared to those who don't. This takes us back to the question of what is a performance enhancement, and where do we draw the line?

Natural lifters need to accept that comparing themselves against AAS users is unfair, as they are not comparing apples with apples. We don't compare male athletes to female athletes, junior athletes to senior athletes, or flyweights to heavyweights, so other major physiological variables, such as the use of AAS, should be treated as entirely separate categories.

Another argument commonly put forward in favour of the use of AAS is that it is not against the rules in sport to use AAS, but it is against the rules to *get caught* using AAS. This is a bizarre argument, as it seems to imply that the use of AAS is acceptable, as long as you don't get caught. This logic however could be applied to the act of breaking any rule or law, which are not to any extent, reduced or removed in terms of their unlawful, prohibited or unethical nature, if that person committing the act does so without detection. *However, getting caught is not the metric we use to differentiate between right and wrong.* If you don't have a problem with the use of AAS, but you have a problem with getting caught, it's pretty simple—don't compete in drug-tested events. I'm not naïve enough to believe that AAS use does not occur in drug-tested events; however, non-drug-tested events are at least open playing fields.

One growing issue among young, natural athletes is looking to elite athletes, not as role models, but as comparisons, and then seeing AAS as a means of attaining the same level. Young and novice athletes need to appreciate that, although the athlete they see is the final result, they do not see the dedication put in, sacrifice made and hard work done in private that has gone in to obtain that level. Young athletes may see a ripped physique or a powerful manoeuvre, but they do not see the ten years of rigorous training, the multitude of injuries and setbacks, the strict dieting and the dozens, if not hundreds, of times they have turned down a night out so they can stay on track for training. Young athletes also need to realise that the vast majority of professional athletes would be professional athletes regardless of whether they have used performance enhancers or not, simply because of their skill development and genetics.

Whatever discipline an individual chooses to engage in, the sticking points, plateaus and weak points experienced by all athletes are not reasons to start using AAS. They are signs to get smarter, look up programs, switch things up and try something different. For those who have hit a wall, the best program is probably the one you aren't doing and have never done!

It should be stressed to young people that although the chances of 'making it' as a professional athlete are exceptionally remote, let alone making any money from that profession, that's no reason to give up on their training or dreams. Sixty million people play tennis throughout the world, and of that group, about 300 men and women break even financially. Certainly, half of this group make extremely good money, and the top few are exceptionally wealthy, but if you crunch the numbers on likelihood of making money, 300 out of 60,000,000 is a 0.0005 per cent chance. Even among the 3,000 tennis 'professionals', ninety per cent struggle to get by. And this analogy can be made in any sport.

The most gifted baseballer is highly unlikely to make it to major leagues, the most talented soccer player will almost certainly never play in the English Premier League, and even for the most dedicated basketballer, the odds of getting into the National Basketball Association are exponentially against them. There are numerous forces outside an individual's control—staying injury free, getting a lucky draw or break or getting noticed by a manager. It is short-sighted for an individual to quit their sport, or choose not to take up a sport because the chances of turning pro are so slim. The benefits of recreational and non-professional competitive physical activity are endless. Quitting a sport because of the realisation that professionalism is highly improbable shows that the initial perspective was idealistic. Dreams need to be viewed through a realistic lens.

⁂

One industry that has grown exponentially over the past few decades is the dietary supplement industry. This has developed into a multi-billion-dollar industry, manufacturing and selling tens of thousands of different products every year. A handful of dietary supplements have been recognised for several hundred years but technological advancements have allowed the industry to diversify rapidly, particularly though the extraction and isolation of specific compounds. Products are intended to supplement deficiencies in an individual's diet. However, if an individual is not deficient in these vitamins or minerals, enhancing intake through supplements, resulting in a surplus, does not improve health and can often cause negative side effects, as for all compounds ingested, there is a recommended daily intake. Additionally, if a study demonstrates that individuals with specific deficiencies benefit from supplementation, that is only relevant to other individuals experiencing the same deficiency, not the entire population. We don't use the example of depressed individuals taking antidepressants as justification for the general populace to take antidepressants, just as we shouldn't use the example of anaemic individuals taking iron supplements to justify the general public taking iron supplements. The vast majority can obtain necessary levels of nutrients through a balanced and healthy diet. However, individuals who have specific needs, such as anaemic individuals, post-operative patients, vegetarians/vegans or individuals competing in strength/power-based sport, may benefit from certain supplements.

The most commonly used supplements are multivitamins, calcium, vitamin D, omega-3 (fish oil, krill oil, cod liver oil), glucosamine, magnesium, probiotics and protein powder. All of these can be obtained through a balanced diet. Despite claims made by supplement manufacturers, many of these claims are based on limited, preliminary or poor research. Far too often, supplements are unfortunately examples of significant overreach in terms of declared health benefits.

For example, research has found little to no evidence of vitamin C preventing or treating the common cold, and excessive doses of vitamin C may cause diarrhoea and kidney stones. There is little to no evidence that green tea or its extracts prevent cancer, and there is good evidence of potential liver toxicity. I am an avid green tea drinker, and I really want to believe that the antioxidants will make me healthier; however, the human studies just aren't there to cement that notion! Despite being marketed as a testosterone booster, there is no evidence to prove that the bindii plant *Tribulus terrestris* raises testosterone in humans; side effects can include stomach cramps, reflux and nausea.

One of my personal concerns about testosterone and hormone boosters is that they attempt to legally achieve the same outcomes as AAS, they are labelled like AAS (product name prefixes such as 'testa', 'growth factor', 'GH', 'testo', or 'anabol' and suffixes such as 'one' and 'bol'), and they are often marketed or owned by people who use AAS (Arnold Schwarzenegger, Victor Martinez, Ronnie Coleman, Jay Cutler, Christian Boeving, Rich Piana and many more). Is it any wonder that performance enhancement-type drug seizures (including beta-2 agonists and peptides) in Australia increased by approximately 800 per cent between 2002 and 2012? Many of these products rely heavily on a placebo effect, as they are marketed effectively with significant flair, and this is particularly the case with sports supplements.

Sports supplements essentially fall into four categories: pre-workouts, intra-workouts, post-workouts and inter-workouts.

Pre-workouts typically contain a range of chemicals, basically none of which, with the exception of caffeine, have been proven to improve performance in any way. The average serve of a pre-workout may contain the caffeine equivalent of a few cups of coffee, which in terms of performance may increase alertness, responsiveness and perspiration. There are some safety concerns surrounding the level of caffeine used in pre-workouts, particularly if used in conjunction with other caffeinated products, such as energy drinks, or even other compounds used within the pre-workout blend, such as beta-alanine and theobromine, as they can cause paraesthesia and trembling. Caffeine in high doses can induce seizures as the drug has been used to produce and lengthen seizures for patients undergoing ECT. Some governments and sports-drug-testing authorities have banned compounds such as dimethylamine due to concerns surrounding increases in blood pressure and other cardiovascular problems.

Intra-workouts consist of products that are supposed to be taken during a training session, and typically consist of electrolytes and branched chain amino acids (BCAA). The five electrolytes are sodium, potassium, chlorine, magnesium and calcium, which are naturally present in milk, nuts, fruits, and vegetables. When individuals exercise, both water and electrolytes are lost through perspiration, as perspiration is the body's natural cooling system. Individuals can get away with consuming only water if the exercise is light, short in duration and in a cool and dry climate. However, if this is not the case, electrolytes need to be replenished. If electrolytes are not replenished, performance tends to drop due to poorer muscle function and fatigue. This is due to the fact that electrolytes create electrically conductible solutions when dissolved in substances, such as water, and communications between cells that control bodily functions are facilitated by electrical impulses. When electrolyte levels in the body drop, cells cannot communicate efficiently, which means that the voluntary nervous system controlling muscle function is compromised, impeding performance. To avoid this, electrolytes should be consumed in the early phase of exercise and later again if the individual sweats heavily.

BCAAs are proteinogenic compounds, meaning that they facilitate the creation of proteins through enzymatic reactions. Proteins are then used in muscle protein synthesis and other functions, such as cellular communication and organ regulation. Despite proteins being made up of hundreds of amino acid units, only twenty different amino acids exist. Of these, nine can only be obtained through diet as the body cannot produce them naturally, and only three amino acids are BCAAs—leucine, isoleucine and valine. These three BCAAs account for almost forty per cent of essential amino acids in muscle proteins, which is why the notion of consuming BCAAs as a muscle-building supplement has gained significant traction. While building muscle is practically impossible without consumption of BCAAs (especially leucine) as they are not naturally produced in the human body and are critical to protein synthesis, if an individual is consuming adequate amounts of protein, particularly through animal products, BCAA supplementation is entirely unnecessary. BCAAs are present in a wide variety of products, such as chicken, fish, eggs, beans, nuts and protein powders. Additional supplementation will not hurt performance but it is essentially overkill. A handful of studies have shown that taking BCAAs before as well as during exercise does not improve performance. The only justification for BCAA supplementation would be because the individual's diet is BCAA deprived. There is some evidence to support the use of BCAAs for retaining muscle mass in individuals on weight loss programs; however, this evidence is not without its critics. Unfortunately, claimed benefits of BCAA supplementation have often been based on research using animals or untrained study populations, whose performance, even with a poor diet, will improve rapidly due to adaptions in neuromuscular coordination and muscle stimulation.

Post-workout supplements typically contain high amounts of protein, and it is advised that individuals consume these products shortly after exercise. Individuals often believe that consuming a large amount of protein immediately after exercise will translate to better muscle gains faster. This is because post-workout supplements are typically in the form of a liquid (protein shake), so they are consumed and absorbed faster. In short, higher-than-average levels of total protein will result in greater muscle mass development. However, the effect of a high protein meal immediately after exercise is insignificant when compared to total protein intake. Essentially, individuals need to ensure that over a twenty-four-hour period, they are consuming adequate levels of protein for their athletic needs, rather than being overly concerned about consuming a large portion of protein immediately after exercise. Total protein is more important than timing of protein. Individuals may feel hungry and/or fatigued after exercise, and there is nothing wrong with immediately consuming a large amount of protein at that time. However, athletes should not get bent out of shape if they are unable to consume protein straight away. A 2013 meta-analysis by Schoenfeld et al. covering about twenty studies found that individuals who consumed protein immediately after training showed no greater increases in lean muscle mass than the control group who did not and simply consumed protein throughout the day. Protein synthesis occurs for at least twenty-four hours after training, and consuming in excess of twenty to twenty-five grams of protein post-workout may actually hinder performance—excess protein is processed by the liver, where the nitrogen component of protein is excreted as urea, and the carbon skeleton is converted into and stored as fat.

The final group of supplements is inter-workouts, which may include creatine, testosterone boosters, immune/joint health aids and fat burners. In regards to testosterone boosters, there is virtually zero evidence to support that use of any of the compounds in these products will raise testosterone levels. Increases in testosterone from booster compounds, such as d-aspartic acid, have only been reported in animal studies. Human studies have shown decreases or no change in testosterone levels, and the only study showing an increase was in 2009, using sedentary individuals with low testosterone, and shortly after the increase, levels declined to prior baseline. Fat burners contain a myriad of compounds, basically none of which produce any measurable change, and the reports of weight loss have occurred due to dietary and fitness changes. Even though caffeine may slightly raise metabolic rate in the short term, the effect is trivial and is not sustained long term. Fat burners are marketed as appetite suppressants and metabolic stimulants, but the effects on heart rate, blood pressure, and levels of hydration have given rise to significant concerns surrounding the safety of compounds present within fat burners.

In regards to immune boosters, zinc is the only compound for which there is evidence in reducing the duration and/or severity of an illness, which in the case of zinc is for the common cold and diarrhoea. The term 'boosts immune system' is also a misnomer—the only things that legitimately boost the immune system are vaccines. Zinc is also used topically for the prevention of sunburn, windburn and dandruff. Like all vitamins and minerals, however, zinc is toxic in high doses.

In regards to joint support, the primary marketed products are glucosamine, chondroitin, different fish oil products and magnesium. Evidence surrounding the effectiveness of chondroitin and glucosamine is inconclusive, while magnesium has been demonstrated to aid in reducing muscle soreness. Despite various claims made about the benefits of fish oil, there is no convincing evidence to recommend their use (particularly in high doses) for cancer or cardiovascular disease (unless possibly if the individual has high triglyceride levels), and evidence surrounding its use for inflammation and joint pain is at this stage tentative. If an individual wishes to increase omega 3 fatty acid consumption for any potential benefits, they are advised to add food to their diet that are high in omega 3 fatty acids, such as fish, flaxseeds, walnuts and soybeans, instead of a fish oil supplement, as non-prescription fish oils are notoriously disposed to spoilage. Researchers at this stage are also uncertain as to whether any of the claimed benefits of fish or fish oil consumption are due to the omega 3 fatty acids present in these products, or if it is due to the fact that these individuals are healthier because they consume less meat. As the benefits of fish oil are still inconclusive, it may be too soon to throw out any fish oil supplements, as future research may potentially prove benefits.

One of the other popular supplement products is creatine, which the body produces naturally and is involved in regulating cellular energy. Creatine is also found in foods, such as red meat and fish. Creatine is one of the supplements most widely used by athletes, particularly those who participate in strength or power-based sport, such as bodybuilding, weightlifting, powerlifting, American football and track and field sports, such as shot put, sprinting, high jump, long jump and javelin.

Athletes are often advised to 'load' creatine initially by using the '5x5x5' method (five grams, five times a day, for the first five days = 125 grams total), and then following this by ingesting approximately five grams once per day for maintenance. Although twenty-five grams per day for five days is unlikely to cause any substantial harms (based on the small amount of evidence we have), some individuals experience bloating, nausea, diarrhoea and dizziness, and the actual loading phase is highly unlikely to improve any performance markers other than weight gain. For individuals participating in physical activity requiring shorts bursts of explosive power, creatine supplementation marginally improves maximal power output and lean body mass among most individual test subjects; however, not all studies have shown this, and some studies showed no effect or the studies have been too small or simplistic to draw conclusions.

Research into the long-term effect of creatine supplementation has not been done, therefore individuals who have either pre-existing or hereditary renal and/or liver dysfunctions are advised to avoid creatine. Although creatine supplementation can improve maximal power output during short, intense exercise, it produces no substantial effects on aerobic endurance. Creatine produces no psychoactive effects and therefore does not improve performance instantaneously. It is rather difficult to consume a level of creatine through diet that would improve performance; however, in terms of creatine consumption timing, there is no strong evidence to support the notion that creatine must be consumed either directly before or after exercise. It is also claimed that performance improves when creatine is taken with fruit juice or carbohydrates, but results with this assertion are inconsistent, and it is uncertain as to whether the creatine is actually working better or whether higher carbohydrate levels are responsible for the improvements. As it is advised to increase water consumption when using creatine supplements, it is possible that performance improvements among creatine users may be partially as a result of better hydration levels, as hydration is key to performance, and, therefore, some of the benefits of creatine itself may be somewhat overstated.

Like protein consumption, the most important aspect of creatine supplementation is that it does exist within an athlete's diet and that it is consumed on a consistent basis. Like many sports supplements, creatine often does not exist in an isolated fashion, and this is where consumers must be aware of terms such as 'proprietary', 'support', 'matrix' or 'gear' blend, because these products may state the total amount of each serving, but they may not state every single ingredient or how much of each ingredient is present. A ten-gram serving of a proprietary blend containing creatine may contain five grams of rice flour, 4.9 grams of sugar and 0.1 grams of creatine. Of course, there is no substantial harm in consuming a small amount of sugar and rice flour (unless you're a diabetic). However, if the consumer is going to fork out sixty dollars to purchase a product, they should know that their money would be better spent on either a cheaper container of creatine monohydrate, fish, chicken or red meat, as all of these products contain creatine. One important caveat to add with regards to creatine supplementation is that despite there being some potential advantages to athleticism, nobody can objectively state that long-term use of creatine will have no serious health consequences because no such studies have been conducted as yet. Similarly, there have been no studies on the safety of creatine in individuals under eighteen, therefore children should certainly be advised against taking it.

While I would never use my own subjective experience as evidence, in the early days of my weight training, I used creatine and protein powder and found that when I swapped out these products for real food, all of my training markers increased. This is not to say that stopping the supplements caused the improvements, but a number of other factors listed below are very likely to be the drivers of performance. Just because there are muscular and/or high-performing athletes who take supplements does not mean that the supplements are the cause or have any contributory role in their performance level—many are simply getting paid to market the product. It's also easy and lucrative to market supplements, while the crucial factors—sacrifices, rigorous training, sleep, water intake and eight meals a day of meat and vegetables—cannot be marketed.

Additionally, it is almost impossible to find any research or evidence covering the harms or benefits of some of the additive compounds in these products, and misleading claims are rife. For example, many testosterone boosters claim to release luteinising hormone, and luteinising hormone stimulates testosterone production. So, if taking a product releases luteinising hormone and this hormone regulates testosterone production, then why not just say that the product increases testosterone? Because not a single study has shown it. What works in a test tube, in animals or in theory does not always work in humans. And the product inconsistencies do not stop there.

Many customers feel somewhat reassured when they purchase a product that is 'Made in Australia', because they assume it would be held to Australian quality standards. However, 'Made in Australia' can simply mean mixed in Australia, and the raw materials can come from overseas in areas such as China, where food supplement regulations are not only poorly regulated, but so too are doping and production regulations.

Alongside a multitude of other products, sports supplements can be produced in enormous international distribution factories, and the products they produce are not always in compliance with outfits such as the World Anti-Doping Agency (WADA) and the Australian Anti-Doping Authority (ASADA). The same machines that produce steroids and other banned substances are also used to produce batches of supplements, and hygiene protocols are seldom followed, meaning they are not cleaned properly, which is where cross-contamination can occur. Brands don't bother testing batches, mandatory testing of source ingredients is poorly regulated, and because the supplement market is so absurdly saturated, brands have been known to be complicit in this process by adding compounds or spiking the strength of the product in the first few batch runs in an attempt to stand out from others.

In the past ten years, the FDA has identified almost 1,000 products with concealed ingredients, and since about only one in one hundred are tested, it is likely there are hundreds more that would contain similar agents. This lack of regulation is not only an issue for the general population in terms of not knowing what they are consuming but is of particular concern for elite athletes whose careers can hinge on a drug test.

Many of these products fall into the category of SARMs (selective androgen receptor modulators), which have been marketed as healthy alternatives to steroids under the banner of research chemicals. Some are available on prescription, while others require licenses or permits from the Office of Drug Control.

Those purchasing SARMs such as GVS111, SR9009 or MK677 online through rogue sellers, body-building supplement suppliers or anti-aging clinics can have their orders seized by border force, face fines or imprisonment and are using themselves as guinea pigs, given that all research has been conducted in pre-clinical animal models, and the alleged benefits have been in the form of subjective anecdotes.

Although it is ultimately up to the individual to be their own health advocate and to conduct due diligence when purchasing products, it is wrong for companies to let financial inventiveness get in the way of objective health outcomes. It is unacceptable that retail representatives not only 'prescribe' things to or advise customers based on flimsy or pseudoscientific evidence, but they also have absolutely no medical authority whatsoever to do so.

This unregulated market is not, however, an entirely new market. In 1976, Eric Fauchner, a reporter for USA magazine *National Enquirer*, visited over a dozen supplement stores in major USA cities to seek help for a variety of symptoms including fatigue, weight loss, insomnia and fever. Despite the fact that presenting to a general practitioner with these symptoms would certainly result in blood tests and/or other scans as these symptoms may indicate the presence of a serious disease, such as cancer, Addison's disease or HIV, only one of the sixteen health store reps actually advised him to see a doctor. Other salespeople made on-the-spot spurious diagnoses, such as energy imbalances or high blood pressure, and recommended taking a handful of supplements including vitamin E.

In the late 1980s, individuals working for the Health Education Council in the US contacted over forty supplement stores within the Houston area to seek help for 'their brother who had AIDS and was still engaging in sexual activity with his wife'. The individuals asked to speak to the store representative who gave nutritional advice as they wanted to find an effective treatment for the man's AIDS as well as protecting the woman from contracting the disease. Every store recommended vitamins and immune boosters, while some recommended additional herbal baths, coenzyme Q10 and homeopathic cell salts. Three quarters claimed they stocked products to cure AIDS, and not a single store mentioned condom use or abstinence.

In the same decade, Julien Devries, a senior medical editor at the *Arizona Star*, visited a supplement store to seek therapy for leg cramps, psoriasis, insomnia and weight loss and was sold over $100 worth of vitamins as well as a book recommending various nutritional cures for every illness that exists. The salesperson insisted their authority was valid because they had taken a three-week vitamin course. Evidence from Australia, New Zealand and Canada has shown that health food retailers almost always recommend store products that are rarely supported by scientific research, and representatives almost never recommended seeking help from a health practitioner.

Other 'health workers' such as trainers and coaches also need to be aware of their professional limitations. In Australia, there are no prerequisites other than high school education and first aid to become a personal trainer or fitness professional; certificates III/IV only take a few months to complete, meaning trainers can have no experience; there are so many certifying bodies; and the standards for certification are low. It worries me when trainers dispense pseudo-medical advice with such blind confidence regarding issues such as nutrition, injuries or medical concerns, when their level of expertise pales in comparison to the years of intensive training that medical practitioners receive. Two examples of this would be advising clients to remove certain foods from their diet or diagnosing them with a medical condition or injury and then recommending specific treatments.

Trainers play a very valuable part in the overall wellbeing of their clients' lives; however, it is important that they stay within the scope of their expertise and do not extend their advice into areas they have limited knowledge of. This is not only to protect the client, but it is also to protect trainer in terms of credibility and liability.

Chiropractors have killed and disabled patients by giving them cervical artery dissections from neck adjustments, and naturopaths have killed patients by injecting them with dangerous concoctions or advising them to delay or not undergo critical medical treatment such as chemo-therapy (whilst at the same time draining their bank accounts on false hope). People have died from acupuncture when needles have punctured their hearts or lungs, homeopathic care has resulted in children dying from conditions that could have easily been prevented or treated such as meningitis or encephalitis, and many others have died or been hospitalised from taking unnecessary unregulated dietary supplements.

What is promoted by the supplement/health food industry appears on the surface to sound innovative or technical, but the majority of products have been rejected by the medical community, particularly when it comes to issues such as anti-pharmaceuticals, anti-medical screening or anti-vaccination.

It is concerning that supplements continue to be pushed despite a consensus in the medical community that they are unnecessary. It is even more concerning that there is a substantial amount of evidence showing that individuals who use supplements are not only not benefitting from the asserted health benefits, but they are also at a higher risk than non-supplement users from other diseases. A 1994 Finnish study took approximately 30,000 male smokers over the age of fifty and split the group into four categories: vitamin E, beta-carotene, both supplements and neither. Individuals who took the supplements were at a higher risk of dying from both heart disease and cancer. An American study in 1996 took another high-risk group, this time just under 20,000 individuals who had been exposed to asbestos, and split the group into four similar categories as above. Those who took the supplements were at a higher risk of dying of both heart disease and cancer. A randomised study in 2004 in Copenhagen took over 150,000 individuals who used vitamins A, C, E and beta-carotene. The study found that the supplements increased overall mortality. A major review in 2008, covering 250,000 subjects, looking into the benefits of antioxidant supplementation found not only no benefit of such supplementation, but an increased risk of cancer and heart disease. And a meta-analysis in 2017 of forty-nine trials covering 287,000 subjects came to similar conclusions—that antioxidant dietary supplements offered no clear benefit, with a number of supplements being associated with a high cancer and all-cause mortality risk.

Whether the supplements were the *cause* is difficult to prove, as those who artificially supplement their diets may have higher rates of drinking and smoking or have poorer diets, less exercise or have pre-existing medical conditions—all of which could cause cancer or heart disease. However, the evidence seems to point towards the supplements being of very little, if any, medical benefit. Many supplements contain disclaimers such as 'these statements have not been evaluated by the Food and Drug Administration' or 'not intended to treat or cure any disease or illness', and this allows the manufacturers to wash their hands of responsibility in a legal sense. Although products contain claims such as 'scientifically proven' or 'backed by science', they are basically unverifiable, or have been conducted in a test tube or in animals. What good is a supplement that, for example, aids in osteoporosis when you are eighty years of age, if you are dead at sixty-five from a heart attack contributed to by the supplement? Save yourself time, effort and money by investing in actual food.

I have no personal beef with the supplement industry as I am sure that the vast majority of people who work within the industry genuinely want to improve the health of the community. They do need to realise, however, that they are not medical professionals and are not in a position to diagnose, prescribe medication for, or treat any illness. The evidence regarding safety and efficacy of the vast majority of products that they sell is slim to non-existent. There is another chapter on supplements in Part Two of this book.

14

CHILL PILLS & MOON GAS – ANALGESICS & INHALANTS

nalgesics are drugs that are specifically used to reduce pain. Inhalants are products that produce vapours, which are often household or industrial goods, such as aerosol sprays, glue and paint thinners. Although nitrous oxide is part of this group, most of the products that fall into the inhalant category are particularly risky because they are not manufactured for human consumption. These two groups have been placed together in the same section, as they are the two most commonly used drugs among young people.

Over ninety-five per cent of secondary school students in Australia have used an analgesic, and just under twenty per cent of secondary students have used an inhalant. Analgesics are, by far, the most commonly misused drug as they are easily available over the counter in pharmacies or in supermarkets; often prescribed by a doctor, implying a level of safety; easily accessible in the home and often the first drug ever used in childhood. The most common analgesics are paracetamol; non-steroidal anti-inflammatory drugs (NSAIDS), such as ibuprofen and aspirin; and opioids. Despite analgesics being the most widely misused group of drugs, more than ninety-five per cent of individuals who have used analgesics have used these drugs for medical purposes, within the pre-scriptive guidelines.

On the other hand, the smaller group of individuals who have used inhalants have done so entirely outside of any medical context, as the vast majority of inhalants with only a few exceptions, such as salbu-tamol (Ventolin) and nitrous oxide, are not used in medicine. Unlike drugs such as alcohol, tobacco or amphetamines, inhalants are the only group of substances used more frequently in younger secondary school students than older secondary school students. From the ages of twelve to seventeen years, all drugs, other than inhalants, increase in use with age. This is likely due to the fact that the substances inhaled are cheap, easy to steal from shops, and ordinarily present within the two environments that young people spend the majority of their time, home and school.

It is also likely that as young students age, they become more inter-ested in actual drugs, rather than non-drug compounds, to become intoxicated. A range of other drugs, such as tobacco and cocaine, can be inhaled, but are not considered inhalants. Although there is a common perception that using inhalants is a low risk and silly behaviour, very real and serious risks exist with the use of almost every inhalant.

One group of products within the inhalant category is aerosol sprays, which, if inhaled, can produce rapid effects similar to that of being intoxicated with alcohol. The effects of such inhalants dissipate quickly. The pharmacological mechanisms behind how inhalants produce psy-choactive effects are largely unclear. Inhaling pressurised aerosol spray directly through the mouth is particularly risky as the temperature of the gas when released is exceedingly cold (about -20°C), therefore potentially freezing the back of the throat, which can stop breathing, and spraying directly onto the skin can cause frostbite. The risk of freeze burns occurring is greater if the individual is already impaired by an inhalant or other substance effecting motor control. In fact, using inhalants in conjunction with other drugs can produce unpredictable effects, and inhalants are particularly risky if used alongside sedatives, such as alcohol, benzodiazepines or opioids, as these depress respiration, increasing the risk of losing consciousness and asphyxiating on vomit. Inhaling gases such as butane can cause VF leading to cardiac arrest as well as laryngospasms leading to users asphyxiating. If other inhalants such as alkyl nitrates are repeatedly inhaled or come into contact with the skin, sores can develop on the nose or mouth, as the substances can be caustic. Inhalants often produce temporary losses in consciousness, increasing the risk of injury if the individual uses the substance while standing up, dancing, near water or located in other precarious areas, such as balconies.

Individuals often try to concentrate the gas or vapour in a confined space, such as a room, face-fixed mask, car, bag or blanket, in an attempt to increase their high. However, if the individual loses consciousness and cannot access oxygen, they can suffer cerebral hypoxia (brain starvation of oxygen), resulting in the brain starting to die within a few minutes. These products also have a number of other risks such as flammability and if swallowed, can cause organ failure, blindness and death.

Organ failure and death from accidently swallowing poppers (alkyl nitrates) has been reported, and this primarily occurs due to methemoglobinemia, which is where red blood cells cannot release oxygen to cells within tissues, resulting in compromised functionality of organs. Poppers cause smooth muscle surrounding blood vessels to relax, resulting in blood pressure dropping, which can lead to dizziness, however, the mechanisms behind other effects are unknown. If inhaled, poppers are considered significantly safer than solvents such as acetone, toluene or turpentine, but even if used only occasionally and within harm-reduction guidelines, they are not without risk.

Recreational substance use, including alkyl nitrates, is more popular among the gay community, and poppers are often used to enhance sexual pleasure by increasing intensity of sex, lengthening orgasm and relaxing muscles around the vagina and anus. Some individuals who use poppers consistently for sexual pleasure may feel reliant on them to create sexual stimulation. However, abstaining for a short period of time creates a reset, and normal sexual response generally returns promptly. In terms of addictiveness, inhalants are not considered to hold significant propensity for addiction, but there have been cases of dentists as well as anaesthetists developing dependence on nitrous oxide, due to consistently being exposed to the gas. Most people run into trouble with nitrous oxide (N2O) if they use it chronically, constrain their supply of oxygen through the use of blankets or bags—where they can pass out and continue to starve their brain of oxygen while unconscious—if they use masks that deliver pure N2O (as medical masks deliver fifty per cent N20/fifty per cent oxygen) or if they use N2O in either confined or precarious places such as a car where a cracked window won't provide enough oxygen or near a balcony where they could fall.

If someone has used inhalants for an extended period of time and then stops abruptly, they may experience withdrawals, which can begin within the first forty-eight hours, lasting for approximately a week. Although multiple areas of the body, such as the brain, kidney and liver, can be permanently damaged from chronic use of specific inhalants such as correction fluid and aerosol sprays, most of the long-term damage can be reversed if the user stops.

The vast majority of products used as inhalants cannot be illegalised as they are needed and safely used in various settings, such as for industrial purposes or household cleaning. The Australian government has banned the sale and distribution of poppers; however, they are reportedly still sold in sex shops or head shops (retail outlets specializing in paraphernalia used for cannabis and tobacco use) under the banner of leather cleaners or room deodorisers. Although there are a handful of harm-reduction messages that I give to young people regarding inhalants, the key take-away message is that, unlike other psychoactive products that were essentially produced for either medical or recreational purposes, these are chemicals that have a wide variety of uses, none of which is for human consumption.

Apart from oxygen starvation, individuals who use inhalants also run the risk of sudden sniffing death syndrome (SSDS), which is typically caused by either uncontrolled muscular contractions in the vocal folds thereby blocking the airway, cardiac arrhythmia resulting in cardiac arrest or oxygen displacement potentially resulting in cerebral hypoxia.

Sniffing petrol still exists to some extent in remote Australian communities; however, in 2005, BP Australia introduced OPAL fuel, which is a low aromatic replacement fuel for unleaded 91, which if sniffed, does not intoxicate. The fuel has since been rolled out to at-risk areas, along with accessibility restrictions for premium forms of unleaded fuel to avoid individuals substituting with another fuel. Although the introduction of OPAL fuel has led to significant reductions in petrol sniffing because removing the intoxicating factor removes the incentive to sniff, inhaling low aromatic fuel still poses substantial health risks.

～℅～

As noted above, the most common analgesics are paracetamol-based products, such as Panadol, Panamax and Panadeine; NSAIDs, such as Advil, Nurofen and Voltaren; and opioid products, such as Panadeine Forte, Nurofen Plus, and Endone/OxyContin. Analgesics form a very broad category, and each of the products within that category produce different effects due to differing mechanisms. This is reflected to an extent in how they are regulated. Apart from caffeine, paracetamol is arguably the least stringently regulated drug in Australia; individuals of any age can purchase the drug from a wide range of facilities, including supermarkets, petrol stations and chemists, in an unlimited supply.

Although serious adverse consequences are very rare, the lax regulations around paracetamol and its widespread use are contributing factors to it being the leading pharmaceutical agent noted in calls to poisons centres in Australia. Accidental paediatric exposures, as young children are much more sensitive to the drug, as well as intentional self-poisonings are further contributing factors. Fatal paracetamol poisonings are rare because a significant amount of the drug must be ingested to induce hepatotoxicity (chemical-driven liver damage).

Individuals often experience excruciating pain over several days, forcing them to seek immediate treatment before it is too late. In some individuals, however, symptoms may not occur for between forty-eight and seventy-two hours. It is also likely that some of the reported cases of paracetamol-related hepatotoxicity are a result of its concomitant use with codeine—either the two drugs existing in the same medication, such as Panadeine Forte or in separate medications, such as Panadol alongside Nurofen Plus.

Apart from being a weak analgesic, paracetamol is also an anti-pyretic (anti = against, pyretic = fever). Paracetamol and NSAIDs work similarly in terms of their function, as they both inhibit cyclooxygen-ase (COX) enzymes, which are involved in various biological func-tions. Although not perfectly understood, it is thought that paracetamol selectively inhibits COX-3, which is found in the cerebral cortex. This may explain why paracetamol is more efficacious than NSAIDs in treat-ing fever and headaches. On the other hand, NSAIDs tend to target COX-1 and COX-2, which are expressed at sites of inflammation and therefore involved in pain signalling. This could be the reason NSAIDs are more effective than paracetamol in treating pain from tissue inju-ries. NSAIDs can selectively target specific COX enzymes, or they can be non-selective. As COX-1 is involved in gastrointestinal functions, NSAIDs that specifically target COX-1, such as low-dose aspirin, show a slightly higher risk of gastrointestinal bleeding and ulcers. NSAIDs that specifically target COX-1 also block thromboxane A2 production, thus increasing the risk of bleeding. This is due to thromboxane A2 stimulating platelet aggregation in blood vessels, and with less throm-boxane A2 production, blood vessels become dilated, increasing blood flow. Non-selective COX inhibitors, such as peroxicam, indomethacin and ibuprofen, may increase risk of kidney injury if used chronically, in high doses or among at-risk individuals, due primarily to NSAIDs reducing prostaglandin production. Since prostaglandin dilates efferent arterioles, which are blood vessels connected to the kidneys that play a vital role in kidney functionality, the reduction in prostaglandin means that blood flow to the kidneys becomes compromised, increasing the risk of injury. Under normal conditions in healthy individuals, prostaglandin plays a fairly small role in dilating blood vessels connected to the kidneys; however, for at-risk individuals, such as the elderly, those with heart problems or a family history of kidney disease, prostaglandin plays a much more important role.

For these individuals, if the protective role of prostaglandin is reduced, they face a significantly greater risk of kidney injury. Selective COX-2 inhibitors, such as meloxicam and celecoxib, may increase the risk of cardiovascular events, such as heart attacks and strokes, as these inhibitors increase production of thromboxane A2, increasing platelet aggregation, which constricts blood flow. Under normal conditions, there is an even homeostatic balance between thromboxane A2 and prostaglandin, meaning that blood flow is neither constricted nor over stimulated. Tipping the balance in favour of either thromboxane A2 or prostaglandin produces different risks among different populations.

Opioids function differently to paracetamol and NSAIDs in terms of their analgesic function. Opioids can be naturally occurring, such as morphine and codeine; semi-synthetic, as in the case of buprenorphine and diamorphine; or synthetic, such as methadone and pethidine. Opioids produce analgesia through different mechanisms; however, a region of the brain known as the periaqueductal gray (PAG) is thought to be the most important area affected as this governs descending pain modulation. When administered, opioids activate descending inhibitory controls in the midbrain, which suppress pain sensation. Blocking or suppressing pain sensation can be effective as treatment. However, as pain is the body's 'alert' system, masking very hot and cold temperatures, sores, cuts or other injuries can lead to other illnesses if ignored. The two pain pathways are ascending (from the body to the brain through the spinal cord) and descending (from the brain to the body through the spinal cord). Essentially, when a harmful stimulus, such as an abrasion on the skin, takes place, sensory neurons known as nociceptors send threat signals from the affected site to the spinal cord and brain.

When the spinal cord and brain receive this signal, a number of processes take place before the brain is able to produce sensations of pain directed towards the affected area. Opioid drugs bind to and activate opioid receptors, which are densely expressed in the PAG, and when the opioid receptors are activated in the PAG, this inhibits the ability of other areas of the brain to interpret the signal as pain. The reason opioid receptors exist is because the body naturally produces other compounds such as endorphins, dynorphins and enkephalins that all bind to opioid receptors.

This also highlights that while opioid drugs may block sensations of pain, they do not fix underlying physiological problems causing the pain. NSAIDs also do not fix underlying problems. However, they do reduce inflammation that produces pain, which like the effects of opioids, can allow individuals to function at a reduced level of pain while the body repairs itself.

Opioids not only function differently to NSAIDs in terms of analgesic function but also in terms of potential risks. The greatest risk associated with opioid use is that of respiratory depression, but other non-analgesic side effects can also occur such as fatigue, gastrointestinal pain, confusion and constipation, due to slowing down bowel movements. Although these side effects seem rather mild, if an individual uses opioids in either high doses or chronically, or if they are using a stronger opioid, these side effects can be very serious. Cancer patients are given strong opioids to manage pain, but this can often result in bowel obstructions. If the individual needs to undergo treatment or surgery to remove the obstruction, they are often not physically well enough at the same time to continue chemotherapy or radiotherapy, increasing the risk of the cancer growing. Fatigue and confusion may seem to be rather mild effects. However, if the individual relies on operating machinery or driving a motor vehicle for work, for example, they may be at a greater risk of errors while operating machinery or having a serious car accident. The sedative and depressant effects of opioids are potentiated with alcohol consumption, and respiratory depression arising from opioids limits their use for providing effective and safe analgesia. Many practitioners also fear prescribing opioids because of the risk of respiratory depression and addiction, which often means that patients in pain are undertreated and left suffering. Respiratory depression essentially means a reduced urge to breathe, and the relationship between opioid use and level of respiration is dose dependent. Increases in pain result in increases in respiration, and opioids that reduce pain also reduce respiration.

Opioids in small doses may result in minimal respiratory depression, which can go unnoticed, and as the dose increases, individuals are more likely to notice respiratory changes such as the rate, depth and regularity. Individuals may however still breathe with ease and obtain adequate oxygen at this level. At high doses, individuals can feel like they are short of air and sedated, and they need to consciously focus on consistent breathing. The fact that the person has to consciously focus on breathing often brings a level of anxiety, as they can feel as though they would stop breathing if they stopped focusing on it. I experienced this when I developed a major infection after wisdom teeth surgery and was prescribed a large dose of oxycodone. I vividly remember having slow breathing before going to sleep and jumping awake a few seconds after falling asleep because I stopped breathing and felt like I was suffocating.

If the individual becomes sedated to the point they lose or have lapses in consciousness, there is a chance they will die, as breathing is no longer automatic and involuntary due to no hypoxic drive (respiratory regulation), and the individual is not conscious to manually regulate their breathing. There are various pharmacological mechanisms in which opioids suppress breathing; however, it is believed that opioid-induced respiratory depression primarily occurs in the pre-bötzinger complex (PBC).

The PBC makes up part of the bötzinger complex, located in the medulla as part of the brain stem. The medulla regulates involuntary biological functions like heart rate and vomiting, and the PBC complex located in the medulla is characterised as a group of neurons that generate respiratory rhythm. It is believed that opioid administration inhibits the function of NK1R receptors located in this region, thereby slowing and ultimately arresting normal respiratory rhythm. There are additional opioid-induced mechanisms that can potentially suppress respiration such as the dampening down of brainstem arousal centres and the inhibition of hypoglossal motor neurons (nerves controlling tongue muscles), which increase the risk of fatal airway obstruction.

Looking forward from an Australian public health perspective, there are a number of concerns regarding opioid use. One of these concerns is the online purchasing of pharmaceuticals, particularly in the wake of codeine now only being available on prescription. Another major concern is the rise of fentanyl/fentanyl analogues. Fentanyl poses a very complex challenge for Australia as well as the rest of the world for a variety of reasons. However, much of the challenge stems from the fact that fentanyl itself is an incredibly potent drug, and the dozens of related analogues multiply the toxicity to a whole other level. Approximately fifty to seventy fentanyl analogues have been reported to drug control agencies such as the EMCDDA. It is, however, possible that hundreds of different analogues exist.

The potency of these chemicals simply cannot be overstated. Keep in mind that since some of these products are tens of thousands of times more potent than morphine or heroin, an amount equal to the size of a grain of sand would be lethal to a human. Even policing and customs officials need to take significant precautions when handling the product. Fentanyl analogues can also be synthesised with relative ease, and the precursor chemicals are legally available. Attacking opium cultivation has driven much of the rise in fentanyl, as shortages in natural opioids, such as morphine, have led to criminal manufacturers looking for more powerful alternatives that deliver more bang for their buck. Fentanyl poses not only a challenge to government authorities due to detection difficulties and potential for mass fatalities (through street use or use by rogue/terrorist groups), but also to individuals working 'on the ground' in the community. There are basically no harm-reduction messages that would have a significant impact due to the drug's high potency. Because we are dealing with compounds that are more than 1000 times as potent as heroin in terms of lethality, not only is it impossible for users to see the drug or weigh the substance out on digital scales reliably, but it is also almost impossible for criminals to weigh the drug out on scales. So even those involved in manufacturing are largely unable to provide an accurate and consistent product.

Increasing the pharmaceutical availability of naloxone (fentanyl antidote), improving and/or expanding injection centres in areas containing a significant number of illicit opioid users and outlawing all fentanyl precursors may be appropriate measures. It was originally thought that allowing take-home naloxone would increase harms, because opioid users might feel as though they had a safety net if they were to increase their dosage, but this has not been substantiated by evidence. Taking an opioid alone or in an unfamiliar place, however, is dangerous, because if the user becomes unconscious, they cannot self-administer naloxone. Additionally, taking an opioid after naloxone is very risky because naloxone only stays in the body for about ninety minutes, meaning that if they have taken an opioid that stays in the body for a lengthy time, such as heroin or oxycodone, re-dosing could result in a second overdose—even if the first one is prevented. In 2016, Australia became the second country to make naloxone an OTC substance (Schedule 3).

Policy makers also need to get real with their support of opioid substitution therapy and do away with the fixation on abstinence-based approaches, as this stands in the way of reducing deaths. Although I would be against banning precursors, it is very unlikely that criminal manufacturers would be able to produce more toxic substitutes than fentanyl and the related analogues.

In regards to online purchasing of opioids, government authorities have been able to clamp down on much of this; however, those who are willing to break the rules are often one step ahead. Data surrounding this issue is fairly limited, but it appears that the quality of online opioids is rather erratic. This is reflective of the logistical difficulty in regulating online pharmaceutical products. In light of regulatory changes to codeine, recent concerning data has emerged showing that some individuals have not only switched to obtaining opioids through illicit means but are also obtaining more potent opioids. This may be due to a number of individual factors such as pain being originally undertreated or the individual seizing the opportunity to get the most powerful painkilling product they can obtain since they are taking the risk anyway. Purchasing a more powerful product may also reduce the risk of getting caught, because if an individual purchases codeine, tramadol or even morphine illegally, then they have to either purchase a very large amount or make consistent purchases, compared to if they had just got a smaller amount of diamorphine or fentanyl less frequently, as these drugs are far more potent.

The growth of cryptocurrencies, which are essentially digital assets, as well as anonymous communication networks have fuelled the online sale of illicit opioids (among other drugs), as they facilitate basically untraceable transactions in terms of location and/or identity. Although cryptocurrencies, such as Bitcoin, Litecoin and SwiftCoin, are regulated to some extent if purchased through a currency exchange, there are many ways individuals can purchase and trade cryptocurrencies with anonymity.

Some argue that purchasing drugs (including opioids) online is a safer alternative than through a classical street sale exchange as it avoids any confrontation, violence or risks associated with physically meeting a drug dealer. This does not remove any risks related to the drug itself. However, there are some online spaces that may either show customer reviews, or at the very least, individuals can do some basic research through websites, such as wedinos.org, pillreports.net or ecstasydata. org, to gather information on product safety. Some individuals may actually prefer meeting a dealer in person to complete an exchange as the face-to-face contact provides a sense of security, instead of purchasing though the internet, where the transaction is not tangible and unable to be discussed. Individuals also need to realise that anything suspicious typed into search engines or accessed online may be watched by authorities, and anything that the individual posts or admits to online may be used as evidence against them if prosecuted.

On a wider platform regarding analgesics, these are a group of drugs that are addressed extensively in primary school as they are the group of drugs young people are most like to initially use and misuse. Once the analgesic box is ticked in primary school, however, these drugs are, for the most part, ignored. The key message given to young individuals is that analgesics are not 'bad' drugs if they are used within their prescriptive or 'use as directed' guidelines. Job done, right? As young people progress through life, however, school work builds up, relationships spark, hormones kick in and the pressures of life begin to increase. This is when young people are more likely to reach for an analgesic as a means of coping or self-medication.

Practitioners and other professionals can certainly play a role here in educating young people, not only around the safe use of medications, but also non-drug alternatives in situations where they are likely to reach for a drug, such as when they have a headache. The importance of the basics, adequate sleep, exercise, water and nutrition, needs to be reinforced. If the individual does have a headache or feels stressed, alternative strategies such as lying down with a cool drink, listening to relaxing music, meditating or doing a yoga routine may do the trick. These activities are not only harmless and helpful in the short term, but they also lay down the basis for a healthier routine for responding to minor ailments in the long term.

This is not to dismiss the benefit of pharmaceuticals for conditions like headaches, particularly if the pain does not dissipate. However, the individual may be able to achieve relief without pharmaceutical aid, and generally speaking, the less the individual is popping pills the better off they will be.

15

VITAMIN K & GRIEVOUS BODILY HARM – KETAMINE & GHB

B oth ketamine and gamma hydroxybutyrate (GHB) have a place in medicine, though with GHB, to a much lesser extent. Ketamine is an essential drug for both human and veterinary anaesthetic purposes, and as ketamine only causes minor respiratory depression and has no effect on the gag reflex, it is the drug of choice in settings where there is no access to electronic anaesthetic machines or trained medical workers.

Ketamine was used in combat zones during the Vietnam War, and even though it was a drug of abuse shortly after the war, recreational use dropped until the 1990s when it rose in popularity among clubbers. Unlike some other anaesthetics, ketamine enables patients' airways to stay open, which is why it has been used at accident scenes where there is no oxygen available (war, car crashes etc.). Ketamine is very similar to the compound methoxetamine; the chemical difference is simply that ketamine has a 2-chloro group on the phenyl ring and methoxetamine has a 3-methoxy. Methoxetamine became available after the ban on mephedrone and was a much more potent drug than ketamine—a gram of ketamine could get a few people high, but a gram of methoxetamine could intoxicate 100.

In Australia, ketamine is basically used only for veterinary purposes due to the risk of hallucinogenic experiences when patients awake and recover from anaesthetic. Australia is fortunate to have highly trained anaesthetists with access to first-class medical equipment that enables monitoring and support of respiration without the use of ketamine. Ketamine is effective for rapidly lifting an individual's depression, but it is not used to treat depressed people as large-scale studies are yet to be done, and the drug does not appear to be a long-term solution. However, it may benefit sufferers of depression in the short term, as antidepressants can take a significant amount of time to work, and symptoms often get worse before getting better. As antidepressants take some time to kick in, the interim treatment measure is benzodiazepines. For humans, both of these drugs are taken orally, and ketamine is administered through injection in a veterinary setting. In the 2010s, analogues of ketamine were being studied as potential treatments for pain and depression. However, due to the fact that a handful ended up being sold on the recreational market, all analogues in the country of study (UK) were placed into Schedule 1, making them virtually impossible to study.

GBL (gamma butyrolactone) is a GHB prodrug, and although more research is currently underway to look the drug's medical utility for conditions such as alcohol withdrawal and fibromyalgia, its use in medicine is rather limited, with narcolepsy and cataplexy being the only illnesses the drug is used for. For other conditions, the risk of GHB appears to outweigh the benefits, and the drug will have to prove itself as being more effective in terms of a cost/benefit ratio if it is to take the place of current treatments. GHB also has a very low safety ratio, between five and eight, which is similar to heroin. GHB often comes in salt form, but when used to spike drinks as a 'date rape' drug, it comes in a clear liquid, or drink spikers dissolve the salt in water or alcohol. Rohypnol (flunitrazepam) is one of the other illicit drugs used in date rape. However, the drug most commonly found in drink spiking is alcohol.

Both ketamine and GHB are extremely risky when mixed with other drugs, and the majority of people who are hospitalised for these drugs have almost always used other drugs alongside. Mixing ketamine with depressants, such as alcohol, heroin, benzodiazepines or GHB, can render someone unconscious fairly easily and stop respiration, while mixing ketamine with stimulants, such as MDMA or cocaine, can strain and possibly overload the heart. The safety ratio of ketamine is estimated to be twenty-five to thirty.

As GHB is a strong sedative, other depressants like alcohol potentiate the effects of the drug, while stimulants can mask its effects. This can make the user feel more alert and as if they can tolerate more GHB. If the stimulant wears off too quickly, however, the user may be lapse into unconsciousness. When mixing drugs, it is extremely risky to assume that one drug will cancel out the effect of another.

Individuals can overdose on GHB without alcohol. However, the risk of overdose is drastically increased when it is used alongside any other depressant, including alcohol. BDO (1,4-butanediol) is converted to GHB in the body by the same enzymes that breaks down alcohol, so it is likely that this would substantially increase the depressant risks associated with GHB.

At the end of 2017, Australian police seized 2,000 litres of BDO, which was about to be divided into thousands of fish-shaped soy sauce dispensers. BDO is attractive to criminal enterprises because while it is illegal for individuals to possess GHB or BDO for human consumption, it is not illegal to import BDO for industrial purposes under Commonwealth legislation.

GHB is a depressant, and its effects are similar to alcohol. However, GHB is a much more potent drug, and the dose-effect relationship is exponential. This is why GHB is commonly used in drink spiking, as one swig may produce little to no effect, two swigs may produce a mild effect, and the third swig may unexpectedly render the individual unconscious. The effects of GHB are predictable to an extent, as higher doses lead to higher depressant and euphoric effects, but the effects of ketamine change depending on the size of the dose. It is a dissociative anaesthetic, meaning that it can give users the feeling their mind is separate from their body, and it can block sensations of pain. In low doses, ketamine can alter or muddle thoughts and induce feelings of lightness and euphoria. Some individuals who use ketamine aim to enter a phase known as the 'k-hole', which can be achieved at high doses, and essentially encompasses the individual in a feeling of detaching entirely from their existence. Individuals who are k-holing can be totally unresponsive to stimuli, such as other people talking to them, and to hazards, such as roads or areas of water, which can greatly increase the risk of accidents. The experience of k-holing can range from being profoundly magical to frightening.

Some may argue that the ketamine experience is similar to that of the psychedelic experience, but psychedelics are not physiologically toxic like ketamine. Other than large doses of ketamine, or mixing ketamine with another drug putting the user at risk, the anaesthetic effects of the drug can mask sensory signals, such as pain, heat or cold, blinding the user to hazards. There have been cases of people losing substantial amounts of blood, dying after lying outside in freezing temperatures or drowning in swimming pools or bathtubs when unconscious.

Like all drugs, some people who use GHB or ketamine do not become addicted, but both drugs hold addiction propensity as they both can cause withdrawals, anxiety and a range of other symptoms if the user lowers their dosage quickly. Limited research into long-term use, coupled with the fact that only a very small number of people have become dependent on GHB, means that there is inadequate evidence covering the long-term harms of the drug other than the severe effects of addiction.

Although quality of life can be severely damaged from being addicted to any drug, more evidence is needed to ascertain whether GHB causes physiological damage that is not reversed after the user stops using. The number of people who have used GHB is very difficult to determine, because although it is reported that only 0.1 per cent of

Australians aged fourteen and over have used GHB at some point in the previous year, some individuals may incorrectly assume they have had their drink spiked with GHB, while others may have actually ingested the drug unknowingly, possibly assuming they were affected by another drug, such as sleeping tablets or alcohol. GHB was used widely as an anaesthetic in clinical settings throughout the 1960s, but usage is now by three distinct groups:

- bodybuilders looking to raise growth hormone
- sexual predators as a means of facilitating sexual assault through the sedative properties of the drug
- ravers or clubbers as a means of enhancing euphoria on nights out.

One common myth that exists regarding GHB is that the drug is a good supplement for building muscle because it is a depressant, therefore promoting deep sleep, and deep sleep is associated with increases in growth hormone. Several studies have demonstrated that GHB does sink individuals into a deep sleep and does allow for acute secretions of growth hormone. However, this evidence is comparable to evidence supporting the consumption of alcohol after exercise to raise testosterone. Neither are long-term solutions nor likely to result in any significant improvements, and the risks most certainly outweigh the benefits. Acute spikes in growth hormone secretion produce negligible effects on muscle growth. Using GHB for bodybuilding purposes is more likely to make the individual addicted to GHB than improve muscle size, just as using alcohol for testosterone increases is more likely to make the individual dependent on alcohol or gain excess fat than improve physique.

As the drug is an illegal drug, there is no purity guarantee, and as the dose-effect relationship is very steep, the same dosing to give an individual one night of solid sleep, may place them into a coma another night. There are simply other perfectly safe ways of getting into a deep sleep to secrete greater levels of growth hormone. GHB is not a steroid, and if someone begins to use GHB frequently, they may struggle to sleep without it. In fact, bodybuilders who take the drug regularly are more likely to become addicted than someone who takes it sporadically for recreational purposes.

Essentially, the benefits of using GHB as a muscle-building supplement are uncertain at best, but its harms are very well established. Those looking for a muscular edge are far more likely to end up addicted to GHB or suffering another harm, such as an accident or unexpected unconsciousness.

⁓

Building on GBL, GHB was first synthesised in the early 1960s by French surgeon, Dr Henri Laborit, in an attempt to create an anaesthetic that would cross the blood-brain barrier, but the drug was never used for human anaesthesia in isolation. The purpose of synthesising GHB was not only to discover its anaesthetic properties, but also to study and understand the workings of gamma aminobutyric acid (GABA) in the brain, as GABA is a key neurotransmitter in reducing neuronal excitability. Since the discovery of GHB, the drug has shown protective effects in settings of stroke, sepsis, heart attack and other conditions. However, despite these potential benefits as well as its anaesthetic properties, GHB administered to animals resulted in electroencephalographic (brain electrical activity) abnormalities, and this, coupled with the side effects of GHB in humans, meant that the drug was not viewed in good light.

In the 1980s, GHB was readily available over the counter (OTC) in health food stores throughout the US, but following concerns surrounding the potential risks of the drug, OTC sale of GHB was increasingly restricted, and the drug was placed in Schedule 1 alongside marijuana, heroin and ecstasy in 2000. The restrictions on OTC sale of GHB in the 1990s led to manufacturers switching to GBL and BDO as alternatives. Fairly soon, GHB had moved out of medicine, out of sport, and into use purely for its psychoactive effects.

The two groups who then used GHB were agreeable users and unaware victims. Agreeable users are those who willingly take the drug, typically in rave or club settings as a means of enhancing euphoria. The drug is popular among ravers due to its simple administration, supposed lack of hangover and powerful effects, but it is particularly attractive because of cost. A single dose of GHB may cost as little as two alcoholic drinks, and the effect will be more powerful and last significantly longer.

Although GHB may also produce an aphrodisiac effect, the chemical nature of the drug makes this effect exceptionally risky. GHB can decrease an individual's capacity to consent, and since the drug causes short-term memory loss, those involved in sexual activity may not recall events. Within club settings, individuals may also take part in sexual activity inside locked cubicles, which can make it difficult to call for help if something goes wrong. Even if the individual is not engaging in sexual activity behind the door of a cubicle, they may slip and hurt themselves or go unconscious, potentially choking on vomit, particularly if they have been drinking alcohol as well. Nightclubs are also loud and poorly lit, and other clients are often intoxicated and may be unaware that someone is in danger.

Although in its liquid form GHB has a salty taste, the drug itself is colourless and odourless, without a strong taste and does not leave gritty sediment. As a result, it is largely undetectable, particularly if the individual is already disinhibited from consuming alcohol. These reasons make the substance particularly attractive to sexual predators. GHB is also eliminated quickly, with the drug only being detectable in urine for six to twelve hours after a single dose. That is why it is extremely important, as difficult as it is, for anyone who believes they have been drugged and potentially sexually assaulted to report to the police as soon as possible.

Unlike GHB, there are a number of well-documented, long-term physiological impacts of ketamine use. Ketamine appears to have a negative impact on memory, and even though memory deficits appear to dissipate when the individual stops using the drug, this is likely to affect a number of areas within the individual's life, such as work or education. Individuals who suffer from schizophrenia, psychosis or anxiety are very likely to have their symptoms brought back by ketamine, even after the drug is cleared from the body. Using ketamine in high doses and/or frequently is also very likely to damage the bladder, resulting in significant damage to the urinary tract. Consistent use of ketamine causes cystitis (inflammation of the bladder) and bladder fibrosis (thickening and scarring of tissue). Both of these conditions lead to the bladder shrinking in volume capacity, meaning that the bladder can only hold a small amount of urine at a time. This causes a range of symptoms:

- needing to urinate often, as frequently as every few minutes
- sudden and forceful need to urinate, which is difficult to hold in
- urinary incontinence (poor/unstable bladder control)
- unrelenting drive to urinate, which is not relived by urinating
- pain in the bladder, pelvic and urethral region, which often intensifies as the bladder fills and during urination
- blood in urine.

One of the problems with ketamine-induced urinary problems is that treatment options are either largely ineffective, or very invasive. Abstaining from using ketamine is difficult for those who are addicted, and even in the case of those who do quit ketamine, symptoms do not always improve or can take a very long time to improve. Those who are unable to gain relief from symptoms may have to use a catheter or undergo more invasive treatment, such as a cystectomy (bladder removal) or reconstructive surgery. Pain relief medication may be prescribed, such as pentosan polysulfate, however, the successfulness of alleviating pain is a bit hit and miss. The earlier the patient is diagnosed, the better chance they have of favourable outcomes.

Like GHB, ketamine was synthesised in the early 1960s for use as anaesthetic. Dr Calvin Stevens, who was a chemical consultant to Parke-Davis, conducted research into reducing the side effects of PCP (phencyclidine), an anaesthetic used throughout the 1950s. PCP was primarily studied in animals, and when the drug was administered, the animals kept their eyes open but were in a cataleptic state, a condition characterised by an immobile posture with muscle rigidity and decreased response to stimuli.

Under the brand name of Sernyl, the first human studies of PCP were published in 1958, and by 1959, it was seen as the most potent analgesic in medicine. Despite PCP not causing respiratory depression, the majority of patients were postoperatively unmanageable due to severe psychological reactions, such as paranoia, hallucinations, ego death (loss of self-identity) as well as complete analgesia and detachment from the self and reality. PCP is still sold on the illicit market in a liquid and rock/powdered form, as well as 'dippers', which are cigarettes dipped in PCP liquid. With PCP deemed largely unsuitable for human use, this prompted research into alternatives. Through this research, a number of PCP derivatives were synthesised, one being ketamine in 1962. Human studies of ketamine, however, did not commence until 1964–1965, with the first group to receive ketamine being Michigan State volunteer prisoners. Approximately thirty per cent of patients experienced adverse effects, with reports of feeling like they lost sensation in their limbs and that they were floating. Ketamine was not as potent as PCP, and also had a shorter duration of action. As the researchers noted that patients appeared to be disconnected as well as anaesthetised, the term 'dissociative anaesthetic' was coined.

Research into ketamine spread through clinical networks in Europe and Asia. However, human trials in 1969–1970 resulted in significant side effects. Subjects reported powerful hallucinations to the point where patient acceptance was lower than that for barbiturates. By this time, ketamine had already been in use as a veterinary anaesthetic for a few years in Belgium, and the FDA officially approved the drug for human consumption in 1970. Ketamine was used during the Vietnam War as a field anaesthetic, but due to its abuse among soldiers as well as the arrival of other anaesthetics and hypnotics such as propofol, it became a Schedule 3 drug in 1999. During the 1990s, numerous scientific advancements were made that gave rise to the use of the fentanyl patch as well as potent fentanyl analogues, such as remifentanil, alfentanil and sufentanil, which were often administered to cancer patients and post-operative/peri-operative patients.

The focus for analgesia had shifted away from ketamine towards opioids. However, chronic use of opioids can produce a paradoxical effect, known as hyperalgesia, which is where patients become sensitised (more sensitive) to specific pain stimuli, potentially drawing them towards stronger painkillers. Little was known about the mechanisms behind hyperalgesia; however, it was discovered that ketamine actually held anti-hyperalgesic properties, which led to a comeback of ketamine use, particularly for patients suffering from chronic pain. Ketamine today is, however, not used within the developed world for human medical purposes and is classified as a Schedule 8 drug in Australia.

The United Nations Commission on Narcotic Drugs planned to ban ketamine globally in 2015, illustrating an immense lack of foresight and understanding of its usefulness in veterinary medicine, as well as for physicians working in areas of the world that use ketamine for pain management, due to opioid unavailability. Some countries, such as the UK, did follow suit leading to perverse outcomes, such as at the Glastonbury Music Festival, where medical staff were denied being able to hold ketamine, in the event it was needed to anaesthetise one of the 140,000 attendees in an emergency. Thankfully this manoeuvre did not eventuate. However, it highlights that the UN's blinkered approach towards drugs is at odds with the medical community as it damages research, harms patients and does nothing to reduce recreational use.

In early 2018, the Black Dog Institute and University of NSW teamed up to run a pilot study looking into the efficacy of a ketamine nasal spray to treat treatment-resistant depression. Despite previous studies showing promise, the study was aborted because some of the participants suffered side effects. Researchers at the Black Dog Institute are currently recruiting for the largest independent trial of ketamine to treat depression, this time using injection as the ROA.

This comes thirty-three years after the first experimental observation into the potential antidepressant utility of ketamine. Although the antidepressant effect of ketamine is short lasting, the drug can provide rapid relief within a few hours, and may be of particular benefit to patients with a high risk of suicide. Ketamine holds a firm place in veterinary medicine as well as in developing parts of the world, where adequate anaesthesia is not possible. However, in terms of human use for its anti-hyperalgesia and antidepressant properties, the future is uncertain.

16

Downers & Downers – Benzodiazepines & Barbiturates

The parent compound of barbiturates, malonylurea, was first synthesised in the 1860s by German scientist Adolf Von Baeyer, and this group of drugs began to be used in clinical settings during the early 1900s.

Excluding a handful of uses, such as capital punishment, epilepsy and euthanasia, barbiturates have largely been replaced by benzodiazepines since the 1950s, primarily due to barbiturates being riskier than benzodiazepines in terms of overdose and addiction propensity. In fact, the ban on barbiturates may represent the only time in history when the prohibition of a drug actually had beneficial outcomes, as people moved away from barbiturates towards benzodiazepines, which, generally speaking, are safer drugs. Drug prohibition can work if demand is relatively weak, easily influenced and highly elastic, if supply is easily interrupted, if the drugs that replace the prohibited drugs are not as harmful or—as in the case of barbiturates—if the drugs are difficult to synthesise.

The two main issues with benzodiazepine prescriptions are patients who take too much and become dependent, and non-patients who use other individuals' prescribed benzodiazepines for non-medical purposes.

Benzodiazepine overdoses can be treated with either activated charcoal or flumazenil, while barbiturate overdoses are more difficult to manage, with activated charcoal being the only potential treatment. Opioid antagonists or methylethylglutarimide may be used to reverse respiratory depression, however there appears to be little research in this area. Even the effectiveness of activated charcoal as an antidote in a barbiturate overdose is unreliable, which further supports the replacing of barbiturates by benzodiazepines in medicine, as the options to pharmacologically reverse the respiratory depression and unconsciousness in barbiturate overdose is very limited compared to benzodiazepine overdose.

Although flumazenil is effective in treating the respiratory depression associated with a benzodiazepine overdose, its administration is controversial due to several contraindications. Contraindications are factors or reasons to withhold treatment due potential risks to the patient, and in the case of flumazenil, this particularly includes those patients with histories of tachycardia and seizures. Contraindications can be either relative, where the treatment may still proceed if caution is taken and if the benefits outweigh the risks, or absolute, where treatment must be avoided due to significant danger, that is, life threatening or significant impairment.

Contraindications can also exist if there is a risk to an unborn baby (teratogenics), as in the case of tretinoin, misoprostol, warfarin, lithium and many other drugs. As the risks associated with flumazenil often outweigh the benefits, only a small proportion of individuals are suitable candidates, and in these cases, it is strongly recommended that toxicologists oversee and advise patients in terms of treatment.

Although the use of barbiturates in medicine is very limited today, they were initially deemed a breakthrough, as patients who suffered from various illnesses such as sleep disorders or epilepsy were largely untreatable. Since their inception, over 2,000 barbiturates have been synthesised, with only two per cent making it to the market and only about twenty per cent of that group being regularly used in clinical settings.

Although they have been largely substituted by benzodiazepines, barbiturates temporarily replaced alkaloids, such as morphine, which were widely used throughout the second half of the nineteenth century.

Bromides, and particularly potassium bromide, were also widely used throughout the nineteenth century for their sedative, anti-epileptic and anti-headache properties. However, in the late 1900s, they were withdrawn from OTC sale due to emerging evidence of toxicity from chronic use. Long-term use of bromides results in bromism, which produces neurological, psychiatric, gastrointestinal and dermatological complications, which in severe cases can be fatal.

⁓

Approximately forty-five years after malonylurea was synthesised, Heinrich Hörlein, a scientist working for Bayer Pharmaceuticals, synthesised phenobarbital, which would later go on to be known as 'the king of barbiturates'. Phenobarbital was commercialised under the name Luminal by Bayer during 1911-1912, which led to it being used extensively among both inpatients and outpatients. Butobarbital was the second barbiturate to be used frequently in therapeutic settings, and the drug was effectively brought to the market by circumstances surrounding World War I.

During this time, the British armed forces used large amounts of acetone in explosive manufacturing. One of the suppliers of acetone discovered that the bacteria clostridium acetobutylicum could easily and inexpensively transform products high in starch into butyric alcohol as well as acetone. As the industrial cost of butyric alcohol fell after the war, this allowed it to be used as a base for producing various synthetic drugs. A number of different research groups took steps towards butobarbital; however, Arthur Dox from Parke-Davis was the first scientist to synthesise the compound in 1922. The drug was marketed the following year under the brand names Neonal, Butethal and Soneryl. Butobarbital was triple the potency of barbital (Veronal), the first barbiturate to be brought to the market in 1903-1904. In the decades following, a number of other barbiturates were brought to the market, such as amobarbital in 1923, secobarbital in 1929, pentobarbital in 1930 and thiopental in the early 1930s.

Barbiturates were used up to the 1950s when they began to be slowly replaced by benzodiazepines. However, a number of other drugs with a similar pharmacological action were also introduced during this transitional period as well, such as glutethimide, chlormethiazole and methaqualone. Although these drugs offered a greater margin of safety than barbiturates, most were taken out of medicine years later due to the fact that the addiction and severe withdrawals associated with their use were like that of barbiturates.

In the UK from the early 1900s to the 1930s, barbiturates were only involved in a handful of deaths every year. However, in the 1940s, this had risen to approximately 100 deaths annually. This number increased over six-fold to almost 700 deaths during the 1950s, and by 1960, almost 1,400 people were dying each year in the UK as a result of barbiturate overdoses, of which a large portion were suicide.

Between 1965 and 1970, over 12,300 deaths in the UK were wholly attributable to barbiturates. This is hardly surprising given that during this period, over 20,000,000 barbiturate prescriptions were handed out annually. This equated to approximately forty per cent of the population at the time obtaining a barbiturate prescription every year. The death of Marilyn Monroe from a barbiturate over-dose in 1962 brought the lethality of barbiturates to public attention and prompted the scientific community to look for safer alternatives. In current medicine, the use of barbiturates is constrained to specific therapeutic applications.

The revolution in psychiatric therapy, away from barbiturates and towards benzodiazepines, had already begun in 1952 with the discovery of chlorpromazine, leading to the commercialisation of the first benzodiazepine, chlordiazepoxide. Hoffmann-La Roche was the first pharmaceutical company to bring a benzodiazepine to the market in the late

1950s, that being the benzheptoxdiazine derivative, chlordiazepoxide, which was primarily prescribed for anxiety and insomnia.

Hoffmann-La Roche researcher Leo Sternbach discovered chlordiazepoxide almost by accident, as it was a leftover substance from previous animal studies. During the time however, rigorous drug testing was not needed for sale approval, which allowed this drug, branded Librium, to enter the market hitch-free. Only a few years later, diazepam entered the market and was quickly followed by nitrazepam, clonazepam, flunitrazepam and flurazepam.

Benzodiazepines are typically used as a short-term treatment for insomnia and anxiety, but they also possess muscle relaxant and anticonvulsant properties, which is why they are used to treat alcohol withdrawal symptoms, such as seizures and shaking. Benzodiazepines are sometimes prescribed for long-term use, although this increases the risk for tolerance and dependence.

Two decades after their initial clinical implementation, benzodiazepines were among the most prescribed drugs by practitioners due to perceived safety and the immediate relief they provided. The enthusiasm and overprescribing of benzodiazepines from the medical community meant that these drugs were dispensed in volume and with laxity, leading to patients becoming dependent and abusing them, even with it being reported that low doses were often prescribed. Despite big pharma and the medical community being aware of emerging evidence around potential risks, this was largely ignored. Practitioners were eager to replace barbiturates due to the drug's potential for addiction and overdose, the interactions and contraindications with various other drugs and the requirement to constantly increase the dosage.

This haste amounted to negligence. Multiple pharmaceutical companies were sued for failing to inform practitioners of the risks, and dozens of patients sued their practitioners after they became dependent for failing to warn them of the risks. Although there was a level of dependence on benzodiazepines, pharmaceutical companies attempted to reassure the community that these drugs were not addictive, because there was no evidence to suggest patients were demanding increases in dosage.

Approximately 7,000,000 prescriptions in Australia and approximately 150,000,000 prescriptions in the USA for benzodiazepines are now issued every year, and it is estimated that somewhere between thirty and forty per cent of patients with prescriptions experience withdrawals, while approximately one in six patients meet the criteria for dependence.

Although benzodiazepines were considered a breakthrough, particularly as the class of drugs expanded, it took almost two decades for researchers to determine that the primary mechanism of action was their potentiating effect on GABA. Although GABA settles the brain, which can be effective in calming anxiety or seizures, as all drugs that work on GABA downregulate the receptor, repeated dosage results in tolerance, and if too much is taken, respiration and heart rate can drop to dangerously low levels. Barbiturates also bind to GABA receptors. However, the two classes of drugs differ in terms of specific site of action, specific mechanism of action, and the curve slope measuring intensity of CNS depression in relation to increased dosage.

Both barbiturates and benzodiazepines are GABA agonists, but barbiturates additionally bind to other sites, such as AMPA, kainate and nicotinic acetylcholine receptors. Benzodiazepines appear to increase the frequency at which GABA ion channels open and close; however, barbiturates appear to increase the duration at which the ion channels are open, which leads to lengthy sedation. The shorter the duration of action, the greater control in administering sedation and anaesthesia.

Barbiturates also have a much narrower therapeutic index than benzodiazepines, meaning that toxicity can be achieved quite easily, particularly if used in conjunction with another sedative or if there are errors in dosing. Neither drug is perfect, as they both possess considerable risk for a number of reasons; however, benzodiazepines are considered the lesser of two evils. Despite benzodiazepines being deemed comparably safer than barbiturates, a handful of these drugs have hit considerable hurdles, which has led to a decline in the overall level of benzodiazepine prescriptions over the past decade or so.

One of the drugs to strike trouble was flunitrazepam (rohypnol), as it became a substance commonly used alongside alcohol and GHB/GBL as a date rape drug. Flunitrazepam has been commonly used as a date rape drug because it is soluble in alcohol and can cause amnesia. Triazolam and lorazepam are two other drugs that have struck challenges—triazolam for its adverse psychiatric side effects and lorazepam for its higher risk for withdrawal compared to other benzodiazepines, even though its amnesic properties can make it an effective drug for individuals suffering from phobias. There has also been a shadow cast over temazepam due to its illicit intravenous use and the ability of this drug to potentiate the sedative effects of other depressants such as heroin and morphine.

It has taken a significant period of time for the medical community to observe and respond to the negative effects of sedative drugs, including barbiturates, and this applies to benzodiazepines as well, even though they are still used extensively today. The majority of benzodiazepines are classified Schedule 4 in the SUSMP, except for flunitrazepam and alprazolam, which are both Schedule 8 substances. Practitioners and those who work in pharmacies throughout Australia have become increasingly conscious of how liberally benzodiazepines are prescribed and dispensed. It is unknown whether prescriptions will increase or decrease in the future—some may argue that with mental illness becoming a major global health burden, benzodiazepine prescriptions may rise. However, it is my hope that the proportion of prescriptions will slowly drop over time. This is likely to occur if safer treatments and interventions are discovered and if medical access to technically illegal drugs such as psychedelics, mephedrone and cannabis is expanded, or at the very least, initiated.

17

DRUG SALAD – POLYDRUG USE

Polydrug use refers to combining two or more drugs, and although some drug users engage in this activity consciously to achieve a particular effect, many individuals are unaware that they are combining drugs. In the past decade or so, a large proportion of high-profile individuals reported to have died from drug-related reasons have actually died from polydrug use. These include Michael Jackson, Phillip Seymour Hoffman, Prince, Health Ledger, Andy Irons, Tom Petty, Whitney Houston and Anna Nicole Smith.

Multiple agents can be used in conjunction with each other to treat ailments more effectively, such as NSAIDs, paracetamol and salbutamol to treat bronchitis; antipsychotics and antidepressants to treat bipolar disorder; or amoxicillin, benzocaine and opioids to treat ear infections.

The risk associated with using alcohol with other commonly used drugs cannot be understated. These drugs include stimulants such as caffeine or MDMA, which can reduce subjective intoxication without affecting objective intoxication; sedatives such as benzodiazepines or opioids, which can potentiate the effects of alcohol; and other drugs such as cocaine, resulting in the body metabolising cocaethylene, or cannabis, potentially causing someone to 'green out', that is feel nauseous or dizzy.

Generally speaking, the drugs posing the greatest risk in terms of potential interactions with other agents are alcohol, GHB/GBL, opioids (particularly tramadol), benzodiazepines and some antidepressant drugs, such as MAOIs. Other than antidepressants, drugs such as tramadol, heroin, GHB and alcohol are of particular concern because there are a large number of other drugs for which they potentiate the sedative effects, meaning that the threshold for dangerously low respiration and unconsciousness becomes much lower. An example of this is combining alcohol with methaqualone, as eight grams of methaqualone is the approximate lethal dose for an adult. However, if the individual consumes alcohol in conjunction, only one-quarter of the dose (two grams) is needed to induce a coma.

The primary concern with antidepressants such as SSRIs and MAOIs when mixed with other drugs that release serotonin, such as cocaine or amphetamines, is the potential for serotonin syndrome. This is a term used to describe an excessive and toxic level of serotonin neurotransmission, and is characterised by neuromuscular excitation (sudden involuntary jerking and contractions of muscles, rigidity and hyperreflexia), autonomic stimulation (hyperthermia, sweating and flushing) and a different psychological state (anxiety and confusion etc.). Serotonergic activity is different between antidepressants and other serotonin-releasing drugs like amphetamines and cocaine. While antidepressants largely work by gradually increasing the extracellular level of serotonin in the brain through inhibiting reuptake of the neurotransmitter, other drugs such as cocaine and amphetamines trigger acute surges in serotonin. Apart from the brain, serotonin receptors are also located in the heart and stomach.

⌒⌒⌒

There is a wide variety of drugs that raise the risk of serotonin syndrome, including MAOIs, TCIs, SSRIs, SNRIs, lithium (mood stabiliser), bupropion (noradrenaline-dopamine reuptake inhibitor), pethidine (opioid analgesic), tapentadol (opioid analgesic), MDMA and other amphetamines, ondansetron (antiemetic—vomiting and nausea prevention medication), cocaine, metoclopramide (antiemetic) and many others.

Symptoms can range from mild to severe, with severe cases generally occurring as a result of using potent or multiple serotonergic agents acting at different sites. The first line of treatment for all cases of serotonin syndrome, severe or mild, is to cease all serotonergic medications and provide supportive care including cooling the patient and intubation (facilitate ventilation). In severe cases, patients may be administered with benzodiazepines to control agitation and anxiety as well as antipsychotic and antiserotonergic drugs, such as chlorpromazine or cyproheptadine. It is advised, however, that pharmacological agents used to reverse serotonin syndrome only be administered after consulting with a toxicologist.

Some individuals argue that antidepressant drugs increase the risk of suicide; however, this is only true in vulnerable patients, which is why patients are extensively screened before prescription is dispensed. There are also a number of other elements to this issue:

- Depressed individuals are twelve to thirty times more likely to end their life.
- After treatment, depressed individuals end their life because they did not have the energy to plan and/or carry out the attempt before treatment; this is known as the energisation effect.

This is where a clinician's skills are crucial in identifying if an attempt is imminent. A patient's symptoms can appear to be rapidly improving; however, the patient may just be calm and at peace because they have decided to end their life.

It is extremely important with mental health illnesses that patients are active in their own treatment in terms of balancing the risks and benefits of different drug and non-drug interventions, because unlike other illnesses where a blood test or scan can detect and measure improvements, the patient is the only one who can gauge if they are getting better or not.

In many instances, it can be a challenge for physicians to judge when a patient can guide their own treatment, and the process of stabilising the patient requires a trusting therapeutic relationship. Consider an individual with anorexia nervosa, the potentially life-threatening eating disorder, where the patient has an obsessive irrational fear of gaining weight. Patients are often highly restrictive in food consumption, exercise obsessively and induce vomiting or use laxatives after bingeing. If the patient loses enough weight, their brain doesn't work properly, meaning they can't think logically and are largely disengaged from treatment. Since they are unable to make decisions for themselves, the patient can be force-fed until their brain functions properly. Once their brain is working properly, however, practitioners often want to maintain control over their patient, and if this distresses the patient, it decreases the likelihood that the treatment will work. For these types of illnesses, patients seldom get better if they expect the drugs to 'fix them' and are not actively engaged in their treatment.

Some individuals also use drugs with contrasting effects in an attempt to cancel out the negative effects of one another. This includes combinations such as 'speedballing' (heroin and cocaine together), 'Calvin Klein/CK1' (cocaine and ketamine) and 'Cherry Meth' (GHB and methamphetamine). This practice is highly risky as objective intoxication can be masked by a contrasting drug, and if one of the contrasting drugs wears off too quickly, the individual can overdose easily. This is of particular concern with regard to illicit drugs, as purity levels rise and fall depending on various factors, including reductions in supply following law enforcement operations.

Using other drugs while under the effect of alcohol can also be very risky because of the judgement-impairing nature of alcohol, meaning that the user may be more likely to use another drug or a higher amount of another drug if they are intoxicated. A significant proportion of drug-related deaths and hospitalisations in Australia and through-out the world involve more than one drug, and the most commonly reported drug in these cases is alcohol.

In 2010, two teenagers from a small town in North Lincolnshire, Louis Wainwright and Nicholas Smith, received widespread media attention in the UK after fatally combining methadone and alcohol. Both had consumed a large amount of alcohol at various licensed venues, and then afterwards, scored some methadone, which ultimately lead to their death.

It was initially reported that the two teens were looking for and had died from another drug called mephedrone. Mephedrone was the first downloadable drug available to the masses—it was only available online and was hidden inside other branded products. It is unclear whether the two boys were actually looking for mephedrone but accidentally took methadone because of the name synchronicity, if their level of intoxication impaired their judgement of how much methadone they took, or if they wouldn't have taken any other drugs if they were sober. Any of these circumstances is possible; however, the case certainly does high-light the risk of using other drugs while under the effect of alcohol.

When an individual has died from mixing two or more drugs together, it is also almost impossible to say which individual drug was responsible for causing the death. The media however, tend to blame either the newest drug, or the drug that is generating the most current social concern.

In mid-2018, a fifteen year old girl in west Sydney died after mixing energy drinks with alcohol; it was reported she obtained the recipe online. She was found unconscious with a BAC of 0.4 (eight times the legal driving limit). However, it is likely that after consuming a large amount of caffeine, she would have inaccurately judged her level of intoxication. If she had not consumed the caffeine, then it is likely that the signs of intoxication, such as confusion, disorientation, and fatigue, would have been more noticeable, which would have been a marker for her to slow down or stop drinking, possibly saving her life.

It is generally considered that the risks of using two or more drugs together for psychoactive effects is greater than using either drug alone, as stacking multiple compounds together increases physiological strain on the body and also increases unpredictability in terms of effects.

One of the most commonly used drug combinations is alcohol and caffeine, and the partnerships forged between alcohol companies and energy drink companies has led to a growing number of individuals combining these two drugs. Energy drinks originally emerged as a sub-category of the soft drink industry in the early 1900s, but it was not until the 1990s that the term 'energy drink' began to be used in specific reference to caffeinated soft drinks.

Pepsi and Coca-Cola were originally promoted as energy boosters, particularly as Coca-Cola historically contained both a higher level of caffeine compared to today's standards and just less than ten milligrams of cocaine per bottle (equivalent to approximately fifteen to twenty per cent of one average line of cocaine). Despite the US government's unsuccessful attempt in the early 1900s to forcibly remove caffeine from Coca-Cola, the soft drink company later decided to reduce the amount of caffeine, which in a way brought an end to the first group of energy boosting drinks.

Later, a number of other products emerged, and were marketed as energy boosters, energy replenishments, nutritional drinks and energy shots. Energy shots and energy powders have primarily been introduced for both fast consumption convenience (marketed as instant energy) and as low-calorie alternatives. On the other hand, due to regulations around levels of caffeine per serving, a handful of energy drink companies, such as Hype Energy Drinks, Red Bull GmbH, Monster Beverage Corporation and Rockstar Energy, have introduced large cans that can contain double the caffeine and calories, across two servings. Outside of the disclosed caloric breakdown of the product, energy drinks like sports supplements list other unique ingredients that make up the total 'energy blend' sum, but often it is not revealed how much of each ingredient exists and how much is recommended to take.

Although the energy drink and alcohol companies would never admit to it, the partnership enables a mutual benefit, as using these drugs in combination allows the individual to consume more of both products. In the US, certain states have banned caffeinated alcoholic beverages following pressure from the FDA. Despite their removal, however, no dent on actual levels of consumption were made because bartenders and consumers simply combined alcoholic products with separate caffeinated products to produce drinks such as excitabulls (vodka and Red Bull), Jägerbombs (Jägermeister and energy drink), blue bulls (rum, vodka and Red Bull) and espresso/Kahlua martinis (vodka, Kahlua and coffee liquor). Although combining alcohol and caffeine is a relatively modern trend, therefore requiring more research into the long-term risks, early evidence shows that mixing alcohol and caffeine together poses a greater risk than either drug in isolation.

Caffeinated alcoholic drinks are available in Australia, and consumption trends in terms of demographics are consistent with other areas of the world, such as Europe, the US and Canada, with young adults/university and college students being the highest consumers. Those who consume caffeinated alcoholic drinks (either pre-mixed or consumer/bartender mixed) have been shown to be heavier episodic (binge or hazardous) drinkers as well as more likely to become dependent drinkers than alcohol alone drinkers; however, caffeine as an independent causative factor for both is yet to be proven.

Hazardous and/or binge drinkers may be more inclined to consume caffeinated alcoholic products, or it may be that caffeinated alcoholic products increase hazardous drinking. A combination of both is also possible. It is unlikely that caffeine actually increases alcohol consumption. It is, however, likely that the stimulatory effects of caffeine result in individuals underestimating their level of intoxication, which in turn facilitates continued alcohol consumption. Whether caffeine itself causes dependence is difficult to say, but given that heavier episodic drinking increases the risk of dependence and consuming caffeine alongside alcohol is associated with heavier episodic drinking, it is probably safer to avoid mixing alcohol and caffeine when it comes to the risk of becoming dependent.

Caffeinated alcoholic beverages may also increase thirst due to dehydration, which increases the likelihood that individuals will drink more. This is almost entirely due to the alcohol. Although caffeine may have a negligible diuretic effect, it does not appear to cause dehydration, and for every SD of alcohol that someone consumes, they excrete an additional 120 ml of urine (on top of other fluid). So, in essence, if someone consumes 300 ml of beer, and the beer contains one SD (ten grams or approximately twelve millilitres of alcohol), that individual would excrete over 400 ml in urine. Drinking water alongside or between each drink will help, however the person will still end up dehydrated at the end of the night.

Although the primary focus in this situation is directed towards the health risks associated with alcohol, it cannot be ignored that there are risks associated with excessive consumption of caffeine. This includes insomnia, restlessness, and with higher doses, seizures and cardiovascular problems, such as arrhythmias, can arise. The increase in energy drink consumption has coincided with an increase in energy drink-related emergency department admissions, but only some of the increase is directly due to energy drinks. There is limited data in this area; however, of the 20,000 annual hospital admissions in the US where caffeinated drinks were noted, caffeine was the only drug consumed in approximately fifty per cent of these admissions. For the other fifty per cent, other stimulants or drugs had also been consumed. In regards to the group that had consumed no drugs other than the caffeinated drinks, these admissions were a mixture of adverse reactions and misuse or abuse.

Although all illicit drugs are erratic in purity and overall contents, if taken in isolation from any other drugs, the effects are generally predictable. Once an individual introduces additional compounds, drug effects can become unpredictable. Other than the aforementioned risks and the fact that most fatal overdoses involve multiple substances, polydrug use can exacerbate or lengthen the hangover effect, increase the user's propensity for becoming dependant and increase the risk of developing or exacerbate existing mental health problems. It would be ideal if nobody used illicit drugs and, from a public health perspective, if nobody used any drug *at all* for recreational purposes. However, if someone is going to use a drug, they greatly reduce their risk of something going wrong if they use only one drug with the safest ROA, as mixing drugs for any purpose will always increase risks.

18

THE BEGINNING OF THE END?

The aim of this book has been to take a diagnostic and historical look at drugs through a broad lens. What is to follow this book will be more prescriptive. In the time it has taken for me to put this together, much has happened in Australia and indeed throughout the entire world within the drug space. However, even though there has been progress, it has been extremely slow, with every step forward followed by half a step back. Despite some changes, much is still the same.

This chapter was written approximately three weeks after the 2018 Defqon.1 music festival took place in Sydney, NSW, where two young people died, three were left in intensive care and hundreds sought medical help. Despite large-scale music festivals being held throughout Australia for at least fifty years, with the number of events growing, the music diversifying and the majority of people attending these events enjoying being a part of the festival experience, festivals have been cast in an increasing negative light, as each and every year a number of drug-related deaths occur during the festival season.

Since the inception of these events and the subsequent deaths, the knee-jerk response from the government and law enforcement authorities has been largely to ban their way out of trouble. Whether it be Gemma Thoms dying after the Big Day Out music festival, Georgina

Bartter dying after the Harbourlife music festival or Stefan Woodward and Sylvia Choi dying after Stereosonic music festival, the state and federal government remain fundamentally unhinged in their commitment to zero tolerance. This is reflected in a number of ways—the increase in police presence and sniffer dogs, the attempts to close festivals down, the crackdowns on supply and the ruling out of harm-reduction measures such as pill testing. The response following the deaths of Joseph Pham and Diana Nguyen after Defqon.1 was no exception.

The government was, as they were in the 1980s with HIV, in the 1990s with heroin and in recent times with the issue of cannabis and pill testing, being tested again concerning their true position. Do they have zero tolerance to people dying or being harmed by illicit drugs or zero tolerance to people using illicit drugs?

The comments from Troy Grant, the NSW Minister for Police, Gladys Berejiklian, the NSW Premier, and media outlets following the death of these two individuals can be described as nothing other than the recycled rhetoric of 'don't do drugs'. This is like a doctor continuing to prescribe the same medication to a patient who keeps getting worse. If this was the case, the treatment would be changed or the patient would get a second opinion.

The Premier was interviewed shortly after the news surfaced regarding the events at Defqon.1, and the take-away messages from the interview were that everything would be done to shut the event down and that the government has a zero-tolerance approach to illicit drugs. These messages are alarming for a number of reasons.

Firstly, the government will do everything it can to shut the event down, but it will not do everything it can to prevent deaths of young people. In essence, it's more important to reiterate the message that the government disapproves of events where some people use drugs, than it is to change the message or implement measures that may save lives.

Secondly, banning the festival would not eliminate the demand for the festival or drugs. Demand drives a market, not supply. The event would most likely continue, albeit in an underground and unregulated form, where the risk of things going wrong would actually be much greater.

Thirdly, the government has a zero tolerance to illicit drugs, but it actively tolerates drugs that cause much more harm. So, the government is selective in the drugs it dislikes irrespective of the objective damage. In fact, in one of Ms Berejiklian's interviews, when asked if her government had a zero tolerance to drugs, Ms Berejiklian interjected with, 'Yes, to illicit drugs'. And yet in the same week, the NSW government watered down drink-driving laws so that low-range drink driving was no longer dealt with by a criminal conviction, but instead with a reduced on-the-spot fine and licence suspension.

Around fifteen Australians die every year from ecstasy-related causes, however, twenty-five to thirty per cent of fatal car accidents in Australia involve alcohol, which with over 1,200 road fatalities equates to over 350 deaths every year (twenty-three times more than ecstasy deaths). Low-range drink driving triples the risk of a car accident, and the risk increases exponentially with consumption. Leaving out alcohol-related homicides, suicides, cancers, other accidents and other diseases that kill over 5,000 Australians annually, alcohol-related traffic accidents are responsible for twenty-three times the number of ecstasy deaths. If low-range drink driving contributed to one tenth of these deaths, that would still be more than double the amount of total ecstasy-related deaths. Increasing zero tolerance for drugs such as ecstasy that kill a handful of people, while increasing tolerance for other drugs such as alcohol that kill hundreds if not thousands more is inconsistent, non-scientific policy.

In mid-2019, the NSW government arranged a cross-party parliamentary committee to examine the effectiveness of the Sydney lockout laws, and despite the evidence being as clear as day, the laws were partially rolled back—alcohol-fuelled violence had been thrown a lifeline. If one person dies at a music festival, all efforts are made to shut the event down, yet if sixteen people die every day from alcohol, the government dances to the tune of the alcohol industry. During the parliamentary enquiry, Justin Hemmes, the CEO of Merivale—one of the largest hospitality groups in the nation—stated that the 'lockout laws must go now', because they are an 'embarrassment on an international scale'. What's embarrassing is that prior to the lockout laws, you couldn't turn on the news after a weekend without hearing a news story about someone getting murdered in an alcohol-related incident. Hemmes also mentioned that his position was 'not about our business'. About half of his eighty-nine venues exist within the CBD area, many of which are subject to the lockout laws. One of his biggest money-spinners was the Ivy complex, which experienced more than a fifty per cent decline in revenue since lockouts. During the same inquiry, the head of Solotel, which owns over thirty hospitality venues across Sydney, Justine Baker, complained that the 'micro-regulations' have been too difficult for staff to regulate. Hemmes and Baker both stated that repealing lockouts would bring about a $16,000,000,000 injection into Sydney's economy. But that is gross income, not net income—it fails to take into account alcohol related costs such as extra police patrols, hospital, emergency and ambulance costs, long term costs arising from heavy or binge drinking such as chronic conditions as well as enduring consequences of severe acute events such as brain trauma, costs of workplace absenteeism, not to mention the unquantifiable emotional costs of alcohol-related incidents. The lockout laws are actually one of the very rare instances where law enforcement and the medical community are both on the same song sheet. The alcohol industry and the government are together on a different song sheet. It is estimated that between 2,500 and 3,000 assaults have been avoided since the lockout laws were implemented, and there has not been one single death.

The justification for having zero tolerance to illicit drugs is that 'young lives are lost' and that 'families of loved ones will be devastated and their lives will change forever', all of which is true. *However, if deaths and devastated families are the basis for cracking down on illicit drugs, then why are other drugs that cause more harm exempt or given different treatment?*

It is because drugs are not treated according to their harm. Many people have a very puritanical philosophy, essentially wanting to rid society of pleasurable behaviours that you don't have to work for, even if the behaviour causes no harm or is less harmful than other activities we tolerate and/or promote. Drug use consistently comes under fire for separating reward from effort, which is also an argument trotted out against the sexual revolution. I am not singling out the NSW Premier, because other politicians, such as Daniel Andrews, the Victorian Labor Premier, Anthony Albanese, the Federal Opposition Leader and the Australian Conservatives have expressed identical views. However, politicians need to be honest when it comes to their reasons as to why they express inconsistent attitudes towards different drugs. When all politicians spit out the same rhetoric of 'just say no/don't take drugs and you won't die', it creates a united political barrier, which the medical community finds almost impenetrable.

What is interesting is that many politicians and media personnel have used drugs in the past, and this can paradoxically make them less likely to hold compassionate views because they did it, didn't get into trouble with the law or their health, stopped doing it and expect that others should be able to do the same.

In the same week as the deaths at Defqon.1 music festival and the uproar that followed, conservative journalist Miranda Devine interviewed the NSW Minister for Police, Troy Grant, on radio. Both Devine and Grant expressed their support for the NSW government to shut the event down, to get tougher on illicit drugs and to rule out pill testing. Devine opened the interview by claiming that if the event were a licensed venue, they would have been closed down immediately, which is entirely untrue.

To my knowledge, there have only been four entertainment venues that have been forcibly closed in Sydney – The Imperial Hotel at Erskineville, as well as Bada Bing, DreamGirls and Candys Apartment in Kings Cross. Each of these clubs were closed only temporarily, and largely due to illicit drug supply concerns. What is interesting is that over the years within the vicinity of these venues, many people have been killed and thousands have been hospitalised for alcohol-related reasons, but none of these incidents resulted in clubs being forcibly closed.

I wouldn't support shutting down venues, but I would support regulatory changes to make them as safe as possible. Ironically when I first listened to this interview online, the show opened with and paused several times for advertising. Each of the advertisements was for a liquor store! Both Devine and Grant suggest withdrawing police from festivals so events cannot get council approval as an option. This, as stated previously, would push the events to a less safe location, without any security or harm-reduction measures.

Following the Defqon.1 deaths, a reader from south-west Sydney made similar suggestion in a Sydney newspaper:

> *I think it's time that the dangers of drug abuse are handed back to the users rather than everyone else... Announce at the next music event that the ambulance service would be in attendance, however, will not have any overdose reversing medications. We would just treat the death as a suicide.*

Perhaps we should take the same approach in the event of a major car accident. The ambulance service will attend, but will simply watch the driver, who shouldn't have been speeding, bleed to death in the car. Or maybe for smokers—the ambulance service will attend if the smoker experiences chest pains, but will not make any effort to treat the individual if they have a heart attack, because they shouldn't have smoked. Or deny obese people insulin if they develop diabetes. Or for someone who drifted out of the surf lifesaving flags at the beach, let them struggle and drown, because they should have swum between the flags.

The idea of actively choosing to not aid someone facing death is a grossly disproportionate and inhumane response. Personal responsibility is important, and the event coordinators should not be held responsible, but what kind of person considers death a fitting punishment for someone ingesting a drug that is different from more popularly consumed drugs? If it were that newspaper reader's child, parent, sibling or friend, I'm sure that they would want the person they care about to be treated and saved, rather than for an emergency worker to consciously and actively not treat them, so they die. Would they feel content that their loved one's death was an appropriate outcome?

People should never be denied treatment if their illness is to some extent self-inflicted. Grant makes the comment that all options will be explored to address this issue, but that's not true because the government refuses to look at pill testing, which is by no means a silver bullet. However, the concept is a part of a more pragmatic solution. It is also the one thing that AMA, the Royal Australian College of General Practitioners, the Royal Australasian College of Physicians, the Australian Drug Foundation, the former AFP Commissioner and the National Drug and Alcohol Research Centre is calling for. It's easy for politicians to physically hear the evidence, but it is extremely hard for them to actually listen without bias, as they only take in what their mind is willing to comprehend.

The NSW government added pill testing to the 2018/2019 Special Inquiry into methamphetamine; however, all that this token gesture will achieve is time for the government. The public's animosity towards the government's stance on pill testing will dwindle (particularly with the 2018/2019 summer period at a close), and when the Inquiry's findings are released in October, six months will have passed, and the primary focus of the inquiry will be on methamphetamine, not pill testing. This is a common ploy—shift the public focus to one arena, so it distracts away from the fact that nothing is being done about another issue that they don't want to deal with. The government doesn't need to make an inquiry into methamphetamine, it doesn't need an inquiry into drug checking, and it doesn't need to buy time in the hope that the public will forget the fact that ignoring all medical advice has resulted in numerous preventable young deaths.

When the president of The Law Society of NSW, Doug Humphreys, was interviewed on ABC radio in the wake of the government's proposal to increase penalties following the deaths at Defqon.1., he said that not only is the proposed strict liability legislation problematic, but also that the formal inquiry in response to the overdoses was extremely short and limited in terms of its consultations with either legal or medical experts. And this is the most infuriating aspect of this issue—*the government is not even open or willing to have a discussion regarding alternative solutions.*

Although I will discuss this further in the book to follow, the evidence is overwhelmingly positive, and yet critics repeatedly cast fear-driven dark shadows over the measure, stating that 'it sends the wrong message', or my personally most hated one 'the jury is still out'. What that really means is that we know the evidence shows it works, but we are waiting and hoping for something to go wrong. This is like setting up a red-light speed camera at an intersection where a high number of fatal crashes have occurred, and the camera prevents thousands of crashes, but as soon as one accident occurs, critics cheer 'ha! We told you it wouldn't work!' (meanwhile, ignoring the thousands of accidents and deaths that have been prevented).

Somehow the idea persists that if you push harder on the zero-tolerance accelerator, eventually you can punish or frighten the public into submission.

Miranda Devine comments that drug liberalisers were opportunistic and were out ready with their opinion pieces before the bodies from Defqon.1 were even cold. The reality is that all of these deaths have continued to occur under the watch of the government. Yet both Grant and Devine agree with government's approach to this situation, which essentially is to ignore expert medical advice and continue to let people die so they can send a strong message that drugs are bad to the majority of people in the community who don't use drugs. *If people are dying and you seek medical advice, and you are provided with unequivocal medical and scientific advice and continue to ignore that advice, then the blood of those people is on your hands.*

Drugs are not the exception though—history is littered with examples of politicians and governments actively ignoring expert evidence because they are pursuing other agendas.

Troy Grant comments that the drug liberalisers were preying on, and politicising the misery of the families, despite the fact that parents who have lost children in situations such as this are the strongest advocates of pill testing—parents like Adriana Buccianti, who lost her son Daniel in 2002 at the Rainbow Serpent music festival. Grant's comment is also hypocritical because medical authorities are rightly claiming that the current approach is not working, giving examples that reflect this and providing solutions, and yet on the grounds of politically expediency, the government chooses to reject the suggestions!

He responds to Devine's assertion that the (drug) problem is 'out of control' by admitting that we cannot arrest our way out of the problem and that it is not a law enforcement or policing issue. Yet, in the next breath, he says that we need to get tougher on supply.

It is strange how we are continually told that illicit drug use is 'out of control', but at the same time, there is the belief that society can cope no matter what the scale. And if it's not a law enforcement and policing issue, then why not heed the one suggestion that the medical community has been suggesting for years? The reason it has not been adopted is because the government is afraid it will work. Grant also claims that pill testing would result in a proliferation of drug use, even though the evidence shows no effect on the level of drug possession and a reduction in the number of people who use drugs, the number of drugs mixed and the amount of drugs used—each of which are independent risk factors for fatalities. He is, however, obviously aware of the benefit of drug checking in other nations. During a separate interview in mid-September 2018, he stated 'those people out there who are calling for pill testing are talking about models in European communities that may have had some success'.

There are individuals within the community, such as News Limited editor-in-chief, David Penberthy, who simply deny evidence ('Pill testing needs to be supported by science, not vibes'). However, when you are aware of the evidence and block the measure regardless, that is a disservice to the community—exactly the opposite of what a government minister is supposed to do.

Grant reiterates, 'The drugs are illegal. They are illegal because they are likely to harm you and cause you death'. The Australian Federal Health Minister, Greg Hunt, made an almost identical statement a few weeks later, 'There are no safe levels of illicit drugs. And the reason they're illicit is because they aren't safe.'

These statements could not be more factually incorrect. Drugs like MDMA are illegal because of historical anomalies. The drugs that the media gets hysterical about were banned in haste, on unscientific grounds, and their objective harm is in no way tied to or reflected in their legal standing. Are they likely to cause you harm and death?

Here's some data you don't want to hear. One of the most commonly used illicit drugs at dance music events is ecstasy. Approximately ten per cent of Australians aged fourteen and over have tried ecstasy at some point in their life, with three per cent using within the past year. Even if we take the three per cent, which equals about 750,000 Australians who are annual users of ecstasy, and if fifteen Australians die from ecstasy every year, that means that of all people who have used ecstasy in the past year, 99.998 per cent have survived—a 0.002 per cent death rate is not a 'likely' death rate. These deaths are nothing short of heartbreaking tragedies, however, the survival rate is similar to that of scuba diving, horse riding, mountain climbing, rock fishing, boxing, skiing or hang gliding and many other recreational activities that are legal and that we engage in.

It is also a much better survival rate than drinking alcohol, because even though the entire population does not consume alcohol on a yearly basis, if 25,000,000 people do consume alcohol in Australia, and 5,800 die as a result, that means 99.9768 per cent have survived, indicating a 0.0232 per cent death rate. If you were to calculate the proportion of drinkers who die from alcohol, the death rates are even higher.

Approximately seventy per cent of Australians eighteen years and older consumed alcohol in the past year (17,500,000 people), and of this group, 5,800 die, resulting in a death rate of 0.0331 per cent and a survival rate 99.9669 per cent.

The next time someone tells you more people die because it's more widely used, read them the above paragraph, and tell them that the proportion of drinkers who die from their drinking is sixteen times greater than the proportion of ecstasy users who die from ecstasy.

～✺～

In the early 2000s, leader of the UK Conservative Party, David Cameron, suggested that ecstasy be downgraded from Class A because evidence clearly demonstrated it being less harmful than other Class A drugs. However, being castigated by anti-drugs activists in the midst of a highly charged political debate led to him backpedalling and effectively retracting his comments. In a wider sense, however, how harmful is ecstasy compared to alcohol? Take a look at the table below from a 2006 article in the *Journal of Psychopharmacology* entitled 'A tale of two Es'.

Drug	Premature deaths	Overdose safety	Brain damage	Violence cases	RTA deaths	Cirrhosis	Heart damage	Costs £B	Contribution £B
Alcohol	22,000	10x	Yes	>10,000	1,500	++ and growing	++	18.5	50
Ecstasy	10	15x	Unknown	0	0	0	0	0.01	0

I vividly remember on my eighteenth birthday that one of my friends took a few ecstasy tablets—one before the party and then one or two during the party. He was happy the entire night and did not suffer any adverse health effects throughout the evening or in the days following. I would never use this as a reason to advise someone that ecstasy is safe; however, on the same night, the vast majority of people, including me, were intoxicated on alcohol. At the end of the evening, I was attempting to hail a taxi at about 3am. Because it was a changeover, taxi availability was limited. One taxi appeared in the distance, but because it was raining so heavily, I was worried that the driver would not be able to see me, so the way I hailed the taxi was by running onto the road in front of the taxi and putting my hands up as a stop sign. The taxi hit the brakes and stopped in time, and everyone (including myself) got home safely. I woke up the next morning and didn't think much of it.

It was only recently that I began to conceptualise how distorted my perception of harm was on that particular night. I and all of my friends were so concerned and focused on the one person who used an illegal drug that night, who suffered no harm, yet I was encouraged to become intoxicated and disinhibited enough to throw myself in front of a moving car in the rain. *This is exactly how people die. Yet for many, that's just something that you do when on the drink.*

✦

We don't ban drinking, and we don't have zero tolerance to other activities. A 2009 UK study comparing the harms of ecstasy and horse riding showed that horse riding is a much more objectively dangerous activity, with one in every 10,000 ecstasy pill exposures causing acute harm, whereas one in every 350 horse riding exposures caused acute harm.

This paper generated an enormous amount of political hysteria because it challenged the integrity of the UK drugs policy, and on an objective analysis, made it almost impossible for the government to defend the illegal status of ecstasy. These are reasonable comparisons to make on objective measures, and contesting this means that morality is the underpinning reason as to why people object to drugs when other riskier activities are allowed. There are those who claim that this kind of data comparison 'trivialises' illicit drug deaths, but ignoring deaths from other activities, such as horse riding, is treating these deaths with equal triviality. In fact, NSW Minister for Police, Troy Grant, actually drew the analogy of the road toll and said that their attitude towards drugs is similar to that of the road toll in that the aim is 'towards zero' (which is different to zero tolerance).

Interestingly, around the same period of time, the NSW government announced a 'towards zero' strategy on suicide. Let us say, for example, that the government was not willing to accept the 1,200 annual road fatalities, so instead of implementing rational harm-reduction measures, such as seatbelts, properly regulated and manufactured cars and roads, age and license restrictions and speed zones, the government imposed a blanket ban on cars. This, of course, would not stop people driving, and instead, drivers would not be regulated based on age, driving history or intoxication. They would drive poorly manufactured cars, on isolated roads, under the effects of alcohol, and the risk of accidents would be much greater.

This is obviously an irrational response. Because it's not going to stop people driving, the risks and harms would increase, and the policing efforts would be enormous. *Why can't we apply this logic to drugs?* We don't want people to die on the roads, so we implement harm-reduction measures to keep people as safe as possible.

Over the 2018 Christmas break, I travelled interstate by car to visit family, and at least a dozen brightly lit signs above the highway read 'Let's keep driving towards zero this summer'. With regard to music festivals, why can't we implement a slogan 'Let's keep dancing towards zero this summer'?

We don't say to society that there will be no seatbelts because that would be tacit support of speeding. There are countless examples of where harm reduction is not an encouragement to engage in that behaviour. Regulation of medical procedures is not encouraging cosmetic surgery, condoms and morning-after pills are not encouraging sex, swimming between the flags is not encouraging swimming in the surf, bike helmets are not an encouragement to go as fast as you want and air bags are not an encouragement to speed.

We don't ban horse riding or close horse-riding facilities when someone falls from a horse and breaks their neck. We don't close roads or ban driving when someone dies in a car accident. We don't shut down nightclubs when someone out the front of the club is bashed to death. We don't ban casinos or gambling, even though it costs the Australian community just under $5,000,000,000 per year. And we don't ban various other activities noted above even though there is obvious harm caused.

Some refute these analogies by arguing that unlike using ecstasy, these activities are not illegal. That is not entirely true. Many people die on the roads because of speeding, drink driving and distracted and dangerous driving, which are all illegal activities, just as many of the alcohol-related violence deaths are caused by serving alcohol to people who are already intoxicated, which is illegal. The illegality of an activity is also irrelevant when it comes to public health and safety, because legality does not necessarily mean safe, illegal does not necessarily mean unsafe, and the law needs to be dictated by harm, not the reverse.

So, if we don't want people to die from drugs, and we can't arrest our way out of the problem, why can't measures such as pill testing be implemented to save lives? The comment by Troy Grant is similar to that made by NSW Police Acting Assistant Commissioner, Stuart Smith, on ABC television in February 2019: 'When we introduced RBT, we saved a thousand lives the following year... Quit smoking—seventy-five per cent of males were smoking, and we brought it down to fourteen per cent. That was through prohibition.' A thousand lives were saved, and smoking rates did decline, but to suggest that was caused by prohibition is an absurd statement and blatantly, factually wrong.

Smoking rates and drink driving deaths were brought down, not by prohibiting alcohol, tobacco or even alcohol before driving—we still allow a limit of 0.05 per cent prescribed concentration—but by introducing sensible harm-reduction measures. During the 1970s, between twenty-five to thirty people per 100,000 died on Australian roads, and now we are down to about four per 100,000, which represents an eighty per cent reduction, despite more car ownership and usage. We achieved this through five things—seatbelts, RBTs, speed cameras, safer cars and better roads. Notice how nowhere in there says 'banning cars'. The community was initially against seatbelts because they thought it would make people drive faster. How absurd we view this attitude now. For tobacco, this has come in the form of plain packaging, no advertising, restrictions on where people can smoke and at what age, etc. In the case of alcohol, trading hours were restricted, we implemented the 'RBT means you need a plan B' campaign, and we restrict intoxication levels to 0.05 per cent for unrestricted license holders (not for provisional or learners). We didn't ban either. Prohibition is really the only policy that by virtually all metrics has been comprehensively disproved, yet continues to be enforced. The profile of harm reduction needs to be raised at a policy level even if it means the sacrifice of supply reduction, because it is a tangible and quantifiable measurement of the effect on quality of life and life expectancy. And just because, alongside prevention as best practice, we implement other harm reduction measures, that does not mean we are tacitly encouraging drug use.

One of Miranda Devine's go-to pieces of evidence to support the argument of zero tolerance is that during the John Howard government years (late 1990s to the mid-2000s), when zero tolerance was the key focus, drug use dropped. Despite the policy framework in Australia since 1985 being harm minimisation, the Howard government adopted a tough-on-drugs campaign. However, being tough on drugs and harm minimisation are largely incompatible in principle and practice. When we talk about a tough-on-drugs strategy, we are speaking about being tough on *illicit* drugs, as there is no evidence of being tough on tobacco or alcohol, the two drugs responsible for approximately ninety-seven per cent of drug-related deaths in Australia.

Conceptually, zero tolerance refers to the authoritarian nature of policing, implemented by the New York City Police Department, particularly during the office of Mayor Rudy Giuliani from 1994 to

2001. There are a number of examples that illustrate the fact that although the Howard government was very much aligned with zero tolerance in a political sense, this was essentially a marketing strategy, and the marketing strategy was the only product differentiation between the Liberal Party and the ALP at the time. This is reflected across the board in reductions in funding for the AFP and National Crime Authority, the increases in funding for diverting offenders away from court to treatment, the funding for NSPs as well as the praise and support from the government and Minister for Foreign Affairs for the implemented harm-reduction measures in Asia to counteract the spread of HIV. What is fascinating is that Prime Minister Howard, in a number of speeches, confirmed that the tough-on-drugs policy *was a moral crusade, rather than a public health campaign.* That admission is admirable because the Prime Minister was at least being honest and explicit about the grounds for the policy, unlike current representatives who clothe their moral beliefs in the robes of bogus evidence.

During the Howard years, Major Brian Watters was appointed the head of the Australian National Council on Drugs and was a zealous supporter of zero tolerance. Unfortunately, the then head of the AFP, Mick Palmer, the then Director of Public Prosecutions, Nicholas Cowdery and the then Director of the NSW Bureau of Crime Statistics, Dr Don Weatherburn, all agree that zero tolerance has done little to stop supply or use. It has, however, caused significant harm to individuals and communities.

Despite falls in certain areas of drug use coinciding with harm reduction still being maintained in practice (despite a surface shine of zero tolerance), we cannot conclude that harm-reduction programs were the reason for the drop in use. It is very likely that some of the harm-reduction measures put in place suppressed total drug harms. However, the immediate reduction in drug harms was principally caused by massive supply reductions of opium and heroin from Myanmar (formally Burma).

If we take out alcohol and tobacco, opioid deaths account for approximately eighty per cent of drug-related deaths, so if a big dent is made in the number of opioid deaths, that in turn makes a big dent in the number of all drug deaths, particularly illicit drug deaths. In terms of overall drug harm before, during and after the Howard government, alcohol-related deaths have continued to rise due to gradual increases in total consumption, tobacco-related deaths have continued to fall due to gradual falls in use, and illicit drug-related deaths peaked in the late 1990s followed by a fall in the early 2000s due to a key supply country changing production.

Drug-related deaths (other than alcohol or tobacco) rose again after the recorded plunge around 2000. However, the increase in deaths was almost entirely due to the overprescribing of opioids, other sedatives and antidepressants, such as from the doubling of prescriptions of oxycodone between 2010 and 2015. Although some minor changes in consumption were recorded, such as lower cannabis use in certain age groups, the tough-on-drugs campaign had at best a minimal impact on use and harm.

There are a handful of areas in the world with very strict drug laws that have very low rates of drug use, but there are other areas of the world that have strict laws yet high rates of drug use as well as areas that have liberal laws with very low rates of drug use and harm. It is clear from looking at every country throughout the world that the legal environment has very little to do with levels of consumption. While it may sound as though I am singling out and hammering specific people in the media who are avid supporters of zero tolerance, I am defending those on the other side of this argument, as they have come under heavier fire and often in a quite personal manner.

Harm-reduction programs and the harm minimisation framework is often criticised for not prioritising hard-line interventions that prevent drug use, which is theorised to result in harm maximisation. It's interesting that many individuals I speak to often fall on either extreme ends of the spectrum, with advocates of harm reduction believing there's no point trying to stop people taking drugs because they are going to do it anyway or as television personality Osher Gunsberg stated in late 2018 on a Channel 10 panel discussion on pill testing: 'People are always going to take drugs. Everyone on this panel has taken drugs. Your grandkids and your kids are going to take drugs. It is going to happen.' On the other hand, critics of harm reduction believe that what you're telling young people is that there is this inevitability of drug use, and you should just surrender and let drugs off the chain.

I personally don't like either of those stances because the majority (approximately sixty-five per cent) of Australians have never used an illicit drug in their life, and the first message of harm reduction is that the only way to avoid all harms is to not take any drug as there is no safe level of drug use. Parents, teachers and anyone who works with young people need to reinforce the message that despite what you hear in the media, illicit drug use is not inevitable, and the majority of Australians never use illicit drugs. That is consistently backed by data, year in, year out. We need to do away with the fixation on the group who are doing it and draw at least the same amount of attention to the group who are not doing it.

As those in favour of prohibition do tolerate legal drugs, just not illegal drugs, you can argue that since the majority of people will never use illegal drugs, why shouldn't the majority be empowered with skills, strategies and information to reduce drug harm to the minority of people who do use drugs? Unfortunately, *while some level of drug use is inevitable, a large proportion of the harm that results from that drug use is not and is entirely avoidable.* Those who dispute this, simply do not want to look at the evidence (see Part Two of this book).

We should be embracing programs and measures that understand and are likely to achieve this, particularly when best practice prevention and early interventions fail. In essence, the government's current line in the sand comes after drug education—from that point the message is: 'we have told you these drugs are harmful, and you didn't listen, so now you face the consequences'. Now those consequences might be nothing, they might be hospitalisation, they might be prison time or a criminal record or they might be death—but by the time you find out, it's too late.

Those who advocate for these kinds of punishing measures undermine two parts of our overarching framework, demand reduction and supply reduction. They need to understand that harm reduction is another pillar and that harm reduction exists at all levels. If we can't destroy every clandestine laboratory, let's try to stop the drugs from reaching the streets. If we can't stop all drugs from reaching the streets, let's try to reduce the number of people who get their hands on drugs. If we can't stop everyone from getting their hands on drugs, then let's try to interrupt their decision to ingest the drug. If we can't stop individuals ingesting drugs, then let's try to reduce the amount of the drug they use or have them switch to a safer method. If individuals still use in a harmful way such as injecting, then let's ensure we can reduce those risks through measures such as providing clean needles and safe injecting facilities. If individuals don't want to use these facilities, we still keep them alive through emergency healthcare services.

We don't, at some random point in this process, cease efforts because previous measures have failed and those who harm themselves don't forfeit the right to help. The government can't be blamed for these events as the responsibility falls at the feet of the user, which is often a very difficult pill for the family to swallow. However, in all other activities that are both risky and illegal, we bend over backwards to ensure that the community is kept safe.

∽≈∽

I grew up with the say no/drugs are bad/don't do drugs message at home, and even though that wasn't the reason for me never using any illegal drug, that certainly was the message I attempted to give young people when I initially started running sessions. Very quickly I realised that not only have they heard that message before, but the majority of students who have never, and will never, use drugs in their lives were not empowered or equipped to look after their friends or to respond to or prevent a drug-related situation. I often think that if I had been given information on how to look after a friend, then perhaps my friend Lilly would still be alive today. I also think that if Lilly had supportive networks around her, which pulled her up instead of pushing her down, perhaps she wouldn't have gone down the road she did.

In closing this book, I recall a recent broadcast that 2GB radio presenter Ray Hadley made in reference to his son who had been charged for possessing a small quantity of cocaine that month. This story gained widespread media attention, as Ray Hadley is well known for his strong opinions on law and lawbreakers, and his son was a police officer.

In his initial press conference, Ray Hadley described the different stages of his reaction to learning of his son Daniel's charges, and how he moved from being puzzled, to being angry, to being deeply concerned, sad and crushed, and considered himself inadequate as a father. Daniel Hadley was caught off-duty with a small amount of cocaine near a licensed venue in north west Sydney in early August 2018. When Hadley was discussing his son's arrest on air, he mentioned an email from a listener, who detailed an incident five years ago, where Daniel Hadley, through his duties as an officer, had saved the life of a fourteen year old girl. The listener spoke highly of Daniel in terms of his caring nature and said that for months after, he checked on the young girl's welfare. When reading this email on air, Ray commented that the boy who was described in the email was the boy he knew.

It came to light that Daniel Hadley had been suffering from mental health issues for some time. When listening to Mr Hadley's original press conference, I immediately flashed back to the many instances I had heard him on the radio slam someone who had been caught up in a drug-related event. It made me wonder why his reaction was different this time. Of course, it was because it was his son. *We all have family, and if it were one of our family members, we would pray that if they were in this situation that they would be pulled up by the system, not pushed down.*

Daniel Hadley had his charges dropped. He was an exception to the rule; for the vast majority of people in his situation, that is not their experience. The Illicit Drug Data Report 2016–2017 released in mid-2018, indicates that there were a record number of illicit drug arrests with almost 155,000 arrests made, as well as a record weight of illicit drugs seized—27.4 tonnes (across 113,533 seizures). Cannabis made up approximately fifty per cent of these arrests, while about thirty per cent were amphetamine, and other drugs such as heroin, cocaine and new psychoactives made up the remaining arrests. For all drug arrests made, almost ninety per cent were for possession, and for cannabis, over ninety per cent of arrests were for possession. *One cannabis possession arrest takes approximately five hours of a police officer's time.*

However, if arrests continue to increase, where do you incarcerate all of these offenders? Here enters the highly controversial issue of privatised prisons. Australia holds the highest percentage of prisoners in private facilities in the world. However, the US holds the highest total number of prisoners in privatised facilities. This is due to both sheer population size, and because the US has an imprisonment rate of about 700 per 100,000, whereas Australia is approximately 210 per 100,000. The US has approximately five per cent of the total world population, but twenty-five per cent of the world's prison population.

Australia currently has a record number of prisoners, with a prison population increase of fifty per cent in the past ten years, even though population has increased at less than half that rate in the same time. The exponential growth in both the Australian and US prison population is almost entirely due to illicit drug charges. (More on cannabis and incarceration in Part Two.)

In 1993, there were 40,408 illicit drug arrests in Australia, which increased to 85,046 in 1997 (approx. 110 per cent increase). This was driven by cannabis arrests more than doubling (33,765 in 1993 to 69,136 in 1997), and heroin arrests almost tripling (2,502 in 1993 to 7,140 in 1997). Heroin arrests peaked at 14,341 in 1999 and declined to 3,691 in 2004. Illicit drug arrests hovered between 78,000 and 85,000 for almost a decade due to the sharp decline in heroin supply and subsequent arrests. However, the shortfall in heroin arrests since the early 2000s has since been filled by other drugs.

In the decade from 2006 to 2016, drug arrests in several categories increased dramatically:

- Amphetamine-type stimulant arrests increased by approximately 210 per cent.
- Cannabis arrests increased by approximately forty per cent.
- Cocaine arrests increased by approximately 270 per cent.
- Heroin/other opioid arrests increased by approximately thirty-seven per cent.
- Other/unknown (steroid, NPS etc.) arrests increased by approximately 191 per cent.

From 1993, illicit drug arrests increased from approximately 40,000 to 155,000 (287.5 per cent increase).

In 1974–1975 in Australia, the rate of recorded drug offences was 71.6 per 100,000, which more than doubled in 1980 to 161.6 per 100,000. This figure doubled again over the next four years to 335.8 in 1984, and fast forward to 2016, the rate of recorded drug offences was just under 400 per 100,000. The increase consists almost entirely of consumer arrests, not supplier arrests. So not only are we arresting more people, we are arresting a greater proportion of the population.

In NSW alone, prisons are currently operating above capacity at about 110 per cent, and overcrowded prisons are incredibly difficult to manage. It is also extremely expensive to incarcerate someone, with current estimates put at around $290 per day, meaning that an eighteen-month sentence for one offender costs the public about $160,000. Incarceration also has substantial negative knock-on effects to the community as those who were incarcerated find it extremely difficult to return to work or obtain employment or education, sustain relationships and integrate back into the community, which increase welfare, public health and public housing costs, not to mention the loss in economic productivity.

Previously incarcerated women are about fourteen times more likely to end their life, men are about five times more likely to end their life, and overall, released prisoners are about ten times more likely to self-harm than the general population. Prisoners can develop mental illnesses while incarcerated, while others have their existing mental health conditions exacerbated. This is due to the nature of prison being highly volatile in terms of violence, the enforced solitude, as well as, paradoxically, the lack of privacy, social networking isolation, absence of meaningful activities, inadequacy of prison mental health services and enormous insecurity about future prospects, such as relationships and career. Prisoners are also likely to come across hard drugs while incarcerated, or they abstain and return to using drugs when released and may overdose due to a loss in tolerance. Australian prisons also have a hepatitis C prevalence of thirty per cent. Overall, prison is probably the worst place on the planet for someone's health, particularly if that person has an existing mental health issue.

Private prisons are highly controversial due to the existence of a profit motive in incarcerating people. The easiest way to ensure that prisons remain at capacity so they are financially viable is to get low-hanging fruit, which are the drug users. Australia is also not obliged under the UN convention to enforce criminal sanctions on drug users—all that is required is that the drugs scheduled are not sold openly in a free market and that a penalty is put in place. In terms of treaty compliance, criminal sanctions must be applied to manufacturers, distributors and traffickers, whereas for possession, a non-criminal penalty is sufficient. Although civil sanctions would meet UN treaty compliance, countries such as Australia elect to incarcerate drug users. It is a complete myth that countries are handcuffed to the prohibition, criminalisation and incarceration of drug users through compliance with UN convention. It is also worth noting that none of the UN conventions define what a drug is, and Australia's National Drug Strategy does not include a plan of action.

The International Narcotics Control Board has stated that countries that facilitate or provide mechanisms where people can use illicit drugs such as injection centres and NSPs are in breach of international drug treaties. This is not entirely true and is likely fuelled by the prohibitive approach that the UN has had towards drugs throughout its entire history. It is not relevant to countries that have simply depenalised or decriminalised use yet are not actually providing society with a legal means of obtaining the drug. Injection centres such as the MSIC have specific amendments in domestic legislation (such as the Drug Misuse and Trafficking Act NSW). In fact, denying people access to NSPs is a direct breach of basic human rights and international law that ascribes the right to health care, which includes prison populations. And even if it were in breach, this is not a reflection on the initiatives, but instead it means the international law is wrong and needs to change. NSPs are not perfect, but no medical intervention is, particularly considering that the clientele is extremely difficult to work with.

Most countries throughout the world have an incarceration rate of less than 150 per 100,000, however it is thought that Australia's high imprisonment rate is due to the fact that Australia originally existed as a penal colony. Nations like Australia, the UK and the US with prohibition as the primary focus in drug policy, have steadily been increasing their prison population, and this has led to some perverse examples of societal damage.

In 2008, two Pennsylvania judges, Mark Ciavarella and Michael Conahan, were sentenced to almost thirty years and twenty years respectively for receiving significant financial kickbacks in exchange for handing down disproportionately harsh sentences to juveniles so that two juvenile detention centres remained at capacity. Ciavarella was appointed as President Judge of Luzerne County, and the community welcomed his zero-tolerance approach to juvenile offenders with open arms in the aftermath of the 1999 Columbine High School massacre. Real estate developer Robert Mericle, who constructed the two facilities and was also involved in the scandal, was fined $250,000, was ordered to pay $2,000,000 to child welfare programs and a further $17,000,000 to former juvenile offenders and was imprisoned for one year. The attorney who co-owned the facility and who was also involved in the scandal, Robert Powell, was sentenced to eighteen months prison and ordered to pay several million dollars in restitution.

Ciavarella imprisoned over 3,000 children, and the scandal is estimated to have involved approximately 2,500 juveniles, the majority of whom were non-violent, first time, minor offenders, who now have irreversibly damaged lives. Most of these kinds of offenders never return to school, progress to further crime and some even kill themselves.

A large proportion of incarceration rate increases are illicit drug related, and the two fastest growing incarcerated groups by offence type in Australia are acts intended to cause injury and illicit drug offences. In areas around the world that focus on prohibition, new prisons continue to be opened. However, in places like the Netherlands that focus on harm reduction and treatment, prisons are being closed. In fact in 2013, almost twenty prisons in the Netherlands were closed, and the country now imports prisoners from other European nations such as Norway just to maintain capacity.

Although it is very difficult to get specific data in terms of total crime across Australia, the offence rate is estimated to be approximately 1,870 per 100,000 individuals, or 1.87 per cent. Across all crimes, the most common type of offence is illicit drug related, and the vast majority of these people have drug-related criminal records for simply possessing drugs. They can't get jobs, or in many cases, they lose their jobs. They are barred from travelling to many parts of the world, and they lose or can't obtain accommodation due to landlords or homeowners not wanting convicted individuals living in their property. If relationships break down and there are children involved, individuals can lose custody, and the perception that others have of the convicted changes, becoming always suspicious of them. Educational institutions may not accept applications or may expel students, and financial institutions do not look favourably upon criminal records.

These examples point to a system that places punishment above reducing harm, because for many of these convicted individuals, the effects of a criminal record are going to damage their health and their future significantly more than the drug is going to damage their health or wider society. Why are individuals being arrested and given criminal records for possessing drugs that, for the most part, are causing less harm than either the drugs' criminalisation or the six-pack of beers that the arresting police officers consume on a Friday or Saturday night?

In 2015, a Victorian man was pulled over for driving with a broken headlight on a main road in north-western NSW. Due to prior minor drug charges, the car was searched. The driver, Daniel Witham, was found in possession of twenty-eight grams of psilocybin, which included the five-gram plastic bag that packaged the psilocybin—the police counted this in the total amount nevertheless. As the weight exceeded twenty-five grams, this meant that the amount was deemed a commercial quantity of psilocybin by the *Drug Misuse and Trafficking Act 1985,* meaning that the law interprets the amount as intending to distribute. This can result in a jail sentence of fifteen to twenty years— a lengthier sentence than rape. This is despite the fact that the same piece of legislation considers 250 grams of heroin an equally indictable commercial quantity—the threshold is ten times higher for a drug that addicts and kills easily.

The day of his arrest, Witham was transported to Moree Community Corrections Office where he was remanded for three days, then sent to Tamworth Correctional Centre for one month and then to Cessnock Correctional Centre for three weeks. He made bail purely on medical grounds but effectively lost two months of his life and has since documented the damage that prison caused him.

Apart from incarcerating someone for three weeks in a 'supermax' prison for possessing native fungi being absurdly unnecessary in itself, he has not been the same since. After sleeping in the freezing cold every night and seeing inmates share the same syringe twenty times and get bashed or stabbed for food, it took years for him to begin treatment. Witham used a multitude of sedatives (flunitrazepam, heroin etc.) to hide from his experience, and he had to re-learn how to function around his family and friends again—not to mention his daughter—whose first birthday he missed while incarcerated. He would probably never have been exposed to harder drug use if he weren't incarcerated. *The most incredible aspect of his story, however, is that despite being arrested for possession of psilocybin, he was able to overcome his prison-induced trauma by taking psilocybin.*

So not only did prison fail to deter him from taking psilocybin, it caused a great deal more harm to him than the drug itself. There are many extreme examples of absurdly disproportionate punishments in other countries as well, such as Lee Otis Johnson, who was incarcerated for thirty years in the US for selling one joint and Atiba Parker who is currently serving a forty-two-year sentence in the US for possessing and selling a small amount of crack cocaine.

What's more is that the harm caused by the law and his punishment was undone by Witham taking the product that he was incarcerated for! The harms of incarceration also often endure long—obtaining employment, particularly in NSW, will be extremely difficult. Because of his criminal record, chances are he will never be able to obtain a level of employment with a high enough salary to be able to repay the fine for his possession charge. He is indebted to the government, probably for the rest of his life. This can be compounded by the fact that late payments incur further penalties, and interest may be charged on an outstanding amount. Building and maintaining healthy relationships can be a challenge due to the enormous level of support needed. Employers, friends, family, and other individuals in his network will never view him in the same light.

This is also the case for other entities, such as insurers who provide security, financial institutions who provide finance, educational institutions who provide internships, education, volunteering etc., and property owners who provide accommodation. The police and criminal justice system err on the side of guilt rather than innocence, which filters into other issues, such as child custody. The domino effect is seemingly never-ending, and not only does society view individuals associated with illegality differently, but they also perceive drugs associated with illegality differently—drugs can never be seen in the same light once they have been illegalised. Illegality can distort rational perceptions of drug harms, just as illegality can distort rational perceptions of an individual's character.

If President Obama had been prosecuted and done time for using cannabis and cocaine (which he has admitted to using), he would not have become President, and neither would have George Bush or Bill Clinton, nor would David Cameron have become UK Prime Minister. Yet all of these leaders have made significant efforts in hypocritically furthering attacks on illicit drugs, such as George Bush as governor of Texas, signing legislation that mandated that users of cocaine must face six months in prison. Why those who rise to power change their mind about drug law reform when they come to power is a difficult question to answer. However, if an individual rises to power on the promise of making change, they should not forget that promise and keep in mind that one of the biggest reasons behind losing the support of the electorate and ultimately losing office is dishonesty. Many politicians believe in the concept of punishing others until it happens to someone close to them.

⁓

One of the limitations that I see from those who argue from a reformist perspective is that they often focus very heavily on dependent or addicted individuals who are not the majority of drug users. Recidivists and problematic drug users do make up a significant proportion of arrests; however, the vast majority of people who use drugs—legal or illegal— are not dependent. For those who are dependent, criminal records only create further damage, and for those who are not dependent, criminal records often cause more damage than the actual drugs. The past and current policy of simply arresting, fining and criminalising users represents a missed opportunity for intervening with constructive education. While Drug Courts are effective in this manner, the vast majority of drug users are not eligible, because they do not suffer from dependence, and because they are not dependant or addicted, they often get the book thrown at them. In fact, the majority of drug users will not experience significant harm, unless they come into contact with the criminal justice system. The law also pushes people into consuming alcohol (which is physiologically more harmful than most illicit drugs), pushes others into sourcing illicit drugs from dealers who sell much more dangerous products than what a regulated market could provide and complicates access to treatment. This is why we have to be very careful about using the law to damage people, especially those who may not be being harmed significantly by the drugs they are using.

This is not to say that the law has no role when it comes to the regulation of drugs. It does, particularly when it comes to manufacture and distribution, however, it is not the primary role. But as the law has been in the primary role, and looks to continue to be in the primary role, we will continue to have an underclass. As a society when it comes to punishing people into submission, we have dug ourselves a hole, and the first step to getting out of a hole is to stop digging.

Some may say that a reform or a change in drug policy will see the end of the world as we know it. I think maybe that's not a bad thing. I do not consider myself either an intelligent or wise human being, but in the short period of time I have been working within the alcohol and other drugs space, my perspective and approach towards drugs in society has changed dramatically because I have learnt from my mistakes. I learnt that my best friend died, not because she was morally weaker than the rest of us, but because she did not have supportive networks around to protect her, and her friends did not know how to look after her. I learnt that some of the people I studied with at university, who had exceptionally promising futures, have now had their entire future thrown into question because they have been caught with drugs on them or passing on drugs to a friend. I learnt that despite thinking illegal drugs were harmful, on several occasions, I was probably one or two drinks away from being hospitalised because of drinking too much. I have learnt many things, but what saddens me the most is that many people in society with much more intelligence and wisdom than me have not learnt.

We continue to double down on approaches that over half a century have proven to do more harm than good. People should not be able to do whatever they want, however, the punishments and negative outcomes as a result of current policy are disproportionally greater than the harms of the drug themselves. For many politicians, the passage of legislation is more important than the outcome of its enforcement. If politicians are conscious that the legislation they implement is increasing harms and not actually in the best interest of the community, then what is driving this incessantly stubborn position?

This last paragraph comes shortly after the tragic death of Sydney teenager, Hamish Bidgood, who while on the Gold Coast celebrating schoolies week, fell to his death from a balcony. The press immediately placed the blame on nitrous oxide, calling for it to be banned and cracked down on, as it was alleged that he had been inhaling the gas shortly before his fall. The story was even picked up by the UK's *Daily Mail*, which had previously referred to nitrous oxide as 'hippie crack'.

Like most of these stories, they ignore the involvement of alcohol, call for crackdowns and bans on other drugs (in this case nitrous oxide), and continue on the path of what one anonymous schoolie told the *Gold Coast Bulletin* 'cope with it and just say no'. The problem is for those who say 'yes' is that they were never given any harm-reduction advice in how to look after themselves or their friends in drug-related situations. For example, don't do other drugs if you are intoxicated. Or, if you are going to use nangs (nitrous oxide canisters), then make sure you are away from any hazards such as roads, pools or balconies. If you are going to use an inhalant, make sure you are seated to minimise the risk of falling if you have a lapse in consciousness.

The vast majority of Australians choose to say no to drugs. If after a hundred years we still have a group of people saying yes, then perhaps it's time to give that group of people a Plan B so that they or their friends do not become another statistic within an impractical system we blindly continue to defend.

ABOUT THE AUTHOR

Tom Reynolds is the founder of Independent Drug Education Australia (IDEA). He has undergraduate as well as postgraduate health-related qualifications (Bachelor of Health & Master of Public Health) and has worked in drug rehabilitation.

In his role in IDEA, he runs drug education sessions with school communities across Australia, where he provides high quality information to teachers and parents, as well as helping young people to develop the skills they need to protect themselves and their friends in all drug-related situations.

Tom lives in Sydney with his wife, Sarah, and cocker spaniel, Bentley.

Acronyms Used

AAS	Anabolic androgenic steroid
ADHD	Attention deficit hyperactivity disorder
AFP	Australian Federal Police
AHA	Australian Hotels Association
AIDS	Acquired immune deficiency syndrome
AIHW	Australian Institute of Health and Welfare
ALDH	Alcohol dehydrogenase
ALP	Australian Labor Party
AMA	Australian Medical Association
ATP	Adenosine triphosphate
BAC	Blood alcohol content
BCAA	Branched chain amino acid
BDO	1,4 butanediol
BHO	Butane hash oil
BMJ	British Medical Journal
BOCSAR	Bureau of Crime Statistics and Research
CBD	Cannabidiol
CDC	Centres for Disease and Control and Prevention
CNS	Central nervous system

COPD	Chronic obstructive pulmonary disease
COX	Cyclooxygenase
DEA	Drug enforcement Administration
DCM	Dilated cardiomyopathy
DFA	Drug Free Australia
DMT	Dimethyltriptamine
DOB	Dimethoxybromoamphetamine
ECT	Electro-convulsive therapy
ED	Emergency department
EFA	Essential fatty acid
EMCDDA	European Monitoring Centre for drugs and drug addiction
EU	European Union
FASD	Foetal alcohol spectrum disorder
FDA	Food and Drug Administration
GABA	Gama-aminobutryic acid
GBL	Gamma butyrolactone
GDP	Gross domestic product
GHB	Gamma hydroxybutyrate
HDL	High density lipoprotein
HIV	Human immunodeficiency virus
HPPD	Hallucinogen persisting perception disorder
ICU	Intensive care unit
LDL	Low density lipoprotein
LSD	Lysergic acid diethylamide
MAOI	Monoamine oxidase inhibitor
MCDA	Multi criteria decision analysis

MDA	Methylenedioxyamphetamine
MDMA	Methylenedioxymethamphetamine
MDT	Mobile drug testing
MPTP	1-methyl-4-phenyl-1,2,3,6-tetrahydropyridine
MPP+	1-methyl-4-phenylpyridinium
MPPP	1-methyl-4-proprionoxypiperidine
MRI	Magnetic resonance imaging
MSIC	Medically Supervised Injecting Centre
NAD+	Nicotinamide adenine dinucleotide
NBOMe	N-methoxybenzyl
NIDA	National Institute on Drug Abuse
NIH	National Institute of Health
NO	Nitric oxide
NPS	Novel psychoactive substance
NRT	Nicotine replacement therapy
NSAID	Non-steroidal anti-inflammatory
NSP	Needle syringe program
OCD	Obsessive compulsive disorder
OFC	Orbitofrontal cortex
OSA	Obstructive sleep apnoea
OTC	Over the counter
PAG	Periaqueductal gray
PCD	Programmed cell death
PCP	Phencyclidine
PD	Parkinson's Disease
PDR	Physicians' Desk Reference

PMA	Paramethoxyamphetamine
PMMA	Paramethoxymethamphetamine
POMC	Proopiomelanocortin
PTSD	Post traumatic stress disorder
RBT	Random breath testing
ROA	Route of administration
RSA	Responsible service of alcohol
RTD	Ready to drink
SAD	Social anxiety disorder
SC	Synthetic cannabinoids
SD	Standard drink
SDRI	Serotonin-dopamine reuptake inhibitor
SIDS	Sudden infant death syndrome
SNRI	Serotonin-noradrenaline reuptake inhibitor
SUSMP	Standard for Uniform Scheduling of Medicines and Poisons
SSRI	Selective-serotonin reuptake inhibitor
TCA	Tricyclic antidepressant
TGA	Therapeutic Goods Administration
THC	Tetrahydrocannabinol
UN	United Nations
UNCPS	United Nations Convention on Psychotropic Substances
UNODC	United Nations Office of Drugs and Crime
VF	Ventricular fibrillation
YPLL	Years of potential life lost

Bibliography

Journal Articles

- Amato, L et al. (2005). An overview of systematic reviews of the effectiveness of opiate maintenance therapies: available evidence to inform clinical practice and research. *Journal of Substance Abuse.* 28 (4).

- Anderson D.M et al. (2013). Medical marijuana laws, traffic fatalities and alcohol consumption. *The Journal of Law and Economics.* 56: 2, 333-369.

- Attwood, A.S et al. (2009). Effects of acute alcohol consumption on processing of perceptual cues of emotional expression. *Journal of Psychopharmacology.* 23(1).

- Aydelotte, J et al. (2017). Crash fatality rates after recreational marijuana legalization in Washington and Colorado. *The American Journal of Public Health.* 107, no. 8, 1329-1331.

- Aydelotte, J.D et al. (2017). Crash fatality rates after recreational marijuana legalisation in Washington and Colorado. *American Journal of Public Health.* 107. Number 8. 1329-1331.

- Banks, E et al. (2015). Tobacco smoking and all-cause mortality in a large Australian cohort study: findings from a mature epidemic with current low smoking prevalence. *BMC Medicine.* 13. Article 38.

- Batrinos M.L (2012). Testosterone and aggressive behavior in man. *International Journal Endocrinology and Metabolism.* 10(3):563–568. doi:10.5812/ijem.3661

- Bellew, B et al. (2015). Health 'benefits' of smoking? *Tobacco in Australia: Facts and issues.* Melbourne: Cancer Council Victoria.

- Benzenhöfer, U and Passie, T (2010). Rediscovering MDMA (ecstasy): the role of the American chemist Alexander T. Shulgin. *Addiction.* 105(8):1355-1361. doi: 10.1111/j.1360-0443.2010.02948.x.

- Beta Carotene Cancer Prevention Study Group (1994). The effect of vitamin E and beta carotene on the incidence of lung cancer and other cancers in male smokers. *New England Journal of Medicine.* 330(15):1029-1035.

- Bjelakovic, G et al. (2004). Antioxidant supplements for prevention of gastrointestinal cancers: A systematic review and meta-analysis. *Lancet.* 8;364(9441). 1219-1228.

- Book, A.S, Starzyk, K.B and Quinsey, V.L (2001). The relationship between testosterone and aggression: a meta-analysis. *Aggression and Violent Behaviour.* Volume 6. Issue 6. 579-599.

- Branch, D (2003). Effect of creatine supplementation on body composition and performance: a meta-analysis. *International Journal of Sports Nutrition and Exercise Metabolism.* 13(2). 198-226.

- Britton A, and McPherson, K (2001). Mortality in England and Wales attributable to current alcohol consumption. *Journal of Epidemiology & Community Health.* 55:383-388.

- Brook, H (2002). Governing failure: Politics, heroin, families. *International Journal of Drug Policy.* 13, 175–184.

- "Brunt, T and Niesink, R (2011). The Drug Information and MonitoringSystem (DIMS) in the Netherlands: Implementation, results, and international comparison. *Drug Testing and Analysis.* 621-634.

- Brunt, T et al. (2010). Instability of the ecstasy market and the new kid on the block: mephedrone. *Journal of Psychopharmacology.* Volume 25. Issue 11. 1543-1547.

- Buchanan, J and Young, L (2000). The war on drugs—a war on drug users? *Drugs: Education, Prevention & Policy.* 7, 409–422.

- Buchanan, T et al. (2006). Dancing hot on Ecstasy: physical activity and thermal comfort ratings are associated with the memory and other psychobiological problems reported by recreational MDMA users. *Human Psycho- pharmacology: Clinical and Experimental.* 21: 285–98.

- Bullington, B (2004). Drug policy reform and its detractors: The United States as the elephant in the closet. *Journal of Drug Issues.* 34, 687–721.

- Burris, S et al. (2004). Addressing the 'risk environment' for injection drug users: The mysterious case of the missing cop. *The Milbank Quarterly.* 82(1), 125–156.

- Campeny, E et al. (2020). The blind men and the elephant: Systematic review of systematic reviews of cannabis use related health harms. *European Neuropsychopharmacology.* Volume 33. 1-35.

- Carhart-Harris, R (2012). Neural correlates of the psychedelic state as determined by fMRI studies with psilocybin. *Proceedings of the National Academy of Sciences. USA* vol. 109 no. 6 2138–2143.

- Chan, B.S et al. (1998). Serotonin syndrome resulting from drug interactions. *Medical Journal of Australia.* 169:523–525.

- Charlton, A (2004). Medicinal uses of tobacco in history. *Journal of the Royal Society of Medicine.* 97 (6).

- Choi, P.Y and Pope, H.G (1994). Violence Toward Women and Illicit Androgenic-Anabolic Steroid Use. *Annals of Clinical Psychiatry.* 6(1):21-25.

- Clemesha, C.G, Thaker, H and Samplaski, M.K (2020). 'Testosterone boosting' supplements composition and claims are not supported by the academic literature. *The World Journal of Men's Health.* 38(1):115-122.

- Collins, D.J and Lapsley, H.M (1996). The social costs of drug abuse in Australia in 1988 and 1992 (National Drug Strategy Monograph Series No. 3). *Canberra: Commonwealth Department of Human Services and Health.*

- Colombo, G et al. (1999). Cross-tolerance to ethanol and γ-hydroxybutyric acid. *Alcoholism: Clinical and Experimental Research.* Volume 23 (10).

- Coral, E et al. (2017). Projecting the future smoking prevalence in Norway. *European Journal of Public Health.* Volume 27, Issue 1, 139–144.

- Coutts, A.S and La Thangue, N.B (2005). The p53 response: emerging levels of co-factor complexity (2005). *Biochemical and Biophysical Research and Communications.* Division of Biochemistry and Molecular Biology, Davidson Building, University of Glasgow.

- Crane, K (2010). Palliative care gains ground in developing countries. *Journal of the National Cancer Institute.* Volume 102, Issue 21, 1613–1615.

- Dabbs, J.M et al. (1995). Testosterone, crime, and misbehavior among 692 male prison inmates. *Elsevier.* Department of Psychology, Georgia State University. Volume 18, Issue 5, 627-633.

- Das, S et al. (2016). Lysergic acid diethylamide: a drug of 'use'? *Therapeutic Advances in Psychopharmacology.* 6(3):214–228. doi:10.1177/2045125316640440.

- Degenhardt, L et al. (2006). The "lessons" of the Australian "heroin shortage". *Substance Abuse Treatment Prevention Policy.* 1:11. doi:10.1186/1747-597X-1-11.

- Dellazizzo, L et al. (2019). Cannabis use and violence in patients with severe mental illnesses: A meta-analytical investigation. *Psychiatry Research.* Volume 274. 42-48.

- Devries, M and Phillips, S (2014). Creatine supplementation during resistance training in older men – A meta-analysis. *Medicine and Science in Sports and Exercise.* Volume 46. Number 6. 1194-1203.

- Di Cicco M.E et al. (2016). Mortality in relation to smoking: the British Doctors Study. *Breathe (Sheff).* 12(3):275–276.

- Doll, R et al. (2004). Mortality in relation to smoking: 50 years' observations on male British doctors. *British Medical Journal (Clinical research ed.)*. 328.

- Drucker, E (1995). Drug prohibition and public health: It's a crime. *Australian and New Zealand Journal of Criminology*. 28, S67–73.

- Drucker, E and Clear, A (1999). Harm reduction in the home of the war on drugs: Methadone and needle exchange in the USA. *Drug and Alcohol Review*. 18, 103–112.

- Elvik, R (2013). Risk of road accident associated with the use of drugs: A systematic review and metaanalysis of evidence from epidemiological studies. *Accident Analysis and Prevention*. Vol 60, 254–267.

- Filbey, F.M et al. (2014). Marijuana and the orbitofrontal cortex. *Proceedings of the National Academy of Sciences*. 111 (47) 16913-16918; DOI:10.1073/pnas.1415297111.

- Ford, T et al. (2005). Service contacts among the children participating in the British Child and Adolescent Mental Health Surveys. *Child and Adolescent Mental Health*. 10.

- Forsyth, A (2001). Distorted? a quantitative exploration of drug fatality reports in the popular press. *International Journal of Drug Policy*. (12).

- Foster, J and Ferguson, C.S (2012). Home Drinking in the UK: Trends and Causes. *Alcohol and Alcoholism*. Volume 47, Issue 3, 355–358.

- Frisher, M et al. (2009). Assessing the impact of cannabis use on trends in diagnosed schizophrenia in the United Kingdom from 1996 to 2005. *Schizophrenia Research*. 113: 123–128.

- Gable, R (2004). Comparison of acute lethal toxicity of commonly abused psychoactive substances. *Addiction*. 99(6):686-696.

- Gao, C et al. (2014). Alcohol's burden of disease in Australia. *Canberra: FARE and VicHealth in collaboration with Turning Point*.

- Gilman, J.M et al. (2014). Cannabis use is quantitatively associated with nucleus accumbens and amygdala abnormalities in young adult recreational users. *Journal of Neuroscience.* 34 (16) 5529-5538.

- Gonzalez, R and James M (2012). Swanson Impact of early onset and regular cannabis use. *Proceedings of the National Academy of Sciences* 109(40), 15970-15971. DOI:10.1073/pnas.1214124109.

- Gore, F.M et al. (2011). Global burden of disease in young people aged 10-24 years: a systematic analysis. *Lancet.* Volume 377, issue 9783. 2093-2102.

- Gorelick, D.A et al. (2011). Antagonist-elicited cannabis withdrawal in humans. *Journal of Clinical Psychopharmacology.* 31(5).

- Gornall, J (2014). Consultation on minimum unit price for alcohol was a sham, *BMJ* investigation shows. 348. *BMJ.* DOI: https://doi.org/10.1136/bmj.g72.

- Gossop M. (2006). Classification of illegal and harmful drugs. *British Medical Journal.* 333(7562):272–273.doi:10.1136/bmj.38929.578414.80.

- Gossop, M et al. (2002). Factors associated with abstinence, lapse or relapse to heroin use after residential treatment: protective effect of coping responses. *Addiction* (97).

- Graham, G.G and Scott, K.F (2005). Mechanism of action of paracetamol. *American Journal of Therapeutics.* 12(1):46-55.

- Grotenhermen, F, and Muller-Vahl, K (2012). The therapeutic potential of cannabis and cannabinoids. *Deutsches Arzteblatt International.* 109: 495-501.

- Gustavsson, A et al. (2011). Cost of disorders of the brain in Europe 2010. *European Neuropsychopharmacology.* 718-779.

- Guzey, C and Spigset, O (2002). Genotyping of Drug Targets: A Method to Predict Adverse Drug Reactions? *Drug Safety.* (25). 8.

- Hall, W (1995). Variations in prohibition: Harm minimisation and drug wars in Australia and the United States in *Australian and New Zealand Journal of Criminology,* 28, S74–77.

- Halpern, J.H et al. (2005). Psychological and cognitive effects of long-term peyote use among Native Americans. *Biological Psychiatry.* 15;58(8):624-631.

- Hansen, B (2018). Early evidence on recreational marijuana legalisation and traffic fatalities. *Economic Inquiry.* Volume 58. Issue 2. 547-568.

- Hemby, S.E et al. (1997). Differences in extracellular dopamine concentrations in the nucleus accumbens during response dependent and response independent cocaine administration in the rat. *Psychopharmacology* (Berlin). 133(1).

- Hickman, M et al. (2009). If cannabis caused schizophrenia — How many cannabis users may need to be prevented in order to prevent one case of schizophrenia? England and Wales calculations. *Addiction.* 104: 1856-1861.

- HIV Hotline (1998). Hepatic effects of 17 alpha-alkylated anabolic-androgenic steroids. 8(5-6):2-5.

- Ho, J et al. (2007). Cannabinoid-induced hyperphagia: correlation with inhibition of proopiomelanocortin neurons? *Physiology and Behaviour.* 92(3):507–519. doi:10.1016/j.physbeh.2007.04.028.

- Hoge, C et al. (2004). Combat duty in Iraq and Afghanistan, mental health problems, and barriers to care. *The New England Journal of Medicine.* (351).

- Isbister, G.K et al. (2003). Moclobemide poisoning: toxicokinetics and occurrence of serotonin toxicity. *British Journal of Clinical Pharmacology.* 56(4):441–450. doi:10.1046/j.1365-2125.2003.01895.x

- Jones, A.W (2017). Review of Caffeine-Related Fatalities along with Postmortem Blood Concentrations in 51 Poisoning Deaths. *Journal of Analytical Toxicology.* Volume 41, Issue 3, 167–172. DOI: https://doi.org/10.1093/jat/bkx011.

- Joossens, L and Raw, M (2000). How can cigarette smuggling be reduced? *BMJ.* 321(7266): 947–950.

- Karch, S.B (1999). Cocaine: History, use, abuse. *Journal of the Royal Society of Medicine.* 92(8). 393-397.

- Karlson–Stiber, C and Persson, H (2003). Cytotoxic fungi – an overview. *Toxicon.* 42 (4): 339-349.

- Kaye, S et al. (2009). Methylenedioxymethamphetamine (MDMA)-related fatalities in Australia: Demographics, circumstances, toxicology and major organ pathology. *Drug and Alcohol Dependence.* 104(3): 254-261.

- Klein, A.S et al. (1989). Amanita poisoning: treatment and the role of liver transplantation. *American Journal of Medicine.* 86 (2): 187-193.

- Knop, J (2011). The Danish longitudinal study of alcoholism 1978–2008. *Danish Medical Bulletin.* (58) 8.

- Koch, M et al. (2015). Hypothalamic POMC neurons promote cannabinoid-induced feeding. *Nature.* 519(7541):45–50. doi:10.1038/nature14260.

- Koob G.F and Le Moal, M. (2008). Review: Neurobiological mechanisms for opponent motivational processes in addiction. *Philosophical Transactions of the Royal Society London B: Biological Sciences.* 363(1507):3113–3123.

- Krebs, T.S and Johansen, P (2011). Lysergic acid diethylamide (LSD) for alcoholism: a meta-analysis of randomized controlled trials. *Journal of Psychopharmacology.* Volume 26. Issue 7. 994-1002

- Kreuz, L.E and Rose, R.M (1972). Assessment of aggressive behavior and plasma testosterone in a young criminal population. *Psychosomatic Medicine.* 34(4):321–32.

- Lachenmeier, D.W and Rehm, J (2015). Comparative risk assessment of alcohol, tobacco, cannabis and other illicit drugs using the margin of exposure approach. *Scientific Reports.* 5:8126. doi:10.1038/srep08126.

- Lane, D and Crawford, L (1979). Mutations in the p53 gene occur in diverse human tumor types. *Nature.* 342, 705 – 708. December 1989.

- Langston, W.L (2017). The MPTP story. *Journal of Parkinson's Disease.* 7(Suppl. 1): S11–S19.

- Levine, H.G and Reinarman, C (1991). From Prohibition to Regulation: Lessons from Alcohol Policy for Drug Policy. *The Milbank Quarterly.* Vol. 69, No. 3, Confronting Drug Policy: Part 1 (1991), 461-494.

- Lindfors, P et al. (2012). Fears for the future among Finnish adolescents in 1983-2007: from global concerns to ill health and loneliness. *Journal of Adolescence.* 35(4):991-9. doi: 10.1016/j.adolescence.2012.02.003.

- Litten, W (1975). The most poisonous mushrooms. *Scientific American.* 232 (3): 90-101.

- Livingston, M and Callinan, S (2019). Examining Australia's heaviest drinkers. *Australian and New Zealand Journal of Public Health.* 43: 451-456.

- Lopez-Larson, M.P et al. (2015). Aberrant orbitofrontal connectivity in marijuana smoking adolescents. *Developmental Cognitive Neuroscience.* 16:54–62. doi: 10.1016/j.dcn.2015.08.002.

- López-Muñoz, F et al. (2005). The history of barbiturates a century after their clinical introduction. *Neuropsychiatric Disease and Treatment.* 1(4):329–343.

- Lucas, P et al. (2013). Cannabis as a substitute for alcohol and other drugs: A dispensary-based survey of substitution effect in Canadian medical cannabis patients. *Addiction Research and Theory.* 21(5).

- Lunze, K et al. (2014). Punitive policing and associated substance use risk among HIV-positive people in Russia who inject drugs. *Journal of International AIDS Society.* 17:19043.

- Lyon, E (1999). A review of the effects of nicotine on schizophrenia and antipsychotic medications. *Psychiatric Services.* 1346-1350.

- Maag, V (2003). Decriminalisation of cannabis use in Switzerland from an international perspective - European, American and Australian experiences. *International Journal of Drug Policy.* 14, 279–281.

- MacDonald, M et al. (2003). Effectiveness of needle and syringe programmes for preventing HIV transmission. *International Journal of Drug Policy.* 14, 353–357.

- Marangoni, C, Hernandez, M and Faedda, G.L (2016). The role of environmental exposures as risk factors for bipolar disorder: A systematic review of longitudinal studies. *Journal of Affective Disorders.* 193:165-174

- Marchese, R et al. (2006). Low correspondence between K-ras mutations in pancreatic cancer tissue and detection of K-ras mutations in circulating DNA. *Pancreas.* 32(2):171-177. FBF S. Pietro Hospital AFAR Research Centre, University of Rome La Sapienza, Rome, Italy.

- Marmer, M.J (1959). A barbiturate antidote – Use of methylethylglutarimide in barbiturate intoxication and in terminating barbiturate anaesthesia. *Western Journal of Medicine.* 91(5). 266-269.

- Mars, S (2003). Heroin Addiction Care and Control: the British System 1916 to 1984. *Journal of the Royal Society of Medicine.* 96(2):99–100.

- Mattay, V.S et al. (2003). Catechol O-methyl transferase val158-met genotype and individual variation in the brain response to amphetamine. *Proceedings of the National Academy of Sciences USA.* 100 (10). 6186-6191.

- Mayo, L.D et al. (2005). Phosphorylation of human p53 at serine 46 determines promoter selection and whether apoptosis is attenuated or amplified. *The Journal of Biological Chemistry.* Department of Radiation Oncology, Case Comprehensive Cancer Center, Case Western Reserve University, Cleveland, Ohio.

- Measham, F (2010). Tweaking, bombing, dabbing and stockpiling: the emergence of mephedrone and the perversity of prohibition. *Drugs and Alcohol Today.* 10 (1).

- Mehra, R et al. (2006). The Association Between Marijuana Smoking and Lung Cancer: A Systematic Review. *Journal of the American Medical Association.* 166(13):1359-1367.

- Meier, M.H et al. (2012). Persistent cannabis users show neuropsychological decline from childhood to midlife. *Proceedings of the National Academy of Sciences.* 109 (40) E2657-E2664; DOI:10.1073/pnas.1206820109.

- Melamede R (2005). Cannabis and tobacco smoke are not equally carcinogenic. *Harm Reduction Journal.* 2:21. doi:10.1186/1477-7517-2-21.

- Mhillaj E et al. (2015). Effects of anabolic-androgens on brain reward function. *Frontiers in Neuroscience.* 9:295. doi:10.3389/fnins.2015.00295.

- Miller, W et al. (2001). How effective is alcoholism treatment in the United States? *Journal Studies of Alcohol.* 62 (2). 211-220.

- Mithoefer M.C et al. (2013). Durability of improvement in post-traumatic stress disorder symptoms and absence of harmful effects or drug dependency after 3,4-methylenedioxymethamphetamine-assisted psychotherapy: a prospective long-term follow-up study. *Journal of Psychopharmacology.* 27(1):28–39. doi:10.1177/0269881112456611.

- Mithoefer, M et al. (2010). The safety and efficacy of 3,4-methylenedioxymethamphetamine-assisted psychotherapy in subjects with chronic, treatment-resistant post-traumatic stress disorder: the first randomized controlled pilot study. *Journal of Psychopharmacology.* 25 (4) 439–452.

- Morgan, C and Curran, V (2010). Ketamine: a scientific review. *Addiction.* ISCD.

- Mweni-fumbo, J.C and Tyndale, R.F (2007). Genetic variability in CYP2A6 and the pharmacokinetics of nicotine. *Pharmacogenomics.* 8(10).

- Nader, M et al. (2010). Characterizing organism x environment interactions in non-human primate models of addiction: PET imaging studies of D2 receptors. *The Neurobiology of Addiction.* Oxford University press.

- Nonnekes, J et al. (2018). MPTP-induced parkinsonism: An historical case series. *Lancet Neurology.* Volume 17, Issue 4, 300-301.

- Nutt D, King L.A, and Nichols D.E (2013). Effects of Schedule I drug laws on neuroscience research and treatment innovation. *Nature Reviews Neuroscience.* 14. 577-585

- Nutt, D (2003). Death and dependence: current controversies over the selective serotonin reuptake inhibitors. *Journal of Psychopharmacology* 17(4).

- Nutt, D (2006). A tale of two Es. *Journal of Psychopharmacology.* 20(3). 315-317.

- Nutt, D (2006). Informed consent – a new approach to drug regulation? *Journal of Psychopharmacology.* Volume 20. Issue 1. 3-4.

- Nutt, D (2007). Blockade of alcohol's amnestic activity in humans by an a5subtype benzodiazepine receptor inverse agonist. *Neuropharmacology.*Volume 53. Issue 7. 810-820.

- Nutt, D (2009). Equasy: an overlooked addiction with implications for the current debate on drug harms. *Journal of Psychopharmacology.* 23 (1).

- Nutt, D (2015). Illegal drug laws: Clearing a 50-year-old obstacle to research. *PLoS Biology.* 13(1): e1002047.

- Nutt, D and Chick, J (2011). Substitution therapy for alcoholism: time for a reappraisal? *Journal of Psychopharmacology.* 205-212.

- Nutt, D et al. (2004). Evidence-based guidelines for the pharmacological management of substance misuse, addiction and comorbidity: recommendations from the British Association for Psychopharmacology. *Journal of Psychopharmacology.* (18) 3.

- Nutt, D et al. (2006). Evidence-based guidelines for management of attention-deficit/hyperactivity disorder in adolescents in transition to adult services and in adults: recommendations from the British Association for Psychopharmacology. *Journal of Psychopharmacology.* (21).

- Nutt, D et al. (2007). Development of a rational scale to assess the harm of drugs of potential misuse. *Lancet.* Volume 369. Issue 9566. 1047-1053.

- Nutt, D et al. (2007). Problem Gambling and Other Behavioural Addictions. *Drugs and the Future: Brain Science, Addiction and Society.*

- Nutt, D et al. (2010). Association of the anxiogenic and alerting effects of caffeine with ADORA2A and ADORA1 polymorphisms and habitual level of caffeine consumption. *Neuropsychopharmacology.* 35: 1973–83.

- Nutt, D et al. (2010). Drug harms in the UK: a multicriteria decision analysis. *Lancet.* ISCD.

- Nutt, D et al. (2014). Estimating the harms of nicotine-containing products using the MCDA approach. *European Addiction Research.* 20:218-225.

- Nutt, D et al. (2014). Estimating the harms of niotine-containing products using the MCDA approach. *European Addiction Research.* 20:218-225.

- Olive, M et al. (2001). Stimulation of endorphin neurotransmission in the nucleus accumbens by ethanol, cocaine, and amphetamine. *Journal of Neuroscience.* 21 (1).

- Omenn, G.S et al. (1996). Effects of a combination of beta carotene and vitamin A on lung cancer and cardiovascular disease. *New England Journal of Medicine.* 2;234(18). 1150-1155.

- Opeskin, K and Anderson, R.M (1997). Suspected MPTP-induced parkinsonism. *Journal of Clinical Neuroscience.* 4(3): 366-370.

- Orsolini, L et al. (2017) Is there a teratogenicity risk associated with cannabis and synthetic cannabimimetics' ('Spice') Intake? *CNS and Neurological Disorders Drug Targets.* 16(5): 585-591.

- Panlilio, L.V et al. (2015). Cannabinoid abuse and addiction: Clinical and preclinical findings. *Clinical Pharmacology and Therapeutics.* 97(6):616–627. doi:10.1002/cpt.118.

- Pavlatos, A.M et al. (2001). Review of oxymetholone: a 17alpha-alkylated anabolic-androgenic steroid. *Clinical Therapy.* 23:789–801.

- Perry, P.J et al. (2003). Measures of aggression and mood changes in male weightlifters with and without androgenic anabolic steroid use. *Journal of Forensic Science.* 48:646–651.

- Pey, A et al. (2003). Effects of prolonged stanozolol treatment on antioxidant enzyme activities, oxidative stress markers, and heat shock protein HSP72 levels in rat liver. *Journal of Steroid Biochemical Molecular Biology.* 87:269–277.

- Pham-Huy, L.A et al. (2008). Free radicals, antioxidants in disease and health. *International Journal Biomedical Science.* 4(2):89–96.

- Pinna, G (2005). Changes in brain testosterone and allopregnanolone biosynthesis elicit aggressive behaviour. *Proceedings of the National Academy of Sciences USA.* 102:2135–2140.

- Pinson, C.W et al. (1990). Liver transplantation for severe Amanita phalloides mushroom poisoning. *American Journal of Surgery.* 159 (5): 493-439.

- Pope, H.G and Katz, D.L (1994). Psychiatric and medical effects of anabolic androgenic steroid use: a controlled study of 160 athletes. *Archives of General Psychiatry.* 51:375–382.

- Pope, H.G et al. (2000a). Effects of supraphysiologic doses of testosterone on mood and aggression in normal men: a randomized controlled trial. *Archives of General Psychiatry.* 57:133–140; discussion 155-136.

- Rasmussen, N (2008). America's first amphetamine epidemic 1929-1971: a quantitative and qualitative retrospective with implications for the present. *American Journal of Public Health.* 98(6):974–985. doi:10.2105/AJPH.2007.110593.

- Regier, D et al. (1990). Comorbidity of Mental Disorders with Alcohol and Other Drug Abuse. *Journal of the American Medical Association.* (264).

- Ressler, K.J et al. (2004). Use of D-Cycloserine in Phobic Individuals to Facilitate Extinction of Fear. *Archives of General Psychiatry.* 1136-1144.

- Reynolds, J.R (1890). On the therapeutic uses and toxic effects of cannabis indica. *Lancet.*

- Ricaurte, G (2002). Severe dopaminergic neurotoxicity in primates after a common recreational dose regimen of MDMA. *Science.* 2260-2263."

- Ricaurte, G (2003). Retraction: Severe dopaminergic neurotoxicity in primates after a common recreational dose regimen of MDMA. *Science.* 301 (5639). 1479.

- Robins, L.N et al. (1975). Narcotic use in South- east Asia and afterward: An interview study of 898 Vietnam returnees. *Archives of General Psychiatry.* 32(8), 955–961.

- Rogers, G et al. (2009). The harmful health effects of recreational ecstasy: a systematic review of observational evidence. *Health Technology Assessment.*

- Roxburgh, A and Lappin J (2020). MDMA-related deaths in Australia 2000 to 2018. *International Journal of Drug Policy.* 76. 102630.

- Santaella-Tenorio, J et al. (2017). US traffic fatalities 1985-2014, and their relationship to medical marijuana laws. *American Journal of Public Health.* 107, Number 2, 336-342.

- Santos, G.S et al. (2007). Effects of ayahuasca on psychometric measures of anxiety, panic-like and hopelessness in Santo Daime members. *Journal of Ethnopharmacology.* 112, 507–513.

- Sasco, A et al. (2004). Tobacco Smoking and Cancer: A brief review of recent epidemiological evidence. *Lung Cancer.* International Agency for Research on Cancer, France.

- Schilt, T et al. (2007). Cognition in novice ecstasy users with minimal exposure to other drugs: a prospective cohort study. *Archives of General Psychiatry.* 64(6):728-736.

- Schoenfeld, B.J, Aragon, A.A and Krieger, J.W (2013). The effect of protein timing on muscle strength hypertrophy: A meta-analysis. *Journal of the International Society of Sports Nutrition.* 10(1). 53.

- Schuckit, M (1988). Reactions to Alcohol in Sons of Alcoholics and Controls. *Alcoholism: Clinical and Experimental Research.* Vol. 12.

- Schwingshackl, L et al. (2017). Dietary supplements and risk of cause-specific death, cardiovascular disease, and cancer: A systematic review and meta-analysis of primary prevention trials. *Advances In Nutrition.* 8(1). 27-39.

- Sciol, G.A (2014). A study on the perception of the stigma related to drug use in a sample of Italians and Belgians. *Psychology, Society and Education.* Vol.7, No 1, 1-8.

- Shaw, M et al. (2000). Time for a smoke? One cigarette reduces your life by 11 minutes. *British Medical Journal.* 320(7226).

- Siegel, M et al. (2008). Local Restaurant Smoking Regulations and the Adolescent Smoking Initiation Process. *Archives of Pediatric and Adolescent Medicine.* 162 (5).

- Silver J.R and Parry J.M (1991). Hazards of horse-riding as a popular sport. *British Journal of Sports Medicine.* 25(2):105–110. doi:10.1136/bjsm.25.2.105

- Silverman, J (2010) Addicted to distortion: the media and UK drugs policy, Jon Silverman. *Safer Communities.* 9 (4).

- Simmons, D et al. (2000). Nonsteroidal Anti-Inflammatory Drugs, Acetaminophen, Cyclooxygenase 2, and Fever. *Clinical Infectious Diseases.* Volume 31, Issue Supplement 5, S211–S218.

- Smeenk, L et al. (2010). Role of p53 Serine 46 in p53 Target Gene Regulation. *Plus one.* Department of Molecular Biology, Faculty of

Science, Nijmegen Centre for Molecular Life Sciences, Radboud University Nijmegen, Nijmegen, The Netherlands.

- Solly, S et al. (1856). The Great Tobacco Question: is Smoking Injurious to Health? *Lancet.*

- Stanton, C.A et al. (2019). Longitudinal e-cigarette and cigarette use among US youth in the PATH study (2013-2015). *Journal of the National Cancer Institute.* Volume 111. Issue 10. 1088-1096.

- Stein, D.J et al. (2006). Warriors versus worriers: the role of COMT genevariants. *CNS Spectrums.* 745-748.

- Stockwell, T et al. (2012). The raising of minimum alcohol prices in Saskatchewan, Canada: impacts on consumption and implications for public health. *American Journal of Public Health.* 102(12):e103–e110. doi:10.2105/AJPH.2012.301094.

- Strang, J et al. (2010). Supervised injectable heroin or injectable methadone versus optimised oral methadone as treatment for chronic heroin addicts in England after persistent failure in orthodox treatment (RIOTT): a randomised trial. *Lancet* 375: 1885–95.

- Szatkowski, L et al. (2011). The impact of the introduction of smoke freelegislation on prescribing of stop-smoking medications in England. *Addiction.* Volume 106. Issue 10. 1827-1834."

- Temple, J.L et al. (2017). The Safety of Ingested Caffeine: A Comprehensive Review. *Frontiers in Psychiatry.* 8:80. doi:10.3389/fpsyt.2017.00080

- Thanos, P.K (2001). Overexpression of dopamine D2 receptors reduces alcohol self-administration. *Journal of Neurochemistry.* (78).

- Thomas, S and Williams, T (2013). Khat (*Catha edulis*): A systematic review of evidence and literature pertaining to its harms to UK users and society. *Sage Journals.* Volume: 1.

- Topo, E et al. (2009). The role and molecular mechanism of D-aspartic acid in the release and synthesis of LH and testosterone in humans and rats. *Reproductive Biology and Endocrinology.* 7:120. doi:10.1186/1477-7827-7-120.

- Townsend, M (2010). Black people six times more likely to face drug arrest. *The Observer.*

- Van Amsterdam, J et al. (2015). European rating of drug harms. *Journal of Psychopharmacology.* 29(6): 655-660.

- Volkow, N et al. (1999). Methylphenidate and cocaine have a similar in vivo potency to block dopamine transporters in the human brain. *Life Sciences.* 65 (1).

- Weatherburn, D (2001). Has the war on drugs failed? *Australian Journal of Forensic Sciences.* 33, 15–21.

- Weissenborn, R and Nutt, D (2008). Popular intoxicants: what lessons canbe learned from the last 40 years of alcohol and cannabis regulation? *Journal of Psychopharmacology.* Volume 26. Issue 2. 213-220.

- White, I.R et al. (2002). Alcohol consumption and mortality: modelling risks for men and women at different ages. *British Medical Journal.* 325.

- Williams, T et al. (2007). Brain opioid receptor binding in early abstinence from opioid dependence. *British Journal of Psychiatry.* (191).

- Winstock, A, Mitcheson, L and Marsden, J (2010) Mephedrone: Still available and twice the price. *Lancet.* Volume 376. Issue 9752. 1537.

- Wood, A.M. et al. (2018). Risk thresholds for alcohol consumption: Combined analysis of individual-participant data for 599,912 current drinkers in 83 prospective studies. *Lancet.* Volume 391, Issue 10129, 1513-1523.

- Wynder, E.L and Graham, E.A (1950). Tobacco smoking as a possible aetiological factor in bronchiogenic carcinoma: a study of 684 provencases. *Journal of the American Medical Association.* 143 (4). 329-336.

- Yucel, M et al. (2008). Regional brain abnormalities associated with long-term heavy cannabis use. *Archives of General Psychiatry*. 65(6):694-701. doi: 10.1001/archpsyc.65.6.694.

- Zahra, E et al. (2020). Rates, characteristics and manner of cannabis-related deaths in Australia 2000-2018. *Drug and Alcohol Dependence*. DOI: 10.1016/j.drugalcdep.2020.108028.

- Zammit, S et al. (2002). Self-reported cannabis use as a risk factor for schizophrenia in Swedish conscripts of 1969: historical cohort study. *British Medical Journal*. 325 :1199.

- Zubieta, J et al. (2003). COMT val158met Genotype Affects u-Opioid Neurotransmitter Responses to a Pain Stressor. *Science*. 299 (5160).1240-1243."

Online Articles

- A frank statement to cigarette smokers (1954). *Truth tobacco industry documents*. University of California San Francisco. URL: https://www.industrydocuments.ucsf.edu/tobacco/docs/#id=zkph0129

- Associated Press. (2010). AP Impact: After 40 years, $1 trillion, US War on Drugs has failed to meet any of its goals. *Fox News*. URL: https://www.foxnews.com/world/ap-impact-after-40-years-1-trillion-us-war-on-drugs-has-failed-to-meet-any-of-its-goals

- Aubusson, K (2019). 'Evidence backs pill testing trials': physicians tell Berejiklian. *The Sydney Morning Herald*. URL: https://www.smh.com.au/national/nsw/evidence-backs-pill-testing-trials-physicians-tell-berejiklian-20190117-p50s1i.html

- Australian Associated Press. (2013). Synthetic LSD didn't kill Henry: Eros. *The Sydney Morning Herald*. URL: https://www.smh.com.au/national/nsw/synthetic-lsd-didnt-kill-henry-eros-20130617-2oct8.html

- Australian Associated Press. (2019). NSW Premier Gladys Berejiklian stands firm on pill testing opposition. *Illawarra Mercury*. URL: https://www.illawarramercury.com.au/story/5849504/

family-plead-for-pill-testing-after-suspected-festival-drug-over-dose/

- Banned drug may have saved lives, not cost them. (2010) *Straight Statistics.* URL: https://straightstatistics.fullfact.org/article/banned-drug-may-have-saved-lives-not-cost-them

- Barrett, S (2016). Don't Trust Advice from Dietary Supplement Retailers! *Quackwatch.* URL: https://www.quackwatch.org/01QuackeryRelatedTopics/hfsadvice.html

- Beaumont, P (2010). What Britain could learn from Portugal's drugs policy. *The Guardian.* URL: https://www.theguardian.com/world/2010/sep/05/portugal-drugs-debate

- Bebergal, P (2008). Will Harvard Drop Acid Again? *The Boston Phoenix.* URL: http://thephoenix.com/News/62230-Will-Harvard-drop-acid-again/

- Biello, D (2006). Large Study Finds No Link between Marijuana and Lung Cancer. *Scientific American.* URL: https://www.scientificamerican.com/article/large-study-finds-no-link/

- Billings, P (2014). Northern Tasmanian Ice Avalanche. *The Examiner.* URL: https://www.examiner.com.au/story/2532711/northern-tasmanian-ice-avalanche/

- Blake, E (2019). The Science of cannabis and driving. *The University of Sydney.* URL: https://sydney.edu.au/news-opinion/news/2019/05/07/the-science-of-cannabis-and-driving.html

- Boffey, D (2011). Andrew Lansley forced to make U-turn on public health campaign cuts. *The Guardian.* URL: https://www.theguardian.com/politics/2011/may/28/andrew-lansley-u-turn-public-health-cuts

- Borland, S (2011). Tens of thousands of surgical patients dying needlessly because of poor. NHS care, says Royal College of Surgeons. *The Daily Mail.* URL: www.dailymail.co.uk/health/article-2042963/

- Boyd, E (2019). Doctors say hospitals could become a conveyer belt of carnage if lockout laws are repealed. *The Daily*

Telegraph. URL: https://www.dailytelegraph.com.au/sub-scribe/news/1/?sourceCode=DTWEB_WRE170_a_GGL&dest=https%3A%2F%2Fwww.dailytelegraph.com.au%2Fnews%2Fnsw%2Fdoctors-say-hospitals-could-become-a-conveyor-belt-of-carnage-if-lockouts-are-repealed%2Fnews-story%2F967d92876bb049a196ede597c5ddc090&memtype=anonymous&mode=premium

- Byrne, P (2014). Children as young as 10 using ice in Ballarat. *The Courier.* URL: https://www.thecourier.com.au/story/2380969/children-as-young-as-10-using-ice-in-ballarat/

- Carroll, L (2017). Doctors debate whether baby died from mari-juana overdose. *NBC News.* URL: https://www.nbcnews.com/health/kids-health/doctors-debate-whether-baby-died-marijuana-overdose-n821801

- Carter, J (2011). Call Off the Global Drug War. *The New York Times.* URL: https://www.nytimes.com/2011/06/17/opinion/17carter.html

- Causes of Death - Deaths due to harmful alcohol consump-tion in Australia. (2018). *Australian Bureau of Statistics.* URL: https://www.abs.gov.au/ausstats/abs@.nsf/Lookup/by%20Subject/3303.0~2017~Main%20Features~Deaths%20due%20to%20harmful%20alcohol%20consumption%20in%20Australia~4

- Clarke's vision: A return to Victorian-style prisons where inmates will find hard work, discipline... and NO drugs. (2010). *The Daily Mail.* URL: https://www.dailymail.co.uk/news/article-1320494/Kenneth-Clarke-Return-Victorian-style-prisons-hard-work-NO-drugs.html

- Colyer, S (2018). Bottom line: Sydney's "lockout laws" reduce assaults. *Insight: Medical Journal of Australia.* URL: https://insightplus.mja.com.au/2018/7/bottom-line-sydneys-lockout-laws-reduce-assaults/

- Cormack, L (2018). Online alcoholic drink recipe examined after death of 15-year-old Sydney girl. *The Sydney Morning Herald.* URL: https://www.smh.com.au/national/nsw/online-alcoholic-drink-recipe-examined-after-death-of-15yo-sydney-girl-20180612-p4zky8.html

- Costa, A.M (2007). International Conference on Drug Trafficking in Guinea-Bissau. *United Nations Office on Drugs and Crime.* URL: https://www.unodc.org/unodc/en/frontpage/assisting-guinea-bissau.html

- Critique of Lancet study of Vancouver's supervised injection site and overdose: Authors' response. (2011). *Urban Health Research Initiative – British Columbia Centre for Excellence in HIV/AIDS.* URL: https://www.scribd.com/document/72458826/Insite-Response-to-Allegations

- Dalzell, S (2017). Ice addiction 'pales into insignificance' compared to harms linked to alcohol abuse, AMA says. *ABC News.* URL: https://www.abc.net.au/news/2017-08-02/governments-focus-on-methamphetamine-misplaced,-ama-says/8767664

- Daniel and Murray Witham. *Earth Frequency.* URL: https://www.earthfrequency.com.au/lecture/daniel_and_murray_witham

- Davies, L (2013). 'Was that one of my fights? I don't know. It fits my description'. *The Sydney Morning Herald.* URL: https://www.smh.com.au/national/nsw/was-that-one-of-my-fights-i-dont-know-it-fits-my-description-20130909-2tgeo.html

- Dick, S (2019). Alcohol does the most damage to Australians, but we won't stop drinking. *The New Daily.* URL: https://thenewdaily.com.au/news/national/2019/05/03/alcohol-abuse-australia/

- Drug-related hospitalisations. (2018). *Australian Institute of Health and Welfare.* URL: https://www.aihw.gov.au/reports/alcohol-other-drug-treatment-services/drug-related-hospitalisations/contents/content

- Drug-related hospitalisations. (2018). *Australian Institute of Health and Welfare.* URL: https://www.aihw.gov.

au/reports/alcohol-other-drug-treatment-services/
drug-related-hospitalisations/contents/content

- Editorial: Drugs drive politicians out of their minds. (2009). *New Scientist.* URL: https://www.newscientist.com/article/mg20126953-300-editorial-drugs-drive-politicians-out-of-their-minds/

- Ellson, A and Smyth, C (2018). Decriminalize cannabis, urges psychosis expert Sir Robin Murray. *The Times.* URL: https://www.thetimes.co.uk/article/decriminalise-cannabis-urges-psychosis-expert-sir-robin-murray-z6zjrcsqm

- Fleming, N (2010) Mephedrone: the anatomy of a media drug scare. *The Guardian.* URL: https://www.theguardian.com/media/2010/apr/05/mephedrone-drug-media-scare-newspapers?cat=media&type=article

- Forsberg, A (2011). The Wonders of the Coca Leaf. *Boliviamundo.net.* URL: http://www.boliviamundo.net/wp-content/uploads/2011/02/Wonders-of-the-Coca-Leaf.pdf

- Freud, S (1884). Cocaine 1884. *Heretical.com.* 'Über Coca,' Centralblatt für die ges. Therapie, 2, 289–314. URL: http://www.heretical.com/freudian/coca1884.html

- Gallagher, P (2011). Drug Free Australia manipulate, misrepresent data to discredit Insite. *Losing in the lucky country – Skeptical musings of the denial of evidence.* URL: https://luckylosing.com/2011/11/16/drug-free-australia-manipulate-misrepresent-data-to-discredit-insite/

- Gallagher, P. and Christian, G. Losing in the Lucky Country's unsubstantiated responses regarding Lancet's Insite study. *Drug Free Australia.* URL: https://www.drugfree.org.au/images/pdf-files/library/Injecting_Rooms/DFA_Lancet_Response_Update2.pdf

- Government adviser Eric Carlin quits over mephedrone. (2010). *BBC News.* URL: http://news.bbc.co.uk/2/hi/uk_news/8601315.stm

- Greenfield, P and Busby, M (2018). Cannabis oil row: Billy Caldwell 'under hospital arrest', says mother. *The Guardian.* URL: https://www.theguardian.com/society/2018/jul/05/cannabis-oil-row-billy-caldwell-under-hospital-arrest-says-mother

- Growing Tobacco. *World Health Organisation.* URL: https://www.who.int/tobacco/en/atlas16.pdf

- Haddou, J.B (2019). Alcohol Violence Drops. *NT News.* URL: https://www.ntnews.com.au/subscribe/news/1/?sourceCode=NTWEB_WRE170_a_GGL&dest=https%3A%2F%2Fwww.ntnews.com.au%2Fnews%2Fcentralian-advocate%2Falcoholic-violence-drops%2Fnews-story%2F14ceb6a76adba00a3eee740093123146&memmtype=anonymous&mode=premium

- Hansen, J (2011). Questions are being asked about the connections between the O'Farrell Government and the Australian Hotels Association. *The Daily Telegraph.* URL: https://www.dailytelegraph.com.au/news/opinion/questions-are-being-asked-about-the-connections-between-the-ofarrell-government-and-the-australian-hotels-association/news-story/75bd55de6b4b73b9234651f04296088c

- Heart attacks fall after smoking ban. (2010). *UK National Health Service.* URL: https://www.nhs.uk/news/heart-and-lungs/heart-attacks-fall-after-smoking-ban/

- Hitchens, P (2017). Stupid Arguments for Drug Legalization Examined and Refuted. *The Daily Mail – Peter Hitchens Blog.* URL: https://hitchensblog.mailonsunday.co.uk/2017/02/stupid-arguments-for-drug-legalisation-examined-and-refuted.html

- Industrial Hemp in the United States: Status and Market Potential. (2000). *United States Department of Agriculture.* URL: https://www.ers.usda.gov/webdocs/publications/41740/15867_ages001e_1_.pdf?v=0

- Kelly, C (2019). The harsh reality for magic mushroom possession: A true story of jail time and becoming a fugitive in Australia. *Medium.* URL: https://medium.com/@ck.medicinepath/the-harsh-reality-for-magic-mushroom-possession-a-true-story-of-jail-time-becoming-a-fugitive-fb465ffd3108

- Kelly, J and Brown, G (2018). Shorten slams Greens weed push at 'political clickbait'. *The Australian.* URL: https://www.theaustralian.com.au/nation/politics/di-natale-plan-to-decriminalise-marijuana-use/news-story/49429f339de72d936fe0e7ae71e0d7c2

- Knapton, S (2010). Wake up and smell the coffee in Turkey's beautiful Izmir. *The Telegraph.* URL: https://www.telegraph.co.uk/travel/destinations/europe/turkey/8678795/Wake-up-and-smell-the-coffee-in-Turkeys-beautiful-Izmir.html

- Knaus, C (2019). Liquor and gaming lobby pumped more than $1m into Liberal, Labor and far-right parties. *The Guardian.* URL: https://www.theguardian.com/australia-news/2019/apr/29/liquor-and-gaming-lobby-pumped-more-than-1m-into-liberal-labor-and-far-right-parties

- Kolata, G (1996). Studies Find Beta Carotene, Used by Millions, Doesn't Forestall Cancer or Heart Disease. *The New York Times.* URL: https://www.nytimes.com/1996/01/19/us/studies-find-beta-carotene-used-millions-doesn-t-forestall-canceror-heart.html

- Kruszelnicki, K (2012). Why does drinking alcohol cause dehydration?. *ABC Science.* URL: https://www.abc.net.au/science/articles/2012/02/28/3441707.htm

- Lambert, O (2015). Sale: The country town being overtaken by ice. *News.com.au.* URL: https://www.news.com.au/lifestyle/health/health-problems/sale-the-country-town-being-overtaken-by-ice/news-story/d8eea81a9cf4fb2460a45f3d23e6c2f0

- Lancet Editorial. A collapse in integrity of scientific advice in the UK. (2010). *Lancet*. URL: https://www.thelancet.com/journals/lancet/article/PIIS0140-6736(10)60556-9/fulltext

- Laurance, J (2008). Britain benefits by giving up. *The Independent*. URL: https://www.independent.co.uk/life-style/health-and-families/health-news/smoking-ban-has-saved-40000-lives-856885.html

- Lavelle, C (2018). Frosty Jack's cider sales in Scotland plummets massive 70 per cent following minimum booze pricing laws. *The Scottish Sun*. URL: https://www.thescottishsun.co.uk/news/3455232/frosty-jacks-cider-sales-scotland-70-down-minimum-price/

- Lynch, G (2013). Are there vested interests in fueling the 'ice epidemic'? *AOD Mediawatch*. URL: https://www.aodmediawatch.com.au/are-there-vested-interests-in-fuelling-the-ice-epidemic/

- MacDonald, H (2017) Death of Matthew Dawson-Clarke a stark warning about dangers of hallucinogenic drug ayahuasca. *The Sydney Morning Herald*. URL: https://www.smh.com.au/national/death-of-matthew-dawsonclarke-a-warning-about-dangers-of-psychedelic-drug-ayahuasca-20170310-guvmsb.html

- Martin Bryant Psychiatric Report. URL: http://members.iinet.net.au/~nedwood/psycho.html

- Mason, R (2014). Alcohol pricing: government 'dancing to the tune of drinks industry'. *The Guardian*. URL: https://www.theguardian.com/society/2014/jan/08/government-dancing-tune-drinks-industry-doctors

- McCoy, T (2014). Even casually smoking marijuana can damage your brain, study says. *The Washington Post*. URL: https://www.washingtonpost.com/news/morning-mix/wp/2014/04/16/even-casually-smoking-marijuana-can-change-your-brain-study-says/

- McGregor, I (2019). Study casts doubt on accuracy of mobile drug testing devices. *The University of Sydney*. URL: https://sydney.edu.au/news-opinion/news/2019/09/12/

study-casts-doubt-on-accuracy-of-mobile-drug-testing-devices-.html

- Mill, J.S (2007 Reprint). Mill's moral and political philosophy. *Stanford Encyclopedia of Philosophy.* URL: https://plato.stanford.edu/entries/mill-moral-political/

- Mims, C (2007). Strange but True: Testosterone Alone Does Not Cause Violence. *ScientificAmerican.* URL:https://www.scientificamerican.com/article/strange-but-true-testosterone-alone-doesnt-cause-violence/

- Misuse of drugs: Temporary class drugs. (2011). *Home Office.* Policy Reform and Social Responsibility Bill – Clause 152/Schedule 17. URL: https://assets.publishing.service.gov.uk/government/uploads/system/uploads/attachment_data/file/98007/temporary-class-drugs.pdf

- Murray, P (2017). Paul Murray: Too many people take drugs but why do they do it. *Tweed Daily News.* URL: https://www.tweeddailynews.com.au/news/paul-murray-too-many-people-take-drugs-why-do-they/3229636/

- Mythbusters: Cannabis 20 times more carcinogenic than tobacco? (2012). *New Zealand Drug Foundation.* URL: https://www.drugfoundation.org.nz/matters-of-substance/august-2012/cannabis-20-times-more-carcinogenic-than-tobacco/

- Naturopath gets in over his head when pilot asks if anyone on board is a doctor.(2017). *TheBigSmoke.* URL:thebigsmoke.com.au/2017/08/11/naturopath-gets-head-pilot-asks-anyone-board-doctor/

- Northern Territory Alcohol Policies and Legislation Reform. (2018). *Northern Territory Government.* URL: https://alcoholreform.nt.gov.au/milestones/floor-price

- Norton, A (2008). Minimum drinking age of 21 cuts road deaths. *Reuters.* URL: https://www.reuters.com/article/us-minimum-drinking-age/minimum-drinking-age-of-21-cuts-road-deaths-idUSARM15193120080701

- Nutt, D (2010) Mephedrone: the class D solution. *The Guardian.* URL: https://www.theguardian.com/commentisfree/2010/mar/17/mephedrone-class-d-solution-criminalise?cat=commentisfree&type=article

- Nutt, D (2010) Necessity or nastiness? The hidden law denying cannabis for medicinal use. *David Nutt's Blog: Evidence not exaggeration.* URL: https://profdavidnutt.wordpress.com/2010/12/13/necessity-or-nastiness-the-hidden-law-denying-cannabis-for-medicinal-use/

- Nutt, D (2011) Teaching the tricks of the liquor trade. *David Nutt's Blog: Evidence not exaggeration.* URL: https://profdavidnutt.word-press.com/2011/01/19/teaching-the-tricks-of-the-liquor-trade/

- Nutt, D (2011). There is no such thing as a safe level of alcohol consumption. *The Guardian.* URL: https://www.theguardian.com/science/2011/mar/07/safe-level-alcohol-consumption

- Offit, P (2013). The Vitamin Myth: Why We Think We Need Supplements. *The Atlantic.* URL: https://www.theatlantic.com/health/archive/2013/07/the-vitamin-myth-why-we-think-we-need-supplements/277947/

- Pareene, A (2011). DEA head: A thousands dead children means we're winning war on drugs. *Salon.* URL: https://www.salon.com/2011/04/15/dea_children/

- Penberthy, D (2018). Pill testing must be supported by science not vibes. *Adelaide Now.* URL: https://www.adelaidenow.com.au/subscribe/news/1/?%3FsourceCode=AAWEB_WRE170_a_GGL&dest=https%3A//www.adelaidenow.com.au/rendezview/david-penberthy-pill-testing-must-be-supported-by-science-not-vibes/news-story/8ec71aaf61d57861a3a09664be8f09b6&memtype=anonymous&mode=premium&v21suffix=51-a

- Phenylketonuria. *UK National Health Service.* URL: https://www.nhs.uk/conditions/phenylketonuria/

- Police Reform and Social Responsibility Bill – Clause 152 / Schedule 17. (2011). *Home Office.*

- Priestly, R (2019). Cannabis testing unjust? Make your vote count. *Echo Net Daily.* URL: https://www.echo.net.au/2019/01/cannabis-testing-unjust-make-vote-count/

- Ravens, T (2007) Opal fuel can kill sniffers: inquest. *The Sydney Morning Herald.* URL: https://www.smh.com.au/national/opal-fuel-can-kill-sniffers-inquest-20071211-1gel.html

- Reed, J (2010). Ecstasy 'disappearing' from British clubs. *BBC Newsbeat.* URL: http://www.bbc.co.uk/newsbeat/article/10353130/ecstasy-disappearing-from-british-clubs

- Rees, A (2004). Nobel Prize Genius Crick was High on LSD when he discovered the secret of life. *Mail on Sunday.* URL: https://maps.org/research/psilo-lsd/lsd-news-timeline/2054-nobel-prize-genius-crick-was-high-on-lsd-when-he-discovered-dna

- Reid, M (2011). Spinal column: horse sense. *The Times.* URL: https://www.thetimes.co.uk/article/spinal-column-horse-sense-f2rh5xznt9s

- Ritter, A (2014). Six reasons should pilot pill testing party drugs. *National Drug and Alcohol Research Centre.* URL: https://ndarc.med.unsw.edu.au/node/301000974

- Smee, B (2018). 'Backlash': Northern Territory alcohol floor price divides community. *The Guardian.* URL: https://www.theguardian.com/australia-news/2018/oct/21/backlash-northern-territory-alcohol-floor-price-divides-community

- Stastna, K (2011). The Cartels behind Mexico's drug war. *CBC News.* URL: http://www.cbc.ca/news/world/story/2011/08/28/f-mexico-drug-cartels.html

- Study: No psychological or cognitive deficits from peyote. (2005). *The Harvard Gazette.* URL: https://news.

harvard.edu/gazette/story/2005/11/study-no-psychological-or-cognitive-deficits-from-peyote/

- Suddath, C (2009). The War on Drugs. *Time*. URL: http://content.time.com/time/world/article/0,8599,1887488,00.html

- Surgeon General (2010). How Tobacco Smoke Causes Disease: The Biology and Behavioural Basis for Smoking-Attributable Disease. *US Department of Health and Human Services*. URL: https://www.surgeongeneral.gov/library/reports/

- Teenagers' deaths 'not caused by mephedrone'. (2010). *BBC News*. URL: https://www.bbc.com/news/10184803

- Teens Spend Thousands on Nangs and Booze. (2018). *Gold Coast Bulletin*. URL: https://www.goldcoastbulletin.com.au/subscribe/news/1/?sourceCode=GCWEB_WRE170_a_GGL&dest=https%3A%2F%2Fwww.goldcoastbulletin.com.au%2Fnews%2Fschoolies%2Fschoolies-on-gold-coast-claim-they-spent-thousands-on-nangs-and-alcohol%2Fnews-story%2F52f56ad580b33eed16b6dc8d89704aa5&memtype=anonymous&mode=premium

- Temko, M and Smith, D (2007). Cameron admits: I used dope at Eton. *The Guardian*. URL: https://www.theguardian.com/politics/2007/feb/11/uk.drugsandalcohol1

- The Effects of Cannabis Use on Creativity (2010). *The Beckley Foundation*. URL: http://archive.beckleyfoundation.org/2010/09/the-effects-of-cannabis-use-on-creativity/

- The Nation: The New Public Enemy No. 1. (1971). *Time*. URL: www.time.com/time/magazine/article/0,9171,905238,00.html

- Tobacco and cancer. *American Cancer Society*. URL: https://www.cancer.org/cancer/cancer-causes/tobacco-and-cancer.html

- Travis, A (2010). Official drug advisers reject time limit on methadone substitution for addicts. *The Guardian*. URL: https://www.theguardian.com/politics/2014/nov/06/drug-advisers-time-limit-methadone-substitution-heroin-addicts

- U.S v. Forty Barrels and Twenty Kegs of Coca Cola (1916). *FindLaw.* URL: https://caselaw.findlaw.com/us-supreme-court/241/265.html

- UK Parliament. Dealing with the health effects of secondhand smoke (2005). *Select Committee on health – First Report.* URL: https://publications.parliament.uk/pa/cm200506/cmselect/cmhealth/485/48506.htm

- Underwood, E (2016). Twin study finds no evidence that marijuana lowers IQ in teens. *Science Mag.* URL: https://www.sciencemag.org/news/2016/01/twins-study-finds-no-evidence-marijuana-lowers-iq-teens

- Untitled Article – Medcave. (1970). *Forensic Research and Criminology International Journal.* eISSN: 2469-2794. URL: https://medcraveonline.com/FRCIJ/FRCIJ-01-00009

- Vincent, M (2018). Cannabis is the only thing easing their chronic pain. Now their father is facing jail. *ABC News.* URL: https://www.abc.net.au/news/2018-03-07/father-faces-jail-for-medicating-daughters-with-cannabis-juice/9523898

- Vulliamy, E (2011). How a big US bank laundered billions from Mexico's murderous drug gangs. *The Guardian.* URL: https://www.theguardian.com/world/2011/apr/03/us-bank-mexico-drug-gangs?cat=world&type=article

- Walters, A (2009). Lunch with Barry O'Farrell to sledge Labor - for $70,000. *The Daily Telegraph.* URL: https://www.dailytelegraph.com.au/lunch-with-ofarrell-for-70k/news-story/634926cd6242f2e54e9b0200698b298d?sv=d289e93d6ced1dc1508cbc022804bb72

- What is Schizophrenia? *National Institute of Mental Health.* URL: http://www.nimh.nih.gov/health/publications/schizophrenia/complete-index.shtml

- When Bobby Kennedy Defended LSD. (2012). *Multidisciplinary Association for Psychedelic Studies.* URL: https://maps.org/news/media/3152-when-bobby-kennedy-defended-lsd

- Who is behind Mexico's drug-related violence? (2014). *BBC News.* URL: https://www.bbc.com/news/world-latin-america-10681249

- Wintour, P (2005). MPs to challenge ministers' veto on total smoking ban. *The Guardian.* URL: https://www.theguardian.com/society/2005/dec/17/health.politics

- Wodak, A (2004). Is the Howard Government tough on drugs? *National Centre in HIV Social Research - NSW Department of Health.* URL: https://pdfs.semanticscholar.org/55f4/7ce3db78661af16ad8 b9e291d86b1cfc6491.pdf?_ga=2.204167257.87974524.1596373670- 2040659490.1596373670

- Woolf, M (2005). Tory Contender calls for more liberal drugs laws. *The Independent.* URL: https://www.independent.co.uk/news/uk/politics/ tory-contender-calls-for-more-liberal-drug-laws-505824.html

- Young, S (2013). Marijuana stops child's severe seizures. *CNN Health.* URL: https://edition.cnn.com/2013/08/07/health/charlotte-child-medical-marijuana/index.html

- Videos and Lectures

- A Speech on Australia's Experience of Methamphetamine Control by Dr Alex Wodak. (2016). *Conference on World Drug Policy – UNGASS.* URL: https://www.youtube.com/watch?v=AIx-5wNBd-c&t=745s

- Addiction: From Brain Mechanisms to new Treatments. (2019). *National Drug and Alcohol Research Centre.* URL: https://ndarc.med.unsw.edu.au/news/online-now-ndarc-seminar-presented-professor-david-nutt

- Alcohol 'more harmful than heroin' says Prof David Nutt. (2010). *BBC News.* URL: https://www.bbc.com/news/uk-11660210

- Alcohol: Unhealthy Behaviours, Toxic Environments and Vested Interests. Dr Nick Sheron. (2014). *Southampton Education School.* URL: https://www.youtube.com/watch?v=swsGJGLYIvo

- Are we losing the war on drugs? (2012). *Sunrise.* URL: https://www. youtube.com/watch?v=Li6XGTkSD08&t=287s

- Big nicotine executive "Nicotine is not addictive". (2010). *C-SPAN Today*. URL: https://www.youtube.com/watch?v=A6B1q22R438
- Bigger, Stronger, Faster*. (2018). *Madman Films*. URL: http://watch-documentaries.com/bigger-stronger-faster/
- BNA Public Lecture by Prof David Nutt 12 April 2015. (2019). *British Neuroscience Association*. URL: https://www.youtube.com/watch?v=EezgNZgZW-o
- Breaking the Taboo. (2013) *The Wilson Centre*. URL: https://www.wilsoncenter.org/event/breaking-the-taboo
- Cannabis Debate with Peter Hitchens and Peter Reynolds – Southampton Debating Union Southampton Debating Union. (2016). *Southampton Debating Union*. URL: https://www.youtube.com/watch?v=M76LEySMxU8&t=2426s
- Cannabis is a gateway drug: Hunt. (2018). *The Sydney Morning Herald*. URL: https://www.smh.com.au/politics/federal/cannabis-is-a-gateway-drug-hunt-20180417-546x7.html
- Cannabis Question in the House. (2011). URL: https://vimeo.com/23580287
- Dangerous drugs in the spotlight. (2013). *Ten Network*. URL: https://www.youtube.com/watch?v=QYjkE1uGxj4
- David Nutt: Decision making about illegal drugs: Time for science to take the lead. (2013). *Nobel Forum, Karolinska Institutet*. URL: https://www.youtube.com/watch?v=mDo09IBVHZw&t=120s
- Dr Alex Wodak – The Current State of Medicinal Cannabis in Australia. (2016). *Entheogenesis Australis November*. URL: https://www.youtube.com/watch?v=GPXNmjxkj_0
- Dr Alex Wodak Discusses Drug Reform in Studio with Tom Elliott. (2018). *3AWRadio*. URL: https://www.youtube.com/watch?v=IKSadZ7HN8A&t=49s

- Dr Alex Wodak: Drug Law Reform – The End of The Beginning. (2013). *Entheogenesis Australis*. URL: https://www.youtube.com/watch?v=0ummIefqGwM

- Dr David Caldicott – Return to Terra Nullius redux. (2015). *Entheogenesis Australis*. URL: https://www.youtube.com/watch?v=VxYjOVFw9tc&t=3066s

- Dr David Caldicott: When the Search for Enlightenment Finds the Emergency Room. (2014). *Entheogenesis Australis*. URL: https://www.youtube.com/watch?v=SPHjj50tvlo

- Dr. Robin Carhart-Harris – Psychedelics as medicine | London Real. (2013). *London Real*. URL: https://www.youtube.com/watch?v=GMjtAu1JqOg&t=4483s

- Drug Law Reform Panel – What Does Regulation Look Like? (2015). *Entheogenesis Australis*. URL: https://www.youtube.com/watch?v=YSVfIOynzm4

- E453: Alcohol with no hangover? Professor David Nutt Fmr UK Drugs Czar. (2017). *Going Underground*. URL: https://www.youtube.com/watch?v=Cy79qAdF3xQ&t=1495s

- *Faculty of Biology, Medicine and Health. University of Manchester*. URL: https://www.youtube.com/watch?v=A16Tb7DaMcs&t=2573s

- Festival of Dangerous Ideas 2013: Peter Hitchens – There is no war on drug. (2013). *Festival of Dangerous Ideas – Sydney Opera House*. URL: https://www.youtube.com/watch?v=36L0p2w_jtA&t=2705s

- Government Pill Testing is NOT the answer. (2018). *Australian Conservatives*. URL: https://www.youtube.com/watch?v=DDSqqlO2ynM

- Greens MP Cate Faehrmann, the first Australain politician to admit to taking the illicit drug MDMA. (2019). *Sky News - News Bite Global*. URL: https://www.youtube.com/watch?v=Xbblp5ba5Rw&t=340s

- Hannity Stoned America. (2016). *Fox News*. URL: https://www.youtube.com/watch?v=lVVROXUTx34

- Hoffman's Potion. (2002). *Connie Littlefield*. URL: https://www.nfb.ca/film/hofmanns_potion/
- How illegal drugs can help our brains|David Nutt|TEDxBrussles. (2017). *TEDxTalks*. URL: https://www.youtube.com/watch?v=WOxSQHtJW1o
- Manocha, R (2012). Online Access of Licit an Illicit Substances – Paul Dillon. *Generation Next*. URL: https://www.generationnext.com.au/2012/04/video-interview-online-access-to-licit-and-illicit-substances-paul-dillon/
- Matthew Perry Debates Drug Courts with Peter Hitchens – BBC Newsnight. *BBC Newsnight*. URL: https://www.youtube.com/watch?v=CDtIZZiySgA
- Medical Cannabis and GPs: Alex Wodak. (2015). *Healthy North Coast*. URL: https://www.youtube.com/watch?v=sKjFOSD4S-8
- Medical Marijuana Irrelevant to Romney. (2012). *CBS News*. URL: https://www.youtube.com/watch?v=8GRLD0pz0bo
- Methamphetamine Fact VS Fiction and Lessons from the Crack Hysteria by Professor Dr. Carl Hart. (2016). *Conference on World Drugs Policy*. URL: https://www.youtube.com/watch?v=o97xuEtbkKg&t=2473s
- Misuse of over the counter drugs by young people. (2012). *Generation Next*. URL: https://www.generationnext.com.au/2012/04/misuse-of-over-the-counter-drugs-by-young-people/
- More Doctors Smoke Camels Than Any Other Cigarette. (2006). URL: https://www.youtube.com/watch?v=gCMzjJjuxQI
- North West Alcohol Conference 2014 – Nick Sheron. (2014). *University of Southampton*. URL: https://www.youtube.com/watch?v=Lc0ORa_MRoY&t=1233s
- NSW Premier Doubles Down on Pill Testing Stance Following Horror Drug Weekend. (2019). *SBS News*. URL: https://www.sbs.com.au/news/

nsw-premier-doubles-down-on-pill-testing-stance-following-hor-ror-drug-weekend

- Nutt, D (2017). Why we should decriminalize possession of all drugs. *Drugscience.* URL: https://www.drugscience.org.uk/assets/files/ decriminalise-all-drugs-addaction-lecture.pdf

- Peter Hitchens Debating Prof. Nutt on Drugs + Aftermath. (2010). *BBC Radio 4.* URL: https://www.youtube.com/watch?v=aynpyOhUV80

- Piers, Coulter battle over 'potheads'. (2014). *CNN.* URL: https:// www.youtube.com/watch?v=tTlRulEFFgc

- Premier Gladys Berejiklian Rejects Pill Testing & Will Ban Defqon.1 Festival. (2018). *ABC News.* URL: https://www.youtube.com/ watch?v=XTX4k7EEAj0

- Prentice, A (2018). Gunsberg slams officials who say pill testing won't save lives. (2018). *The Daily Mail.* URL: https://www.daily-mail.co.uk/news/article-6481743/Bachelor-host-Osher-Gunsberg-slams-officials-insist-pill-testing-wont-save-lives.html

- President's Lecture: With Professor David Nutt (London). (2018). *Royal College of Psychiatrists.* February. URL: https://www.youtube. com/watch?v=aySOu0nr_fY

- President's Lecture: With Professor David Nutt. (2018). *Future of Psychiatry Conference.* URL: https://www.youtube.com/ watch?v=IMpUjGUeihI&t=1819s

- Prof. David Nutt – The Brain and Drugs: Time for a Neuroscience enlightenment? 19.01.15. (2015). *UCL Neuroscience Society.* URL: https://www.youtube.com/watch?v=FYcBxYe7X-s

- Professor David Nutt – 'Not all in the mind' public lecture. (2019). *Faculty of Biology, Medicine and Health. University of Manchester.* URL: https://www.youtube.com/watch?v=kZpUXHyQWqA&t=2119s

- Professor David Nutt – The Truth About Drugs, Isle of man Lecture, 2014. (2015). URL: https://www.youtube.com/ watch?v=fi5LjgK8_Ys&t=1546s

- Professor David Nutt – The Truth About Drugs. (2016). *London Real*. URL: https://londonreal.tv/e/professor-david-nutt-the-truth-about-drugs/

- Professor David Nutt at the 2015 Science Festival. (2015). *Edinburgh Science*. URL: https://www.youtube.com/watch?v=XFu8W3DqXVg

- Professor David Nutt. Drug Science | London Real. (2013). *London Real*. URL: https://www.youtube.com/watch?v=lhx_zAauays

- Prohibition. (2011). Burns, K and Novick, L. Accessed via Netflix.

- Psychedelics: Lifting the Veil. Robin Carhart-Harris. TEDx-Warwick. (2016). *TEDxTalks*. URL: https://www.youtube.com/watch?v=MZIaTaNR3gk

- Q&A on drugs|18th February 2019. (2019). *ABC Q&A*. URL: https://www.youtube.com/watch?v=7FgA3yK1ob4&t=3433s

- Rave On. (1996). *Nine Network*. URL: https://www.9now.com.au/60-minutes/rewind/clip-cjdmjnn8r000c0nmvzkbv3kf0

- Richard Calls for Pill Testing at Festivals. (2018). *The Australian Greens*. URL: https://www.youtube.com/watch?v=2QROInKwewg

- Talking Drugs – Dr Kevin Morgan in conversation with professor David Nutt. (2014). *University of Westminster*. URL: https://www.youtube.com/watch?v=HmExDibZMpw

- Testing Times. (2015). *Nine Network*. URL: https://www.9now.com.au/60-minutes/2015/clip-cikyzehz50039s3nn11y7n9pm

- The Culture High Cannabis Documentary. (2014). Brett Harvey. URL: https://www.youtube.com/watch?v=zLT6AFsTm74

- The Dalgarno Institute - Bill Hearing 2018 – Against Removing Commonwealth Restrictions on Cannabis (2018). *Australian Senate*. URL: https://www.youtube.com/watch?v=X7uKj3lt5so&t=1130s

- The drug trial that went wrong: Emergency at the hospital (Medical Documentary). (2018). *Real stories*. URL: https://www.youtube.com/watch?v=a9_sX93RHOk

- The Equalizer. (2014). *Village Roadshow Pictures*

- The Global War on Drugs. Alex Wodak (Pt.1). (2013). *The Lowy Institute.* URL: https://www.youtube.com/watch?v=6o1IuVBNrT4&t=358s

- The Global War on Drugs. Alex Wodak (Pt.2). (2013). *The Lowy Institute.* URL: https://www.youtube.com/watch?v=B1ZF05RCF0g&t=1537s

- Time to put science, not politics, at the heart of UK drugs policy – David Nutt. (2018). *Faculty of Biology, Medicine and Health. University of Manchester.* URL: https://www.youtube.com/watch?v=A16Tb7DaMcs&t=2573s

- Torsten Passie: History of MDMA – An Overview. *Multidisciplinary Association for Psychedelic Studies.* URL: https://www.youtube.com/watch?v=r72hZzJGsNU

- Troy Grant is against pill testing. (2018). *ABC News.* URL: https://www.msn.com/en-au/video/news/troy-grant-is-against-pill-testing/vi-BBNrcW8

- Turbo HIV Film. (2010). *International Treatment Preparedness Coalition.* URL: https://www.youtube.com/watch?v=kCtxrm4cWPM

- Webinar: Parties, gatherings and sleepovers: How can parents keen their kids safe? (2018). *Positive Choices.* URL: https://positivechoices.org.au/teachers/parties-gatherings-and-sleepovers

Reports

- A review of the Second Report of the Interdepartmental Committee on Addiction. (2001). *United Nations Office on Drugs and Crime.* URL: https://www.unodc.org/unodc/en/data-and-analysis/bulletin/bulletin_1966-01-01_2_page006.html

- ACMD Technical Committee: Report on Ketamine. (2004). *Advisory Council on the Misuse of Drugs - Technical Committee.* URL: https://assets.publishing.service.gov.uk/government/uploads/system/uploads/attachment_data/file/119098/ketamine-report.pdf

- Alcohol: First Report of Session 2009–10. (2009). *House of Commons.* URL: https://publications.parliament.uk/pa/cm200910/cmselect/cmhealth/151/151i.pdf

- Analysis of KPMG evaluation of the Sydney Medically Supervised Injecting Centre. (2010). *Drug Free Australia.* URL: https://www.drugfree.org.au/images/13Books-FP/pdf/DFA_Analysis_Injecting_Room_2010.pdf

- Australian National Drugs Strategy 2017-2026. (2017). *Australian Department of Health.* URL: https://beta.health.gov.au/file/9871/download?token=kkKW6Fht

- Baldock, M.R.J (2007). A review of the literature on cannabis and crash risk. *Centre for Automotive Safety Research – University of Adelaide.* URL: http://casr.adelaide.edu.au/casrpubfile/36/CASR010.pdf

- Cannabis: classification and public health. (2008). *Advisory Council on the Misuse of Drugs.* URL: https://assets.publishing.service.gov.uk/government/uploads/system/uploads/attachment_data/file/119174/acmd-cannabis-report-2008.pdf

- Consideration of the Cathinones. (2010). *Advisory Council on the Misuse of Drugs.* URL: https://assets.publishing.service.gov.uk/government/uploads/system/uploads/attachment_data/file/119173/acmd-cathinodes-report-2010.pdf

- Country Progress Report of the Russian Federation on the Implementation of the Declaration of Commitment to HIV/AIDS. (2008). *UNAIDS.* URL: http://data.unaids.org/pub/report/2008/russia_2008_country_progress_report_en.pdf

- DEA History Book, 1876–1990. (1991). US Department of Justice.

- Donaldson, L (2008). Chief Medical Officer 150th annual report. *UK Government.* URL: https://webarchive.nationalarchives.gov.uk/20130105045448/http://www.dh.gov.uk/prod_consum_dh/groups/dh_digitalassets/documents/digitalasset/dh_096231.pdf

- Drug Deaths in the UK. Annual Report 2010. (2010). *International Centre for Drug Policy*. URL: http://www.sgul.ac.uk/images/docs/idcp%20 pdfs/National%20programme%20on%20substance%20abuse%20 deaths/np-SAD_11th_annual_report_2010_FinalCopy.pdf

- European Drug Report. (2017). *European Monitoring Centre for Drugs and Drug Addiction*. URL: http://www.emcdda.europa.eu/system/ files/publications/4541/TDAT17001ENN.pdf

- Final Report of the evaluation of the Sydney Medically Supervised Injecting Centre. (2003). *MSIC evaluation committee*. URL: https:// www.drugsandalcohol.ie/5706/1/MSIC_final_evaluation_report.pdf

- Gabler, N and Katz, D (2010). Contraband tobacco in Canada. *Fraser Institute*. URL: https://www.fraserinstitute.org/sites/default/files/ contraband-tobacco-in-canada.pdf

- Harm reduction measures. *Parliament of Australia*. URL: https:// www.aph.gov.au/Parliamentary_Business/Committees/Joint/ Law_Enforcement/Crystalmethamphetamine45/Final_Report/c04

- Havelock, E (1898). Mescal: A new artificial paradise. *The Contemporary Review*. URL: https://www.samorini.it/doc1/alt_aut/ek/ellis-mescal-a-new-artificial-paradise.pdf

- Illicit Drug Data Report: 2014 – 2015. (2016). *Australian Criminal Intelligence Commission*. URL: https://www.acic.gov.au/sites/ default/files/2016/08/acic-iddr-2014-15.pdf?v=1498017786

- Illicit Drug Data Report: 2015 – 2016. (2017). *Australian Criminal Intelligence Commission*. URL: https://www.acic.gov.au/sites/default/ files/2017/06/illicit_drug_data_report_2015-16_full_report. pdf?v=1498019727

- Illicit Drug Data Report: 2016 – 2017. (2018). *Australian Criminal Intelligence Commission*. URL: https://www.acic.gov.au/sites/default/ files/iddr_2016-17_050718.pdf?v=1536906944

- Khat (Qat): Assessment of the risk to individuals and communities in the UK. (2005). *Advisory Council on the Misuse of Drugs.* URL: http://www.dldocs.stir.ac.uk/documents/khat.pdf

- Matthews, A and Bruno, R (2010). Mephedrone use among regular ecstasy users in Australia. EDRS Drug Trends Bulletin. *National Drug and Alcohol Research Centre.* URL: https://ndarc.med.unsw.edu.au/sites/default/files/ndarc/resources/EDRS%20Bulletin%20Dec%202010.pdf

- MDMA ("ecstasy"): a review of its harms and classification under the Misuse of Drugs Act 1971. (2008). *Advisory Council on the Misuse of Drugs.* URL: https://assets.publishing.service.gov.uk/government/uploads/system/uploads/attachment_data/file/119088/mdma-report.pdf

- Measuring different aspects of problem drug use: methodological developments. (2006). *Home Office.* URL: https://webarchive.nationalarchives.gov.uk/20110218140138/http://rds.homeoffice.gov.uk/rds/pdfs06/rdsolr1606.pdf

- Misuse of Drugs Act 1971. *Home Office.* URL: https://www.legislation.gov.uk/ukpga/1971/38/contents

- National Drug Strategy Household Survey 2016. (2017). *Australian Institute of Health and Welfare.* URL: https://www.aihw.gov.au/getmedia/15db8c15-7062-4cde-bfa4-3c2079f30af3/21028a.pdf.aspx?inline=true

- Peters, G (2009). How Opium Profits the Taliban. *United States Institute of Peace.* URL: https://www.usip.org/sites/default/files/resources/taliban_opium_1.pdf

- Poisons Standard. (2019). *Australian Department of Health.* URL: https://www.legislation.gov.au/Details/F2019L00032

- Public Acts. (1897). *Parliament of Queensland.* URL: https://aiatsis.gov.au/sites/default/files/catalogue_resources/54692.pdf

- Regulation: The responsible control of drugs. (2018). *Global Commission on drug policy.* URL: http://www.globalcommissionondrugs. org/wp-content/uploads/2018/09/ENG-2018_Regulation_Report_ WEB-FINAL.pdf

- Reporting rates of assaults at The Star casino by licensed premises staff. (2016). *NSW Bureau of Crime Statistics and Research.* URL: https://www.bocsar.nsw.gov.au/Documents/BB/Report-2016-Reporting-rates-of-assaults-at-The-Star-casino-BB121.pdf

- Return of Investment 2: Evaluating the cost-effectiveness of needle and syringe programs in Australia. *Australian Department of Health and Ageing.* URL: http://www.health.gov.au/internet/main/publishing.nsf/content/A407CF4FECBDC715CA257BF0001F98B2/%2 4File/return2.pdf

- Sheron, N. Alcohol in a general hospital. *University of Southampton and Royal College of Physicians.* URL: https://www.stap.nl/content/ bestanden/nick-sheron---alcohol-in-a-general-hospital.pdf

- Sheron, N. Alcohol, liver disease and dinosaurs. *University of Southampton and Royal College of Physicians.* URL: https://www.rcplondon. ac.uk/file/2266/download?token=f5be4K8x

- Smith, K and Flatley, J (2011). Drug Misuse Declared: Findings from the 2010/2011 British Crime Survey. *Home Office.* URL: https:// assets.publishing.service.gov.uk/government/uploads/system/ uploads/attachment_data/file/116333/hosb1211.pdf

- Sydney Medically Supervised Injecting Centre Evaluation Report No. 4: Evaluation of service operation and overdose-related events. (2007). *National Centre in HIV Epidemiology and Clinical Research.* URL: https://kirby.unsw.edu.au/sites/default/files/kirby/report/ EvalRep4SMSIC.pdf

- The effect of lockout and last drinks laws on non-domestic assaults in Sydney: An update to September 2016. (2017). *NSW Bureau of Crime Statistics and Research.* URL: https://www.bocsar.nsw.gov.au/

Documents/CJB/Report-2017-Effect-of-lockout-and-last-drinks-laws-on-non-domestic-assaults-cjb201.pdf

- The Health Effects of Passive Smoking: A Scientific Information Paper. (1997). *National Health & Medical Research Council*. URL: https://trove.nla.gov.au/work/24711351?q&versionId=45626318

- White, V et al. (2016). Australian Secondary School Students' use of tobacco, alcohol, OTC and illicit substances in 2014. *Australian Government Department of Health and Cancer Council*. URL: https://www.health.gov.au/sites/default/files/secondary-school-students-use-of-tobacco-alcohol-and-other-drugs-in-2014.pdf

- Youth Violence: A report of the Surgeon General. (2001). *Office of the Surgeon General*. URL: https://www.ncbi.nlm.nih.gov/books/NBK44294/

Books

- Abel, E (1980). *Marijuana - the first twelve thousand years*. Plenum Press

- Adler, I and Green, L (1912). *Primary malignant growth of the lung and bronchi*. New York

- Babor, T (2003). *Alcohol: no ordinary commodity*. Oxford University Press.

- Baum, D (1997). Smoke and Mirrors: *The War on Drugs and the Politics of Failure*. Back Bay Books.

- Brownlee, N (2011). *This is cannabis*. Sanctuary Publishing

- Cocks, G (1997). *Psychotherapy in the Third Reich: the Göring Institute*. New Brunswick.

- de Mondernard, Jean Pierre (2000). *Dopage: l'imposture des performances*. Chiron.

- Doweiko, Harold E (2009). *Concepts of Chemical Dependency*. Cengage Learning.

- Eisner, B (1993). *Ecstasy: The MDMA story.* Ronin Publishing
- Elliott, F (2007). *Cameron – the rise of the new conservative.* Fourth Estate
- Ghalinger, P.M (2003). *Illegal drugs: a complete guide to their history, chemistry, use and abuse.* Plume
- Hill, J (1714). *Cautions against the immoderate use of snuff.* Printed for R. Baldwin
- Hitchens, P (2016). *The war we never fought: The British Establishments Surrender to Drugs.* Bloomsbury
- Holland, J (2001). *Ecstasy: The complete guide; A comprehensive look at the risks and benefits of MDMA.* Park Street Press.
- Iverson, L.I (2000). *The Science of Marijuana.* Oxford University Press
- Jay, M (2010). *High Society.* Thames & Hudson.
- Laserna, R (1997) *20 (mis)conceptions on coca and cocaine.* Plural Publishers
- Mackeganey, N (2009). *Controversies in Drug Policy and Practice.* Palgrave
- Medical Economics (2003). *Physicians' desk reference* (2003 ed.)
- Nutt, D (2012). *Drugs without the hot air.* UIT Cambridge
- Pariente, R and Lagorce, G (2004). *La Fabuleuse Histoire des Jeux Olympiques.* Minerva.
- Porter, R and Teich, M (1995). *Exotic Substances: in introduction and global spread of tobacco, coffee, cocoa, tea and distilled liquor, sixteenth to eighteenth centuries.* Cambridge University Press.
- Power, M (2013). *Drugs 2.0: The Web Revolution That's Changing how the World Gets High.* Portobello Books
- Rusby H. (1933). *Jungle Memories.* New York: McGraw; Hill.
- Sabet, K (2013). *Reefer Sanity: Seven Great Myths About Marijuana.* Beaufort Books

- Shiloh, R and Nutt, D (2006). *The Atlas of Psychiatric Pharmacotherapy.* CRC Press

- Stafford, P.G and Golightly, B.H (1967). *LSD - The Problem Solving Psychedelic.* Award Books

- Twenge, J (2014). *Generation Me: Why Todays Young American's are More Confident, Assertive, Entitled – and More miserable than ever.* Atria Books.

- Twenge, J and Campbell, K (2009). *The Narcissism Epidemic: Living in the Age of Entitlement.* Atria Books

- Winter, J (2000). *Tobacco use by Native Americans: sacred smoke and silent killer.* University of Oklahoma Press.

Radio Recordings

- Federal liberals against pill testing. *Nights with Steve Price.* URL: https://omny.fm/shows/nights-with-steve-price/federal-liberals-against-pill-testing

- Interview with David Nutt. (2019). ABC Radio – *All in the Mind.* URL: https://abcmedia.akamaized.net/rn/podcast/2019/02/aim_20190224.mp3

- Interview with Doug Humphreys. (2018). *ABC Radio.* URL: https://abcmedia.akamaized.net/rn/podcast/2018/10/bst_20181024_0835.mp3

- Stanley, J (2017). We're losing the war on drugs. *2GB873.* URL: https://www.2gb.com/podcast/were-losing-the-war-on-drugs/

- Tony Wood Joins Miranda Live. *Miranda Devine Live.* URL: https://player.whooshkaa.com/episode?id=242821

- Troy Grant on how the state government plans to stop drug deaths. (2018). *Miranda Live.* URL: https://www.news.com.au/national/nsw-act/miranda-live-troy-grant-on-how-the-state-government-plans-to-stop-drug-deaths/live-coverage/2c8e04aaa724fda3f46a79c9232ebd32

- Troy Grant says pill testing will not happen on my watch. (2018). *Miranda Live*. URL: https://www.dailytelegraph.com.au/ blogs/miranda-devine/miranda-live-troy-grant-says-pilltesting-will-not-happen-on-my-watch/news-story/a864f43777 f28168c3cfede37ba6c224

www.ingramcontent.com/pod-product-compliance
Lightning Source LLC
Chambersburg PA
CBHW071532200326

41519CB00021BB/6459